Java Performance:
The Definitive Guide

Scott Oaks

Beijing · Cambridge · Farnham · Köln · Sebastopol · Tokyo

Java Performance: The Definitive Guide
by Scott Oaks

Copyright © 2014 Scott Oaks. All rights reserved.

Printed in the United States of America.

Published by O'Reilly Media, Inc., 1005 Gravenstein Highway North, Sebastopol, CA 95472.

O'Reilly books may be purchased for educational, business, or sales promotional use. Online editions are also available for most titles (*http://safaribooksonline.com*). For more information, contact our corporate/institutional sales department: 800-998-9938 or *corporate@oreilly.com*.

Editor: Meghan Blanchette	**Indexer:** Judith McConville
Production Editor: Kristen Brown	**Cover Designer:** Karen Montgomery
Copyeditor: Becca Freed	**Interior Designer:** David Futato
Proofreader: Charles Roumeliotis	**Illustrator:** Rebecca Demarest

April 2014:   First Edition

Revision History for the First Edition:

2014-04-09:   First release

2014-12-19:   Second release

See *http://oreilly.com/catalog/errata.csp?isbn=9781449358457* for release details.

ISBN: 978-1-449-35845-7

[LSI]

Table of Contents

Preface

When O'Reilly first approached me about writing a book on Java performance tuning, I was unsure. Java performance, I thought—aren't we done with that? Yes, I still work on performance of Java (and other) applications on a daily basis, but I like to think that I spend most of my time dealing with algorithmic inefficiences and external system bottlenecks rather than on anything directly related to Java tuning.

A moment's reflection convinced me that I was (as usual) kidding myself. It is certainly true that end-to-end system performance takes up a lot of my time, and that I sometimes come across code that uses an $O(n^2)$ algorithm when it could use one with O(log N) performance. Still, it turns out that every day, I think about GC performance, or the performance of the JVM compiler, or how to get the best performance from Java Enterprise Edition APIs.

That is not to minimize the enormous progress that has been made in the performance of Java and JVMs over the past 15-plus years. When I was a Java evangelist at Sun during the late 1990s, the only real "benchmark" available was CaffeineMark 2.0 from Pendragon software. For a variety of reasons, the design of that benchmark quickly limited its value; yet in its day, we were fond of telling everyone that Java 1.1.8 performance was eight times faster than Java 1.0 performance based on that benchmark. And that was true—Java 1.1.8 had an actual just-in-time compiler, where Java 1.0 was pretty much completely interpreted.

Then standards committees began to develop more rigorous benchmarks, and Java performance began to be centered around them. The result was a continuous improvement in all areas of the JVM—garbage collection, compilations, and within the APIs. That process continues today, of course, but one of the interesting facts about performance work is that it gets successively harder. Achieving an eightfold increase in performance by introducing a just-in-time compiler was a straightforward matter of engineering, and even though the compiler continues to improve, we're not going to see an improvement like that again. Parallelizing the garbage collector was a huge performance improvement, but more recent changes have been more incremental.

This is a typical process for applications (and the JVM itself is just another application): in the beginning of a project, it's easy enough to find archictural changes (or code bugs) which, when addressed, yield huge performance improvements. In a mature application, finding such performance improvements is quite rare.

That precept was behind my original concern that, to a large extent, the engineering world might be done with Java performance. A few things convinced me I was wrong. First is the number of questions I see daily about how this or that aspect of the JVM performs under certain circumstances. New engineers come to Java all the time, and JVM behavior remains complex enough in certain areas that a guide to how it operates is still beneficial. Second is that environmental changes in computing seem to have altered the performance concerns that engineers face today.

What's changed in the past few years is that performance concerns have become bifurcated. On the one hand, very large machines capable of running JVMs with very large heaps are now commonplace. The JVM has moved to address those concerns with a new garbage collector (G1), which—as a new technology—requires a little more hand-tuning than traditional collectors. At the same time, cloud computing has renewed the importance of small, single-CPU machines: you can go to Oracle or Amazon or a host of other companies and very cheaply rent a single CPU machine to run a small application server. (You're not actually getting a single-CPU machine: you're getting a virtual OS image on a very large machine, but the virtual OS is limited to using a single CPU. From the perspective of Java, that turns out to be the same as single-CPU machine.) In those environments, correctly managing small amounts of memory turns out to be quite important.

The Java platform also continues to evolve. Each new edition of Java provides new language features and new APIs that improve the productivity of developers—if not always the performance of their applications. Best practice use of these language features can help to differentiate between an application that sizzles, and one that plods along. And the evolution of the platform brings up interesting performance questions: there is no question that using JSON to exchange information between two programs is much simpler than coming up with a highly optimized proprietary protocol. Saving time for developers is a big win—but making sure that productivity win comes with a performance win (or at least breaks even) is the real goal.

Who Should (and Shouldn't) Read This Book

This book is designed for performance engineers and developers who are looking to understand how various aspects of the JVM and the Java APIs impact performance.

If it is late Sunday night, your site is going live Monday morning, and you're looking for a quick fix for performance issues, this is not the book for you.

If you are new to performance analysis and are starting that analysis in Java, then this book can help you. Certainly my goal is to provide enough information and context that novice engineers can understand how to apply basic tuning and performance principles to a Java application. However, system analysis is a very broad field. There are a number of excellent resources for system analysis in general (and those principles of course apply to Java), and in that sense, this book will hopefully be a useful companion to those texts.

At a fundamental level, though, making Java go really fast requires a deep understanding about how the JVM (and Java APIs) actually work. There are literally hundreds of Java tuning flags, and tuning the JVM has to be more than an approach of blindly trying them and seeing what works. Instead, my goal is to provide some very detailed knowledge about what the JVM and APIs are doing, with the hope that if you understand how those things work, you'll be able to look at the specific behavior of an application and understand *why* it is performing badly. Understanding that, it becomes a simple (or at least simpler) task to get rid of undesirable (badly performing) behavior.

One interesting aspect to Java performance work is that developers often have a very different background than engineers in a performance or QA group. I know developers who can remember thousands of obscure method signatures on little-used Java APIs but who have no idea what the flag -Xmn means. And I know testing engineers who can get every last ounce of performance from setting various flags for the garbage collector but who could barely write a suitable "Hello, World" program in Java.

Java performance covers both of these areas: tuning flags for the compiler and garbage collector and so on, and best-practice uses of the APIs. So I assume that you have a good understanding of how to write programs in Java. Even if your primary interest is not in the programming aspects of Java, I do spent a fair amount of time discussing programs, including the sample programs used to provide a lot of the data points in the examples.

Still, if your primary interest is in the performance of the JVM itself—meaning how to alter the behavior of the JVM without any coding—then large sections of this book should still be beneficial to you. Feel free to skip over the coding parts and focus in on the areas that interest you. And maybe along the way, you'll pick up some insight into how Java applications can affect JVM performance and start to suggest changes to developers so they can make your performance-testing life easier.

Conventions Used in This Book

The following typographical conventions are used in this book:

Italic

Indicates new terms, URLs, email addresses, filenames, and file extensions.

Constant width

Used for program listings, as well as within paragraphs to refer to program elements such as variable or function names, databases, data types, environment variables, statements, and keywords.

Constant width bold

Shows commands or other text that should be typed literally by the user.

Constant width italic

Shows text that should be replaced with user-supplied values or by values determined by context.

 This element signifies a tip or suggestion.

 This element signifies a general note.

 This element indicates a warning or caution.

Using Code Examples

Supplemental material (code examples, exercises, etc.) is available for download at *https://github.com/ScottOaks/JavaPerformanceTuning*.

This book is here to help you get your job done. In general, if example code is offered with this book, you may use it in your programs and documentation. You do not need to contact us for permission unless you're reproducing a significant portion of the code. For example, writing a program that uses several chunks of code from this book does not require permission. Selling or distributing a CD-ROM of examples from O'Reilly books does require permission. Answering a question by citing this book and quoting example code does not require permission. Incorporating a significant amount of example code from this book into your product's documentation does require permission.

We appreciate, but do not require, attribution. An attribution usually includes the title, author, publisher, and ISBN. For example: "*Java Performance: The Definitive Guide* by Scott Oaks (O'Reilly). Copyright 2014 Scott Oaks, 978-1-449-35845-7."

If you feel your use of code examples falls outside fair use or the permission given above, feel free to contact us at *permissions@oreilly.com*.

Safari® Books Online

 *Safari Books Online* is an on-demand digital library that delivers expert content in both book and video form from the world's leading authors in technology and business.

Technology professionals, software developers, web designers, and business and creative professionals use Safari Books Online as their primary resource for research, problem solving, learning, and certification training.

Safari Books Online offers a range of plans and pricing for enterprise, government, education, and individuals.

Members have access to thousands of books, training videos, and prepublication manuscripts in one fully searchable database from publishers like O'Reilly Media, Prentice Hall Professional, Addison-Wesley Professional, Microsoft Press, Sams, Que, Peachpit Press, Focal Press, Cisco Press, John Wiley & Sons, Syngress, Morgan Kaufmann, IBM Redbooks, Packt, Adobe Press, FT Press, Apress, Manning, New Riders, McGraw-Hill, Jones & Bartlett, Course Technology, and hundreds more. For more information about Safari Books Online, please visit us online.

How to Contact Us

Please address comments and questions concerning this book to the publisher:

O'Reilly Media, Inc.
1005 Gravenstein Highway North
Sebastopol, CA 95472
800-998-9938 (in the United States or Canada)
707-829-0515 (international or local)
707-829-0104 (fax)

We have a web page for this book, where we list errata, examples, and any additional information. You can access this page at *http://oreil.ly/java-performance-tdg*.

To comment or ask technical questions about this book, send email to *bookques tions@oreilly.com*.

For more information about our books, courses, conferences, and news, see our website at *http://www.oreilly.com*.

Find us on Facebook: *http://facebook.com/oreilly*

Follow us on Twitter: *http://twitter.com/oreillymedia*

Watch us on YouTube: *http://www.youtube.com/oreillymedia*

Acknowledgments

I would like to thank everyone who helped me as I worked on this book. In many ways, this book is an accumulation of knowledge gained over my past 15 years in the Java Performance Group at Sun Microsystems and Oracle, so the list of people who have provided positive input into this book is quite broad. To all the engineers I have worked with during that time, and particularly to those who patiently answered my random questions over the past year, thank you!

I would especially like to thank Stanley Guan, Azeem Jiva, Kim LiChong, Deep Singh, Martijn Verburg, and Edward Yue Shung Wong for their time reviewing draft copies and providing valuable feedback. I am sure that they were unable to find all my errors, though the material here is greatly improved by their input.

The production staff at O'Reilly was as always very helpful, and thanks to my editor Meg Blanchette for all your encouragement during the process. Finally, I must thank my husband James for putting up with the long nights and those weekend dinners where I was in a continual state of distraction.

## CHAPTER 1

Introduction

This is a book about the art and science of Java performance.

The science part of this statement isn't surprising; discussions about performance include lots of numbers and measurements and analytics. Most performance engineers have a background in the sciences, and applying scientific rigor is a crucial part of achieving maximum performance.

What about the art part? The notion that performance tuning is part art and part science is hardly new, but it is rarely given explicit acknowledgment in performance discussions. This is partly because the idea of "art" goes against our training.

Part of the reason is that what looks like art to some people is fundamentally based on deep knowledge and experience. It is said that magic is indistinguishable from sufficiently advanced technologies, and certainly it is true that a cell phone would look magical to a knight of the Round Table. Similarly, the work produced by a good performance engineer may look like art, but that art is really an application of deep knowledge, experience, and intuition.

This book cannot help with the experience and intuition part of that equation, but its goal is to help with the deep knowledge—with the view that applying knowledge over time will help you develop the skills needed to be a good Java performance engineer. The goal is to give you an in-depth understanding of the performance aspects of the Java platform.

This knowledge falls into two broad categories. First is the performance of the Java Virtual Machine (JVM) itself: the way in which the JVM is configured affects many aspects of the performance of a program. Developers who are experienced in other languages may find the need for tuning to be somewhat irksome, though in reality tuning the JVM is completely analogous to testing and choosing compiler flags during compilation for C++ programmers, or to setting appropriate variables in a *php.ini* file for PHP coders, and so on.

The second aspect is to understand how the features of the Java platform affect performance. Note the use of the word *platform* here: some features (e.g., threading and synchronization) are part of the language, and some features (e.g., XML parsing performance) are part of the standard Java API. Though there are important distinctions between the Java language and the Java API, in this case they will be treated similarly. This book covers both facets of the platform.

The performance of the JVM is based largely on tuning flags, while the performance of the platform is determined more by using best practices within your application code. In an environment where developers code and a performance group tests, these are often considered separate areas of expertise: only performance engineers can tune the JVM to eke out every last bit of performance, and only developers worry about whether their code is written well. That is not a useful distinction—anyone who works with Java should be equally adept at understanding how code behaves in the JVM and what kinds of tuning is likely to help its performance. Knowledge of the complete sphere is what will give your work the patina of art.

A Brief Outline

First things first, though: Chapter 2 discusses general methodologies for testing Java applications, including pitfalls of Java benchmarking. Since performance analysis requires visibility into what the application is doing, Chapter 3 provides an overview of some of the tools available to monitor Java applications.

Then it is time to dive into performance, focusing first on common tuning aspects: just-in-time compilation (Chapter 4) and garbage collection (Chapter 5 and Chapter 6). The remaining chapters focus on best practice uses of various parts of the Java platform: memory use with the Java heap (Chapter 7), native memory use (Chapter 8), thread performance (Chapter 9), Java Enterprise Edition APIs (Chapter 10), JPA and JDBC (Chapter 11), and some general Java SE API tips (Chapter 12).

Appendix A lists all the tuning flags discussed in this book, with cross-references to the chapter where they are examined.

Platforms and Conventions

This book is based on the Oracle HotSpot Java Virtual Machine and the Java Platform, Standard Edition (Java SE), versions 7 and 8. Within versions, Oracle provides update releases periodically. For the most part, update releases provide only bug fixes; they never provide new language features or changes to key functionality. However, update releases do sometimes change the default value of tuning flags. Oracle will doubtless provide update releases that postdate publication of this book, which is current as of Java 7 update 40 and Java 8 (as of yet, there are no Java 8 update releases). When an update release provides an important change to JVM behavior, the update release is specified like this: 7u6 (Java 7 update 6).

Sections on Java Enterprise Edition (Java EE) are based on Java EE 7.

This book does not address the performance of previous releases of Java, though of course the current versions of Java build on those releases. Java 7 is a good starting point for a book on performance because it introduces a number of new performance features and optimizations. Chief among these is a new garbage collection (GC) algorithm called G1. (Earlier versions of Java had experimental versions of G1, but it was not considered production-ready until 7u4.) Java 7 also includes a number of new and enhanced performance-related tools to provide vastly increased visibility into the workings of a Java application. That progress in the platform is continued in Java 8, which further enhances the platform (e.g., by introducing lambda expressions). Java 8 offers a big performance advantage in its own right—the performance of Java 8 itself is much faster than Java 7 in several key areas.

There are other implementations of the Java Virtual Machine. Oracle has its JRockit JVM (which supports Java SE 6); IBM offers its own compatible Java implementation (including a Java 7 version). Many other companies license and enhance Oracle's Java technology.

Oracle's Commercial JVM

Java and the JVM are open source; anyone may participate in the development of Java by joining the project at *http://openjdk.java.net*. Even if you don't want to actively participate in development, source code can be freely downloaded from that site. For the most part, everything discussed in this book is part of the open source version of Java.

Oracle also has a commercial version of Java, which is available via a support contract. That is based on the standard, open source Java platform, but it contains a few features that are not in the open source version. One feature of the commercial JVM that is important to performance work is Java Flight Recorder (see "Java Flight Recorder" on page 60).

Unless otherwise mentioned, all information in this book applies to the open source version of Java.

Although all these platforms must pass a compatibility test in order to be able to use the Java name, that compatibility does not always extend to the topics discussed in this book. This is particularly true of tuning flags. All JVM implementations have one or more garbage collectors, but the flags to tune each vendor's GC implementation are product-specific. Thus, while the concepts of this book apply to any Java implementation, the specific flags and recommendations apply only to Oracle's standard (HotSpot-based) JVM.

That caveat is applicable to earlier releases of the HotSpot JVM—flags and their default values change from release to release. Rather than attempting to be comprehensive and cover a variety of now-outdated versions, the information in this book covers only Java 7 (up through 7u40) and Java 8 (the initial release only) JVMs. It is possible that later releases (e.g., a hypothetical 7u60) may slightly change some of this information. Always consult the release notes for important changes.

At an API level, different JVM implementations are much more compatible, though even then there might be subtle differences between the way a particular class is implemented in the Oracle HotSpot Java SE (or EE) platform and an alternate platform. The classes must be functionally equivalent, but the actual implementation may change. Fortunately, that is infrequent, and unlikely to drastically affect performance.

For the remainder of this book, the terms Java and JVM should be understood to refer specifically to the Oracle HotSpot implementation. Strictly speaking, saying "The JVM does not compile code upon first execution" is wrong; there are Java implementations that do compile code the first time it is executed. But that shorthand is much easier than continuing to write (and read) "The Oracle HotSpot JVM…"

JVM Tuning Flags

With a few exceptions, the JVM accepts two kinds of flags: boolean flags, and flags that require a parameter.

Boolean flags use this syntax: `-XX:+FlagName` enables the flag, and `-XX:-FlagName` disables the flag.

Flags that require a parameter use this syntax: `-XX:FlagName=something`, meaning to set the value of `FlagName` to `something`. In the text, the value of the flag is usually rendered with something indicating an arbitrary value. For example, `-XX:NewRatio=N` means that the `NewRatio` flag can be set to some arbitrary value N (where the implications of N are the focus of the discussion).

The default value of each flag is discussed as the flag is introduced. That default is often a combination of different factors: the platform on which the JVM is running and other command-line arguments to the JVM. When in doubt, "Basic VM Information" on page 47 shows how to use the `-XX:+PrintFlagsFinal` flag (by default, `false`) to determine the default value for a particular flag in a particular environment given a particular command line. The process of automatically tuning flags based on the environment is called *ergonomics*.

Client Class and Server Class

Java ergonomics is based on the notion that some machines are "client" class and some are "server" class. While those terms map directly to the compiler used for a particular platform (see Chapter 4), they apply to other default tunings as well. For example, the default garbage collector for a platform is determined by the class of a machine (see Chapter 5).

Client-class machines are any 32-bit JVM running on Microsoft Windows (regardless of the number of CPUs on the machine), and any 32-bit JVM running on a machine with one CPU (regardless of the operating system). All other machines (including all 64-bit JVMs) are considered server class.

The JVM that is downloaded from Oracle and OpenJDK sites is called the "product" build of the JVM. When the JVM is built from source code, there are many different builds that can be produced: debug builds, developer builds, and so on. These builds often have additional functionality in them. In particular, developer builds include an even larger set of tuning flags so that developers can experiment with the most minute operations of various algorithms used by the JVM. Those flags are generally not considered in this book.

The Complete Performance Story

This book is focused on how to best use the JVM and Java platform APIs so that programs run faster, but there are many outside influences that affect performance. Those influences pop up from time to time in the discussion, but because they are not specific to Java, they are not necessarily discussed in detail. The performance of the JVM and the Java platform is a small part of getting to fast performance.

Here are some of the outside influences that are at least as important as the Java tuning topics covered in this book. The Java knowledge-based approach of this book complements these influences, but many of them are beyond the scope of what we'll discuss.

Write Better Algorithms

There are a lot of details about Java that affect the performance of an application, and a lot of tuning flags are discussed. But there is no magical -XX:+RunReallyFast option.

Ultimately, the performance of an application is based on how well it is written. If the program loops through all elements in an array, the JVM will optimize the array bounds-checking so that the loop runs faster, and it may unroll the loop operations to provide an additional speedup. But if the purpose of the loop is to find a specific item, no optimization in the world is going to make the array-based code as fast as a different version that uses a `HashMap`.

A good algorithm is the most important thing when it comes to fast performance.

Write Less Code

Some of us write programs for money, some for fun, some to give back to a community, but all of us write programs (or work on teams that write programs). It is hard to feel like a contribution to the project is being made by pruning code, and there are still those managers who evaluate developers by the amount of code they write.

I get that, but the conflict here is that a small well-written program will run faster than a large well-written program. This is true in general of all computer programs, and it applies specifically to Java programs. The more code that has to be compiled, the longer it will take until that code runs quickly. The more objects that have to be allocated and discarded, the more work the garbage collector has to do. The more objects that are allocated and retained, the longer a GC cycle will take. The more classes that have to be loaded from disk into the JVM, the longer it will take for a program to start. The more code that is executed, the less likely that it will fit in the hardware caches on the machine. And the more code that has to be executed, the longer it will take.

We Will Ultimately Lose the War

One aspect of performance that can be counterintuitive (and depressing) is that the performance of every application can be expected to decrease over time—meaning over new release cycles of the application. Often, that performance difference is not noticed, since hardware improvements make it possible to run the new programs at acceptable speeds.

Think what it would be like to run the Windows Aero interface on the same computer that used to run Windows 95. My favorite computer ever was a Mac Quadra 950, but it couldn't run Mac OS X (and it if did, it would be so very, very slow compared to Mac OS 7.5). On a smaller level, it may seem that Firefox 23.0 is faster than Firefox 22.0, but those are essentially minor release versions. With its tabbed browsing and synced scrolling and security features, Firefox is far more powerful than Mosaic ever was, but Mosaic can load basic HTML files located on my hard disk about 50% faster than Firefox 23.0.

Of course, Mosaic cannot load actual URLs from almost any popular website; it is no longer possible to use Mosaic as a primary browser. That is also part of the general point here: particularly between minor releases, code may be optimized and run faster. As performance engineers, that's what we can focus on, and if we are good at our job, we can win the battle. That is a good and valuable thing; my argument isn't that we shouldn't work to improve the performance of existing applications.

> But the irony remains: as new features are added and new standards adopted—which is a requirement to match competing programs—programs can be expected to get larger and slower.

I think of this as the "death by 1,000 cuts" principle. Developers will argue that they are just adding a very small feature and it will take no time at all (especially if the feature isn't used). And then other developers on the same project make the same claim, and suddenly the performance has regressed by a few percent. The cycle is repeated in the next release, and now program performance has regressed by 10%. A couple of times during the process, performance testing may hit some resource threshold—a critical point in memory use, or a code cache overflow, or something like that. In those cases, regular performance tests will catch that particular condition and the performance team can fix what appears to be a major regression. But over time, as the small regressions creep in, it will be harder and harder to fix them.

I'm not advocating here that you should never add a new feature or new code to your product; clearly there are benefits as programs are enhanced. But be aware of the trade-offs you are making, and when you can, streamline.

Oh Go Ahead, Prematurely Optimize

Donald Knuth is widely credited with coining the term "premature optimization," which is often used by developers to claim that the performance of their code doesn't matter, and if it does matter, we won't know that until the code is run. The full quote, if you've never come across it, is "We should forget about small efficiencies, say about 97% of the time; premature optimization is the root of all evil."

The point of this dictum is that in the end, you should write clean, straightforward code that is simple to read and understand. In this context, "optimizing" is understood to mean employing algorithmic and design changes that complicate program structure but provide better performance. Those kind of optimizations indeed are best left undone until such time as the profiling of a program shows that there is a large benefit from performing them.

What optimization does not mean in this context, however, is avoiding code constructs that are known to be bad for performance. Every line of code involves a choice, and if there is a choice between two simple, straightforward ways of programming, choose the more performant one.

At one level, this is well understood by experienced Java developers (it is an example of their art, as they have learned it over time). Consider this code:

```
log.log(Level.FINE, "I am here, and the value of X is "
        + calcX() + " and Y is " + calcY());
```

This code does a string concatenation that is likely unnecessary, since the message won't be logged unless the logging level is set quite high. If the message isn't printed, then unnecessary calls are also made to the calcX() and calcY() methods. Experienced Java developers will reflexively reject that; some IDEs (such as NetBeans) will even flag the code and suggest it be changed. (Tools aren't perfect, though: NetBeans will flag the string concatenation, but the suggested improvement retains the unneeded method calls.)

This logging code is better written like this:

```
if (log.isLoggable(Level.FINE)) {
    log.log(Level.FINE,
            "I am here, and the value of X is {} and Y is {}",
            new Object[]{calcX(), calcY()});
}
```

This avoids the string concatenation altogether (the message format isn't necessarily more efficient, but it is cleaner), and there are no method calls or allocation of the object array unless logging has been enabled.

Writing code in this way is still clean and easy to read; it took no more effort than writing the original code. Well, OK, it required a few more keystrokes and an extra line of logic. But it isn't the type of premature optimization that should be avoided; it's the kind of choice that good coders learn to make. Don't let out-of-context dogma from pioneering heroes prevent you from thinking about the code you are writing.

We'll see other examples of this throughout this book, including in Chapter 9, which discusses the performance of a benign-looking loop construct to process a Vector of objects.

Look Elsewhere: The Database Is Always the Bottleneck

If you are developing standalone Java applications that use no external resources, the performance of that application is (mostly) all that matters. Once an external resource —a database, for example—is added, then the performance of both programs is important. And in a distributed environment, say with a Java EE application server, a load balancer, a database, and a backend enterprise information system, the performance of the Java application server may be the least of the performance issues.

This is not a book about holistic system performance. In such an environment, a structured approach must be taken toward all aspects of the system. CPU usage, I/O latencies, and throughput of all parts of the system must be measured and analyzed; only then can it be determined which component is causing the performance bottleneck. There are a number of excellent resources on that subject, and those approaches and tools are not really specific to Java. I assume you've done that analysis and determined that it is the Java component of your environment than needs to be improved.

Bugs and Performance Issues Aren't Limited to the JVM

The performance of the database is the example used in this section, but any part of the environment may be the source of a performance issue.

I once faced an issue where a customer was installing a new version of an application server, and testing showed that the requests sent to the server took longer and longer over time. Applying Occam's Razor (see the next tip) led me to consider all aspects of the application server that might be causing the issue.

After those were ruled out, the performance issue remained, and there was no backend database on which to place the blame. The next most likely issue, therefore, was the test harness, and some profiling determined that the load generator—Apache JMeter—was the source of the regression: it was keeping every response in a list, and when a new response came in, it processed the entire list in order to calculate the 90th% response time (if that term is unfamiliar, see Chapter 2).

Performance issues can be caused by any part of the entire system where an application is deployed. Common case analysis says to consider the newest part of the system first (which is often the application in the JVM), but be prepared to look at every possible component of the environment.

On the other hand, don't overlook that initial analysis. If the database is the bottleneck (and here's a hint: it is), then tuning the Java application accessing the database won't help overall performance at all. In fact, it might be counterproductive. As a general rule, when load is increased into a system that is overburdened, performance of that system gets worse. If something is changed in the Java application that makes it more efficient —which only increases the load on an already-overloaded database—overall performance may actually go down. The danger there is then reaching the incorrect conclusion that the particular JVM improvement shouldn't be used.

This principle—that increasing load to a component in a system that is performing badly will make the entire system slower—isn't confined to a database. It applies when load is added to an application server that is CPU-bound, or if more threads start accessing a lock that already has threads waiting for it, or any of a number of other scenarios. An extreme example of this that involves only the JVM is shown in Chapter 9.

Optimize for the Common Case

It is tempting—particularly given the "death by 1,000 cuts" syndrome—to treat all performance aspects as equally important. But focus should be given to the common use case scenarios.

This principle manifests itself in several ways:

- Optimize code by profiling it and focusing on the operations in the profile taking the most time. Note, however, that this does not mean looking at only the leaf methods in a profile (see Chapter 3).

- Apply Occam's Razor to diagnosing performance problems. The simplest explanation for a performance issue is the most conceivable cause: a performance bug in new code is more likely than a configuration issue on a machine, which in turn is more likely than a bug in the JVM or operating system. Obscure bugs do exist, and as more credible causes for a performance issue are ruled out, it does become possible that somehow the test case in question has triggered such a latent bug. But don't jump to the unlikely case first.

- Write simple algorithms for the most common operations in an application. Take the case of a program that estimates some mathematical formula, where the user can decide if she wants an answer within a 10% margin of error, or a 1% margin. If most users will be satisfied with the 10% margin, then optimize that code path— even if it means slowing down the code that provides the 1% margin of error.

Summary

Java 7 and 8 introduce a number of new features and tools that make it even easier to get the best possible performance from a Java application. This book should help you understand how best to use all the features of the JVM in order to end up with fast-running programs.

In many cases, though, remember that the JVM is a small part of the overall performance picture. A systemic, system-wide approach to performance is required in Java environments where the performance of databases and other backend systems is at least as important as the performance of the JVM. That level of performance analysis is not the focus of this book—it is assumed the due diligence has been performed to make sure that the Java component of the environment is the important bottleneck in the system.

However, the interaction between the JVM and other areas of the system is equally important—whether that interaction is direct (e.g., the best way to use JDBC) or indirect (e.g., optimizing native memory usage of an application that shares a machine with several components of a large system). The information in this book should help solve performance issues along those lines as well.

CHAPTER 2

An Approach to Performance Testing

This chapter discusses four principles of getting results from performance testing; these principles form the basis of the advice given in later chapters. The science of performance engineering is covered by these principles.

Most of the examples given in later chapters use a common application, which is also outlined in this chapter.

Test a Real Application

The first principle is that testing should occur on the actual product in the way the product will be used. There are, roughly speaking, three categories of code that can be used for performance testing, each with its own advantages and disadvantages. The category that includes the actual application will provide the best results.

Microbenchmarks

The first of these categories is the microbenchmark. A microbenchmark is a test designed to measure a very small unit of performance: the time to call a synchronized method versus a nonsynchronized method; the overhead in creating a thread versus using a thread pool; the time to execute one arithmetic algorithm versus an alternate implementation; and so on.

Microbenchmarks may seem like a good idea, but they are very difficult to write correctly. Consider the following code, which is an attempt to write a microbenchmark that tests the performance of different implementations of a method to compute the 50th Fibonacci number:

```
public void doTest() {
    // Main Loop
    double l;
    long then = System.currentTimeMillis();
```

```
        for (int i = 0; i < nLoops; i++) {
            l = fibImpl1(50);
        }
        long now = System.currentTimeMillis();
        System.out.println("Elapsed time: " + (now - then));
    }
    ...
    private double fibImpl1(int n) {
        if (n < 0) throw new IllegalArgumentException("Must be > 0");
        if (n == 0) return 0d;
        if (n == 1) return 1d;
        double d = fibImpl1(n - 2) + fibImpl(n  - 1);
        if (Double.isInfinite(d)) throw new ArithmeticException("Overflow");
        return d;
    }
```

This may seem simple, but there are many problems with this code.

Microbenchmarks must use their results

The biggest problem with this code is that it never actually changes any program state. Because the result of the Fibonacci calculation is never used, the compiler is free to discard that calculation. A smart compiler (including current Java 7 and 8 compilers) will end up executing this code:

```
long then = System.currentTimeMillis();
long now = System.currentTimeMillis();
System.out.println("Elapsed time: " + (now - then));
```

As a result, the elapsed time will be only a few milliseconds, regardless of the implementation of the Fibonacci method, or the number of times the loop is supposed to be executed. Details of how the loop is eliminated are given in Chapter 4.

There is a way around that particular issue: ensure that each result is read, not simply written. In practice, changing the definition of l from a local variable to an instance variable (declared with the volatile keyword) will allow the performance of the method to be measured. (The reason the l instance variable must be declared as volatile can be found in Chapter 9.)

Threaded Microbenchmarks

The need to use a volatile variable in this example applies even when the microbenchmark is single-threaded.

Be especially wary when thinking of writing a threaded microbenchmark. When several threads are executing small bits of code, the potential for synchronization bottlenecks (and other thread artifacts) is quite large. Results from threaded microbenchmarks often lead to spending a lot of time optimizing away synchronization bottlenecks that will rarely appear in real code—at a cost of addressing more pressing performance needs.

Consider the case of two threads calling a synchronized method in a microbenchmark. Because the benchmark code is small, most of it will execute within that synchronized method. Even if only 50% of the total microbenchmark is within the synchronized method, the odds that as few as two threads will attempt to execute the synchronized method at the same time is quite high. The benchmark will run quite slowly as a result, and as additional threads are added, the performance issues caused by the increased contention will get even worse. The net is that the test ends up measuring how the JVM handles contention rather than the goal of the microbenchmark.

Microbenchmarks must not include extraneous operations

Even then, potential pitfalls exist. This code performs only one operation: calculating the 50th Fibonacci number. A very smart compiler can figure that out and execute the loop only once—or at least discard some of the iterations of the loop since those operations are redundant.

Additionally, the performance of fibImpl(1000) is likely to be very different than the performance of fibImpl(1); if the goal is to compare the performance of different implementations, then a range of input values must be considered.

To overcome that, the parameter passed to the fibImpl1() method must vary. The solution is to use a random value, but that must also be done carefully.

The easy way to code the use of the random number generator is to process the loop as follows:

```
for (int i = 0; i < nLoops; i++) {
    l = fibImpl1(random.nextInteger());
}
```

Now the time to calculate the random numbers is included in the time to execute the loop, and so the test now measures the time to calculate a Fibonacci sequence nLoops times, plus the time to generate nLoops random integers. That likely isn't the goal.

In a microbenchmark, the input values must be precalculated, for example:

```
int[] input = new int[nLoops];
for (int i = 0; i < nLoops; i++) {
    input[i] = random.nextInt();
}
long then = System.currentTimeMillis();
for (int i = 0; i < nLoops; i++) {
    try {
        l = fibImpl1(input[i]);
    } catch (IllegalArgumentException iae) {
    }
}
long now = System.currentTimeMillis();
```

Microbenchmarks must measure the correct input

The third pitfall here is the input range of the test: selecting arbitrary random values isn't necessarily representative of how the code will be used. In this case, an exception will be immediately thrown on half of the calls to the method under test (anything with a negative value). An exception will also be thrown anytime the input parameter is greater than 1476, since that is the largest Fibonacci number that can be represented in a double.

What happens in an implementation where the Fibonacci calculation is significantly faster, but where the exception condition is not detected until the end of the calculation? Consider this alternate implementation:

```
public double fibImplSlow(int n) {
    if (n < 0) throw new IllegalArgumentException("Must be > 0");
    if (n > 1476) throw new ArithmeticException("Must be < 1476");
    return verySlowImpl(n);
}
```

It's hard to imagine an implementation slower than the original recursive implementation, but assume one was devised and used in this code. Comparing this implementation to the original implementation over a very wide range of input values will show this new implementation is much faster than the original one—simply because of the range checks at the beginning of the method.

If, in the real world, users are only ever going to pass values less than 100 to the method, then that comparison will give us the wrong answer. In the common case, the fibImpl() method will be faster, and as Chapter 1 explained, we should optimize for the common case. (This is obviously a contrived example, and simply adding a bounds test to the original implementation makes it a better implementation anyway. In the general case, that may not be possible.)

What About a Warm-Up Period?

One of the performance characteristics of Java is that code performs better the more it is executed, a topic that is covered in Chapter 4. For that reason, microbenchmarks must include a warm-up period, which gives the compiler a chance to produce optimal code.

The advantages and disadvantages of a warm-up period are discussed in depth later in this chapter. For microbenchmarks, a warm-up period is required; otherwise, the microbenchmark is measuring the performance of compilation rather than the code it is attempting to measure.

Taken all together, the proper coding of the microbenchmark looks like this:

```
package net.sdo;

import java.util.Random;

public class FibonacciTest {
    private volatile double l;
    private int nLoops;
    private int[] input;

    public static void main(String[] args) {
        FibonacciTest ft = new FibonacciTest(Integer.parseInt(args[0]));
        ft.doTest(true);
        ft.doTest(false);
    }

    private FibonacciTest(int n) {
        nLoops = n;
        input = new int[nLoops];
        Random r = new Random();
        for (int i = 0; i < nLoops; i++) {
            input[i] = r.nextInt(100);
        }
    }

    private void doTest(boolean isWarmup) {
        long then = System.currentTimeMillis();
        for (int i = 0; i < nLoops; i++) {
            l = fibImpl1(input[i]);
        }
        if (!isWarmup) {
            long now = System.currentTimeMillis();
            System.out.println("Elapsed time: " + (now - then));
        }
    }

    private double fibImpl1(int n) {
        if (n < 0) throw new IllegalArgumentException("Must be > 0");
        if (n == 0) return 0d;
        if (n == 1) return 1d;
        double d = fibImpl1(n - 2) + fibImpl(n  - 1);
        if (Double.isInfinite(d)) throw new ArithmeticException("Overflow");
        return d;
    }
}
```

Even this microbenchmark measures some things that are not germane to the Fibonacci implementation: there is a certain amount of loop and method overhead in setting up the calls to the fibImpl1() method, and the need to write each result to a volatile variable is additional overhead.

Beware, too, of additional compilation effects. The compiler uses profile feedback of code to determine the best optimizations to employ when compiling a method. The profile feedback is based on which methods are frequently called, the stack depth when they are called, the actual type (including subclasses) of their arguments, and so on—it is dependent on the environment in which the code actually runs. The compiler will frequently optimize code differently in a microbenchmark than it optimizes that same code when used in an application. If the same class measures a second implementation of the Fibonacci method, then all sorts of compilation effects can occur, particularly if the implementation occurs in different classes.

Finally, there is the issue of what the microbenchmark actually means. The overall time difference in a benchmark such as the one discussed here may be measured in seconds for a large number of loops, but the per-iteration difference is often measured in nanoseconds. Yes, nanoseconds add up, and "death by 1,000 cuts" is a frequent performance issue. But particularly in regression testing, consider whether tracking something at the nanosecond level actually makes sense. It may be important to save a few nanoseconds on each access to a collection that will be accessed millions of times (for example, see Chapter 12). For an operation that occurs less frequently—for example, maybe once per request for a servlet—fixing a nanosecond regression found by a microbenchmark will take away time that could be more profitably spent on optimizing other operations.

Writing a microbenchmark is hard. There are very limited times when it can be useful. Be aware of the pitfalls involved, and make the determination if the work involved in getting a reasonable microbenchmark is worthwhile for the benefit—or if it would be better to concentrate on more macro-level tests.

Macrobenchmarks

The best thing to use to measure performance of an application is the application itself, in conjunction with any external resources it uses. If the application normally checks the credentials of a user by making LDAP calls, it should be tested in that mode. Stubbing out the LDAP calls may make sense for module-level testing, but the application must be tested in its full configuration.

As applications grow, this maxim becomes both more important to fulfill and more difficult to achieve. Complex systems are more than the sum of their parts; they will behave quite differently when those parts are assembled. Mocking out database calls, for example, may mean that you no longer have to worry about the database performance—and hey, you're a Java person; why should you have to deal with someone else's performance problem? But database connections consume lots of heap space for their buffers; networks become saturated when more data is sent over them; code is optimized differently when it calls a simpler set of methods (as opposed to the complex code in a JDBC driver); CPUs pipeline and cache shorter code paths more efficiently than longer code paths; and so on.

The other reason to test the full application is one of resource allocation. In a perfect world, there would be enough time to optimize every line of code in the application. In the real world, deadlines loom, and optimizing only one part of a complex environment may not yield immediate benefits.

Consider the data flow shown in Figure 2-1. Data comes in from a user, some proprietary business calculation is made, some data based on that is loaded from the database, more proprietary calculations are made, changed data is stored back to the database, and an answer is sent back to the user. The number in each box is the number of requests per second (e.g., 200 RPS) that the module can process when tested in isolation.

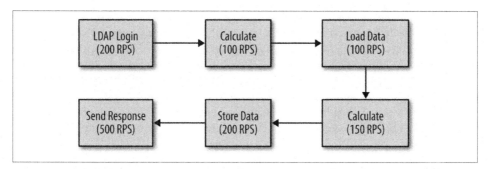

Figure 2-1. Typical program flow

From a business perspective, the proprietary calculations are the most important thing; they are the reason the program exists, and the reason we are paid. Yet making them 100% faster will yield absolutely no benefit in this example. Any application (including a single, standalone JVM) can be modeled as a series of steps like this, where data flows out of a box (module, subsystem, etc.) at a rate determined by the efficiency of that box. (In this model, that time includes the code in that subsystem and also includes network transfer times, disk transfer times, and so on. In a module model, the time includes only the code for that module.) Data flows into a subsystem at a rate determined by the output rate of the previous box.

Assume that an algorithmic improvement is made to the business calculation so that it can process 200 RPS; the load injected into the system is correspondingly increased. The LDAP system can handle the increased load: so far, so good, and 200 RPS will flow into the calculation module, which will output 200 RPS.

But the database can still process only 100 RPS. Even though 200 RPS flow into the database, only 100 RPS flow out of it and into the other modules. The total throughput of the system is still only 100 RPS, even though the efficiency of the business logic has doubled. Further attempts to improve the business logic will prove futile until time is spent improving the other aspects of the environment.

Full System Testing with Multiple JVMs

One particularly important case of testing a full application occurs when multiple applications are run at the same time on the same hardware. Many aspects of the JVM are tuned by default to assume that all machine resources are available to them, and if those JVMs are tested in isolation, they will behave well. If they are tested when other applications are present (including, but not limited to, other JVMs), their performance will be quite different.

Examples of this are given in later chapters, but here is one quick preview: when executing a GC cycle, one JVM will (in its default configuration) drive the CPU usage on a machine to 100% of all processors. If CPU is measured as an average during the program's execution, the usage may average out to 40%—but that really means that the CPU is 30% busy at some times and 100% busy at other times. When the JVM is run in isolation, that may be fine, but if the JVM is running concurrently with other applications, it will not be able to get 100% of the machine's CPU during GC. Its performance will be measurably different than when it was run by itself.

This is another reason why microbenchmarks and module-level benchmarks cannot necessarily give you the full picture of an application's performance.

It's not the case that the time spent optimizing the calculations in this example is entirely wasted: once effort is put into the bottlenecks elsewhere in the system, the performance benefit will finally be apparent. Rather, it is a matter of priorities: without testing the entire application, it is impossible to tell where spending time on performance work will pay off.

Mesobenchmarks

I work with the performance of both Java SE and EE, and each of those groups has a set of tests they characterize as microbenchmarks. To a Java SE engineer, that term connotes an example even smaller than that in the first section: the measurement of something quite small. Java EE engineers tend to use that term to apply to something else: benchmarks that measure one aspect of performance, but that still execute a lot of code.

An example of a Java EE "microbenchmark" might be something that measures how quickly the response from a simple JSP can be returned from an application server. The code involved in such a request is substantial compared to a traditional microbenchmark: there is a lot of socket-management code, code to read the request, code to find (and possibly compile) the JSP, code to write the answer, and so on. From a traditional standpoint, this is not microbenchmarking.

This kind of test is not a macrobenchmark either: there is no security (e.g., the user does not log in to the application), no session management, and no use of a host of other Java EE features. Because it is only a subset of an actual application, it falls somewhere in the middle—it is a mesobenchmark. Mesobenchmarks are not limited to the Java EE arena: it is a term I use for benchmarks that do some real work, but are not full-fledged applications.

Mesobenchmarks have fewer pitfalls than microbenchmarks and are easier to work with than macrobenchmarks. It is unlikely that mesobenchmarks will contain a large amount of dead code that can be optimized away by the compiler (unless that dead code actually exists in the application, in which case optimizing it away is a good thing). Mesobenchmarks are more easily threaded: they are still more likely to encounter more synchronization bottlenecks than the code will encounter when run in a full application, but those bottlenecks are something the real application will eventually encounter on larger hardware systems under larger load.

Still, mesobenchmarks are not perfect. A developer who uses a benchmark like this to compare the performance of two application servers may be easily led astray. Consider the hypothetical response times of two application servers shown in Table 2-1.

Table 2-1. Hypothetical response times for two application servers

Test	App server 1	App server 2
Simple JSP	19 ms	50 ms
JSP with session	75 ms	50 ms

The developer who uses only a simple JSP to compare the performance of the two servers might not realize that server 2 is automatically creating a session for each request. She may then conclude that server 1 will give her the fastest performance. Yet if her application always creates a session (which is typical), she will have made the incorrect choice, since it takes server 1 much longer to create a session. (Whether the performance of subsequent calls differs is yet another matter to consider, but it is impossible to predict from this data which server will do better once the session is created.)

Even so, mesobenchmarks offer a reasonable alternative to testing a full-scale application; their performance characteristics are much more closely aligned to an actual application than are the performance characteristics of microbenchmarks. And there is of course a continuum here. A later section in this chapter presents the outline of a common application used for many of the examples in subsequent chapters. That application has an EE mode, but that mode doesn't use session replication (high availability) or the EE platform-based security, and though it can access an enterprise resource (i.e., a database), in most examples it just makes up random data. In SE mode, it mimics some actual (but quick) calculations: there is, for example, no GUI or user interaction occurring.

Mesobenchmarks are also good for automated testing, particularly at the module level.

Quick Summary

1. Good microbenchmarks are hard to write and offer limited value. If you must use them, do so for a quick overview of performance, but don't rely on them.

2. Testing an entire application is the only way to know how code will actually run.

3. Isolating performance at a modular or operational level—a mesobenchmark—offers a reasonable compromise but is no substitute for testing the full application.

Common Code Examples

Many of the examples throughout the book are based on a sample application that calculates the "historical" high and low price of a stock over a range of dates, as well as the standard deviation during that time. Historical is in quotes here because in the application, all the data is fictional; the prices and the stock symbols are randomly generated.

The full source code for all examples in this book are on my GitHub page (*https://github.com/ScottOaks/JavaPerformanceTuning*), but this section covers basic points about the code. The basic object within the application is a StockPrice object that represents the price range of a stock on a given day:

```
public interface StockPrice {
        String getSymbol();
        Date getDate();
        BigDecimal getClosingPrice();
        BigDecimal getHigh();
        BigDecimal getLow();
        BigDecimal getOpeningPrice();
        boolean isYearHigh();
        boolean isYearLow();
        Collection<? extends StockOptionPrice> getOptions();
}
```

The sample applications typically deal with a collection of these prices, representing the history of the stock over a period of time (e.g., 1 year or 25 years, depending on the example):

```
public interface StockPriceHistory {
        StockPrice getPrice(Date d);
        Collection<StockPrice> getPrices(Date startDate, Date endDate);
        Map<Date, StockPrice> getAllEntries();
        Map<BigDecimal,ArrayList<Date>> getHistogram();
```

```
        BigDecimal getAveragePrice();
        Date getFirstDate();
        BigDecimal getHighPrice();
        Date getLastDate();
        BigDecimal getLowPrice();
        BigDecimal getStdDev();
        String getSymbol();
    }
```

The basic implementation of this class loads a set of prices from the database:

```
public class StockPriceHistoryImpl implements StockPriceHistory {
    ...
    public StockPriceHistoryImpl(String s, Date startDate,
        Date endDate, EntityManager em) {
        Date curDate = new Date(startDate.getTime());
        symbol = s;
        while (!curDate.after(endDate)) {
            StockPriceImpl sp = em.find(StockPriceImpl.class,
                        new StockPricePK(s, (Date) curDate.clone()));
            if (sp != null) {
                Date d = (Date) curDate.clone();
                if (firstDate == null) {
                    firstDate = d;
                }
                prices.put(d, sp);
                lastDate = d;
            }
            curDate.setTime(curDate.getTime() + msPerDay);
        }
    }
    ...
}
```

The architecture of the samples is designed to be loaded from a database, and that functionality will be used in the examples in Chapter 11. However, to facilitate running the examples, most of the time they will use a mock entity manager that generates random data for the series. In essence, most examples are module-level mesobenchmarks that are suitable for illustrating the performance issues at hand—but we would only have an idea of the actual performance of the application when the full application is run (as in Chapter 11).

One caveat is that a number of the examples are therefore dependent on the performance of the random number generator in use. Unlike the microbenchmark example, this is by design, as it allows the illustration of several performance issues in Java. (For that matter, the goal of the examples is to measure the performance of some arbitrary thing, and the performance of the random number generator fits that goal. That is quite different than a microbenchmark, where including the time for generating random numbers would affect the overall calculation.)

The examples are also heavily dependent on the performance of the BigDecimal class, which is used to store all the data points. This is a standard choice for storing currency data; if the currency data is stored as primitive double objects, then rounding of half-pennies and smaller amounts becomes quite problematic. From the perspective of writing examples, that choice is also useful as it allows some "business logic" or lengthy calculation to occur—particularly in calculating the standard deviation of a series of prices. The standard deviation relies on knowing the square root of a BigDecimal number. The standard Java API doesn't supply such a routine, but the examples use this method:

```
public static BigDecimal sqrtB(BigDecimal bd) {
    BigDecimal initial = bd;
    BigDecimal diff;
    do {
        BigDecimal sDivX = bd.divide(initial, 8, RoundingMode.FLOOR);
        BigDecimal sum = sDivX.add(initial);
        BigDecimal div = sum.divide(TWO, 8, RoundingMode.FLOOR);
        diff = div.subtract(initial).abs();
        diff.setScale(8, RoundingMode.FLOOR);
        initial = div;
    } while (diff.compareTo(error) > 0);
    return initial;
}
```

This is an implementation of the Babylonian method for estimating the square root of a number. It isn't the most efficient implementation; in particular, the initial guess could be much better, which would save some iterations. That is deliberate since it allows the calculation to take some time (emulating business logic), though it does illustrate the basic point made in Chapter 1: often the better way to make Java code faster is to write a better algorithm, independent of any Java tuning or Java coding practices that are employed.

The standard deviation, average price, and histogram of an implementation of the StockPriceHistory interface are all derived values. In different examples, these values will be calculated eagerly (when the data is loaded from the entity manager) or lazily (when the method to retrieve the data is called). Similarly, the StockPrice interface references a StockOptionPrice interface, which is the price of certain options for the given stock on the given day. Those option values can be retrieved from the entity manager either eagerly or lazily. In both cases, the definition of these interfaces allows these different approaches to be compared in different situations.

These interfaces also fit naturally into a Java EE application: a user can visit a JSP page that lets her enter the symbol and date range for a stock she is interested in. In the standard example, the request will go through a standard servlet that parses the input parameters, calls a stateless Enterprise JavaBean (EJB) with an embedded Java Persistence API (JPA) bean to get the underlying data, and forwards the response to a JavaServer Pages (JSP) page, which formats the underlying data into an HTML presentation:

```
protected void processRequest(HttpServletRequest request,
        HttpServletResponse response)
        throws ServletException, IOException {
    try {
        String symbol = request.getParameter("symbol");
        if (symbol == null) {
        symbol = StockPriceUtils.getRandomSymbol();
        }
            ... similar processing for date and other params...
        StockPriceHistory sph;
        DateFormat df = localDf.get();
        sph = stockSessionBean.getHistory(symbol, df.parse(startDate),
                    df.parse(endDate), doMock, impl);
    String saveSession = request.getParameter("save");
    if (saveSession != null) {
        .... Store the data in the user's session ....
        .... Optionally store the data in a global cache for
        .... use by other requests
    }
    if (request.getParameter("long") == null) {
        // Send back a page with about 4K of data
        request.getRequestDispatcher("history.jsp").
                forward(request, response);
    }
    else {
        // Send back a page with about 100K of data
        request.getRequestDispatcher("longhistory.jsp").
                forward(request, response);
        }
    }
```

This class can inject different implementations of the history bean (for eager or lazy initialization, among other things); it will optionally cache the data retrieved from the backend database (or mock entity manager). Those are the common options when dealing with the performance of an enterprise application (in particular, caching data in the middle tier is sometimes considered to be the big performance advantage of an application server). Examples throughout the book will examine those trade-offs as well.

System Under Test

Even though this book is primarily focused on software, benchmarks are just as much a measure of the hardware that they are run on.

For the most part, the examples in this book were run on my desktop system, which has an AMD Athlon X4 640 CPU with four cores (four logical CPUs) and 8 GB of physical memory, running Ubuntu Linux 12.04 LTS.

Understand Throughput, Batching, and Response Time

The second principle in performance testing involves various ways to look at the application's performance. Which one to measure depends on which factors are most important to your application.

Elapsed Time (Batch) Measurements

The simplest way of measuring performance is to see how long it takes to accomplish a certain task: retrieve the history of 10,000 stocks for a 25-year period and calculate the standard deviation of those prices; produce a report of the payroll benefits for the 50,000 employees of a corporation; execute a loop 1,000,000 times.

In the non-Java world, this testing is straightforward: the application is written, and the time of its execution is measured. In the Java world, there is one wrinkle to this: just-in-time compilation. That process is described in Chapter 4; essentially it means that it takes a few minutes (or longer) for the code to be fully optimized and operate at peak performance. For that (and other) reasons, performance studies of Java are quite concerned about warm-up periods: performance is most often measured after the code in question has been executed long enough for it to have been compiled and optimized.

Other Factors for a Warm Application

Warming up an application is most often discussed in terms of waiting for the compiler to optimize the code in question, but there are other factors that can affect the performance of code based on how long it has run.

JPA, for example, will typically cache data it has read from the database (see Chapter 11); the second time that data is used, the operation will often be faster since the data can be obtained from the cache rather than requiring a trip to the database. Similarly, when an application reads a file, the operating system typically pages that file into memory. A test that subsequently reads the same file (e.g., in a loop to measure performance) will run faster the second time, since the data already resides in the computer's main memory and needn't actually be read from disk.

In general, there can be many places—not all of them obvious—where data is cached, and where a warm up period matters.

On the other hand, in many cases the performance of the application from start to finish is what matters. A report generator that processes 10,000 data elements will complete in a certain amount of time; to the end user, it doesn't matter if the first 5,000 elements are processed 50% more slowly than the last 5,000 elements. And even in something like an application server—where the server's performance will certainly improve over time—the initial performance matters. It may take 45 minutes for an application server to reach peak performance in certain configurations. To the users accessing the application during that time, the performance during the warm-up period does matter.

For those reasons, many examples in this book are batch-oriented (even if that is a little uncommon).

Throughput Measurements

A throughput measurement is based on the amount of work that can be accomplished in a certain period of time. Although the most common examples of throughput measurements involve a server processing data fed by a client, that is not strictly necessary: a single, standalone application can measure throughput just as easily as it measures elapsed time.

In a client-server test, a throughput measurement means that clients have no think time. If there is a single client, that client sends a request to the server. When it receives a response, it immediately sends a new request. That process continues; at the end of the test, the client reports the total number of operations it achieved. Typically, the client has multiple threads doing the same thing, and the throughput is the aggregate measure of the number of operations all clients achieved. Usually this number is reported as the number of operations per second, rather than the total number of operations over the measurement period. This measurement is frequently referred to as transactions per second (TPS), requests per second (RPS), or operations per second (OPS).

All client-server tests run the risk that the client cannot send data quickly enough to the server. This may occur because there aren't enough CPU cycles on the client machine to run the desired number of client threads, or because the client has to spend a lot of time processing the request before it can send a new request. In those cases, the test is effectively measuring the client performance rather than the server performance, which is usually not the goal.

This risk depends on the amount of work that each client thread performs (and the size and configuration of the client machine). A zero-think-time (throughput-oriented) test is more likely to encounter this situation, since each client thread is performing a lot of work. Hence, throughput tests are typically executed with fewer client threads (less load) than a corresponding test that measures response time.

It is common for tests that measure throughput also to report the average response time of its requests. That is an interesting piece of information, but changes in that number aren't indicative of a performance problem unless the reported throughput is the same. A server that can sustain 500 OPS with a 0.5-second response time is performing better than a server than reports a 0.3-second response time but only 400 OPS.

Throughput measurements are almost always taken after a suitable warm-up period, particularly since what is being measured is not a fixed set of work.

Response Time Tests

The last common test is one that measures response time: the amount of time that elapses between the sending of a request from a client and the receipt of the response.

The difference between a response time test and a throughput test (assuming the latter is client-server based) is that client threads in a response time test sleep for some period of time between operations. This is referred to as *think time*. A response time test is designed to mimic more closely what a user does: she enters a URL in a browser, spends some time reading the page that comes back, clicks on a link in the page, spends some time reading that page, and so on.

When think time is introduced into a test, throughput becomes fixed: a given number of clients executing requests with a given think time will always yield the same TPS (with some slight variance; see sidebar). At that point, the important measurement is the response time for the request: the effectiveness of the server is based on how quickly it responds to that fixed load.

Think Time and Throughput

The throughput of a test where the clients include think time can be measured in two ways. The simplest way is for clients to sleep for a period of time between requests:

```
while (!done) {
    time = executeOperation();
    Thread.currentThread().sleep(30*1000);
}
```

In this case, the throughput is somewhat dependent on the response time. If the response time is 1 second, it means that the client will send a request every 31 seconds, which will yield a throughput of 0.032 OPS. If the response time is 2 seconds, each client will send a request every 32 seconds, yielding a throughput of 0.031 OPS.

The other alternative is known as cycle time (rather than think time). Cycle time sets the total time between requests to 30 seconds, so that the time the client sleeps depends on the response time:

```
while (!done) {
    time = executeOperation();
    Thread.currentThread().sleep(30*1000 - time);
}
```

This alternative yields a fixed throughput of 0.033 OPS per client regardless of the response time (assuming the response time is always less than 30 seconds in this example).

Think times in testing tools often vary by design; they will average a particular value but use random variation to better simulate what users do. In addition, thread scheduling is never exactly real-time, so the actual time between the requests a client sends will vary slightly.

As a result, even when using a tool that provides a cycle time instead of a think time, the reported throughput between runs will vary slightly. But if the throughput is far from the expected value, something has gone wrong in the execution of the test.

There are two ways of measuring response time. Response time can be reported as an average: the individual times are added together and divided by the number of requests. Response time can also be reported as a percentile request, for example the 90th% response time. If 90% of responses are less than 1.5 seconds and 10% of responses are greater than 1.5 seconds, then 1.5 seconds is the 90th% response time.

One difference between the two numbers is in the way outliers affect the calculation of the average: since they are included as part of the average, large outliers will have a large effect on the average response time.

Figure 2-2 shows a graph of 20 requests with a somewhat typical range of response times. The response times range from 1 to 5 seconds. The average response time (represented by the lower heavy line along the x-axis) is 2.35 seconds, and 90% of the responses occur in 4 seconds or less (represented by the upper heavy line along the x-axis).

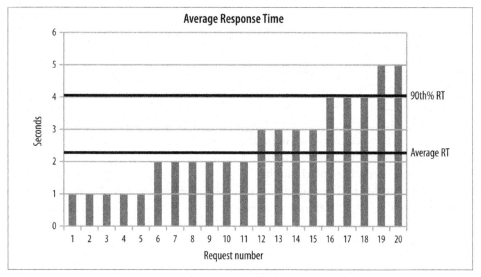

Figure 2-2. Typical set of response times

This is the usual scenario for a well-behaved test. Outliers can skew that analysis, as the data in Figure 2-3 shows.

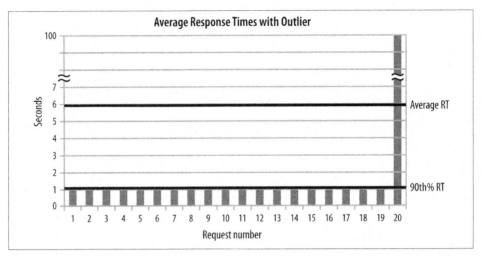

Figure 2-3. Set of response times with an outlier

This data set includes a huge outlier: one request took 100 seconds. As a result, the positions of the 90th% and average response times are reversed. The average response time is a whopping 5.95 seconds, but the 90th% response time is 1.0 second. Focus in this case should be given to reducing the effect of the outlier (which will drive down the average response time).

Outliers like that are rare in general, though they can more easily occur in Java applications because of the pause times introduced by GC. (Not that garbage collection should be expected to introduce a 100-second delay, but particularly for tests with small average response times, the GC pauses can introduce significant outliers.) In performance testing, the usual focus is on the 90th% response time (or sometimes the 95th% or 99th% response time; there is nothing magical about 90%). If you can only focus on one number, a percentile-based number is the better choice, since achieving a smaller number there will benefit a majority of users. But it is even better to look at both the average response time and at least one percentile-based response time, so that you do not miss the case where there are large outliers.

Load Generators

There are many open source and commercial load-generating tools. The examples in this book utilize Faban (*http://faban.org*), an open source, Java-based load generator. Faban comes with a simple program (fhb) that can be used to measure the performance of a simple URL:

```
% fhb -W 1000 -r 300/300/60 -c 25  http://host:port/StockServlet?stock=SDO
ops/sec: 8.247
% errors: 0.0
```

```
avg. time: 0.022
max time: 0.045
90th %: 0.030
95th %: 0.035
99th %: 0.035
```

This example measures 25 clients (-c 25) making requests to the stock servlet (re-questing symbol SDO); each request has a 1-second cycle time (-W 1000). The bench-mark has a 5-minute (300-second) warm-up period, followed by a 5-minute measure-ment period and a 1-minute ramp-down period (-r 300/300/60). Following the test, fhb reports the OPS and various response times for the test (and because this example includes think time, the response times are the important metric, while the OPS will be more or less constant).

fhb can handle POST data with limited substitutions, and limited scripting with multiple URLs. For more complex tests, Faban has a useful framework for defining benchmark load generators in Java.

Quick Summary

1. Batch-oriented tests (or any test without a warm-up period) have been infrequently used in Java performance testing, but they can yield valuable results.

2. Other tests can measure either throughput or response time, depending on whether the load comes in at a fixed rate (i.e., based on emulating think time in the client).

Understand Variability

The third principle involves understanding how test results vary over time. Programs that process exactly the same set of data will produce a different answer each time they are run. Background processes on the machine will affect the application, the network will be more or less congested when the program is run, and so on. Good benchmarks also never process exactly the same set of data each time they are run; there will be some random behavior built into the test to mimic the real world. This creates a problem: when comparing the result from one run to the result from another run, is the difference due to a regression, or due to the random variation of the test?

This problem can be solved by running the test multiple times and averaging those results. Then when a change is made to the code being tested, the test can be rerun multiple times, the results averaged, and then the two averages compared. It sounds so easy.

Unfortunately, it isn't quite as simple as that. Understanding when a difference is a real regression and when it is a random variation is difficult—and it is a key area where science leads the way, but art will come into play.

When averages in benchmark results are compared, it is impossible to know with certainty whether the difference in the averages is real, or whether it is due to random fluctuation. The best that can be done is to hypothesize that "the averages are the same" and then determine the probability that such a statement is true. If the statement is false with a high degree of probability, then we are comfortable in believing the difference in the averages (though we can never be 100% certain).

Testing code for changes like this is called regression testing. In a regression test, the original code is known as the baseline and the new code is called the specimen. Take the case of a batch program where the baseline and specimen are each run three times, yielding the times given in Table 2-2.

Table 2-2. Hypothetical times to execute two tests

	Baseline	Specimen
First iteration	1.0 seconds	0.5 seconds
Second iteration	0.8 seconds	1.25 seconds
Third iteration	1.2 seconds	0.5 seconds
Average	**1 seconds**	**0.75 seconds**

The average of the specimen says there is a 25% improvement in the code. How confident can we be that the test really reflects a 25% improvement? Things look good: two of the three specimen values are less than the baseline average, and the size of the improvement is large—yet when the analysis described in this section is performed on those results, it turns out that the probability the specimen and the baseline have the same performance is 43%. When numbers like these are observed, 43% of the time the underlying performance of the two tests are the same. Hence, performance is different only 57% of the time. This, by the way, is not exactly the same thing as saying that 57% of the time the performance is 25% better, but more about that a little later.

The reason these probabilities seem different than might be expected is due to the large variation in the results. In general, the larger the variation in a set of results, the harder it is to guess the probability that the difference in the averages is real or due to random chance.

This number—43%—is based on the result of Student's t-test, which is a statistical analysis based on the series and their variances. Student, by the way, is the pen name of the scientist who first published the test; it isn't named that way to remind you of graduate school where you (or at least I) slept through statistics class. The t-test produces a number called the *p-value*, which refers to the probability that the null hypothesis for the test is true. (There are several programs and class libraries that can calculate t-test results;

the numbers produced in this section come from using the TTest class of the Apache Commons Mathematics Library.)

The null hypothesis in regression testing is the hypothesis that the two tests have equal performance. The p-value for this example is roughly 43%, which means the confidence we can have that the series converge to the same average is 43%. Conversely, the confidence we have that the series do not converge to the same average is 57%.

What does it mean to say that 57% of the time, the series do not converge to the same average? Strictly speaking, it doesn't mean that we have 57% confidence that there is a 25% improvement in the result—it means only that we have 57% confidence that the results are different. There may be a 25% improvement, there may be a 125% improvement; it is even conceivable that the specimen actually has worse performance than the baseline. The most probable likelihood is that the difference in the test is similar to what has been measured (particularly as the p-value goes down), but certainty can never be achieved.

Statistics and Semantics

The correct way to present results of a t-test is to phrase a statement like this: there is a 57% probability that the specimen differs from the baseline, and the best estimate of that difference is 25%.

The common way to present these results is to say that there is a 57% confidence level that there is a 25% improvement in the results. Though that isn't exactly the same thing and will drive statisticians crazy, it is easy shorthand to adopt and isn't that far off the mark. Probabilistic analysis always involves some uncertainty, and that uncertainty is better understood when the semantics are precisely stated. But particularly in an arena where the underlying issues are well understood, some semantic shortcuts will inevitably creep in.

The t-test is typically used in conjunction with an α-value, which is a (somewhat arbitrary) point at which the the result is assumed to have statistical significance. The α-value is commonly set to 0.1—which means that a result is considered statistically significant if it means that the specimen and baseline will be the same only 10% (0.1) of the time (or conversely, that 90% of the time there is a difference between the specimen and baseline). Other commonly used α-values are 0.05 (95%) or 0.01 (99%). A test is considered statistically significant if the p-value is larger than $1 - \alpha$-value.

Hence, the proper way to search for regressions in code is to determine a level of statistical significance—say, 90%—and then to use the t-test to determine if the specimen and baseline are different within that degree of statistical significance. Care must be taken to understand what it means if the test for statistical significance fails. In the example, the p-value is 0.43; we cannot say that that there is statistical significance within a 90% confidence level that the result indicates that the averages are different. The fact that the test is not statistically significant does not mean that it is an insignificant result; it simply means that the test is inconclusive.

Statistically Important

Statistical significance does not mean statistical importance. A baseline with little variance that averages 1 second and a specimen with little variance that averages 1.01 seconds may have a p-value of 0.01: there is a 99% probability that there is a difference in the result.

The difference itself is only 1%. Now say a different test shows a 10% regression between specimen and baseline, but with a p-value of 0.2: not statistically significant. Which test warrants the most precious resource of all—additional time to investigate?

Although there is less confidence in the case showing a 10% difference, time is better spent investigating that test (starting, if possible, with getting additional data to see if the result is actually statistically significant). Just because the 1% difference is more probable doesn't mean that it is more important.

The usual reason a test is statistically inconclusive is that there isn't enough data in the samples. So far, the example here has looked at a series with three results in the baseline and the specimen. What if three additional results are added—again yielding 1, 1.2, and 0.8 seconds for the baseline, and 0.5, 1.25, and 0.5 seconds for the specimen? With the additional data, the p-value drops from 0.43 to 0.19: the probability that the results are different has risen from 57% to 81%. Running additional tests and adding the three data points again increases the probability to 91%—past the usual level of statistical significance.

Running additional tests until a level of statistical significance is achieved isn't always practical. It isn't, strictly speaking, necessary either. The choice of the α-value that determines statistical significance is arbitrary, even if the usual choice is common. A p-value of 0.11 is not statistically significant within a 90% confidence level, but it is statistically significant within an 89% confidence level.

The conclusion here is that regression testing is not a black-and-white science. You cannot look at a series of numbers (or their averages) and make a judgment that compares them without doing some statistical analysis to understand what the numbers mean. Yet even that analysis cannot yield a completely definitive answer due to the laws of probabilities. The job of a performance engineer is to look at the data, understand those probabilities, and determine where to spend time based on all the available data.

Quick Summary

1. Correctly determining whether results from two tests are different requires a level of statistical analysis to make sure that perceived differences are not the result of random chance.

2. The rigorous way to accomplish that is to use Student's t-test to compare the results.

3. Data from the t-test tells us the probability that a regression exists, but it doesn't tell us which regressions should be ignored and which must be pursued. Finding that balance is part of the art of performance engineering.

Test Early, Test Often

Fourth and finally, performance geeks (including me) like to recommend that performance testing be an integral part of the development cycle. In an ideal world, performance tests would be run as part of the process when code is checked into the central repository; code that introduces performance regressions would be blocked from being checked in.

There is some inherent tension between that recommendation and other recommendations in this chapter—and between that recommendation and the real world. A good performance test will encompass a lot of code—at least a medium-sized mesobenchmark. It will need to be repeated multiple times to establish confidence that any difference found between the old code and the new code is a real difference and not just random variation. On a large project, this can take a few days or a week, making it unrealistic to run performance tests on code before checking it into a repository.

The typical development cycle does not make things any easier. A project schedule often establishes a feature-freeze date: all feature changes to code must be checked into the repository at some early point in the release cycle, and the remainder of the cycle is devoted to shaking out any bugs (including performance issues) in the new release. This causes two problems for early testing:

1. Developers are under time constraints to get code checked in to meet the schedule; they will balk at having to spend time fixing a performance issue when the schedule has time for that after all the initial code is checked in. The developer who checks in code causing a 1% regression early in the cycle will face pressure to fix that issue; the developer who waits until the evening of the feature freeze can check in code that causes a 20% regression and deal with it later.

2. Performance characteristics of code will change as the code changes. This is the same principle that argued for testing the full application (in addition to any

module-level tests that may occur): heap usage will change, code compilation will change, and so on.

Despite these challenges, frequent performance testing during development is important, even if the issues cannot be immediately addressed. A developer who introduces code causing a 5% regression may have a plan to address that regression as development proceeds: maybe her code depends on some as-yet-to-be integrated feature, and when that feature is available, a small tweak will allow the regression to go away. That's a reasonable position, even though it means that performance tests will have to live with that 5% regression for a few weeks (and the unfortunate but unavoidable issue that said regression is masking other regressions).

On the other hand, if the new code causes a regression that can only be fixed with some architectural changes, it is better to catch the regression and address it early, before the rest of the code starts to depend on the new implementation. It's a balancing act, requiring analytic and often political skills.

Early, frequent testing is most useful if the following guidelines are followed:

Automate everything
All performance testing should be scripted (or programmed, though scripting is usually easier). Scripts must be able to install the new code, configure it into the full environment (creating database connections, setting up user accounts, and so on), and run the set of tests. But it doesn't stop there: the scripts must be able to run the test multiple times, perform t-test analysis on the results, and produce a report showing the confidence level that the results are the same, and the measured difference if they are not the same.

The automation must make sure that the machine is in a known state before tests are run: it must check that no unexpected processes are running, that the OS configuration is correct, and so on. A performance test is only repeatable if the environment is the same from run to run; the automation must take care of that.

Measure everything
The automation must gather every conceivable piece of data that will be useful for later analysis. This includes system information sampled throughout the run: CPU usage, disk usage, network usage, memory usage, and so on. It includes logs from the application—both those the application produces, and the logs from the garbage collector. Ideally it can include Java Flight Recorder (JFR) recordings (see Chapter 3) or other low-impact profiling information, periodic thread stacks, and other heap analysis data like histograms or full heap dumps (though the full heap dumps, in particular, take a lot of space and cannot necessarily be kept long term).

The monitoring information must also include data from other parts of the system, if applicable: for example, if the program uses a database, then include the system statistics from the database machine as well as any diagnostic output from the database (including performance reports like Oracle's Automatic Workload Repository [AWR] reports).

This data will guide the analysis of any regressions that are uncovered. If the CPU usage has increased, it's time to consult the profile information to see what is taking more time. If the time spent in GC has increased, it's time to consult the heap profiles to see what is consuming more memory. If CPU time and GC time have decreased, contention somewhere has likely slowed down performance: stack data can point to particular synchronization bottlenecks (see Chapter 9), JFR recordings can be used to find application latencies, or database logs can point to something that has increased database contention.

When figuring out the source of a regression, it is time to play detective, and the more data that is available, the more clues there are to follow. As discussed in Chapter 1, it isn't necessarily the case that the JVM is the regression. Measure everything, everywhere, to make sure the correct analysis can be done.

Run on the target system

A test that is run on a single-core laptop will behave very differently than a test run on a machine with a 256-thread SPARC CPU. That should be clear in terms of threading effects: the larger machine is going to run more threads at the same time, reducing contention among application threads for access to the CPU. At the same time, the large system will show synchronization bottlenecks that would be unnoticed on the small laptop.

There are other performance differences that are just as important even if they are not as immediately obvious. Many important tuning flags calculate their defaults based on the underlying hardware the JVM is running on. Code is compiled differently from platform to platform. Caches—software and, more importantly, hardware—behave differently on different systems, and under different loads. And so on...

Hence, the performance of a particular production environment can never be fully known without testing the expected load on the expected hardware. Approximations and extrapolations can be made from running smaller tests on smaller hardware, and in the real world, duplicating a production environment for testing can be quite difficult or expensive. But extrapolations are simply predictions, and even in the best case, predictions can be wrong. A large-scale system is more than the sum of its parts, and there can be no substitute for performing adequate load testing on the target platform.

Quick Summary

1. Frequent performance testing is important, but it doesn't occur in a vacuum; there are trade-offs to consider regarding the normal development cycle.

2. An automated testing system that collects all possible statistics from all machines and programs will provide the necessary clues to any performance regressions.

Summary

Performance testing involves a number of trade-offs. Making good choices among competing options is crucial to successfully tracking the performance characteristics of a system.

Choosing what to test is the first area where experience with the application and intuition will be of immeasurable help when setting up performance tests. Microbenchmarks tend to be the least helpful test; they are useful really only to set a broad guideline for certain operations. That leaves a quite broad continuum of other tests, from small module-level tests to a large, multitiered environment. Tests all along that continuum have some merit, and choosing the tests along that continuum is one place where experience and intuition will come into play. However, in the end there can be no substitute for testing a full application as it is deployed in production; only then can the full effect of all performance-related issues be understood.

Similarly, understanding what is and is not an actual regression in code is not always a black-and-white issue. Programs always exhibit random behavior, and once randomness is injected into the equation, we will never be 100% certain about what data means. Applying statistical analysis to the results can help to turn the analysis to a more objective path, but even then some subjectivity will be involved. Understanding the underlying probabilities and what they mean can help to lessen that subjectivity.

Finally, with these foundations in place, an automated testing system can be put in place that gathers full information about everything that occurred during the test. With the knowledge of what's going on and what the underlying tests mean, the performance analyst can apply both science and art so that the program can exhibit the best possible performance.

## CHAPTER 3

A Java Performance Toolbox

Performance analysis is all about visibility—knowing what is going on inside of an application, and in the application's environment. Visibility is all about tools. And so performance tuning is all about tools.

In Chapter 2, I stressed the importance of taking a data-driven approach to performance: you must measure the application's performance and understand what those measurements mean. Performance analysis must be similarly data-driven: you must have data about what, exactly, the program is doing in order to make it perform better. How to obtain and understand that data is the subject of this chapter.

There are hundreds of tools that provide information about what a Java application is doing, and of course it is impractical to look at all of them. Many of the most important tools come with the Java Development Kit (JDK) or are developed in open source at *http://java.net*, and even though those tools have other open source and commercial competitors, this chapter focuses mostly on the JDK tools as a matter of expedience.

Operating System Tools and Analysis

The starting point for program analysis is actually not Java-specific at all: it is the basic set of monitoring tools that come with the operating system. On Unix-based systems, these are `sar` (System Accounting Report) and its constituent tools like `vmstat`, `iostat`, `prstat`, and so on. On Windows, there are graphical resource monitors as well as command-line utilities like `typeperf`.

Whenever performance tests are run, data should be gathered from the operating system. At a minimum, information on CPU, memory, and disk usage should be collected; if the program uses the network, information on network usage should be gathered as well. If performance tests are automated, this means relying on command-line tools (even on Windows)—but even if tests are running interactively, it is better to have a command-line tool that captures output, rather than eyeballing a GUI graph and guessing what it means. The output can always be graphed later when doing analysis.

CPU Usage

Let's look first at monitoring the CPU and what it tells us about Java programs. CPU usage is typically divided into two categories: user time and system time (Windows refers to this as privileged time). User time is the percentage of time the CPU is executing application code, while system time is the percentage of time the CPU is executing kernel code. System time is related to the application; if the application performs I/O, for example, the kernel will execute the code to read the file from disk, or write the buffered data to the network, and so on. Anything that uses an underlying system resource will cause the application to use more system time.

The goal in performance is to drive CPU usage as high as possible for as short a time as possible. That may sound a little counterintuitive; you've doubtless sat at your desktop and watched it struggle because the CPU is 100% utilized. So let's consider what the CPU usage actually tells us.

The first thing to keep in mind is that the CPU usage number is an average over an interval—5 seconds, 30 seconds, perhaps even as little as 1 second (though never really less than that). Say that the average CPU usage of a program is 50% for the 10 minutes it takes to execute. If the code is tuned such that the CPU usage goes to 100%, the performance of the program will double: it will run in 5 minutes. If performance is doubled again, the CPU will still be at 100% during the 2.5 minutes it takes the program to complete. The CPU number is an indication of how effectively the program is using the CPU, and so the higher the number the better.

If I run vmstat 1 on my Linux desktop, I will get a series of lines (one every second) that look like this:

```
% vmstat 1
procs -----------memory---------- ---swap-- -----io---- -system-- ----cpu----
 r  b   swpd   free   buff  cache   si   so    bi    bo   in   cs us sy id wa
 2  0      0 1797836 1229068 1508276 0    0     0     9 2250 3634 41  3 55  0
 2  0      0 1801772 1229076 1508284 0    0     0     8 2304 3683 43  3 54  0
 1  0      0 1813552 1229084 1508284 0    0     3    22 2354 3896 42  3 55  0
 1  0      0 1819628 1229092 1508292 0    0     0    84 2418 3998 43  2 55  0
```

This example comes from running an application with one active thread—that makes the example easier to follow, but the concepts apply even if there are multiple threads.

During each second, the CPU is busy for 450 ms (42% of the time executing user code, and 3% of the time executing system code). Similarly, the CPU is idle for 550 ms. The CPU can be idle for a number of reasons:

- The application might be blocked on a synchronization primitive and unable to execute until that lock is released.
- The application might be waiting for something, such as a response to come back from a call to the database.
- The application might have nothing to do.

These first two situations are always indicative of something that can be addressed. If contention on the lock can be reduced, or the database can be tuned so that it sends the answer back more quickly, then the program will run faster and the average CPU use of the application will go up (assuming, of course, that there isn't another such issue that will continue to block the application).

That third point is where confusion often lies. If the application has something to do (and is not prevented from doing it because it is waiting for a lock or another resource), then the CPU will spend cycles executing the application code. This is a general principle, not specific to Java. Say that you write a simple script containing an infinite loop. When that script is executed, it will consume 100% of a CPU. The following batch job will do just that in Windows:

```
ECHO OFF
:BEGIN
ECHO LOOPING
GOTO BEGIN
REM We never get here...
ECHO DONE
```

Consider what it would mean if this script did not consume 100% of a CPU. It would mean that the operating system had something it could do—it could print yet another line saying LOOPING—but it chose instead to be idle. Being idle doesn't help anyone in that case, and if we were doing a useful (lengthy) calculation, forcing the CPU to be periodically idle would mean that it would take longer to get the answer we are after.

If you run this command on a single-CPU machine, much of the time you are unlikely to notice that it is running. But if you attempt to start a new program, or time the performance of another application, then you will certainly see the effect. Operating systems are good at time-slicing programs that are competing for CPU cycles, but there will be less CPU available for the new program, and it will run more slowly. That experience sometimes leads people to think it would be a good idea to leave some idle CPU cycles just in case something else needs them.

But the operating system cannot guess what you want to do next; it will (by default) execute everything it can rather than leaving the CPU idle.

Limiting CPU for a Program

Running a program whenever there are CPU cycles available maximizes the performance of that program. There may be times you don't want that behavior. If, for example, you run *SETI@home*, it will consume all available CPU cycles on your machine. That may be fine when you aren't working, or if you're just surfing the web or writing documents, but it could otherwise hamper your productivity. (And let's not consider what might happen if you are playing a CPU-intensive game!)

A number of operating-system-specific mechanisms can artificially throttle the amount of CPU that a program uses—in effect, forcing the CPU to leave idle cycles just in case something might want to take advantage of them. The priority of processes can also be changed so that those background jobs don't take CPU from what you want to run but still don't leave idle CPU cycles. Those techniques are beyond the scope of our discussion (and for the record, *SETI@home* will let you configure those; it won't really take up all the spare cycles on your machine unless you tell it to do so).

Java and single-CPU usage

To return to the discussion of the Java application—what does periodic, idle CPU mean in that case? It depends on the type of application. If the code in question is a batch-style application where there is a fixed amount of work, you should never see idle CPU because there is no work to do. Driving the CPU usage higher is always the goal for batch jobs, because it means the job will be completed faster. If the CPU is already at 100%, then you can of course still look for optimizations that allow the work to be completed faster (while trying also to keep the CPU at 100%).

If the measurement involves a server-style application that accepts requests from some source, then there may be idle time because no work is available: for example, when a web server has processed all outstanding HTTP requests and is waiting for the next request. This is where the average time comes in. The sample vmstat output was taken during execution of an application server that was receiving one request every second. It took 450 ms for the application server to process that request—meaning that the CPU was actually 100% busy for 450 ms, and 0% busy for 550 ms. That was reported as the CPU being 45% busy.

Although it usually happens at a level of granularity that is too small to visualize, the expected behavior of the CPU when running a load-based application is to operate in short bursts like this. The same macro-level pattern will be seen from the reporting if the CPU received one request every half-second and the average time to process the request was 225 ms. The CPU would be busy for 225 ms, idle for 275 ms, busy again for 225 ms, and idle for 275 ms: on average, 45% busy and 55% idle.

If the application is optimized so that each request takes only 400 ms, then the overall CPU usage will also be reduced (to 40%). This is the only case where driving the CPU usage lower makes sense—when there is a fixed amount of load coming into the system and the application is not constrained by external resources. On the other hand, that optimization also gives you the opportunity to add more load into the system, ultimately increasing the CPU utilization. And at a micro level, optimizing in this case is still a matter of getting the CPU usage to 100% for a short period of time (the 400 ms it takes to execute the request)—it's just that the duration of the CPU spike is too short to effectively register as 100% using most tools.

Java and multi-CPU usage

This example has assumed a single thread running on a single CPU, but the concepts are the same in the general case of multiple threads running on multiple CPUs. Multiple threads can skew the average of the CPU in interesting ways—one such example is shown in Chapter 5, which shows the effect of the multiple GC threads on CPU usage. But in general, the goal for multiple threads on a multi-CPU machine is still to drive the CPU higher by making sure individual threads are not blocked, or to drive the CPU lower (over a long interval) because the threads have completed their work and are waiting for more work.

In a multithreaded, multi-CPU case, there is one important addition regarding when CPUs could be idle: CPUs can be idle even when there is work to do. This occurs if there are no threads available in the program to handle that work. The typical case here is an application with a fixed-size thread pool that is running various tasks. Each thread can execute only one task at a time, and if that particular task blocks (e.g., is waiting for a response from the database), the thread cannot pick up a new task to execute in the meantime. Hence, there can be periods where there are tasks to be executed (work to be done), but no thread is available to execute them; the result is some idle CPU time.

In that example, the size of the thread pool should be increased. However, don't assume that just because idle CPU is available, it means that the size of the thread pool should be increased in order to accomplish more work. The program may not be getting CPU cycles for the other two reasons previously mentioned—because of bottlenecks in locks or external resources. It is important to understand why the program isn't getting CPU before determining a course of action. (See Chapter 9 for more details on this topic.)

Looking at the CPU usage is a first step in understanding application performance, but it is only that: use it to see if the code is using all the CPU that can be expected, or if it points to some synchronization or resource issue.

The CPU Run Queue

Both Windows and Unix systems allow you to monitor the number of threads that can be run (meaning that they are not blocked on I/O, or sleeping, and so on). Unix systems refer to this as the *run queue*, and several tools include the run queue length in their output. That includes the vmstat output in the last section: the first number in each line is the length of the run queue. Windows refers to this number as the *processor queue*, and reports it (among other ways) via typeperf:

```
C:> typeperf -si 1 "\System\Processor Queue Length"
"05/11/2013 19:09:42.678","0.000000"
"05/11/2013 19:09:43.678","0.000000"
```

There is a very important difference in the output here: the run queue length number on a Unix system (which was either 1 or 2 in the sample vmstat output) is the number of all threads that *are* running or that *could run* if there were an available CPU. In that example, there was always at least one thread that wanted to run: the single thread doing application work. Hence, the run queue length was always at least 1. Keep in mind that the run queue represents everything on the machine, so sometimes there are other threads (from completely separate processes) that want to run, which is why the run queue length sometimes was 2 in that sample output.

In Windows, the processor queue length does not include the number of threads that are currently running. Hence, in the typeperf sample output, the processor queue number was 0, even though the machine was running the same single-threaded application with one thread always executing.

If there are more threads to run than available CPUs, performance will begin to degrade. In general, then, you want the processor queue length to be 0 on Windows, and equal to (or less than) the number of CPUs on Unix systems. That isn't a hard and fast rule; there are system processes and other things that will come along periodically and briefly raise that value without any significant performance impact. But if the run queue length is too high for any significant period of time, it is an indication that the machine is overloaded and you should look into reducing the amount of work the machine is doing (either by moving jobs to another machine or optimizing the code).

Quick Summary

1. CPU time is the first thing to examine when looking at performance of an application.

2. The goal in optimizing code is to drive the CPU usage up (for a shorter period of time), not down.

3. Understand why CPU usage is low before diving in and attempting to tune an application.

Disk Usage

Monitoring disk usage has two important goals. The first of these regards the application itself: if the application is doing a lot of disk I/O, then it is easy for that I/O to become a bottleneck.

Knowing when disk I/O is a bottleneck is tricky, because it depends on the behavior of the application. If the application is not efficiently buffering the data it writes to disk (an example of which is in Chapter 12), the disk I/O statistics will be quite low. But if the application is performing more I/O than the disk can handle, the disk I/O statistics will be quite high. In either situation, performance can be improved; be on the lookout for both.

The basic I/O monitors on some systems are better than on others. Here is some partial output of iostat on a Linux system:

```
% iostat -xm 5
avg-cpu:   %user   %nice %system %iowait  %steal   %idle
           23.45    0.00   37.89    0.10    0.00   38.56

           Device:          rrqm/s   wrqm/s    r/s     w/s    rMB/s
           sda                0.00    11.60    0.60   24.20    0.02

           wMB/s avgrq-sz avgqu-sz   await r_await w_await  svctm  %util
           0.14    13.35     0.15    6.06    5.33    6.08   0.42   1.04
```

The application here is writing data to disk sda. At first glance, the disk statistics look good. The w_await—the time to service each I/O write—is fairly low (6.08 ms), and the disk is only 1.04% utilized. (The acceptable values for that depend on the physical disk, but the 5200 RPM disk in my desktop system behaves well when the service time is under 15 ms.) But there is a clue here that something is wrong: the system is spending 37.89% of its time in the kernel. If the system is doing other I/O (in other programs), that's one thing; if all that system time is from the application being tested, then something inefficient is happening.

The fact that the system is doing 24.2 writes per second is another clue here: that is a lot when writing only 0.14 MB per second (MBps). I/O has become a bottleneck, and the next step would be to look into how the application is performing its writes.

The other side of the coin comes if the disk cannot keep up with the I/O requests:

```
% iostat -xm 5
avg-cpu:   %user   %nice %system %iowait  %steal   %idle
           35.05    0.00    7.85   47.89    0.00    9.20

           Device:          rrqm/s   wrqm/s    r/s     w/s    rMB/s
           sda                0.00     0.20    1.00  163.40    0.00

           wMB/s avgrq-sz avgqu-sz   await r_await w_await  svctm  %util
           81.09 1010.19   142.74  866.47   97.60  871.17   6.08 100.00
```

The nice thing about Linux is that it tells us immediately that the disk is 100% utilized; it also tells us that processes are spending 47.89% of their time in iowait (that is, waiting for the disk).

Even on other systems where only raw data is available, that data will tell us something is amiss: the time to complete the I/O (w_await) is 871 ms, the queue size is quite large, and the disk is writing 81 MB of data per second. This all points to disk I/O as a problem, and that the amount of I/O in the application (or, possibly, elsewhere in the system) must be reduced.

A second reason to monitor disk usage—even if the application is not expected to perform a significant amount of I/O—is to help monitor if the system is swapping. Computers have a fixed amount of physical memory, but they can run a set of applications that use a much larger amount of virtual memory. Applications tend to reserve more memory than they actually need, and they usually operate on only a subset of their memory. In both cases, the operating system can keep the unused parts of memory on disk, and page it into physical memory only if it is needed.

For the most part, this kind of memory management works well, especially for interactive and GUI programs (which is good, or your laptop would require much more memory than it has). It works less well for server-based applications, since those applications tend to use more of their memory. And it works particularly badly for any kind of Java application (including a Swing-based GUI application running on your desktop) because of the Java heap. More details about that appear in Chapter 5.

A system that is swapping—moving pages of data from main memory to disk and vice versa—will have generally bad performance. Other system tools can also report if the system is swapping; for example, the vmstat output has two columns (si, for swap in, and so, for swap out) that alert us if the system is swapping. Disk activity is another indicator that swapping might be occurring.

Quick Summary

1. Monitoring disk usage is important for all applications. For applications that don't directly write to disk, system swapping can still affect their performance.

2. Applications that write to disk can be bottlenecked both because they are writing data inefficiently (too little throughput) or because they are writing too much data (too much throughput).

Network Usage

If you are running an application that uses the network—for example, a Java EE application server—then you must monitor the network traffic as well. Network usage is similar to disk traffic: the application might be inefficiently using the network so that bandwidth is too low, or the total amount of data written to a particular network interface might be more than the interface is able to handle.

Unfortunately, standard system tools are less than ideal for monitoring network traffic because they typically show only the number of packets and number of bytes that are sent and received over a particular network interface. That is useful information, but it doesn't tell us if the network is under- or overutilized.

On Unix systems, the basic network monitoring tool is `netstat` (and on most Linux distributions, `netstat` is not even included and must be obtained separately). On Windows, `typeperf` can be used in scripts to monitor the network usage—but here is a case where the GUI has an advantage: the standard Windows resource monitor will display a graph showing what percentage of the network is in use. Unfortunately, the GUI is of little help in an automated performance testing scenario.

Fortunately, there are many open source and commercial tools that monitor network bandwidth. On Unix systems, one popular command-line tool is `nicstat` (*http://sourceforge.net/projects/nicstat*), which presents a summary of the traffic on each interface, including the degree to which the interface is utilized:

```
% nicstat 5
Time      Int      rKB/s   wKB/s   rPk/s   wPk/s   rAvs    wAvs    %Util  Sat
17:05:17  e1000g1  225.7   176.2   905.0   922.5   255.4   195.6   0.33   0.00
```

The `e1000g1` interface is a 1,000 MB interface; it is not utilized very much (0.33%) in this example. The usefulness of this tool (and others like it) is that it calculates the utilization of the interface. In this output, there are 225.7 Kbps of data being written and 176.2 Kbps of data being read over the interface. Doing the division for a 1,000 MB network yields the 0.33% utilization figure, and the `nicstat` tool was able to figure out the bandwidth of the interface automatically.

Tools such as `typeperf` or `netstat` will report the amount of data read and written, but to figure out the network utilization, you must determine the bandwidth of the interface and perform the calculation in your own scripts. Be sure to remember that the bandwidth is measured in bits per second (bps), although tools generally report bytes per second (Bps). A 1,000-megabit network yields 125 megabytes (MB) per second. In this example, 0.22 MBps are read and 0.16 MBps are written; adding those and dividing by 125 yields a 0.33% utilization rate. So there is no magic to `nicstat` (or similar) tools; they are just more convenient to use.

Networks cannot sustain a 100% utilization rate. For local-area Ethernet networks, a sustained utilization rate over 40% indicates that the interface is saturated. If the network is packet-switched or utilizes a different medium, the maximum possible sustained rate will be different; consult a network architect to determine the appropriate goal. This goal is independent of Java, which will simply use the networking parameters and interfaces of the operating system.

Quick Summary

1. For network-based applications, make sure to monitor the network to make sure it hasn't become a bottleneck.

2. Applications that write to the network can be bottlenecked both because they are writing data inefficiently (too little throughput) or because they are writing too much data (too much throughput).

Java Monitoring Tools

To gain insight into the JVM itself, Java monitoring tools are required. A number of tools come with the JDK:

jcmd

Prints basic class, thread, and VM information for a Java process. This is suitable for use in scripts; it is executed like this:

```
% jcmd process_id command optional_arguments
```

Supplying the command help will list all possible commands, and supplying help <command> will give the syntax for a particular command.

jconsole

Provides a graphical view of JVM activities, including thread usage, class usage, and GC activities.

jhat

Reads and helps analyze memory heap dumps. This is a postprocessing utility.

jmap

Provides heap dumps and other information about JVM memory usage. Suitable for scripting, though the heap dumps must be used in a postprocessing tool.

jinfo

Provides visibility into the system properties of the JVM, and allows some system properties to be set dynamically. Suitable for scripting.

jstack

Dumps the stacks of a Java process. Suitable for scripting.

jstat

Provides information about GC and class-loading activities. Suitable for scripting.

`jvisualvm`

A GUI tool to monitor a JVM, profile a running application, and analyze JVM heap dumps (which is a postprocessing activity, though `jvisualvm` can also take the heap dump from a live program).

These tools fits into these broad areas:

- Basic VM information
- Thread information
- Class information
- Live GC analysis
- Heap dump postprocessing
- Profiling a JVM

As you likely noticed, there is not a one-to-one mapping here; many tools perform functions in multiple areas. So rather than exploring each tool individually, we'll take a look at the functional areas of visibility that are important to Java, and discuss how various tools provide that information. Along the way, we'll discuss other tools (some open source, some commercial) that provide the same basic functionality but which have advantages over the basic JDK tools.

Basic VM Information

JVM tools can provide basic information about a running JVM process: how long it has been up, what JVM flags are in use, JVM system properties, and so on.

Uptime

The length of time the JVM has been up can be found via this command:

```
% jcmd process_id VM.uptime
```

System properties

The set of items in `System.getProperties()` can be displayed with either of these commands:

```
% jcmd process_id VM.system_properties
```

or

```
% jinfo -sysprops process_id
```

This includes all properties set on the command line with a -D option, any properties dynamically added by the application, and the set of default properties for the JVM.

JVM version

The version of the JVM is obtained like this:

```
% jcmd process_id VM.version
```

JVM command line

The command line can be displayed in the VM summary tab of jconsole, or via jcmd:

```
% jcmd process_id VM.command_line
```

JVM tuning flags

The tuning flags in effect for an application can be obtained like this:

```
% jcmd process_id VM.flags [-all]
```

Working with tuning flags

There are a lot of tuning flags that can be given to a JVM, and many of those flags are a major focus of this book. Keeping track of those flags and their default values can be a little daunting; those last two examples of jcmd are quite useful in that regard. The command_line command shows which flags were specified directly on the command line. The flags command shows which flags were set on the command line, plus some flags that were set directly by the JVM (because their value was determined ergonomically). Including the -all option lists every flag within the JVM.

There are hundreds of JVM tuning flags, and most of them are very obscure; it is recommended that most of them never be changed (see "Too Much Information?" on page 49). Figuring out which flags are in effect is a frequent task when diagnosing performance issues, and the jcmd commands can do that for a running JVM. Often, what you'd rather figure out is what the platform-specific defaults for a particular JVM are, in which case using the -XX:+PrintFlagsFinal option on the command line is more useful.

A useful way to determine what the flags are set to on a particular platform is to execute this command:

```
% java other_options -XX:+PrintFlagsFinal -version
...Hundreds of lines of output, including...
uintx InitialHeapSize                          := 4169431040      {product}
intx InlineSmallCode                           = 2000             {pd product}
```

You should include any other options you intend to use on the command line because setting some options (particularly when setting GC-related flags) will affect the final value of other options. This will print out the entire list of JVM flags and their values (the same as is printed via the VM.flags -all option to jcmd for a live JVM).

Flag data from these commands is printed in one of the two ways shown. The colon in the first line of included output indicates that a nondefault value is in use for the flag in question. This can happen for the following reasons:

1. The flag's value was specified directly on the command line.
2. Some other option indirectly changed that option.
3. The JVM calculated the default value ergonomically.

The second line (without a colon) indicates that value is the default value for this version of the JVM. Default values for some flags may be different on different platforms, which is shown in the final column of this output. `product` means that the default setting of the flag is uniform across all platforms; `pd product` indicates that the default setting of the flag is platform-dependent.

Too Much Information?

The `PrintFlagsFinal` command will print out hundreds of available tuning flags for the JVM (there are 668 possible flags in JDK 7u40, for example).

The vast majority of these flags are designed to enable support engineers to gather more information from running (and misbehaving) applications. It is tempting upon learning that there is a flag called `AllocatePrefetchLines` (which has a default value of 3) to assume that value can be changed so that instruction prefetching might work better on a particular processor. But that kind of hit-or-miss tuning is not worthwhile in a vacuum; none of those flags should be changed without a compelling reason to do so. In the case of the `AllocatePrefetchLines` flag, that would include knowledge of the application's prefetch performance, the characteristics of the CPU running the application, and the effect that changing the number will have on the JVM code itself.

Other possible values for the last column include `manageable` (the flag's value can be changed dynamically during runtime) and `C2 diagnostic` (the flag provides diagnostic output for the compiler engineers to understand how the compiler is functioning).

Yet another way to see this information for a running application is with `jinfo`. The advantage to `jinfo` is that it allows certain flag values to be changed during execution of the program.

Here is how to retrieve the values of all the flags in the process:

```
% jinfo -flags process_id
```

With the `-flags` option, `jinfo` will provide information about all flags; otherwise it prints only those specified on the command line. The output from either of these commands isn't as easy to read as that from the `-XX:+PrintFlagsFinal` option, but `jinfo` has other features to keep in mind.

`jinfo` can inspect the value of an individual flag:

```
% jinfo -flag PrintGCDetails process_id
-XX:+PrintGCDetails
```

Although `jinfo` does not itself indicate whether a flag is manageable or not, flags that are manageable (as identified when using the `PrintFlagsFinal` argument) can be turned on or off via `jinfo`:

```
% jinfo -flag -PrintGCDetails process_id  # turns off PrintGCDetails
% jinfo -flag PrintGCDetails process_id
-XX:-PrintGCDetails
```

Be aware that `jinfo` can change the value of any flag, but that doesn't mean that the JVM will respond to that change. For example, most flags that affect the behavior of a GC algorithm are used at startup time to determine various ways that the collector will behave. Altering a flag later via `jinfo` does not cause the JVM to change its behavior; it will continue executing based on how the algorithm was initialized. So this technique only works for those flags marked `manageable` in the output of the `PrintFlagsFinal` command.

 Quick Summary

1. `jcmd` can be used to find the basic JVM information—including the value of all the tuning flags—for a running application.

2. Default flag values can be found by including `-XX:+PrintFlags Final` on a command line. This is useful for determining the default ergonomic settings of flags on a particular platform.

3. `jinfo` is useful for inspecting (and in some cases changing) individual flags.

Thread Information

`jconsole` and `jvisualvm` display information (in real time) about the number of threads running in an application.

It can be very useful to look at the stack of running threads to determine if they are blocked. The stacks can be obtained via `jstack`:

```
% jstack process_id
... Lots of output showing each thread's stack ...
```

Stack information can also be obtained from `jcmd`:

```
% jcmd process_id Thread.print
... Lots of output showing each thread's stack ...
```

See Chapter 9 for more details on monitoring thread stacks.

Class Information

Information about the number of classes in use by an application can be obtained from jconsole or jstat. jstat can also provide information about class compilation.

See Chapter 12 for more details on class usage by applications, and Chapter 4 for details on monitoring class compilation.

Live GC Analysis

Virtually every monitoring tool reports something about GC activity. jconsole displays live graphs of the heap usage; jcmd allows GC operations to be performed; jmap can print heap summaries or information on the permanent generation or create a heap dump; and jstat produces a lot of different views of what the garbage collector is doing.

See Chapter 5 for examples of how these programs monitor GC activities.

Heap Dump Postprocessing

Heap dumps can be captured from the jvisualvm GUI, or from the command line using jcmd or jmap. The heap dump is a snapshot of the heap that can be analyzed with various tools, including jvisualvm and jhat. Heap dump processing is one area where third-party tools have traditionally been a step ahead of what comes with the JDK, so Chapter 7 uses a third-party tool—the Eclipse Memory Analyzer Tool—to provide examples of how to postprocess heap dumps.

Profiling Tools

Profilers are the most important tool in a performance analyst's toolbox. There are many profilers available for Java, each with its own advantages and disadvantages. Profiling is one area where it often makes sense to use different tools—particularly if they are sampling profilers. One sampling profiler may find different problems than another one, even on the same application.

Almost all Java profiling tools are themselves written in Java and work by "attaching" themselves to the application to be profiled—meaning that the profiler opens a socket (or other communication channel) to the target application. The target application and the profiling tool then exchange information about the behavior of the target application.

This means you must pay attention to tuning the profiling tool just as you would tune any other Java application. In particular, if the application being profiled is large, it will transfer quite a lot of data to the profiling tool, so the profiling tool must have a sufficiently large heap to handle the data. It is often a good idea to run the profiling tool with a concurrent GC algorithm as well; ill-timed full GC pauses in the profiling tool can cause the buffers holding the data to overflow.

Sampling Profilers

Profiling happens in one of two modes: sampling mode or instrumented mode. Sampling mode is the basic mode of profiling and carries the least amount of overhead. That's important, since one of the pitfalls of profiling is that by introducing measurement into the application, you are altering its performance characteristics. (Still, you must profile: how else will you know if the cat inside your program is still alive?) Limiting the impact of profiling will lead to results that more closely model how the application behaves under usual circumstances.

Unfortunately, sampling profilers can be subject to all sorts of errors. Sampling profilers work when a timer periodically fires; the profiler then looks at each thread and determines which method the thread is executing. That method is then charged with having been executed since the timer previously fired.

The most common sampling error is illustrated by Figure 3-1. The thread here is alternating between executing methodA (shown in the shaded bars) and methodB (shown in the clear bars). If the timer fires only when the thread happens to be in methodB, the profile will report that the thread spent all its time executing methodB; in reality, more time was actually spent in methodA.

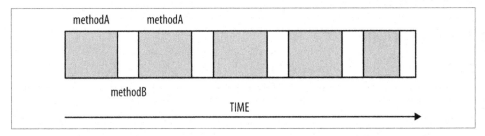

Figure 3-1. Alternate method execution

This is the most common sampling error, but it is by no means the only one. The way to minimize these errors is to profile over a longer period of time, and to reduce the time interval between samples. Reducing the interval between samples is counterproductive to the goal of minimizing the impact of profiling on the application; there is a balance here. Profiling tools resolve that balance differently, which is one reason why one profiling tool may happen to report much different data than another tool.

Figure 3-2 shows a basic sampling profile taken to measure the startup of a domain of the GlassFish application server. The profile shows that the bulk of the time (19%) was spent in the defineClass1() method, followed by the getPackageSourcesInternal()

method, and so on. It isn't a surprise that the startup of a program would be dominated by the performance of defining classes; in order to make this code faster, the performance of classloading must be improved.

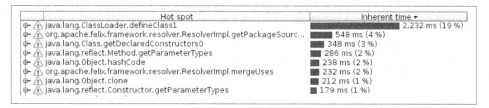

Hot spot	Inherent time ▾
⊙ ⚠ java.lang.ClassLoader.defineClass1	2,232 ms (19 %)
⊙ ⚠ org.apache.felix.framework.resolver.ResolverImpl.getPackageSourc...	548 ms (4 %)
⊙ ⚠ java.lang.Class.getDeclaredConstructors0	348 ms (3 %)
⊙ ⚠ java.lang.reflect.Method.getParameterTypes	286 ms (2 %)
⊙ ⚠ java.lang.Object.hashCode	238 ms (2 %)
⊙ ⚠ org.apache.felix.framework.resolver.ResolverImpl.mergeUses	232 ms (2 %)
⊙ ⚠ java.lang.Object.clone	212 ms (1 %)
⊙ ⚠ java.lang.reflect.Constructor.getParameterTypes	179 ms (1 %)

Figure 3-2. A sample-based profile

Note carefully the last statement: it is the performance of classloading that must be improved, and not the performance of the defineClass1() method. The common assumption when looking at a profile is that improvements must come from optimizing the top method in the profile. However, that is often too limiting an approach. In this case, the defineClass1() method is part of the JDK, and a native method at that; its performance isn't going to be improved without rewriting the JVM. Still, assume that it could be rewritten so that it took 60% less time. That will translate to a 10% overall improvement in the execution time—which is certainly nothing to sneeze at.

More commonly, though, the top method in a profile may take 2% of 3% of total time; cutting its time in half (which is usually enormously difficult) will only speed up application performance by 1%. Focusing only on the top method in a profile isn't usually going to lead to huge gains in performance.

Instead, the top method(s) in a profile should point you to the area in which to search for optimizations. GlassFish performance engineers aren't going to attempt to make class definition faster, but they can figure out how to speed up classloading in general —by loading fewer classes, loading classes in parallel, and so on.

Quick Summary

1. Sampling-based profilers are the most common kind of profiler.

2. Because of their relatively low profile, sampling profilers introduce fewer measurement artifacts.

3. Different sampling profiles behave differently; each may be better for a particular application.

Instrumented Profilers

Instrumented profilers are much more intrusive than sampling profilers, but they can also give more beneficial information about what's happening inside a program. Figure 3-3 uses the same profiling tool to look at startup of the same GlassFish domain, but this time it is using instrumented mode.

Hot spot	Inherent time ▾	Average Time	Invocations
org.apache.felix.framework.resolver.ResolverImpl.getPackageSourcesInternal	11,934 ms (13 %)	356 µs	33,489
org.apache.felix.framework.util.ImmutableMap.get	11,651 ms (12 %)	2 µs	4,769,764
java.lang.Object.equals	5,797 ms (6 %)	0 µs	15,907,963
org.apache.felix.framework.BundleWiringImpl$BundleClassLoader.findClass	4,814 ms (5 %)	1,022 µs	4,710
java.util.Map.get	4,635 ms (5 %)	0 µs	6,783,508
java.util.Iterator.hasNext	4,123 ms (4 %)	0 µs	6,179,992
java.util.Map$Entry.getKey	4,013 ms (4 %)	0 µs	11,126,431
java.util.Iterator.next	3,951 ms (4 %)	0 µs	5,687,480
org.apache.felix.framework.util.ImmutableList$ListItr.hasNext	3,430 ms (3 %)	0 µs	4,591,013
org.apache.felix.framework.resolver.ResolverImpl.mergeUses	2,329 ms (2 %)	8 µs	265,690
java.lang.String.equals	1,988 ms (2 %)	0 µs	5,056,880

Figure 3-3. An instrumented profile

A few things are immediately apparent about this profile. First, notice that the "hot" method is now getPackageSourcesInternal(), accounting for 13% of the total time (not 4%, as in the previous example). There are other expensive methods near the top of the profile, and the defineClass1() method doesn't appear at all. The tool also now reports the number of times each method was invoked, and it calculates the average time per invocation based on that number.

Is this a better profile than the sampled version? It depends; there is no way to know in a given situation which is the more accurate profile. The invocation count of an instrumented profile is certainly accurate, and that additional information is often quite helpful in determining where the code is actually spending more time and which things are more fruitful to optimize. In this case, although the ImmutableMap.get() method is consuming 12% of the total time, it is called 4.7 million times. We can have a much greater performance impact by reducing the total number of calls to this method rather than speeding up its implementation.

On the other hand, instrumented profilers work by altering the bytecode sequence of classes as they are loaded (inserting code to count the invocations, and so on). They are much more likely to introduce performance differences into the application than are sampling profilers. For example, the JVM will inline small methods (see Chapter 4) so that no method invocation is needed when the small-method code is executed. The compiler makes that decision based on the size of the code; depending on how the code is instrumented, it may no longer be eligible to be inlined. This may cause the instrumented profiler to overestimate the contribution of certain methods. And inlining is just one example of a decision that the compiler makes based on the layout of the code; in general, the more the code is instrumented (changed), the more likely it is that its execution profile will change.

There is also an interesting technical reason why the `ImmutableMap.get()` method shows up in this profile and not the sampling profile. Sampling profilers in Java can only take the sample of a thread when the thread is at a safepoint—essentially, whenever it is allocating memory. The `get()` method may never arrive at a safepoint and so may never get sampled. That means the sampling profile can underestimate the contribution of that method to the program execution.

In this example, both the instrumented and sampled profiles pointed to the same general area of the code: classloading and class resolution. In practice, it is possible for different profilers to point to completely different areas of the code. Profilers are good estimators, but they are only making estimates: some of them will be wrong some of the time.

Quick Summary

1. Instrumented profilers yield more information about an application, but can possibly have a greater effect on the application than a sampling profiler.

2. Instrumented profilers should be set up to instrument small sections of the code—a few classes or packages. That limits their impact on the application's performance.

Blocking Methods and Thread Timelines

Figure 3-4 shows the GlassFish startup using a different instrumented profiling tool (the NetBeans profiler). Now the execution time is dominated by the `park()` and `parkNanos()` methods (and to a lesser extent, the `read()` method).

Hot Spots - Method	Self time [%]	Self time	Invocations
java.util.concurrent.locks.LockSupport.**parkNanos** (Object, long)	▓▓▓▓	632,104 ms (57.3%)	470
java.util.concurrent.locks.LockSupport.**park** (Object)	▓▓	350,790 ms (31.8%)	356
java.net.SocketInputStream.**read** (byte[], int, int, int)	▌	60,144 ms (5.5%)	21
org.apache.felix.framework.resolver.ResolverImpl.**getPackageSourcesInternal** (or...		1,562 ms (0.1%)	22,400
java.lang.ClassLoader.**defineClass** (String, byte[], int, int, java.security.ProtectionDo...		1,501 ms (0.1%)	2,447
java.lang.Class.**privateGetDeclaredConstructors** (boolean)		1,282 ms (0.1%)	10,657
java.util.HashMap.**getEntry** (Object)		1,015 ms (0.1%)	1,656,447
java.util.concurrent.LinkedTransferQueue.**awaitMatch** (java.util.concurrent.Linked...		1,007 ms (0.1%)	18
org.apache.felix.framework.resolver.ResolverImpl.**mergeUses** (org.osgi.framewor...		643 ms (0.1%)	182,836
org.apache.felix.framework.util.ImmutableMap.**get** (Object)		608 ms (0.1%)	3,067,340
org.apache.felix.framework.util.ImmutableList$ListItr.**hasNext** ()		605 ms (0.1%)	2,899,072
java.lang.ClassLoader.**getCallerClassLoader** ()		566 ms (0.1%)	18,506
org.apache.felix.framework.BundleWiringImpl$BundleClassLoader.**findClass** (String)		538 ms (0.1%)	2,980
org.apache.felix.framework.util.ImmutableList.**size** ()		524 ms (0%)	2,903,040
org.apache.felix.framework.BundleWiringImpl.**findClassOrResourceByDelegation** ...		455 ms (0%)	8,289
java.util.zip.Inflater.**inflate** (byte[], int, int)		413 ms (0%)	9,988
java.util.HashMap.**hash** (Object)		409 ms (0%)	2,259,411

Figure 3-4. A profile with blocked methods

Those methods (and similar blocking methods) do not consume CPU time, so they are not contributing to the overall CPU usage of the application. Their execution cannot necessarily be optimized. Threads in the application are not spending 632 seconds executing code in the `parkNanos()` method; they are spending 632 seconds waiting for something else to happen (e.g., for another thread to call the `notify()` method). The same is true of the `park()` and `read()` methods.

For that reason, most profilers will not report methods that are blocked; those threads are shown as being idle (and in this case, NetBeans was set to explicitly include those and all other Java-level methods). In this particular example, that is a good thing: the threads that are parked are the threads of the Java threadpool that will execute servlet (and other) requests as they come into the server. No such requests occur during startup, and so those threads remain blocked, waiting for some task to execute. That is their normal state.

In other cases, you do want to see the time spent in those blocking calls. The time that a thread spends inside the `wait()` method—waiting for some other thread to notify it —is a significant determinant of the overall execution time of many applications. Most Java-based profilers have filter sets and other options that can be tweaked to show or hide these blocking calls.

Alternately, it is usually more fruitful to examine the execution patterns of threads rather than the amount of time a profiler attributes to the blocking method itself. Figure 3-5 shows such a thread display from the Oracle Solaris Studio profiling tool.

Figure 3-5. A thread timeline profile

Each horizontal area here is a different thread (so there are two threads in the figure: thread 1.3 and thread 1.2). The colored (or different grayscale) bars represent execution of different methods; blank areas represent places where the thread is not executing. At a high level, observe that thread 1.2 executed a lot of code and then waited for thread 1.3 to do something; thread 1.3 then waited a bit of time for thread 1.2 to do something else, and so on. Diving into those areas with the tool lets us learn how those threads are interacting with each other.

Notice too that there are blank areas where no thread appears to be executing. The image shows only two of many threads in the application, so it is possible that these threads are waiting for one of those other threads to do something, or the thread could be executing a blocking `read()` (or similar) call.

Quick Summary

1. Threads that are blocked may or may not be a source of a performance issue; it is necessary to examine why they are blocked.

2. Blocked threads can be identified by the method that is blocking, or by a timeline analysis of the thread.

Native Profilers

Native profiling tools are those that profile the JVM itself. This allows visibility into what the JVM is doing, and if an application includes its own native libraries, it allows visibility into that code as well. Any native profiling tool can be used to profile the C code of the JVM (and of any native libraries), but some native-based tools can profile both the Java and C/C++ code of an application.

Figure 3-6 shows the now-familiar profile from starting GlassFish in the Oracle Solaris Studio analyzer tool, which is a native profiler that understands both Java and C/C++ code. (Although it has Solaris in its name, this tool works on Linux systems as well; in fact, these images are from profiling on a Linux OS. However, the kernel architecture of Solaris allows the tool to provide even more application visibility when run on Solaris.)

User CPU ▽ (sec.)	User CPU (sec.)	Name
25.105	25.105	*<Total>*
20.064	20.064	*<JVM-System>*
0.550	0.670	java.lang.ClassLoader.defineClass1(java.lang.String, byte[], int, int, java.sec
0.380	0.380	*<no Java callstack recorded>*
0.220	0.220	java.util.jar.Attributes.read(java.util.jar.Manifest$FastInputStream, byte[])
0.120	0.170	java.util.zip.Inflater.inflateBytes(long, byte[], int, int)
0.100	0.100	org.apache.felix.framework.util.ImmutableMap.get(java.lang.Object)

Figure 3-6. A native profiler

The first difference to note here is that there is a total of 25.1 seconds of CPU time recorded by the application, and 20 seconds of that is in JVM-System. That is the code attributable to the JVM itself: the JVM's compiler threads and GC threads (plus a few other ancillary threads). We can drill into that further; in this case, we'd see that virtually all of that time is spent by the compiler (as is expected during startup, when there is a lot of code to compile). A very small amount of time is spent by the GC threads in this example.

Unless the goal is to hack on the JVM itself, that native visibility is enough, though if we wanted, we could look into the actual JVM functions and go optimize them. But the key piece of information from this tool—one that isn't available from a Java-based tool

—is the amount of time the application is spending in GC. In Java profiling tools, the impact of the GC threads is nowhere to be found. (Unless the test is run on a machine which is CPU-bound, the large amount of time in the compiler thread will not matter: that thread will consume a lot of one CPU on the machine, but as long as there are more CPUs available, the application itself won't be impacted, since the compilation happens in the background.)

Once the impact of the native code has been examined, it can be filtered out to focus on the actual startup (Figure 3-7).

User CPU ∇ (sec.)	User CPU (sec.)	Name
5.041	5.041	<Total>
0.550	0.670	java.lang.ClassLoader.defineClass1(java.lang.String, byte[], int, int, java.sec
0.380	0.380	<no Java callstack recorded>
0.220	0.220	java.util.jar.Attributes.read(java.util.jar.Manifest$FastInputStream, byte[])
0.120	0.170	java.util.zip.Inflater.inflateBytes(long, byte[], int, int)
0.100	0.100	org.apache.felix.framework.util.ImmutableMap.get(java.lang.Object)

Figure 3-7. A filtered native profiler

Once again, the sampling profiler here points to the `defineClass1()` method as the hottest method, though the actual time spent in that method and its children—0.67 seconds out of 5.041 seconds—is about 11% (significantly less than what the last sample-based profiler reported). This profile also points to some additional things to examine: reading and unzipping JAR files. As these are related to classloading, we were on the right track for those anyway—but in this case it is interesting to see that the actual I/O for reading the JAR files (via the `inflateBytes()` method) is a few percentage points. Other tools didn't show us that—partly because the native code involved in the Java ZIP libraries got treated as a blocking call and was filtered out.

No matter which profiling tool—or better yet, tools—you use, it is quite important to become familiar with their idiosyncrasies. Profilers are the most important tool to guide the search for performance bottlenecks, but you must learn to use them to guide you to areas of the code to optimize, rather than focusing solely on the top hot spot.

Quick Summary

1. Native profilers provide visibility into both the JVM code and the application code.

2. If a native profiler shows that time in GC dominates the CPU usage, then tuning the collector is the right thing to do. If it shows significant time in the compilation threads, however, that is usually not affecting the application's performance.

Java Mission Control

The commercial releases of Java 7 (starting with 7u40) and Java 8 include a new monitoring and control feature called Java Mission Control. This feature will be familiar to users of JDK 6–based JRockit JVMs (where the technology originated), since it is part of Oracle's merging of technologies for Java 7. Java Mission Control is not part of the open-source development of Java and is available only with a commercial license (i.e., the same procedure as for competitive monitoring and profiling tools from other companies).

The Java Mission Control program (jmc) starts a window that displays the JVM processes on the machine and lets you select one or more processes to monitor. Figure 3-8 shows Java Mission Control monitoring an instance of the GlassFish application server.

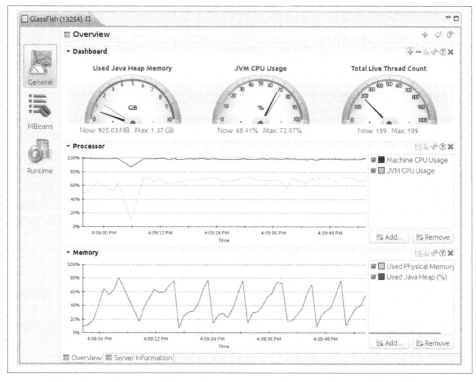

Figure 3-8. Java Mission Control monitoring

This display shows basic information that Java Mission Control is monitoring: CPU usage and heap usage. Note, though, that the CPU graph includes the total CPU on the machine (which is essentially 100%, even though the application being monitored here is using only about 70%). That is a key feature of the monitoring: Java Mission Control has the ability to monitor the entire system, not just the JVM that has been selected. The upper dashboard can be configured to display JVM information (all kinds of statistics about GC, classloading, thread usage, heap usage, and so on) as well as OS-specific information (total machine CPU and memory usage, swapping, load averages, and so on).

Like other monitoring tools, Java Mission Control can make Java Management Extensions calls into whatever managed beans the application has available.

Java Flight Recorder

The key feature of Java Mission Control is the Java Flight Recorder (JFR). As its name suggests, JFR data is a history of events in the JVM that can be used to diagnose the past performance and operations of the JVM.

The basic operation of JFR is that some set of events are enabled (for example, one event is that a thread is blocked waiting for a lock). Each time a selected event occurs, data about that event is saved (either in memory or to a file). The data stream is held in a circular buffer, so only the most recent events are available. Java Mission Control can then display those events—either taken from a live JVM or read from a saved file—and you can perform analysis on those events to diagnose performance issues.

All of that—the kind of events, the size of the circular buffer, where it is stored, and so on—is controlled via various arguments to the JVM, via the Java Mission Control GUI, and by jcmd commands as the program runs. By default, JFR is set up so that it has very low overhead: an impact below 1% of the program's performance. That overhead will change as more events are enabled, or as the threshold at which events are reported is changed, and so on. The details of all that configuration are discussed later in this section, but first we'll examine what the display of these events look like, since that makes it easier to understand how JFR works.

JFR overview

This example uses a JFR recording taken from a GlassFish application server over a 6-minute period. The server is running the stock servlet discussed in Chapter 2. As the recording is loaded into Java Mission Control, the first thing it displays is a basic monitoring overview (Figure 3-9).

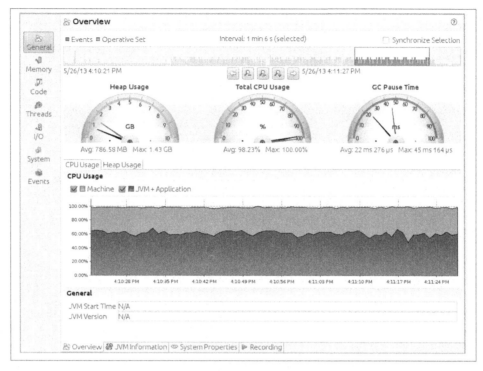

Figure 3-9. Java Flight Recorder general information

This display is quite similar to what Java Mission Control displays when doing basic monitoring. Above the gauges showing CPU and heap usage, there is a timeline of events (represented by a series of vertical bars). The timeline allows us to zoom into a particular region of interest; although in this example the recording was taken over a 6-minute period, I zoomed into a 1:06 interval near the end of the recording.

The graph here for CPU usage is a little clearer as to what is going on; the GlassFish JVM is the bottom portion of the graph (averaging about 70% usage), and the machine is running at 100% CPU usage. Along the bottom, there are some other tabs to explore: information about system properties and how the JFR recording was actually made. The icons that run down the lefthand side of the window are more interesting: those icons provide visibility into the application behavior.

JFR Memory view

The information gathered here is extensive. Figure 3-10 shows just one panel of the Memory view.

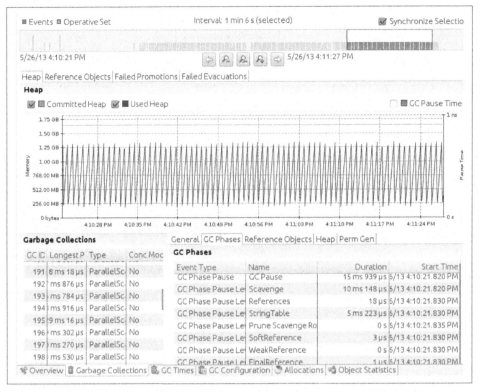

Figure 3-10. Java Flight Recorder Memory panel

The graph here shows that memory is fluctuating fairly regularly as the young generation is cleared (and interestingly enough, there is no overall growth of the heap in this application: nothing is promoted to the old generation). The lower-left panel shows all the collections that occurred during the recording, including their duration and what kind of collection they were (always a `ParallelScavenge` in this example). When one of those events is selected, the bottom-right panel breaks that down even further, showing all the specific phases of that collection and how long each took.

As can be seen from the various tabs on this page, there is a wealth of other available information: how long and how many reference objects were cleared, whether there are promotion or evacuation failures from the concurrent collectors, the configuration of the GC algorithm itself (including the sizes of the generations and the survivor space configurations), and even information on the specific kinds of objects that were allocated. As you read through Chapters 5 and 6, keep in mind how this tool can diagnose the problems that are discussed there. If you need to understand why CMS bailed out and performed a full GC (was it due to promotion failure?), or how the JVM has adjusted the tenuring threshold, or virtually any other piece of data about how and why GC behaved as it did, JFR will be able to tell you.

JFR Code view

The Code page in Java Mission Control shows basic profiling information from the recording (Figure 3-11).

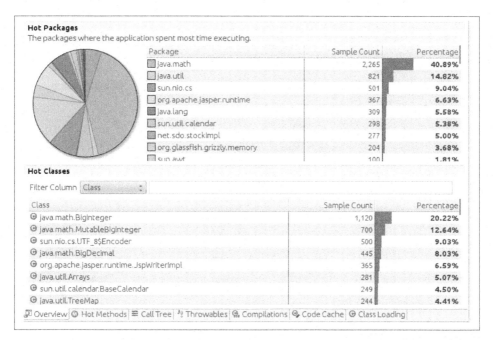

Figure 3-11. Java Flight Recorder Code panel

The first tab on this page shows an aggregation by package name, which is an interesting feature not found in many profilers; unsurprisingly, the stock application spends 41% of its time doing calculations in the java.math package. At the bottom, there are other tabs for the traditional profile views: the hot methods and call tree of the profiled code.

Unlike other profilers, JFR offers other modes of visibility into the code. The Throwables tab provides a view into the exception processing of the application (Chapter 12 has a discussion of why excessive exception processing can be bad for performance). There are also tabs that provide information on what the compiler is doing, including a view into the code cache (see Chapter 4).

There are other displays like this—for threads, I/O, and system events—but for the most part, these displays simply provide nice views into the actual events in the JFR recording.

Overview of JFR events

JFR produces a stream of events that are saved as a recording. The displays seen so far provide views of those events, but the most powerful way to look at the events is on the Event panel itself, as seen in Figure 3-12.

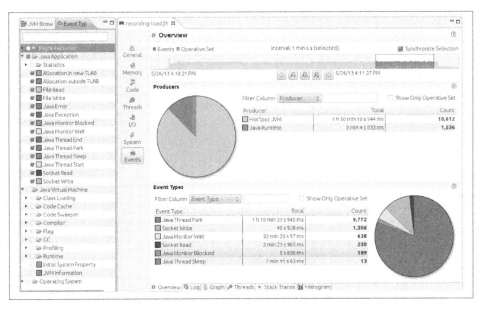

Figure 3-12. Java Flight Recorder Event panel

The events to display can be filtered in the lefthand panel of this window; here, only the application-level events are selected. Be aware that when the recording is made, only certain kinds of events are included in the first place: at this point, we are doing post-processing filtering (the next section will show how to filter the events included in the recording).

Within the 66-second interval in this example, the application produced 10,612 events from the JVM and 1,536 events from the JDK libraries, and the six event types generated in that period are shown near the bottom of the window. I've already discussed why the thread-park and monitor-wait events for this example will be high; those can be ignored (and in fact they are often a good candidate to filter out). What about the other events?

Over the 66-second period, multiple threads in the application spent 40 seconds writing to sockets. That's not an unreasonable number for an application server running across four CPUs (i.e., with 264 seconds of available time), but it does indicate that performance could be improved by writing less data to the clients (using the techniques outlined in Chapter 10).

Similarly, multiple threads spent 143 seconds reading from sockets. That number sounds worse, and it is worthwhile to look at the traces involved with those events, but it turns out that there are several threads that use blocking I/O to read administrative requests that are expected to arrive periodically. In between those requests—for long periods of time—the threads sit blocked on the `read()` method. So the read time here turns out to be acceptable: just as when using a profiler, it is up to you to determine whether a lot of threads blocked in I/O is expected, or if it indicates a performance issue.

That leaves the monitor-blocked events. As discussed in Chapter 9, contention for locks goes through two levels: first the thread spins waiting for the lock, and then it uses (in a process called lock inflation) some CPU- and OS-specific code to wait for the lock. A standard profiler can give hints about that situation, since the spinning time is included in the CPU time charged to a method. A native profiler can give some information about the locks subject to inflation, but that can be hit-or-miss (e.g., the Oracle Studio analyzer does a very good job of that on Solaris, but Linux lacks the operating system hooks necessary to provide the same information). The JVM, though, can provide all this data directly to JFR.

An example of using lock visibility is shown in Chapter 9, but the general takeaway about JFR events is that, since they come directly from the JVM, they offer a level of visibility into an application that no other tool can provide. In Java 7u40, there are 77 event types that can be monitored with JFR. The exact number and types of events will vary slightly depending on release, but here are some of the more useful ones.

The list of events that follows displays two bullet points for each event type. Events can collect basic information that can be collected with other tools like `jconsole` and `jcmd`; that kind of information is described in the first bullet. The second bullet describes information the event provides that is difficult to obtain outside of JFR.

Classloading
- Number of classes loaded and unloaded
- Which classloader loaded the class; time required to load an individual class

Thread statistics
- Number of threads created and destroyed; thread dumps
- Which threads are blocked on locks (and the specific lock they are blocked on)

Throwables
- Throwable classes used by the application
- How many exceptions and errors are thrown and the stack trace of their creation

TLAB allocation
- The number of allocations in the heap and size of thread-local allocation buffers (TLABs)
- The specific objects allocated in the heap and the stack trace where they are allocated

File and socket I/O
- Time spent performing I/O
- Time spent per read/write call, the specific file or socket taking a long time to read or write

Monitor blocked
- Threads waiting for a monitor
- Specific threads blocked on specific monitors and the length of time they are blocked

Code cache
- Size of code cache and how much it contains
- Methods removed from the code cache; code cache configuration

Code compilation
- Which methods are compiled, OSR compilation, and length of time to compile
- Nothing specific to JFR, but unifies information from several sources

Garbage collection
- Times for GC, including individual phases; sizes of generations
- Nothing specific to JFR, but unifies the information from several tools

Profiling
- Instrumenting and sampling profiles
- Not as much as you'd get from a true profiler, but the JFR profile provides a good high-order overview

Enabling JFR

In the commercial version of the Oracle JVM, JFR is initially disabled. To enable it, add the flags `-XX:+UnlockCommercialFeatures -XX:+FlightRecorder` to the command line of the application. This enables JFR as a feature, but no recordings will be made until the recording process itself is enabled. That can occur either through a GUI, or via the command line.

Enabling JFR via Java Mission Control

The easiest way to enable recording is through the Java Mission Control GUI (jmc). When jmc is started, it displays a list of all the JVM processes running on the current system. The JVM processes are displayed in a tree-node configuration; expand the node under the Flight Recorder label to bring up the flight recorder window shown in Figure 3-13.

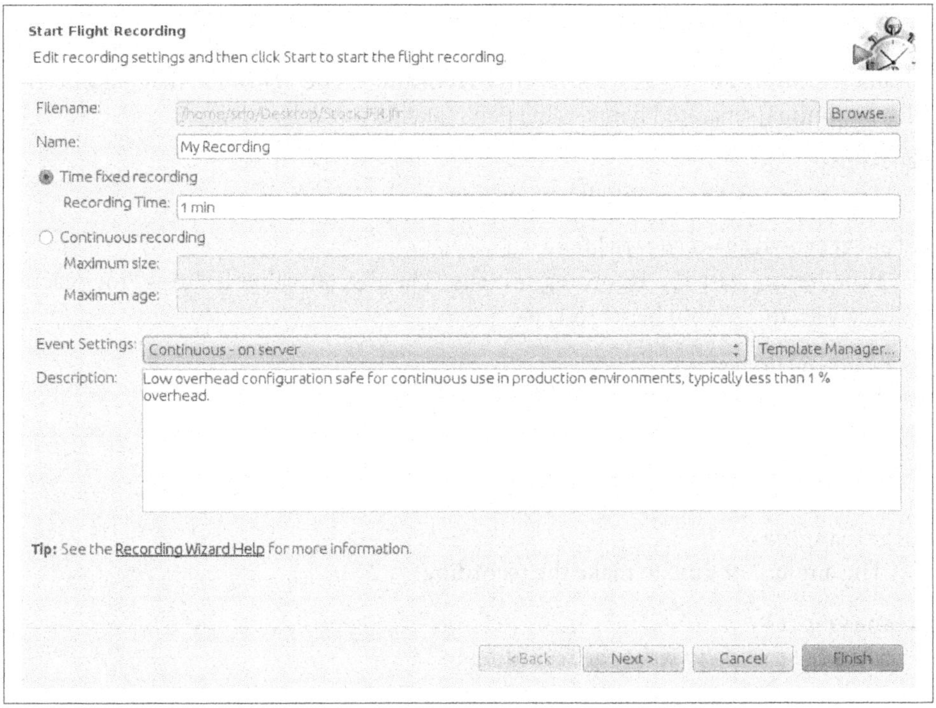

Start Flight Recording
Edit recording settings and then click Start to start the flight recording.

Filename:	/home/sdo/Desktop/StockJFR.jfr [Browse...]
Name:	My Recording

- ● Time fixed recording
  Recording Time: 1 min
- ○ Continuous recording
  Maximum size:
  Maximum age:

Event Settings: Continuous - on server [Template Manager...]
Description: Low overhead configuration safe for continuous use in production environments, typically less than 1 % overhead.

Tip: See the Recording Wizard Help for more information.

[< Back] [Next >] [Cancel] [Finish]

Figure 3-13. JFR Start Flight Recording window

Flight recordings are made in one of two modes: either for a fixed duration (1 minute in this case), or continuously. For continuous recordings, a circular buffer is utilized; the buffer will contain the most recent events that are within the desired duration and size.

To perform proactive analysis—meaning that you will start a recording and then generate some work, or start a recording during a load-testing experiment after the JVM has warmed up—a fixed-duration recording should be used. That recording will give a good indication of how the JVM responded during the test.

The continuous recording is best for reactive analysis. This lets the JVM keep the most recent events, and then dump out a recording in response to some event. For example, the WebLogic application server can trigger that a recording be dumped out in response to an abnormal event in the application server (such as a request that takes more than 5 minutes to process). You can set up your own monitoring tools to dump out the recording in response to any sort of event.

Enabling JFR via the command line

After enabling JFR (with the -XX:+FlightRecorder option), there are two ways to control how and when the actual recording should happen. The recording parameters can be controlled when the JVM starts by using the -XX:+FlightRecorderOptions=*string* parameter; this is most useful for reactive recordings. The *string* in that parameter is a list of comma-separated name-value pairs taken from these options:

name=*name*
> The name used to identify the recording.

defaultrecording=*<true/false>*
> Whether to start the recording initially. The default value is false; for reactive analysis, this should be set to true.

settings=*path*
> Name of the file containing the JFR settings (see next section).

delay=*time*
> The amount of time (e.g., 30s, 1h) before the recording should start.

duration=*time*
> The amount of time to make the recording.

filename=*path*
> Name of the file to write the recording to.

compress=*<true/false>*
> Whether to compress (with gzip) the recording; the default is false.

maxage=*time*
> Maximum time to keep recorded data in the circular buffer.

maxsize=*size*
> Maximum size (e.g., 1024K, 1M) of the recording's circular buffer.

Setting up a default recording like that can be useful in some circumstances, but for more flexibility, all options can be controlled with jcmd during a run (assuming that the -XX:+FlightRecorder option was specified in the first place).

To start a flight recording:

```
% jcmd process_id JFR.start [options_list]
```

The options_list is a series of comma-separated name-value pairs that control how the recording is made. The possible options are exactly the same as those that can be specified on the command line with the -XX:+FlightRecorderOptions=*string* flag.

If a continuous recording has been enabled, the current data in the circular buffer can be dumped to a file at any time via this command:

```
% jcmd process_id JFR.dump [options_list]
```

The list of options includes:

name=*name*
> The name under which the recording was started.

recording=*n*
> The number of the JFR recording (see the next example for JFR.check).

filename=*path*
> The location to dump the file to.

It is possible that multiple JFR recordings have been enabled for a given process. To see the available recordings:

```
% jcmd process_id JFR.check [verbose]
```

Recordings in this case are identified by the name used to begin them, as well as an arbitrary recording number (which can be used in other JFR commands).

Finally, to abort a recording in process:

```
% jcmd process_id JFR.stop [options_list]
```

That command takes the following options:

name=*name*
> The recording name to stop.

recording=*n*
> The recording number (from JFR.check) to stop.

discard=*boolean*
> If true, discard the data rather than writing it to the previously provided filename (if any).

filename=*path*
> Write the data to the given path.

In an automated performance testing system, running these command-line tools and producing a recording is useful when it comes time to examine those runs for regressions.

Selecting JFR Events

JFR (presently) supports approximately 77 events. Many of these events are periodic events: they occur every few milliseconds (e.g., the profiling events work on a sampling basis). Other events are triggered only when the duration of the event exceeds some threshold (e.g., the event for reading a file is triggered only if the read() method has taken more than some specified amount of time).

Other JFR Events

JFR is extensible: applications can define their own events. Hence, your JFR implementation may show many more available event types depending on the application in question. For example, the WebLogic application server enables a number of application server events: JDBC operations, HTTP operations, and so on. These events are treated just like the other JFR events discussed here: they can be individually enabled, may have some threshold associated with them, and so on. Similarly, later versions of the JVM may have additional events that are not discussed here.

Consult the up-to-date product documentation for the most detailed information.

Collecting events naturally involves some overhead. The threshold at which events are collected—since it increases the number of events—also plays a role in the overhead that comes from enabling a JFR recording. In the default recording, not all events are collected (the six most-expensive events are not enabled), and the threshold for the time-based events is somewhat high. This keeps the overhead of the default recording to less than 1%.

There are times when extra overhead is worthwhile. Looking at TLAB events, for example, can help you determine if objects are being allocated directly to the old generation, but those events are not enabled in the default recording. Similarly, the profiling events are enabled in the default recording, but only every 20 ms—that gives a good overview, but it can also lead to sampling errors.

The events (and the threshold for events) that JFR captures are defined in a template (which is selected via the settings option on the command line). JFR ships with two templates: the default template (limiting events so that the overhead will be less than 1%) and a profile template (which sets most threshold-based events to be triggered every 10 ms). The estimated overhead of the profiling template is 2% (though, as always, your mileage may vary, and I typically observe a much lower overhead than that).

Templates are managed by the jmc template manager; you may have noticed a button to start the template manager in Figure 3-13. Templates are stored in two locations: under the *$HOME/.jmc/<release>* directory (local to a user) and in the *$JAVA_HOME/ jre/lib/jfr* directory (global for a JVM). The template manager allows you to select a global template (the template will say that it is "on server"), select a local template, or define a new template. To define a template, cycle through the available events, and enable (or disable) them as desired, optionally setting the threshold at which the event kicks in.

Figure 3-14 shows that the File Read event is enabled with a threshold of 15 ms: file reads that take longer than that will cause an event to be triggered. This event has also been configured to generate a stack trace for the File Read events. That increases the overhead—which in turn is why taking a stack trace for events is a configurable option.

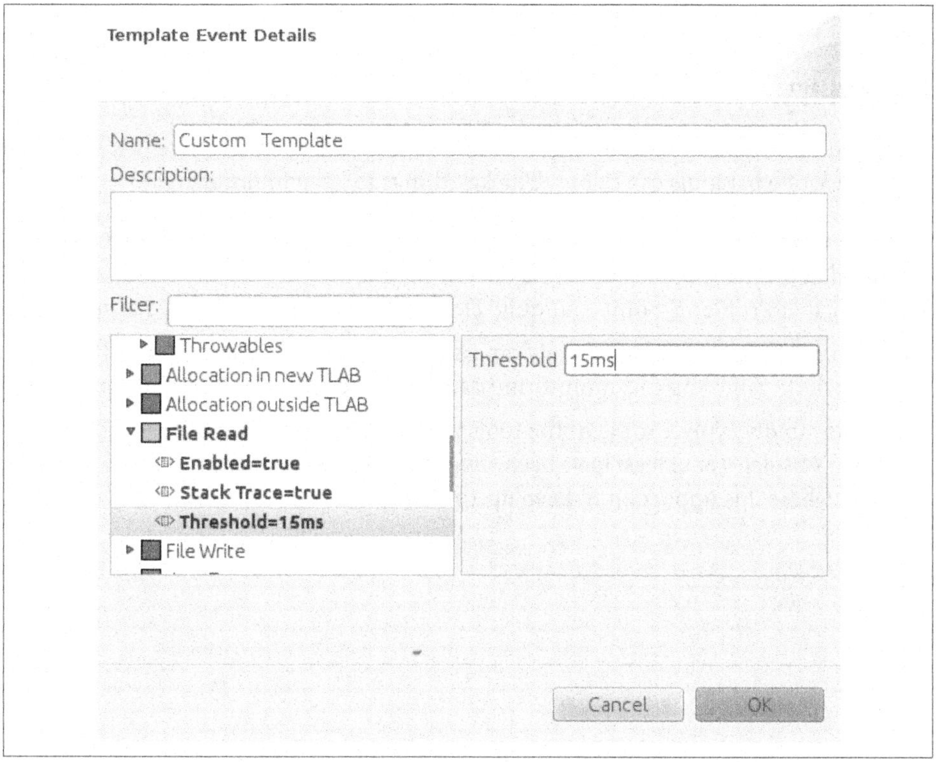

Figure 3-14. A sample JFR event template

The event templates are simple XML files, so the best way to determine which events are enabled in a template (and their thresholds and stack-trace configurations) is to read the XML file. Using an XML file also allows the local template file to be defined on one machine and then copied to the global template directory for use by others on the team.

Quick Summary

1. Java Flight Recorder provides the best possible visibility into the JVM, since it is built into the JVM itself.

2. Like all tools, JFR introduces some level of overhead into an application. For routine use, JFR can be enabled to gather a substantial amount of information with low overhead.

3. JFR is useful in performance analysis, but it is also useful when enabled on a production system so that you can examine the events that led up to a failure.

Summary

Good tools are key to good performance analysis; in this chapter, we've just scratched the surface of what tools can tell us. The key things to keep in mind are:

- No tool is perfect, and competing tools have relative strengths. Profiler X may be a good fit for many applications, but there will always be cases where it misses something that Profiler Y points out quite clearly. Always be flexible in your approach.

- Command-line monitoring tools can gather important data automatically; be sure to include gathering this monitoring data in your automated performance testing.

- Tools rapidly evolve: some of the tools mentioned in this chapter are probably already obsolete (or at least have been superseded by new, superior tools). This is one area where it is important to keep up-to-date.

## CHAPTER 4

Working with the JIT Compiler

The just-in-time (JIT) compiler is the heart of the Java Virtual Machine. Nothing in the JVM affects performance more than the compiler, and choosing a compiler is one of the first decisions made when running a Java application—whether you are a Java developer or an end user. Fortunately, in most situations the compiler needs little tuning beyond some basics.

This chapter covers the compiler in depth. It starts with some information on how the compiler works and discusses the advantages and disadvantages to using a JIT compiler. Then it moves on to which kinds of compilers are present within which versions of Java: understanding this and choosing the correct compiler for a situation is the most important step you must take to make applications run fast. Finally, it covers some intermediate and advanced tunings of the compiler; these tunings can help get those last few percentage points in the performance of an application.

Just-in-Time Compilers: An Overview

Some introductory material first; feel free to skip ahead if you understand the basics of just-in-time compilation.

Computers—and more specifically CPUs—can execute only a relatively few, specific instructions, which are called assembly or binary code. All programs that the CPU executes must therefore be translated into these instructions.

Languages like C++ and Fortran are called compiled languages because their programs are delivered as binary (compiled) code: the program is written, and then a static compiler produces a binary. The assembly code in that binary is targeted to a particular CPU. Complementary CPUs can execute the same binary: for example, AMD and Intel CPUs share a basic, common set of assembly language instructions, and later versions of CPUs almost always can execute the same set of instructions as previous versions of that

CPU. The reverse is not always true; new versions of CPUs often introduce instructions that will not run on older versions of CPUs.

Languages like PHP and Perl, on the other hand, are interpreted. The same program source code can be run on any CPU as long as the machine has the correct interpreter (that is, the program called php or perl). The interpreter translates each line of the program into binary code as that line is executed.

There are advantages and disadvantages to each of these systems. Programs written in interpreted languages are portable: you can take the same code, drop it on any machine with the appropriate interpreter, and it will run. However, it might run slowly. As a simple case, consider what happens in a loop: the interpreter will retranslate each line of code when it is executed in the loop. The compiled code doesn't need to repeatedly make that translation.

There are a number of factors that a good compiler takes into account when it produces a binary. One simple example of this is the order of the binary statements: not all assembly language instructions take the same amount of time to execute. A statement that adds the values stored in two registers might execute in one cycle, but retrieving (from main memory) the values needed for the addition may take multiple cycles.

Hence, a good compiler will produce a binary that executes the statement to load the data, executes some other instructions, and then—when the data is available—executes the addition. An interpreter that is looking at only one line of code at a time doesn't have enough information to produce that kind of code; it will request the data from memory, wait for it to become available, and then execute the addition. Bad compilers will do the same thing, by the way, and it is not necessarily the case that even the best compiler can prevent the occasional wait for an instruction to complete.

For these (and other) reasons, interpreted code will almost always be measurably slower than compiled code: compilers have enough information about the program to provide a number of optimizations to the binary code that an interpreter simply cannot perform.

Interpreted code does have the advantage of portability. A binary compiled for a SPARC CPU obviously cannot run on an Intel CPU. But a binary that uses the latest AVX instructions of Intel's Sandy Bridge processors cannot run on older Intel processors either. Hence, it is common for commercial software to be compiled to a fairly old version of a processor and not take advantage of the newest instructions available to it. There are various tricks around this, including shipping a binary with multiple shared libraries where the shared libraries execute performance-sensitive code and come with versions for various flavors of a CPU.

Java attempts to find a middle ground here. Java applications are compiled—but instead of being compiled into a specific binary for a specific CPU, they are compiled into an idealized assembly language. This assembly language (known as Java bytecodes) is then run by the java binary (in the same way that an interpreted PHP script is run by the php binary). This gives Java the platform independence of an interpreted language. Because it is executing an idealized binary code, the java program is able to compile the code into the platform binary as the code executes. This compilation occurs as the program is executed: it happens "just in time."

The manner in which the Java Virtual Machine compiles this code as it executes is the focus of this chapter.

Hot Spot Compilation

As discussed in Chapter 1, the Java implementation discussed in this book is Oracle's HotSpot JVM. This name (HotSpot) comes from the approach it takes toward compiling the code. In a typical program, only a small subset of code is executed frequently, and the performance of an application depends primarily on how fast those sections of code are executed. These critical sections are known as the hot spots of the application; the more the section of code is executed, the hotter that section is said to be.

Hence, when the JVM executes code, it does not begin compiling the code immediately. There are two basic reasons for this. First, if the code is going to be executed only once, then compiling it is essentially a wasted effort; it will be faster to interpret the Java bytecodes than to compile them and execute (only once) the compiled code.

But if the code in question is a frequently called method, or a loop that runs many iterations, then compiling it is worthwhile: the cycles it takes to compile the code will be outweighed by the savings in multiple executions of the faster compiled code. That trade-off is one reason that the compiler executes the interpreted code first—the compiler can figure out which methods are called frequently enough to warrant their compilation.

The second reason is one of optimization: the more times that the JVM executes a particular method or loop, the more information it has about that code. This allows the JVM to make a number of optimizations when it compiles the code.

A number of those optimizations (and ways to affect them) are discussed later in this chapter, but for a simple example, consider the case of the equals() method. This method exists in every Java object (since it is inherited from the Object class) and is often overridden. When the interpreter encounters the statement b = obj1.equals(obj2), it must look up the type (class) of obj1 in order to know which equals() method to execute. This dynamic lookup can be somewhat time-consuming.

Registers and Main Memory

One of the most important optimizations a compiler can make involves when to use values from main memory and when to store values in a register. Consider this code:

```java
public class RegisterTest {
    private int sum;

    public void calculateSum(int n) {
        for (int i = 0; i < n; i++) {
            sum += i;
        }
    }
}
```

At some point in time, the sum instance variable must reside in main memory, but retrieving a value from main memory is an expensive operation that takes multiple cycles to complete. If the value of sum were to be retrieved from (and stored back to) main memory on every iteration of this loop, performance would be dismal. Instead, the compiler will load a register with the initial value of sum, perform the loop using that value in the register, and then (at an indeterminate point in time) store the final result from the register back to main memory.

This kind of optimization is very effective, but it means that the semantics of thread synchronization (see Chapter 9) are crucial to the behavior of the application. One thread cannot see the value of a variable stored in the register used by another thread; synchronization makes it possible to know exactly when the register is stored to main memory and available to other threads.

Register usage is a general optimization of the compiler, and when escape analysis is enabled (see the end of this chapter), register use is quite aggressive.

Over time, say that the JVM notices that each time this statement is executed, obj1 is of type java.lang.String. Then the JVM can produce compiled code that directly calls the String.equals() method. Now the code is faster not only because it is compiled, but also because it can skip the lookup of which method to call.

It's not quite as simple as that; it is quite possible the next time the code is executed that obj1 refers to something other than a String, so the JVM has to produce compiled code that deals with that possibility. Nonetheless, the overall compiled code here will be faster (at least as long as obj1 continues to refer to a String) because it skips the lookup of which method to execute. That kind of optimization can only be made after running the code for a while and observing what it does: this is the second reason why JIT compilers wait to compile sections of code.

Quick Summary

1. Java is designed to take advantage of the platform independence of scripting languages and the native performance of compiled languages.

2. A Java class file is compiled into an intermediate language (Java bytecodes) that is then further compiled into assembly language by the JVM.

3. Compilation of the bytecodes into assembly language performs a number of optimizations that greatly improve performance.

Basic Tunings: Client or Server (or Both)

The JIT compiler comes in two flavors, and the choice of which to use is often the only compiler tuning that needs to be done when running an application. In fact, choosing your compiler is something that must be considered even before Java is installed, since different Java binaries contain different compilers. That will get sorted out in just a bit; first, let's figure out which one should be used in which circumstances.

The two compilers are known as client and server. These names come from the command-line argument used to select the compiler (e.g., either -client or -server). JVM developers (and even some tools) often refer to the compilers by the names C1 (compiler 1, client compiler) and C2 (compiler 2, server compiler). The names imply that the choice between them should be influenced by the hardware on which the program is running, but that's not really true: especially today, some 15 years after the terms were first utilized, and your "client" laptop has four to eight CPUs and 8 GB of memory (which is more processing power than a midrange server had when Java was first developed).

Compiler Flags Are Different

Unlike most Java flags, the flags to select a compiler are different: most of them do not use -XX. The standard compiler flags are simple words: -client, -server, or -d64.

The exception here is tiered compilation, which is enabled with a flag in the common format: -XX:+TieredCompilation. Tiered compilation implies that the server compiler must be used. The following command silently turns off tiered compilation, because it conflicts with the choice of the client compiler:

```
% java -client -XX:+TieredCompilation other_args
```

The primary difference between the two compilers is their aggressiveness in compiling code. The client compiler begins compiling sooner than the server compiler does. This means that during the beginning of code execution, the client compiler will be faster, because it will have compiled correspondingly more code than the server compiler.

The engineering trade-off here is the knowledge the server compiler gains while it waits: that knowledge allows the server compiler to make better optimizations in the compiled code. Ultimately, code produced by the server compiler will be faster than that produced by the client compiler. From a user's perspective, the benefit to that trade-off is based on how long the program will run, and how important the startup time of the program is.

The obvious question here is why there needs to be a choice at all: couldn't the JVM start with the client compiler, and then use the server compiler as code gets hotter? That technique is known as *tiered compilation*. With tiered compilation, code is first compiled by the client compiler; as it becomes hot, it is recompiled by the server compiler.

Experimental versions of tiered compilation are available in early releases of Java 7. It turns out that there are a number of technical difficulties here (notably in the different architectures of the two compilers), and as a result, tiered compilation didn't perform well in those experimental versions. Starting in Java 7u4, those difficulties have largely been solved, and tiered compilation usually offers the best performance for an application.

In Java 7, tiered compilation has a few quirks, and so it is not the default setting. In particular, it is easy to exceed the JVM code cache size, which can prevent code from getting optimally compiled (though it is easy enough to address that, as is discussed in "Intermediate Tunings for the Compiler" on page 85). To use tiered compilation, specify the server compiler (either with `-server` or by ensuring it is the default for the particular Java installation being used), and ensure that the Java command line includes the flag `-XX:+TieredCompilation` (the default value of which is `false`). In Java 8, tiered compilation is enabled by default.

To understand the trade-offs here, let's look at a few examples.

Optimizing Startup

The client compiler is most often used when fast startup is the primary objective. The difference this makes on various applications is shown in Table 4-1.

Table 4-1. Startup time of various applications

Application	-client	-server	-XX:+TieredCompilation
HelloWorld	0.08	0.08	0.08
NetBeans	2.83	3.92	3.07
BigApp	51.5	54.0	52.0

In a simple HelloWorld application, neither compiler has an advantage because not enough code is run for either compiler to make any contribution. And for a task that lasts only 80 ms, we'd be hard-pressed to notice a difference if it did exist.

NetBeans is a fairly typical, moderately sized Java GUI application. On startup, it loads about 10,000 classes, performs initialization of several graphical objects, and so on. Here, the client compiler offers a significant advantage on startup: the server compiler starts 38.5% slower, and the 1-second difference will certainly be noticeable. Note that the tiered compiler isn't quite as fast, though it is only about 8% slower, a fairly trivial difference.

This is the reason NetBeans—and many GUI programs like it, including the Java plug-in used by web browsers—uses the client compiler by default. Performance is often all about perception: if the initial startup seems faster, and everything else seems fine, users will tend to view the program that has started faster as being faster overall.

Does Startup Time Matter?

A strong argument can be made that for GUI-based programs, overall performance is more important than startup performance, and that the server compiler is more appropriate even in those cases.

If the server compiler optimizes the GUI code in an application, the GUI will end up slightly more responsive, but this difference is unlikely to be noticed by an end user. But if the program performs a lot of other calculations, that work may matter. NetBeans, for example, can perform extensive (and expensive) code refactoring, which will be faster when the server compiler is used.

Program vendors typically make the choice here for what they think their defaults should be (and because startup time is one of the first things reviewers comment about, these programs are often tuned to have the best possible startup time). If your experience of using the program is different, don't hesitate to switch those programs to use the server or tiered compilers.

Finally, there is BigApp: a very large server program that loads more than 20,000 classes and performs extensive initialization. Because it is an application server, it will certainly need to use the server compiler. Even though a lot of processing is going on here, there is still a slightly noticeable benefit to the client compiler. What's interesting about this example is one thing mentioned in Chapter 1: it's not always the JVM that is the problem. In this case, there are so many JAR files that must be read from disk that it is the gating factor for performance (otherwise, the startup difference would have been even more in favor of the client compiler).

Optimizing Batch Operations

For batch applications—those that run a fixed amount of work—the choice of compiler boils down to which gets the best optimization in the amount of time the application runs. Table 4-2 shows an example of that.

Table 4-2. Time to execute batch applications

Number of stocks	-client	-server	-XX:+TieredCompilation
1	0.142 seconds	0.176 seconds	0.165 seconds
10	0.211 seconds	0.348 seconds	0.226 seconds
100	0.454 seconds	0.674 seconds	0.472 seconds
1,000	2.556 seconds	2.158 seconds	1.910 seconds
1,0000	23.78 seconds	14.03 seconds	13.56 seconds

Using the sample stock code discussed in Chapter 2, the application here requests 1 year's history (plus the average and standard deviation of that history) for between 1 and 10,000 stocks.

For 1 to 100 stocks, the faster startup with the client compiler completes the job sooner, and if the goal is to process only 100 stocks, the client compiler is the best choice. After that, the performance advantage swings in favor of the server compiler (and particularly the server compiler with tiered compilation). Even for a limited number of calculations, tiered compilation is pretty close to the client compiler, making it a good candidate for all cases.

It is also interesting that tiered compilation is always slightly better than the standard server compiler. In theory, once the program has run enough to compile all the hot spots, the server compiler might be expected to achieve the best (or at least equal) performance. But in any application, there will almost always be some small section of code that is infrequently executed. It is better to compile that code—even if the compilation is not the best that might be achieved—than to execute that code in interpreted mode. And as is discussed later in this chapter (see "Compilation Thresholds" on page 87), the server compiler will likely never actually compile all the code in an application, even if it runs forever.

Quick Summary

1. For jobs that run in a fixed amount of time, choose the compiler based on which one is the fastest at executing the actual job.
2. Tiered compilation provides a reasonable default choice for batch jobs.

Optimizing Long-Running Applications

Finally, there is the difference that can be expected in the eventual performance of a long-running application when different compilers are used. Performance of long-running applications is typically measured by examining the throughput that an application delivers after it has been "warmed up"—meaning after it has run long enough that the important parts of the code have been compiled.

This example uses the basic stock calculator and puts it in a servlet; each call to the servlet will retrieve information for a random stock symbol for a period of 25 years. Using the fhb program discussed in Chapter 2, Table 4-3 shows how many operations per second the server produced after warm-up periods of 0, 60, and 300 seconds.

Table 4-3. Throughput of server applications

Warm-up period	-client	-server	-XX:+TieredCompilation
0 seconds	15.87	23.72	24.23
60 seconds	16.00	23.73	24.26
300 seconds	16.85	24.42	24.43

The measurement period here is 60 seconds, so even in the case where there is no warm-up, the compilers had an opportunity to get enough information to compile the hot spots; hence the server compilers are always better in this example. (Also, a lot of code was compiled during the startup of the application server.) As before, tiered compilation can compile just a little bit more code and squeeze out just a little more performance than the server compiler alone.

Quick Summary

For long-running applications, always choose the server compiler, preferably in conjunction with tiered compilation.

Java and JIT Compiler Versions

Now that differences between the compilers have been examined, let's look at how to get the desired compiler. When you download Java, you must choose a version; the choice ultimately revolves around the platform you are using. However, the choice also impacts the JIT compiler(s) available to applications. The discussion so far has been about client and server compilers, but there are three versions of the JIT compiler:

- A 32-bit client version (-client)
- A 32-bit server version (-server)
- A 64-bit server version (-d64)

To a certain extent, you choose the compiler you want to use by supplying the given argument (-server, etc.). However, things are not quite so simple.

32-Bit or 64-Bit?

If you have a 32-bit operating system, then you must use a 32-bit version of the JVM. If you have a 64-bit operating system, then you can choose to use either the 32- or 64-bit version of Java. Don't assume that just because you have a 64-bit operating system, you must also use a 64-bit version of Java.

If the size of your heap will be less than about 3 GB, the 32-bit version of Java will be faster and have a smaller footprint. This is because the memory references within the JVM will be only 32 bits, and manipulating those memory references is less expensive than manipulating 64-bit references (even if you have a 64-bit CPU). The 32-bit references also use less memory.

Chapter 8 discusses compressed *ordinary object pointers* (oops), which is a way that the JVM can use 32-bit addresses even within the 64-bit JVM. However, even with that optimization, the 64-bit JVM will have a larger footprint because the native code it uses will still have 64-bit addresses.

The downside to the 32-bit JVM is that the total process size must be less than 4 GB (3 GB on some versions of Windows, and 3.5 GB on some old versions of Linux). That includes the heap, permgen, and the native code and native memory the JVM uses. Programs that make extensive use of long or double variables will be slower on a 32-bit JVM because they cannot use the CPU's 64-bit registers, though that is a very exceptional case.

Programs that fit within a 32-bit address space will run anywhere between 5% and 20% faster in a 32-bit JVM than a similarly configured 64-bit JVM. The stock batching program discussed earlier in this chapter, for example, is 20% faster when run on a 32-bit JVM on my desktop.

When downloading Java for a given operating system, there are only two options: a 32-bit or a 64-bit binary. So clearly, the 32-bit binary can be expected to have (up to) two compilers, while the 64-bit binary will have only a single compiler. (In fact, the 64-bit binary will have two compilers, since the client compiler is needed to support tiered compilation. But a 64-bit JVM cannot be run with only the client compiler.)

Once installed, though, things become a little more complicated. On most platforms, the 32-bit and 64-bit binaries install separately. You can have both binaries installed on your computer, but you must refer to them via separate paths. Hence, on the machine I use for Linux testing, I have binaries installed in */export/VMs/jdk1.7.0-32bit* and */export/VMs/jdk1.7.0-64bit*, and I choose between them by setting my PATH accordingly.

On Solaris, things are different: the 64-bit installation overlays the 32-bit installation. Hence all three compilers are available from the same path. This makes it much easier for the end user; among other things, it means that if Java is installed system-wide in */usr/bin*, a user can always specify via the command line which of the three possible compilers she wants. That kind of installation remains the exception. Things can be further complicated since developers of HotSpot often use Solaris as their primary development system and hence discussions (and sometimes documentation) gets confused by which installation paradigm is in use.

One last complication: for the sake of compatibility, the argument specifying which compiler to use is not rigorously followed. If you have a 64-bit JVM and specify -client, the application will use the 64-bit server compiler anyway. If you have a 32-bit JVM and you specify -d64, you will get an error that the given instance does not support a 64-bit JVM.

To summarize: the selection of the compiler is controlled by which JVM bits are installed and by the compiler argument passed to the JVM. Table 4-4 shows the result when the given argument is specified for the given installation.

Table 4-4. Result of compiler argument for OS combinations

Install bits	-client	-server	-d64
Linux 32-bit	32-bit client compiler	32-bit server compiler	Error
Linux 64-bit	64-bit server compiler	64-bit server compiler	64-bit server compiler
Mac OS X	64-bit server compiler	64-bit server compiler	64-bit server compiler
Solaris 32-bit	32-bit client compiler	32-bit server compiler	Error
Solaris 64-bit	32-bit client compiler	32-bit server compiler	64-bit server compiler
Windows 32-bit	32-bit client compiler	32-bit server compiler	Error
Windows 64-bit	64-bit server compiler	64-bit server compiler	64-bit server compiler

In Java 8, when the server compiler is the default in any of these cases, tiered compilation is also enabled by default.

What if no compiler argument is given at all? Then the JVM uses the default compiler for the machine on which the code is running: the default compiler is a runtime choice.

This choice is made based on whether the JVM considers the machine to be a "client" machine or a "server" machine. That decision is based on a combination of the operating system and number of CPUs on the machine; Table 4-5 lists the various defaults.

Table 4-5. Default compiler based on OS and machine

OS	Default compiler
Windows, 32-bit, any number of CPUs	`-client`
Windows, 64-bit, any number of CPUs	`-server`
MacOS, any number of CPUs	`-server`
Linux/Solaris, 32-bit, 1 CPU	`-client`
Linux/Solaris, 32-bit, 2 or more CPUs	`-server`
Linux, 64-bit, any number of CPUs	`-server`
Solaris, 32-bit/64-bit overlay, 1 CPU	`-client`
Solaris, 32-bit/64-bit overlay, 2 or more CPUs	`-server` (32-bit mode)

Determining the Default Compiler

To determine the default compiler for a particular installation of Java, run this command:

```
% java -version
java version "1.7.0"
Java(TM) SE Runtime Environment (build 1.7.0-b147)
Java HotSpot(TM) Server VM (build 21.0-b17, mixed mode)
```

This example is from my Linux desktop and a 32-bit Java binary. The last line indicates which of the three possible compilers will be used: client (32-bit), server (32-bit), or 64-bit server.

Even if the particular installation doesn't support the specified compiler, the last line will show the actual compiler used:

```
% java -client -version
java version "1.7.0"
Java(TM) SE Runtime Environment (build 1.7.0-b147)
Java HotSpot(TM) 64-Bit Server VM (build 21.0-b17, mixed mode)
```

In this case, the 64-bit version of Java is used, which (on Linux) supports only the 64-bit server compiler.

These defaults are based on the notion that startup time is always the most important thing for 32-bit Windows machines, and Unix-based machines are generally more interested in long-running performance. As always, there are exceptions: certainly modern Windows-based machines can run powerful servers even in 32-bit mode, and in those cases the server compiler should be used. Similarly, many application servers use simple Java-based administrative commands to inspect or change their configuration; even on Unix-based machines, these are better run with the client compiler.

Quick Summary

1. Different Java binaries support different compilers.
2. The compilers supported by different binaries are inconsistent among operating systems and binary architectures.
3. A program doesn't necessarily use the compiler specified depending on the platform support for that compiler.

Intermediate Tunings for the Compiler

For the most part, tuning the compiler is really just a matter of selecting the proper JVM and compiler switch (-client, -server or -XX:+TieredCompilation) for the installation on the target machine. Tiered compilation is usually the best choice for long-running applications and is within a few milliseconds of the performance of the client compiler on short-lived applications.

There are a few cases in which additional tunings are required; those cases are explored in this section.

Tuning the Code Cache

When the JVM compiles code, it holds the set of assembly-language instructions in the code cache. The code cache has a fixed size, and once it has filled up, the JVM is not able to compile any additional code.

It is easy to see the potential issue here if the code cache is too small. Some hot spots will get compiled, but others will not: the application will end up running a lot of (very slow) interpreted code.

This is more frequently an issue when using either the client compiler or tiered compilation. When the regular server compiler is used, it is somewhat unlikely that the number of classes eligible for compilation will fill the code cache; typically only a handful of classes will be compiled. But the number of classes eligible for compilation when using the client compiler (and hence also eligible for compilation when tiered compilation is enabled) is potentially much higher.

When the code cache fills up, the JVM will (usually) spit out a warning to that effect:

```
Java HotSpot(TM) 64-Bit Server VM warning: CodeCache is full.
        Compiler has been disabled.
Java HotSpot(TM) 64-Bit Server VM warning: Try increasing the
        code cache size using -XX:ReservedCodeCacheSize=
```

It is sometimes easy to miss this message, and some versions of Java 7 do not print it correctly when tiered compilation is enabled. Another way to determine if the compiler has ceased to compile code is to follow the output of the compilation log discussed later in this section.

Table 4-6 lists the default value of the code cache for various platforms.

Table 4-6. Default code cache based on platform

JVM type	Default code cache size
32-bit client, Java 8	32 MB
32-bit server with tiered compilation, Java 8	240 MB
64-bit server with tiered compilation, Java 8	240 MB
32-bit client, Java 7	32 MB
32-bit server, Java 7	32 MB
64-bit server, Java 7	48 MB
64-bit server with tiered compilation, Java 7	96 MB

In Java 7, the default size for tiered compilation is often insufficient, and it is often necessary to increase the code cache size. Large programs that use the client compiler may also need to increase the code cache size.

There really isn't a good mechanism to figure out how much code cache a particular application needs. Hence, when you need to increase the code cache size, it is sort of a hit-and-miss operation; a typical option is to simply double or quadruple the default.

The maximum size of the code cache is set via the -XX:ReservedCodeCacheSize=N flag (where N is the default just mentioned for the particular compiler). The code cache is managed like most memory in the JVM: there is an initial size (specified by -XX:InitialCodeCacheSize=N). Allocation of the code cache size starts at the initial size and increases as the cache fills up. The initial size of the code cache varies based on the chip architecture and compiler in use (on Intel machines, the client compiler starts with a 160 KB cache and the server compiler starts with a 2,496 KB cache). Resizing the cache happens in the background and doesn't really affect performance, so setting the ReservedCodeCacheSize size (i.e., setting the maximum code cache size) is all that is generally needed.

Is there a disadvantage to specifying a really large value for the maximum code cache size so that it never runs out of space? It depends on the resources available on the target machine. If a 1 GB code cache size is specified, then the JVM will reserve 1 GB of native memory space. That memory isn't allocated until needed, but it is still reserved, which means that there must be sufficient virtual memory available on your machine to satisfy the reservation.

In addition, if the JVM is 32-bit, then the total process size of the process cannot exceed 4 GB. That includes the Java heap, space for all the code of the JVM itself (including its native libraries and thread stacks), any native memory the application allocates (either directly of via the NIO libraries), and of course the code cache.

Those are the reasons the code cache is not unbounded and sometimes requires tuning for large applications (or even medium-sized applications when tiered compilation is used). Particularly on 64-bit machines, though, setting the value too high is unlikely to have a practical effect on the application: the application won't run out of process space memory, and the extra memory reservation will generally be accepted by the operating system.

The size of the code cache can be monitored using jconsole by selecting the Memory Pool Code Cache chart on the Memory panel.

Quick Summary

1. The code cache is a resource with a defined maximum size that affects the total amount of compiled code the JVM can run.

2. Tiered compilation can easily use up the entire code cache in its default configuration (particularly in Java 7); monitor the code cache and increase its size if necessary when using tiered compilation.

Compilation Thresholds

This chapter has been somewhat vague in defining just what triggers the compilation of code. The major factor involved here is how often the code is executed; once it is executed a certain number of times, its compilation threshold is reached, and the compiler deems that it has enough information to compile the code.

There are tunings that affect these thresholds, which are discussed in this section. However, this section is really designed to give you better insight into how the compiler works (and introduce some terms). There is really only one case where the compilation thresholds might need to be tuned; that is discussed at the end of this section.

Compilation is based on two counters in the JVM: the number of times the method has been called, and the number of times any loops in the method have branched back. Branching back can effectively be thought of as the number of times a loop has completed execution, either because it reached the end of the loop itself or because it executed a branching statement like continue.

When the JVM executes a Java method, it checks the sum of those two counters and decides whether or not the method is eligible for compilation. If it is, the method is queued for compilation (see "Compilation Threads" on page 94 for more details about queuing). This kind of compilation has no official name but is often called standard compilation.

But what if the method has a really long loop—or one that never exits and provides all the logic of the program? In that case, the JVM needs to compile the loop without waiting for a method invocation. So every time the loop completes an execution, the branching counter is incremented and inspected. If the branching counter has exceeded its individual threshold, then the loop (and not the entire method) becomes eligible for compilation.

This kind of compilation is called *on-stack replacement* (OSR), because even if the loop is compiled, that isn't sufficient: the JVM has to have the ability to start executing the compiled version of the loop while the loop is still running. When the code for the loop has finished compiling, the JVM replaces the code (on-stack), and the next iteration of the loop will execute the much-faster compiled version of the code.

Standard compilation is triggered by the value of the -XX:CompileThreshold=N flag. The default value of N for the client compiler is 1,500; for the server compiler it is 10,000. Changing the value of the CompileThreshold flag will cause the the compiler to choose to compile the code sooner (or later) than it normally would have. Note, however, that although there is one flag here, the threshold is calculated by adding the sum of the back-edge loop counter plus the method entry counter.

Changing OSR Compilation

It is very rare to change the threshold for OSR compilation: in fact, though OSR compilation is frequently triggered in benchmarks (and particularly in microbenchmarks), it is triggered less frequently in application code.

To provide complete details, OSR compilation is triggered by the value of three flags:

```
OSR trigger = (CompileThreshold *
        ((OnStackReplacePercentage - InterpreterProfilePercentage)/100))
```

In all compilers, the default value of the -XX:InterpreterProfilePercentage=N flag is 33. In the client compiler, the default value of the -XX:OnStackReplacePercentage=N flag is 933, and so the client compiler requires that the back-edge counter hit 13,500 before it will begin OSR compilation. In the server compiler, OSR compilation begins when the back-edge counter hits 10,700, since the default value for `OnStackReplace Percentage` is 140. Note that for tiered compilation, these decisions are based on different flags altogether, though the concepts are the same; full details are given in "Advanced Compiler Tunings" on page 94.

Changing the `CompileThreshold` flag has been a popular recommendation in performance circles for quite some time; in fact, you may have seen that Java benchmarks often use this flag (e.g., frequently after 8,000 iterations for the server compiler).

We've seen that there is a big difference between the ultimate performance of the client and server compilers, due largely to the information available to the compiler when it compiles a particular method. Lowering the compile threshold, particularly for the server compiler, runs the risk that the code may be compiled a little less optimally than possible—but testing on an application may show that there is in fact little difference between compiling after, say, 8,000 invocations instead of 10,000.

You can bet that vendors who submit benchmark results with that tuning have verified there is no performance difference between the two settings for that benchmark. They use the lower setting for two reasons:

- It saves a little time in how long the application needs to warm up.
- It can compile certain server methods that would otherwise never compile.

The first point here should be well understood, but why would the server never compile an important method? It isn't just that the compilation threshold hasn't been reached yet: it's that the compilation threshold will never be reached. This is because the counter values increase as methods and loops are executed, but they also decrease over time.

Periodically (specifically, when the JVM reaches a safepoint), the value of each counter is reduced. Practically speaking, this means that the counters are a relative measure of the *recent* hotness of the method or loop. One side effect of this is that somewhat-frequently executed code may never be compiled, even for programs that run forever (these methods are sometimes called lukewarm [as opposed to hot]). This is one case where reducing the compilation threshold can be beneficial, and it is another reason why tiered compilation is usually slightly faster than the server compiler alone. The next section will show how to determine if a particular method is not compiled; if methods in the critical path of the profiles for your application show they are not compiled, compilation can sometimes be achieved by reducing the compiler thresholds.

Inspecting the Compilation Process

The last of the intermediate tunings aren't tunings per se: that is, they will not improve the performance of an application. Rather, they are the JVM flags (and other tools) that give visibility into the working of the compiler. The most important of these is -XX:+PrintCompilation (which by default is false).

If PrintCompilation is enabled, every time a method (or loop) is compiled, the JVM prints out a line with information about what has just been compiled. The output has varied somewhat between Java releases; the output discussed here became standardized in Java 7.

Most lines of the compilation log have the following format:

```
timestamp compilation_id attributes (tiered_level) method_name size deopt
```

The timestamp here is the time after the compilation has finished (relative to 0, which is when the JVM started).

The compilation_id is an internal task ID. Usually this number will simply increase monotonically, but sometimes with the server compiler (or anytime the number of compilation threads has been increased), you may see an out-of-order compilation ID. This indicates that compilation threads are running faster or slower relative to each other, but don't conclude that one particular compilation task was somehow inordinately slow: it is usually just a function of thread scheduling (though OSR compilation is slow and often appears out of order).

The attributes field is a series of five characters that indicates the state of the code being compiled. If a particular attribute applies to the given compilation, the character shown in the following list is printed; otherwise, a space is printed for that attribute. Hence, the five-character attribute string may appear as two or more items separated by spaces. The various attributes are:

- %: The compilation is OSR.
- s: The method is synchronized.
- !: The method has an exception handler.
- b: Compilation occurred in blocking mode.
- n: Compilation occurred for a wrapper to a native method.

The first three of these should be self-explanatory. The blocking flag will never be printed by default in current versions of Java; it indicates that compilation did not occur in the background (see "Compilation Threads" on page 94 for more details about that). Finally, the native attribute indicates that the JVM generated some compiled code to facilitate the call into a native method.

If the program is not running with tiered compilation, the next field (tiered_level) will be blank. Otherwise, it will be a number indicating which tier has completed compilation (see "Tiered Compilation Levels" on page 101).

Next comes the name of the method being compiled (or the method containing the loop being compiled for OSR), which is printed as ClassName::method.

Next is the size (in bytes) of the code being compiled. This is the size of the Java bytecodes, not the size of the compiled code (so, unfortunately, this can't be used to predict how large to size the code cache).

Finally, in some cases there will be a message at the end of the compilation line that indicates that some sort of deoptimization has occurred; these are typically the phrases "made not entrant" or "made zombie." See "Deoptimization" on page 98 for more details.

Inspecting Compilation with jstat

Seeing the compilation log requires that the program be started with the -XX:+PrintCompilation flag. If the program was started without that flag, you can get some limited visibility into the working of the compiler by using jstat.

jstat has two options to provide information about the compiler. The -compiler option supplies summary information about how many methods have been compiled (here 5003 is the process ID of the program to be inspected):

```
% jstat -compiler 5003
Compiled Failed Invalid   Time   FailedType FailedMethod
    206      0       0    1.97         0
```

Note this also lists the number of methods that failed to compile and the name of the last method that failed to compile; if profiles or other information lead you to suspect that a method is slow because it hasn't been compiled, this is an easy way to verify that hypothesis.

Alternately, you can use the `-printcompilation` option to get information about the last method that is compiled. Because `jstat` takes an optional argument to repeat its operation, you can see over time which methods are being compiled. In this example, `jstat` repeats the information for process ID 5003 every second (1,000 ms):

```
% jstat -printcompilation 5003 1000
Compiled  Size  Type Method
     207    64     1 java/lang/CharacterDataLatin1 toUpperCase
     208     5     1 java/math/BigDecimal$StringBuilderHelper getCharArray
```

The compilation log may also include a line that looks like this:

```
timestamp compile_id COMPILE SKIPPED: reason
```

This line (with the literal text `COMPILE SKIPPED`) indicates that something has gone wrong with the compilation of the given method. There are two cases where this is expected, depending on the reason specified:

Code cache filled
> The size of the code cache needs to be increased using the `ReservedCodeCache` flag.

Concurrent classloading
> The class was modified as it was being compiled. The JVM will compile it again later; you should expect to see the method recompiled later in the log.

In all cases (except the cache being filled), the compilation should be reattempted again. If it is not, then there is an error that prevents compilation of the code. This is often a bug in the compiler, but the usual remedy in all cases is to refactor the code into something simpler that the compiler can handle.

Here are a few lines of output from enabling `PrintCompilation` on the stock servlet web application:

```
 28015  850          net.sdo.StockPrice::getClosingPrice (5 bytes)
 28179  905  s       net.sdo.StockPriceHistoryImpl::process (248 bytes)
 28226   25  %       net.sdo.StockPriceHistoryImpl::<init> @ 48 (156 bytes)
 28244  935          net.sdo.MockStockPriceEntityManagerFactory$\
                        MockStockPriceEntityManager::find (507 bytes)
 29929  939          net.sdo.StockPriceHistoryImpl::<init> (156 bytes)
106805 1568  !       net.sdo.StockServlet::processRequest (197 bytes)
```

This output includes only a few of the stock-related methods that have been compiled. A few interesting things to note: the first such method wasn't compiled until 28 seconds after the application server was started, and 849 methods were compiled before it. In this case, all those other methods were methods of the application server (filtered out of this output). The application server took about 2 seconds to start; the remaining 26 seconds before anything else was compiled were essentially idle as the application server waited for requests.

The remaining lines are included to point out some interesting features. The `process()` method, as seen here and in the code listing, is synchronized. Inner classes are compiled just like any other class and appear in the output with the usual Java nomenclature: `outer-classname$inner-classname`. The `processRequest()` method shows up with the exception handler as expected.

Finally, recall the implementation of the `StockPriceHistoryImpl` constructor, which contains a large loop:

```
public StockPriceHistoryImpl(String s, Date startDate, Date endDate) {
    EntityManager em = emf.createEntityManager();
    Date curDate = new Date(startDate.getTime());
    symbol = s;
    while (!curDate.after(endDate)) {
        StockPrice sp = em.find(StockPrice.class, new StockPricePK(s, curDate));
        if (sp != null) {
            if (firstDate == null) {
                firstDate = (Date) curDate.clone();
            }
            prices.put((Date) curDate.clone(), sp);
            lastDate = (Date) curDate.clone();
        }
        curDate.setTime(curDate.getTime() + msPerDay);
    }
}
```

The loop is executed more often than the constructor itself, so the loop is subject to OSR compilation. Note that it took a while for that method to be compiled; its compilation ID is 25, but it doesn't appear until other methods in the 900 range are being compiled. (It's easy to read OSR lines like this example as 25% and wonder about the other 75%, but remember that the number is the compilation ID, and the % just signifies OSR compilation.) That is typical of OSR compilation; the stack replacement is harder to set up, but other compilation can continue in the meantime.

Quick Summary

1. The best way to gain visibility into how code is being compiled is by enabling `PrintCompilation`.

2. Output from enabling `PrintCompilation` can be used to make sure that compilation is proceeding as expected.

Advanced Compiler Tunings

This section fills in some remaining details on how compilation works, and in the process explores some additional tunings that can affect it. However, although these values can be changed, there is really little reason to do so; the tunings exist to a large degree to help JVM engineers diagnose the behavior of the JVM. If you're quite curious as to how the compiler works, then this section will be interesting to you; otherwise, feel free to read ahead.

Compilation Threads

"Compilation Thresholds" on page 87 mentioned that when a method (or loop) becomes eligible for compilation, it is queued for compilation. That queue is processed by one or more background threads. This means that compilation is an asynchronous process, which is a good thing; it allows the program to continue executing even while the code in question is being compiled. If a method is compiled using standard compilation, then the next method invocation will execute the compiled method; if a loop is compiled using OSR, then the next iteration of the loop will execute the compiled code.

These queues are not strictly first in, first out: methods whose invocation counters are higher have priority. So even when a program starts execution and has lots of code to compile, this priority ordering helps to ensure that the most important code will be compiled first. (This is another reason why the compilation ID in the `PrintCompila tion` output can appear out of order.)

When the client compiler is in use, the JVM starts one compilation thread; the server compiler has two such threads. When tiered compilation is in effect, the JVM will by default start multiple client and server threads based on a somewhat complex equation involving double logs of the number of CPUs on the target platform. That works out to the values shown in Table 4-7.

Table 4-7. Default number of C1 and C2 compiler threads for tiered compilation

Number of CPUs	Number of C1 threads	Number of C2 threads
1	1	1
2	1	1
4	1	2
8	1	2
16	2	6
32	3	7
64	4	8
128	4	10

The number of compiler threads (for all three compiler options) can be adjusted by setting the `-XX:CICompilerCount=N` flag (with a default value given in the previous table). That is the total number of threads the JVM will use to process the queue(s); for tiered compilation, one-third of them (but at least one) will be used to process the client compiler queue, and the remaining threads (and also at least one) will be used to process the server compiler queue.

When might you consider adjusting this value? If a program is run on a single-CPU system, then having only one compiler thread might be slightly beneficial: there is limited CPU available, and having fewer threads contending for that resource will help performance in many circumstances. However, that advantage is limited only to the initial warm-up period; after that, the number of eligible methods to be compiled won't really cause contention for the CPU. When the stock batching application was run on a single-CPU machine and the number of compiler threads was limited to one, the initial calculations were about 10% faster (since they didn't have to compete for CPU as often). The more iterations that were run, the smaller the overall effect of that initial benefit, until all hot methods were compiled and the benefit was eliminated.

When tiered compilation is used, the number of threads can easily overwhelm the system, particularly if multiple JVMs are run at once (each of which will start many compilation threads). Reducing the number of threads in that case can help overall throughput (though again with the possible cost that the warm-up period will last longer).

Similarly, if lots of extra CPU cycles are available, then theoretically the program will benefit—at least during its warm-up period—when the number of compiler threads is increased. In real life, that benefit is extremely hard to come by. Further, if all that excess CPU is available, you're much better off trying something that takes advantage of the available CPU cycles during the entire execution of the application (rather than just compiling faster at the beginning).

One other setting that applies to the compilation threads is the value of the `-XX:+BackgroundCompilation` flag, which by default is `true`. That setting means that the queue is processed asynchronously as just described. But that flag can be set to `false`, in which case when a method is eligible for compilation, code that wants to execute it will wait until it is in fact compiled (rather than continuing to execute in the interpreter). Background compilation is also disabled when `-Xbatch` is specified.

Quick Summary

1. Compilation occurs asynchronously for methods that are placed on the compilation queue.

2. The queue is not strictly ordered; hot methods are compiled before other methods in the queue. This is another reason why compilation IDs can appear out of order in the compilation log.

Inlining

One of the most important optimizations the compiler makes is to inline methods. Code that follows good object-oriented design often contains a number of attributes that are accessed via getters (and perhaps setters):

```
public class Point {
    private int x, y;

    public void getX() { return x; }
    public void setX(int i)  { x = i; }
}
```

The overhead for invoking a method call like this is quite high, especially relative to the amount of code in the method. In fact, in the early days of Java, performance tips often argued against this sort of encapsulation precisely because of the performance impact of all those method calls. Fortunately, JVMs now routinely perform code inlining for these kinds of methods. Hence, you can write this code:

```
Point p = getPoint();
p.setX(p.getX() * 2);
```

and the compiled code will essentially execute this:

```
Point p = getPoint();
p.x = p.x * 2;
```

Inlining is enabled by default. It can be disabled using the -XX:-Inline flag, though it is such an important performance boost that you would never actually do that (for example, disabling inlining reduces the performance of the stock batching test by over 50%). Still, because inlining is so important, and perhaps because there are many other knobs to turn, recommendations are often made regarding tuning the inlining behavior of the JVM.

Unfortunately, there is no basic visibility into how the JVM inlines code. (If you compile the JVM from source, you can produce a debug version that includes the flag -XX: +PrintInlining. That flag provides all sorts of information about the inlining decisions that the compiler makes.) The best that can be done is to look at profiles of the code, and if there are simple methods near the top of the profiles that seem like they should be inlined, try some experiments with inlining flags.

The basic decision about whether to inline a method depends on how hot it is and its size. The JVM determines if a method is hot (i.e., called frequently) based on an internal calculation; it is not directly subject to any tunable parameters. If a method is eligible for inlining because it is called frequently, then it will be inlined only if its bytecode size is less than 325 bytes (or whatever is specified as the -XX:MaxFreqInlineSize=N flag). Otherwise, it is eligible for inlining only if it is small: less than 35 bytes (or whatever is specified as the -XX:MaxInlineSize=N flag).

Sometimes you will see recommendations that the value of the MaxInlineSize flag be increased so that more methods are inlined. One often overlooked aspect of this relationship is that setting the MaxInlineSize value higher than 35 means that a method might be inlined when it is first called. However if the method is called frequently—in which case its performance matters much more—then it would have been inlined eventually (assuming its size is less than 325 bytes). Otherwise, the net effect of tuning the MaxInlineSize flag is that it might reduce the warm-up time needed for a test, but it is unlikely that it will have a big impact on a long-running application.

Quick Summary

1. Inlining is the most beneficial optimization the compiler can make, particularly for object-oriented code where attributes are well encapsulated.

2. Tuning the inlining flags is rarely needed, and recommendations to do so often fail to account for the relationship between normal inlining and frequent inlining. Make sure to account for both cases when investigating the effects of inlining.

Escape Analysis

The server compiler performs some very aggressive optimizations if escape analysis is enabled (-XX:+DoEscapeAnalysis, which is true by default). For example, consider this class to work with factorials:

```
public class Factorial {
    private BigInteger factorial;
    private int n;
    public Factorial(int n) {
        this.n = n;
    }
    public synchronized BigInteger getFactorial() {
        if (factorial == null)
            factorial = ...;
        return factorial;
    }
}
```

To store the first 100 factorial values in an array, this code would be used:

```
ArrayList<BigInteger> list = new ArrayList<BigInteger>();
for (int i = 0; i < 100; i++) {
    Factorial factorial = new Factorial(i);
    list.add(factorial.getFactorial());
}
```

The `factorial` object is referenced only inside that loop; no other code can ever access that object. Hence, the JVM is free to perform a number of optimizations on that object:

- It needn't get a synchronization lock when calling the `getFactorial()` method.
- It needn't store the field n in memory; it can keep that value in a register. Similarly it can store the `factorial` object reference in a register.
- In fact, it needn't allocate an actual factorial object at all; it can just keep track of the individual fields of the object.

This kind of optimization is quite sophisticated: it is simple enough in this example, but these optimizations are possible even with more complex code. Depending on the code usage, not all optimizations will necessarily apply. But escape analysis can determine which of those optimizations are possible and make the necessary changes in the compiled code.

Escape analysis is enabled by default. In rare cases, it will get things wrong, in which case disabling it will lead to faster and/or more stable code. If you find this to be the case, then simplifying the code in question is the best course of action: simpler code will compile better. (It is a bug, however, and should be reported.)

 Quick Summary

1. Escape analysis is the most sophisticated of the optimizations the compiler can perform. This is the kind of optimization that frequently causes microbenchmarks to go awry.

2. Escape analysis can often introduce "bugs" into improperly synchronized code.

Deoptimization

The discussion of the output of the `PrintCompilation` flag mentioned two cases where the compiler deoptimized the code. Deoptimization means that the compiler had to "undo" some previous compilation; the effect is that the performance of the application will be reduced—at least until the compiler can recompile the code in question.

There are two cases of deoptimization: when code is "made not entrant," and when code is "made zombie."

Not Entrant Code

There are two things that cause code to be made not entrant. One is due to the way classes and interfaces work, and one is an implementation detail of tiered compilation.

Let's look at the first case. Recall that the stock application has an interface StockPriceHistory. In the sample code, this interface has two implementations: a basic one (StockPriceHistoryImpl) and one that adds logging (StockPriceHistoryLogger) to each operation. In the servlet code, the implementation used is based on the log parameter of the URL:

```
StockPriceHistory sph;
String log = request.getParameter("log");
if (log != null && log.equals("true")) {
    sph = new StockPriceHistoryLogger(...);
}
else {
    sph = new StockPriceHistoryImpl(...);
}
// Then the JSP makes calls to:
sph.getHighPrice();
sph.getStdDev();
// and so on
```

If a bunch of calls are made to *http://localhost:8080/StockServlet* (that is, without the log parameter), the compiler will see that the actual type of the sph object is StockPriceHistoryImpl. It will then inline code and perform other optimizations based on that knowledge.

Later, say a call is made to *http://localhost:8080/StockServlet?log=true*. Now the assumption the compiler made regarding the type of the sph object is false; the previous optimizations are no longer valid. This generates a deoptimization trap, and the previous optimizations are discarded. If a lot of additional calls are made with logging enabled, the JVM will quickly end up compiling that code and making new optimizations.

The compilation log for that scenario will include lines such as the following:

```
 841113   25 %           net.sdo.StockPriceHistoryImpl::<init> @ -2 (156 bytes)
                            made not entrant
 841113  937  s          net.sdo.StockPriceHistoryImpl::process (248 bytes)
                            made not entrant
1322722   25 %           net.sdo.StockPriceHistoryImpl::<init> @ -2 (156 bytes)
                            made zombie
1322722  937  s          net.sdo.StockPriceHistoryImpl::process (248 bytes)
                            made zombie
```

Note that both the OSR-compiled constructor and the standard-compiled methods have been made not entrant, and some time much later, they are made zombie.

Deoptimization sounds like a bad thing, at least in terms of performance, but that isn't necessarily the case. The first example in this chapter that used the stock servlet application measured only the performance of the URL that triggers the StockPrice HistoryImpl path. With a 300-second warm-up, recall that test achieved about 24.4 OPS with tiered compilation.

Suppose that immediately after that test, a test is run that triggers the StockPrice HistoryLogger path—that is the scenario I ran to produce the deoptimization examples just listed. The full output of PrintCompilation shows that all the methods of the StockPriceHistoryImpl class get deoptimized when the requests for the logging implementation are started. But after deoptimization, if the path that uses the StockPriceHistoryImpl implementation is rerun, that code will get recompiled (with slightly different assumptions), and we will still end up still seeing about 24.4 OPS (after another warm-up period).

That's the best case, of course. What happens if the calls are intermingled such that the compiler can never really assume which path the code will take? Because of the extra logging, the path that includes the logging gets about 24.1 OPS through the servlet. If operations are mixed, we get about 24.3 OPS: just about what would be expected from an average. Similar results are observed in the batch program. So aside from a momentary point where the trap is processed, deoptimization has not affected the performance in any significant way.

The second thing that can cause code to be made not entrant is due to the way tiered compilation works. In tiered compilation, code is compiled by the client compiler, and then later compiled by the server compiler (and actually it's a little more complicated than that, as discussed in the next section). When the code compiled by the server compiler is ready, the JVM must replace the code compiled by the client compiler. It does this by marking the old code as not entrant and using the same mechanism to substitute the newly compiled (and more efficient) code. Hence, when a program is run with tiered compilation, the compilation log will show a slew of methods that are made not entrant. Don't panic: this "deoptimization" is in fact making the code that much faster.

The way to detect this is to pay attention to the tier level in the compilation log:

```
40915   84 %    3       net.sdo.StockPriceHistoryImpl::<init> @ 48 (156 bytes)
40923 3697      3       net.sdo.StockPriceHistoryImpl::<init> (156 bytes)
41418   87 %    4       net.sdo.StockPriceHistoryImpl::<init> @ 48 (156 bytes)
41434   84 %    3       net.sdo.StockPriceHistoryImpl::<init> @ -2 (156 bytes)
                            made not entrant
41458 3749      4       net.sdo.StockPriceHistoryImpl::<init> (156 bytes)
41469 3697      3       net.sdo.StockPriceHistoryImpl::<init> (156 bytes)
                            made not entrant
42772 3697      3       net.sdo.StockPriceHistoryImpl::<init> (156 bytes)
                            made zombie
42861   84 %    3       net.sdo.StockPriceHistoryImpl::<init> @ -2 (156 bytes)
                            made zombie
```

Here, the constructor is first OSR-compiled at level 3, and then fully compiled also at level 3. A second later, the OSR code becomes eligible for level 4 compilation, so it is compiled at level 4 and the level 3 OSR code is made not entrant. The same process then occurs for the standard compilation, and then finally the level 3 code becomes a zombie.

Deoptimizing Zombie Code

When the compilation log reports that it has made zombie code, it is saying that it has reclaimed some previous code that was made not entrant. In the last example, after a test was run with the StockPriceHistoryLogger implementation, the code for the StockPriceHistoryImpl class was made not entrant. But there were still objects of the StockPriceHistoryImpl class around. Eventually all those objects were reclaimed by GC. When that happened, the compiler noticed that the methods of that class were now eligible to be marked as zombie code.

For performance, this is a good thing. Recall that the compiled code is held in a fixed-size code cache; when zombie methods are identified, it means that the code in question can be removed from the code cache, making room for other classes to be compiled (or limiting the amount of memory the JVM will need to allocate later).

The possible downside here is that if the code for the class is made zombie and then later reloaded and heavily used again, the JVM will need to recompile and reoptimize the code. Still, that's exactly what happened in the scenario described above where the test was run without logging, then with logging, and then without logging; performance in that case was not noticeably affected. In general, the small recompilations that occur when zombie code is recompiled will not have a measurable effect on most applications.

 Quick Summary

1. Deoptimization allows the compiler to back out previous versions of compiled code.

2. Code is deoptimized when previous optimizations are no longer valid (e.g., because the type of the objects in question has changed).

3. There is usually a small, momentary effect in performance when code is deoptimized, but the new code usually warms up quickly again.

4. Under tiered compilation, code is deoptimized when it had previously been compiled by the client compiler and has now been optimized by the server compiler.

Tiered Compilation Levels

The compilation log for a program using tiered compilation prints the tier level at which each method is compiled. In the example from the last section, code was compiled up through level 4, even though to simplify the discussion so far, I've said there are only two compilers (plus the interpreter).

It turns out that there are five levels of execution, because the client compiler has three different levels. So the level of compilation runs from:

- 0: Interpreted code
- 1: Simple C1 compiled code
- 2: Limited C1 compiled code
- 3: Full C1 compiled code
- 4: C2 compiled code

A typical compilation log shows that most methods are first compiled at level 3: full C1 compilation. (All methods start at level 0, of course.) If they run often enough, they will get compiled at level 4 (and the level 3 code will be made not entrant). This is the most frequent path: the client compiler waits to compile something until it has information about how the code is used that it can leverage to perform optimizations.

If the server compiler queue is full, methods will be pulled from the server queue and compiled at level 2, which is the level at which the C1 compiler uses the invocation and back-edge counters (but doesn't require profile feedback). That gets the method compiled more quickly; the method will later be compiled at level 3 after the C1 compiler has gathered profile information, and finally compiled at level 4 when the server compiler queue is less busy.

On the other hand, if the client compiler is full, a method that is scheduled for compilation at level 3 may become eligible for level 4 compilation while still waiting to be compiled at level 3. In that case, it is quickly compiled to level 2 and then transitioned to level 4.

Trivial methods may start in either levels 2 or 3 but then go to level 1 because of their trivial nature. If the server compiler for some reason cannot compile the code, it will also go to level 1.

And of course when code is deoptimized, it goes to level 0.

There are flags that control some of this behavior, but expecting results when tuning at this level is quite optimistic. The best case for performance happens when methods are compiled as expected: tier 0 → tier 3 → tier 4. If methods frequently get compiled into tier 2 and extra CPU cycles are available, consider increasing the number of compiler threads; that will reduce the size of the server compiler queue. If no extra CPU cycles are available, then all you can do is attempt to reduce the size of the application.

Quick Summary

1. Tiered compilation can operate at five distinct levels among the two compilers.
2. Changing the path between levels is not recommended; this section just helps to explain the output of the compilation log.

Summary

This chapter has provided a lot of details about how just-in-time compilation works. From a tuning perspective, the simple choice here is to use the server compiler with tiered compilation for virtually everything; this will solve 90% of compiler-related performance issues. Just make sure that the code cache is sized large enough, and the compiler will provide pretty much all the performance that is possible.

A Final Word on Compiler Performance

If you have some experience with Java performance, you may be surprised that compilation has been discussed for an entire chapter without mentioning the final keyword. In some circles, the final keyword is thought to be an important factor in performance because it is believed to allow the JIT compiler to make better choices about inlining and other optimizations.

That idea may have had some validity in the dim past, but it has not been true for many, many years (if it ever was). Still, it is a persistent rumor. For the record, then, you should use the final keyword whenever it makes sense: for an immutable object or primitive value you don't want to change, for parameters to certain inner classes, and so on. But the presence or absence of the final keyword will not affect the performance of an application.

This chapter also contains a lot of background about how the compiler works. One reason for this is so you can understand some of the general recommendations made in Chapter 1 regarding small methods and simple code, and the effects of the compiler on microbenchmarks that were described in Chapter 2. In particular:

1. Don't be afraid of small methods—and in particular getters and setters—because they are easily inlined. If you have a feeling that the method overhead can be expensive, you're correct in theory (we showed that removing inlining has a huge impact on performance). But it's not the case in practice, since the compiler fixes that problem.

2. Code that needs to be compiled sits in a compilation queue. The more code in the queue, the longer the program will take to achieve optimal performance.

3. Although you can (and should) size the code cache, it is still a finite resource.

4. The simpler the code, the more optimizations that can be performed on it. Profile feedback and escape analysis can yield much faster code, but complex loop structures and large methods limit their effectiveness.

Finally, if you profile your code and find some surprising methods at the top of your profile—methods you expect shouldn't be there—you can use the information here to look into what the compiler is doing and to make sure it can handle the way your code is written.

## CHAPTER 5

An Introduction to Garbage Collection

This chapter covers the basics of garbage collection within the JVM. Short of rewriting code, tuning the garbage collector is the most important thing that can be done to improve the performance of a Java application.

There are four main garbage collectors available in current JVMs: the serial collector (used for single-CPU machines), the throughput (parallel) collector, the concurrent (CMS) collector, and the G1 collector. Their performance characteristics are quite different, so each will be covered in depth in the next chapter. However, they share basic concepts, so this chapter provides a basic overview of how the collectors operate.

Garbage Collection Overview

One of the most attractive features of Java is that developers needn't explicitly manage the lifecycle of objects: objects are created when needed, and when the object is no longer in use, the JVM automatically frees the object. If, like me, you spend a large amount of time optimizing the memory use of Java programs, this whole scheme might seem like a weakness instead of a feature (and the amount of time I'll spend covering GC might seem to lend credence to that position). Certainly it can be considered a mixed blessing, though I'd say I've personally spent less time dealing with Java memory issues in the past 15 years than I spent during 10 years of finding and fixing bugs caused by dangling and null pointers in other languages.

At a basic level, GC consists of finding objects that are no longer in use, and freeing the memory associated with those objects. The JVM starts by finding objects that are no longer in use (garbage objects). This is sometimes described as finding objects that no longer have any references to them (implying that references are tracked via a count). That sort of reference counting is insufficient, though: given a linked list of objects, each object in the list (except the head) will be pointed to by another object in the list—but if nothing refers to the head of the list, the entire list is not in use and can be freed. And if the list is circular (i.e., the tail of the list points to the head), then every object in the list has a reference to it—even though no object in the list can actually be used, since no objects reference the list itself.

So references cannot be tracked dynamically via a count; instead, the JVM must periodically search the heap for unused objects. When it finds unused objects, the JVM can free the memory occupied by those objects and use it to allocate additional objects. However, it is usually insufficient simply to keep track of that free memory and use it for future allocations; at some point, memory must be coalesced to prevent memory fragmentation.

Consider the case of a program that allocates an array of 1,000 bytes, then one of 24 bytes, and repeats that process in a loop. When that process fills up the heap, it will appear like the top row in Figure 5-1: the heap is full, and the allocations of the array sizes are interleaved.

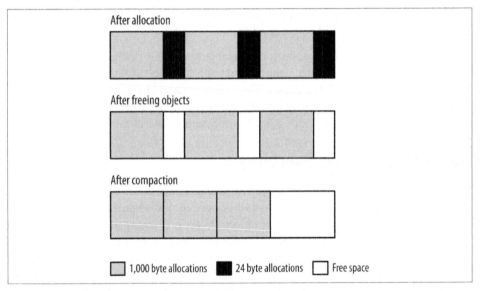

Figure 5-1. Idealized GC heap during collection

When the heap is full, the JVM will free the unused arrays. Say that all the 24-byte arrays are no longer in use, and the 1,000-byte arrays are still all in use: that yields the second row in Figure 5-1. The heap has free areas within it, but it can't actually allocate anything larger than 24 bytes—unless the JVM moves all the 1,000-byte arrays so that they are contiguous, leaving all the free memory in a region where it can be allocated as needed (the third row in Figure 5-1).

The implementations are a little more detailed, but the performance of GC is dominated by these basic operations: finding unused objects, making their memory available, and compacting the heap. Different collectors take different approaches to these operations, which is why they yield different performance characteristics.

It is simpler to perform these operations if no application threads are running while the garbage collector is running. Java programs are typically heavily multithreaded, and the garbage collector itself often runs multiple threads. This discussion considers two logical groups of threads: those performing application logic, and those performing GC. When GC tracks object references, or moves objects around in memory, it must make sure that application threads are not using those objects. This is particularly true when GC moves objects around: the memory location of the object changes during that operation, and hence no application threads can be accessing the object.

The pauses when all application threads are stopped are called *stop-the-world pauses*. These pauses generally have the greatest impact on the performance of an application, and minimizing those pauses is the key consideration when tuning GC.

Generational Garbage Collectors

Though the details differ somewhat, all garbage collectors work by splitting the heap into different generations. These are called the old (or tenured) generation, and the young generation. The young generation is further divided into sections known as eden and the survivor spaces (though sometimes, eden is incorrectly used to refer to the entire young generation).

The rationale for having separate generations is that many objects are used for a very short period of time. Take, for example, the loop in the stock price calculation where it sums the square of the difference of price from the average price (part of the calculation of standard deviation):

```
sum = new BigDecimal(0);
for (StockPrice sp : prices.values()) {
    BigDecimal diff = sp.getClosingPrice().subtract(averagePrice);
    diff = diff.multiply(diff);
    sum = sum.add(diff);
}
```

Like many Java classes, the BigDecimal class is immutable: the object represents a particular number and cannot be changed. When arithmetic is performed on the object, a new object is created (and often, the previous object with the previous value is then discarded). When this simple loop is executed for a year's worth of stock prices (roughly 250 iterations), 750 BigDecimal objects are created to store the intermediate values just in this loop. Those objects are discarded on the next iteration of the loop. Within the add() and other methods, the JDK library code creates even more intermediate BigDecimal (and other) objects. In the end, a lot of objects are created and discarded very quickly in this very small amount of code.

This kind of operation is quite common in Java and so the garbage collector is designed to take advantage of the fact that many (and sometimes most) objects are only used temporarily. This is where the generational design comes in. Objects are first allocated in the young generation, which is some subset of the entire heap. When the young generation fills up, the garbage collector will stop all the application threads and empty out the young generation. Objects that are no longer in use are discarded, and objects that are still in use are moved elsewhere. This operation is called a minor GC.

There are two performance advantages to this design. First, because the young generation is only a portion of the entire heap, processing it is faster than processing the entire heap. This means that the application threads are stopped for a much shorter period of time than if the entire heap were processed at once. You probably see a trade-off there, since it also means that the application threads are stopped more frequently than they would be if the JVM waited to perform GC until the entire heap were full; that trade-off will be explored in more detail later in this chapter. For now, though, it is almost always a big advantage to have the shorter pauses even though they will be more frequent.

The second advantage arises from the way objects are allocated in the young generation. Objects are allocated in eden (which comprises the vast majority of the young generation). When the young generation is cleared during a collection, all objects in eden are either moved or discarded: all live objects are moved either to one of the survivor spaces or to the old generation. Since all objects are moved, the young generation is automatically compacted when it is collected.

All GC algorithms have stop-the-world pauses during collection of the young generation.

As objects are moved to the old generation, eventually it too will fill up, and the JVM will need to find any objects within the old generation that are no longer in use and discard them. This is where GC algorithms have their biggest differences. The simpler algorithms stop all application threads, find the unused objects and free their memory, and then compact the heap. This process is called a full GC, and it generally causes a long pause for the application threads.

On the other hand, it is possible—though more computationally complex—to find unused objects while application threads are running; CMS and G1 both take that approach. Because the phase where they scan for unused objects can occur without stopping application threads, CMS and G1 are called concurrent collectors. They are also called low-pause (and sometimes—incorrectly—pauseless) collectors, since they minimize the need to stop all the application threads. Concurrent collectors also take different approaches to compacting the old generation.

When using the CMS or G1 collector, an application will typically experience fewer (and much shorter) pauses. The trade-off is that the application will use more CPU overall.

CMS and G1 may also perform a long, full GC pause (and avoiding those is one of the key factors to consider when tuning those algorithms).

As you consider which garbage collector is appropriate for your situation, think about the overall performance goals that must be met. There are trade-offs in every situation. In an application (such as a Java EE server) measuring the response time of individual requests, consider these points:

- The individual requests will be impacted by pause times—and more importantly by long pause times for full GCs. If minimizing the effect of pauses on response times is the goal, a concurrent collector will be more appropriate.
- If the average response time is more important than the outliers (i.e., the 90th% response time), the throughput collector will usually yield better results.
- The benefit of avoiding long pause times with a concurrent collector comes at the expense of extra CPU usage.

Similarly, the choice of garbage collector in a batch application is guided by the following trade-off:

- If enough CPU is available, using the concurrent collector to avoid full GC pauses will allow the job to finish faster.
- If CPU is limited, then the extra CPU consumption of the concurrent collector will cause the batch job to take more time.

 Quick Summary

1. All GC algorithms divide the heap into old and young generations.
2. All GC algorithms employ a stop-the-world approach to clearing objects from the young generation, which is usually a very quick operation.

GC Algorithms

The JVM provides four different algorithms for performing GC.

The serial garbage collector

The serial garbage collector is the simplest of the four. This is the default collector if the application is running on a client-class machine (32-bit JVMs on Windows or single-processor machines).

The serial collector uses a single thread to process the heap. It will stop all application threads as the heap is processed (for either a minor or full GC). During a full GC, it will fully compact the old generation.

The serial collector is enabled by using the -XX:+UseSerialGC flag (though usually it is the default in those cases where it might be used). Note that unlike with most JVM flags, the serial collector is not disabled by changing the plus sign to a minus sign (i.e., by specifying -XX:-UseSerialGC). On systems where the serial collector is the default, it is disabled by specifying a different GC algorithm.

The throughput collector

This is the default collector for server-class machines (multi-CPU Unix machines, and any 64-bit JVM).

The throughput collector uses multiple threads to collect the young generation, which makes minor GCs much faster than when the serial collector is used. The throughput collector can use multiple threads to process the old generation as well. That is the default behavior in JDK 7u4 and later releases, and that behavior can be enabled in earlier JDK 7 JVMs by specifying the -XX:+UseParallelOldGC flag. Because it uses multiple threads, the throughput collector is often called the parallel collector.

The throughput collector stops all application threads during both minor and full GCs, and it fully compacts the old generation during a full GC. Since it is the default in most situations where it would be used, it needn't be explicitly enabled. To enable it where necessary, use the flags -XX:+UseParallelGC -XX:+UseParallelOldGC.

The CMS collector

The CMS collector is designed to eliminate the long pauses associated with the full GC cycles of the throughput and serial collectors. CMS stops all application threads during a minor GC, which it also performs with multiple threads. Notably, though, CMS uses a different algorithm to collect the young generation (-XX:+UseParNewGC) than the throughput collector uses (-XX:+UseParallelGC).

Instead of stopping the application threads during a full GC, CMS uses one or more background threads to periodically scan through the old generation and discard unused objects. This makes CMS a low-pause collector: application threads are only paused during minor collections, and for some very short periods of time at certain points as the background threads scan the old generation. The overall amount of time that application threads are stopped is much less than with the throughput collector.

The trade-off here comes with increased CPU usage: there must be adequate CPU available for the background GC thread(s) to scan the heap at the same time the application threads are running. In addition, the background threads do not perform any compaction, which means that the heap can become fragmented. If the CMS background threads don't get enough CPU to complete their tasks, or if the heap becomes too fragmented to allocate an object, CMS reverts to the behavior of the serial collector: it stops all application threads in order to clean and compact the old generation using a single thread. Then it begins its concurrent, background processing again (until, possibly, the next time the heap becomes too fragmented).

CMS is enabled by specifying the flags `-XX:+UseConcMarkSweepGC -XX:+UseParNewGC` (both of which are `false` by default).

The G1 collector

The G1 (or Garbage First) collector is designed to process large heaps (greater than about 4 GB) with minimal pauses. It divides the heap into a number of regions, but it is still a generational collector. Some number of those regions comprise the young generation, and the young generation is still collected by stopping all application threads and moving all objects that are alive into the old generation or the survivor spaces. As in the other algorithms, this occurs using multiple threads.

G1 is a concurrent collector: the old generation is processed by background threads that don't need to stop the application threads to perform most of their work. Because the old generation is divided into regions, G1 can clean up objects from the old generation by copying from one region into another, which means that it (at least partially) compacts the heap during normal processing. Hence, a G1 heap is much less likely to be subject to fragmentation—though that is still possible.

Like CMS, the trade-off for avoiding the full GC cycles is CPU time: the multiple background threads must have CPU cycles available at the same time the application threads are running. G1 is enabled by specifying the flag `-XX:+UseG1GC` (which by default is `false`).

Causing and Disabling Explicit Garbage Collection

GC is typically caused when the JVM decides GC is necessary: a minor GC will be triggered when the new generation is full, a full GC will be triggered when the old generation is full, or a concurrent GC (if applicable) will be triggered when the heap starts to fill up.

Java provides a mechanism for applications to force a GC to occur: the `System.gc()` method. Calling that method is almost always a bad idea. This call always triggers a full GC (even if the JVM is running with CMS or G1), so application threads will be stopped for a relatively long period of time. And calling this method will not make the application any more efficient; it will cause a GC to occur sooner than might have happened otherwise, but that is really just shifting the performance impact.

There are exceptions to every rule, particularly when doing performance monitoring or benchmarking. For small benchmarks that run a bunch of code to properly warm up the JVM, forcing a GC before the measurement cycle may make sense. Similarly when doing heap analysis, it is usually a good idea to force a full GC before taking the heap dump. Most techniques to obtain a heap dump will perform a full GC anyway, but there are also other ways you can force a full GC: you can execute **jcmd <process id> GC.run**, or you can connect to the JVM using jconsole and click the Perform GC button in the Memory panel.

Another exception is RMI, which calls System.gc() every hour as part of its distributed garbage collector. That timing can be changed by setting a different value for these two system properties: -Dsun.rmi.dgc.server.gcInterval=*N* and -Dsun.rmi.dgc.client.gcInterval=*N*. The values for *N* are in milliseconds, and the default value in Java 7 (which is changed from earlier releases) is 3600000 (one hour).

If you end up running third-party code that incorrectly calls the System.gc() method, those GCs can be prevented entirely by including -XX:+DisableExplicitGC in the JVM arguments; by default that flag is false.

Quick Summary

1. The four available GC algorithms take different approaches toward minimizing the effect of GC on an application.

2. The serial collector makes sense (and is the default) when only one CPU is available and extra GC threads would interfere with the application.

3. The throughput collector is the default on other machines; it maximizes the total throughput of an application but may subject individual operations to long pauses.

4. The CMS collector can concurrently collect the old generation while application threads are running. If enough CPU is available for its background processing, this can avoid full GC cycles for the application.

5. The G1 collector also concurrently collects the old generation while application threads are running, potentially avoiding full GCs. Its design makes it less likely to experience full GCs than CMS.

Choosing a GC Algorithm

The choice of a GC algorithm depends in part on what the application looks like, and in part on the performance goals for the application.

The serial collector is best used only in those cases where the the application uses less than 100 MB. That allows the application to request a small heap, one that isn't going to be helped by the parallel collections of the throughput collector, nor by the background collections of CMS or G1.

That sizing guideline limits the usefulness of the serial collector. Most programs will need to choose between the throughput collector and a concurrent collector; that choice is most influenced by the performance goals of the application.

An overview of this topic was discussed in Chapter 2: there is a difference in measuring an application's elapsed time, throughput, or average (or 90th%) response times.

GC algorithms and batch jobs

For batch jobs, the pauses introduced by the throughput collector—and particularly the pauses of the full GC cycles—are a big concern. Each one adds a certain amount of elapsed time to the overall execution time. If each full GC cycle takes 0.5 seconds and there are 20 such cycles during the 5-minute execution of a program, then the pauses have added a 3.4% performance penalty: without the pauses, the program would have completed in 290 rather than 300 seconds.

If extra CPU is available (and that might be a big if), then using a concurrent collector will give the application a nice performance boost. The key here is whether adequate CPU is available for the background processing of the concurrent GC threads. Take the simple case of a single-CPU machine where there is a single application thread that consumes 100% of the CPU. When that application is run with the throughput collector, then GC will periodically run, causing the application thread to pause. When the same application is run with a concurrent collector, the operating system will sometimes run the application thread on the CPU, and sometimes run the background GC thread. The net effect is the same: the application thread is effectively paused (albeit for much shorter times) while the OS is running other threads.

The same principle applies in the general case when there are multiple application threads, multiple background GC threads, and multiple CPUs. If the operating system can't run all the application threads at the same time as the background GC threads, then the competition for the CPU has effectively introduced pauses into the behavior of the application threads.

Table 5-1 shows how this trade-off works. The batch application calculating stock data has been run in a mode that saves each set of results in memory for a few minutes (to fill up the heap); the test was run with a CMS and throughput GC algorithm.

Table 5-1. Batch processing time with different GC algorithms

GC algorithm	4 CPUs (CPU utilization)	1 CPU (CPU utilization)
CMS	78.09 (30.7%)	120.0 (100%)
Throughput	81.00 (27.7%)	111.6 (100%)

The times in this table are the number of seconds required to run the test, and the CPU utilization of the machine is shown in parentheses. When four CPUs are available, CMS runs a batch of operations about 3 seconds faster than the throughput collector—but notice the amount of CPU utilized in each case. There is a single application thread that will continually run, so with four CPUs that application thread will consume 25% of the available CPU.

The extra CPU reported in the table comes from the extra processing introduced by the GC threads. In the case of CMS, the background thread periodically consumes an entire CPU, or 25% of the total CPU available on the machine. The background thread here runs periodically—it turned out to run about 5% of the time—leaving an average CPU utilization of 30%.

Similarly, the throughput collector runs four GC threads. During GC cycles, those threads consume 100% of the four available CPUs, leaving a 28% average usage during the entire test. During minor collections, CMS will also run four GC threads that consume 100% of the four CPUs.

When only a single CPU is available, the CPU is always busy—whether running the application or GC threads. Now the extra overhead of the CMS background thread is a drawback, and the throughput collector finishes 9 seconds sooner.

Average CPU Usage and GC

Looking at only the average CPU during a test misses the interesting picture of what happens during GC cycles. The throughput collector will (by default) consume 100% of the CPU available on the machine while it runs, so a more accurate representation of the CPU usage during this test is shown in Figure 5-2.

Most of the time, only the application thread is running, consuming 25% of the total CPU. When GC kicks in, 100% of the CPU is consumed. Hence, the actual CPU usage resembles the sawtooth pattern in the graph, even though the average during the test is reported as the value of the straight dashed line.

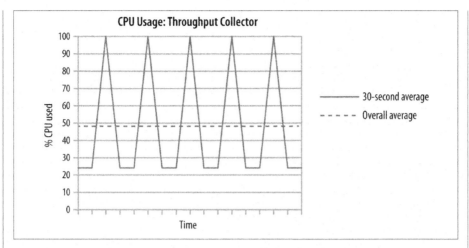

Figure 5-2. Actual versus average CPU usage (throughput)

The effect is different in a concurrent collector, when there are background thread(s) running concurrently with the application threads. In that case, a graph of the CPU might look like Figure 5-3.

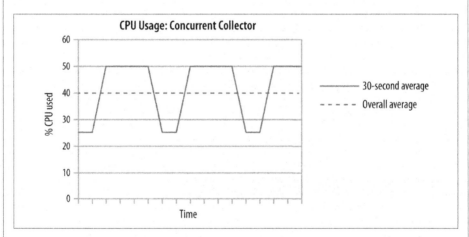

Figure 5-3. Actual versus average CPU usage (CMS)

The application thread starts by using 25% of the total CPU. Eventually it has created enough garbage for the CMS background thread to kick in; that thread also consumes an entire CPU, bringing the total up to 50%. When the CMS thread finishes, CPU usage drops to 25%, and so on. Note that there are no 100% peak-CPU periods, which is a little bit of a simplification: there will be very short spikes to 100% CPU usage during the CMS young generation collections, but those are short enough that we can ignore them for this discussion.

There can be multiple background threads in a concurrent collector, but the effect is similar: when those background threads run, they will consume CPU and drive up the long-term CPU average.

This can be quite important when you have a monitoring system triggered by CPU usage rules: you want to make sure CPU alerts are not triggered by the 100% CPU usage spikes in a full GC, or the much longer (but lower) spikes from background concurrent processing threads. These spikes are normal occurrences for Java programs.

Quick Summary

1. Batch jobs with application threads that utilize most of the CPU will typically get better performance from the throughput collector.

2. Batch jobs that do not consume all the available CPU on a machine will typically get better performance with a concurrent collector.

GC algorithms and throughput tests

When a test measures throughput, the basic trade-offs in GC algorithms are the same as for batch jobs, but the effect of the pauses is quite different. The overall system impact on CPU still plays an important role.

This section uses the stock servlet as the basis for its testing; the servlet is run in a GlassFish instance with a 2 GB heap, and the previous 10 requests are saved in each user's HTTP session (to put more pressure on the GC system). Table 5-2 shows the throughput the test achieves when running with the throughput and CMS collectors. In this case, the tests are run on a machine with four CPUs.

Table 5-2. Throughput with different GC algorithms

Number of clients	Throughput TPS (CPU usage)	CMS TPS (CPU usage)
1	30.43 (29%)	31.98 (31%)
10	81.34 (97%)	62.20 (85%)

Two tests are run to measure the total throughput. In the first test, a single client is emulated by the fhb program; the second case drives the load from 10 clients so that the target-machine CPU is fully utilized.

When there are available CPU cycles, CMS performs better here, yielding 5% more TPS than the throughput collector. The throughput collector in this test had 24 full GC pauses during which it could not process requests; those pauses were about 5% of the total steady-state time of the test. By avoiding those pauses, CMS provided better throughput.

When CPU was limited, however, CMS performed much worse: about 23.5% fewer TPS. Note too that CMS could not keep the CPU close to 100% busy in this experiment. That's because there were not sufficient CPU cycles for the background CMS threads, and so CMS encountered concurrent mode failures. Those failures meant the JVM had to perform a single-threaded full GC, and those periods of time (during which the four-CPU machine was only 25% busy) drove down the average CPU utilization.

GC algorithms and response time tests

Table 5-3 shows the same test with a think time of 250 ms between requests, which results in a fixed load of 29 TPS. The performance measurement then is the average, 90th%, and 99th% response times for each request.

Table 5-3. Response time with different GC algorithms

Session size	Throughput				CMS			
	Avg	90th%	99th%	CPU	Avg	90th%	99th%	CPU
10 items	0.092	0.171	0.813	41%	0.104	0.211	0.260	46%
50 items	0.180	0.218	3.617	55%	0.107	0.222	0.315	53%

The first test saves the previous 10 requests in the user's session state. The result here is typical when comparing the two collectors: the throughput collector is faster than the concurrent collector in terms of an average response time and even the 90th% response time. The 99th% response time shows a significant advantage for CMS: the full GCs in the throughput case made 1% of the operations (those that were stopped during a full GC) take significantly longer. CMS uses about 10% more CPU to get that improvement in the 99th% result.

When 50 items were saved in the session data, GC cycles had a much bigger impact, particularly in the throughput case. Now the average response time for the throughput collector is much higher than CMS, and all because of the very large outliers that drove the 99th% response time over 3 seconds. Interestingly, the 90th% response time for the throughput collector is lower than for CMS—when the JVM isn't doing those full GCs, the throughput collector still shows an advantage.

Cases like that certainly occur from time to time, but they are far less common than the first case. In a sense, CMS was lucky in the last case too: often when the heap contains so much live data that the full GC time dominates the response times for the throughput collector, the CMS collector experiences concurrent mode failures as well. In this example, the CMS background processing was sufficient to keep up with the demands of the application.

These are the sort of trade-offs to consider when deciding which GC algorithm suits your performance goals. If the average time is all you care about, then the throughput collector will likely look similar to a concurrent collector, and you can consider the CPU usage instead (in which case, the throughput collector will be the better choice). If you're interested in the 90th% or other percentile-based response times, then only testing can see where those line up with the number of full GC cycles the application needs to perform its job.

Quick Summary

1. When measuring response time or throughput, the choice between throughput and concurrent collectors is dependent on the amount of CPU available for the background concurrent threads to run.

2. The throughput collector will frequently have a lower average response time than a concurrent collector, but the concurrent collector will often have a lower 90th% or 99th% response time.

3. When the throughput collector performs excessive full GCs, a concurrent collector will often have lower average response times.

Choosing between CMS and G1

The tests in the last section used CMS as the concurrent collector. As a basic rule of thumb, CMS is expected to outperform G1 for heaps that are smaller than 4 GB. CMS is a simpler algorithm than G1, and so in simple cases (i.e., those with small heaps), it is likely to be faster. When large heaps are used, G1 will usually be better than CMS because of the manner in which it can divide work.

CMS background thread(s) must scan the entire old generation before any objects can be freed. The time to scan the heap is obviously dependent on the size of the heap. If the CMS background thread does not finish scanning the heap and freeing objects before the heap fills up, CMS will experience a concurrent mode failure: at that point, CMS has to revert to doing a full GC with all application threads stopped. That full GC is done only with a single thread, making it a very severe performance penalty. CMS can be tuned to utilize multiple background threads to minimize that change, but the larger the heap grows, the more work those CMS threads have to do. (The chance that CMS experiences a concurrent mode failure also depends on the amount of allocation that the application does.)

G1, on the other hand, segments the old generation into regions, so it is easier for multiple background threads to divide the necessary work of scanning the old generation. G1 can still experience concurrent mode failures if the background threads can't keep up, but the G1 algorithm makes that less likely to occur.

CMS can also revert to a full GC because of heap fragmentation, since CMS does not compact the heap (except during the lengthy full GCs). G1 compacts the heap as it goes.

G1 can still experience heap fragmentation, but its design again reduces the chance of that compared to CMS.

There are ways to tune both CMS and G1 to attempt to avoid these failures, but for some applications, that will not always work. As heaps grow larger (and the penalty for a full GC grows larger), it is easier to use G1 to avoid these issues. (On the other hand, for some applications it is impossible to tune either collector to avoid concurrent mode failures. Hence, even if the performance goals for an application seem to be in line with the goals of a concurrent collector, the throughput collector may still be the better choice.)

Finally, there are some slightly intangible factors to consider among all three collectors. The throughput collector is the oldest of the three, which means the JVM engineers have had more opportunity to ensure it is written to perform well in the first place. G1, as a relatively new algorithm, is more likely to encounter corner cases that its design didn't anticipate. G1 has fewer tuning knobs to affect its performance, which may be good or bad depending on your perspective. G1 was considered experimental until Java 7u4, and some of its tuning features aren't available until Java 7u10. G1 has significant performance benefits in Java 8 compared to earlier Java 7 releases, and future work on G1 can also be expected to improve its performance on smaller heaps relative to CMS.

Quick Summary

1. CMS is the better of the concurrent collectors when the heap is small.
2. G1 is designed to process the heap in regions, so it will scale better than CMS on large heaps.

Basic GC Tuning

Although GC algorithms differ in the way they process the heap, they share basic configuration parameters. In many cases, these basic configurations are all that is needed to run an application.

Sizing the Heap

The first basic tuning for GC is the size of the application's heap. There are advanced tunings that affect the size of the heap's generations; as a first step, this section will discuss setting the overall heap size.

Like most performance issues, choosing a heap size is a matter of balance. If the heap is too small, the program will spend too much time performing GC and not enough time performing application logic. But simply specifying a very large heap isn't necessarily the answer either. The time spent in GC pauses is dependent on the size of the heap, so as the size of the heap increases, the duration of those pauses also increases. The pauses will occur less frequently, but their duration will make the overall performance lag.

A second danger arises when very large heaps are used. Computer operating systems use virtual memory to manage the physical memory of the machine. A machine may have 8 GB of physical RAM, but the OS will make it appear as if there is much more memory available. The amount of virtual memory is subject to the OS configuration, but say the OS makes it look like there is 16 GB of memory. The OS manages that by a process called swapping. (Or paging, though there is also a technical difference between those two terms that isn't important for this discussion.) You can load programs that use up to 16 GB of memory, and the OS will copy inactive portions of those programs to disk. When those memory areas are needed, the OS will copy them from disk to RAM (usually it will first need to copy something from RAM to disk to make room).

This process works well for a system running lots of different applications, since most of the applications are not active at the same time. It does not work so well for Java applications. If a Java program with a 12 GB heap is run on this system, the OS can handle it by keeping 8 GB of the heap in RAM and 4 GB on disk (that simplifies the actual situation a little, since other programs will use part of RAM). The JVM won't know about this; the swapping is transparently handled by the OS. Hence, the JVM will happily fill up all 12 GB of heap it has been told to use. This causes a severe performance penalty as the OS swaps data from disk to RAM (which is an expensive operation to begin with).

Worse, the one time this swapping is guaranteed to occur is during a full GC, when the JVM must access the entire heap. If the system is swapping during a full GC, pauses will be an order of magnitude longer than they would otherwise be. Similarly, if a concurrent collector is used, when the background thread sweeps through the heap, it will likely fall behind due to the long waits for data to be copied from disk to main memory—resulting in an expensive concurrent mode failure.

Hence, the first rule in sizing a heap is never to specify a heap that is larger than the amount of physical memory on the machine—and if there are multiple JVMs running, that applies to the sum of all their heaps. You also need to leave some room for the JVM itself, as well as some memory for other applications: typically, at least 1 GB of space for common OS profiles.

The size of the heap is controlled by two values: an initial value (specified with -XmsN) and a maximum value (-XmxN). The defaults for these vary depending on the operating system, the amount of system RAM, and the JVM in use. The defaults can be affected by other flags on the command line as well; heap sizing is one of the JVM's core ergonomic tunings.

The goal of the JVM is to find a "reasonable" default initial value for the heap based on the system resources available to it, and to grow the heap up to a "reasonable" maximum if (and only if) the application needs more memory (based on how much time it spends performing GC). Absent some of the advanced tuning flags and details discussed later in this and the next chapters, the default values for the initial and maximum sizes are given in Table 5-4. (The JVM will round these values down slightly for alignment purposes; the GC logs that print the sizes will show that the values are not exactly equal to the numbers in this table.)

Table 5-4. Default heap sizes

Operating system and JVM	Initial heap (Xms)	Maximum heap (Xmx)
Linux/Solaris, 32-bit client	16 MB	256 MB
Linux/Solaris, 32-bit server	64 MB	Min (1 GB, 1/4 of physical memory)
Linux/Solaris, 64-bit server	Min (512 MB, 1/64 of physical memory)	Min (32 GB, 1/4 of physical memory)
MacOS 64-bit server JVMs	64 MB	Min (1 GB, 1/4 of physical memory)
Windows 32-bit client JVMs	16 MB	256 MB
Windows 64-bit server JVMs	64 MB	Min (1 GB, 1/4 of physical memory)

On a machine with less than 192 MB of physical memory, the maximum heap size will be half of the physical memory (96 MB or less).

Having an initial and maximum size for the heap allows the JVM to tune its behavior depending on the workload. If the JVM sees that it is doing too much GC with the initial heap size, it will continually increase the heap until the JVM is doing the "correct" amount of GC, or until the heap hits its maximum size.

For many applications, that means a heap size doesn't need to be set at all. Instead, you specify the performance goals for the GC algorithm: the pause times you are willing to tolerate, the percentage of time you want to spend in GC, and so on. The details of that will depend on the GC algorithm used and are discussed in the next chapter (though even then, the defaults are chosen such that for a wide range of applications, those values needn't be tuned either).

That approach usually works fine if an application does not need a larger heap than the default maximum for the platform it is running on. However, if the application is spending too much time in GC, then the heap size will need to be increased by setting the -Xmx flag. There is no hard-and-fast rule on what size to choose (other than not specifying a size larger than the machine can support). A good rule of thumb is to size the heap so that it is 30% occupied after a full GC. To calculate this, run the application until it has reached a steady-state configuration: a point at which it has loaded anything it caches, has created a maximum number of client connections, and so on. Then connect to the application with jconsole, force a full GC, and observe how much memory is used when the full GC completes. (Alternately, for throughput GC, you can consult the GC log if it is available.)

Be aware that automatic sizing of the heap occurs even if you explicitly set the maximum size: the heap will start at its default initial size, and the JVM will grow the heap in order to meet the performance goals of the GC algorithm. There isn't necessarily a memory penalty for specifying a larger heap than is needed: it will only grow enough to meet the GC performance goals.

On the other hand, if you know exactly what size heap the application needs, then you may as well set both the initial and maximum values of the heap to that value (e.g., -Xms4096m -Xmx4096m). That makes GC slightly more efficient, because it never needs to figure out whether the heap should be resized.

Quick Summary

1. The JVM will attempt to find a reasonable minimum and maximum heap size based on the machine it is running on.

2. Unless the application needs a larger heap than the default, consider tuning the performance goals of a GC algorithm (given in the next chapter) rather than fine-tuning the heap size.

Sizing the Generations

Once the heap size has been determined, you (or the JVM) must decide how much of the heap to allocate to the young generation, and how much to allocate to the old generation. The performance implication of this should be clear: if there is a relatively larger young generation, then it will be collected less often, and fewer objects will be promoted into the old generation. But on the other hand, because the old generation is relatively smaller, it will fill up more frequently and do more full GCs. Striking a balance here is the key.

Different GC algorithms attempt to strike this balance in different ways. However, all GC algorithms use the same set of flags to set the sizes of the generations; this section covers those common flags.

The command-line flags to tune the generation sizes all adjust the size of the young generation; the old generation gets everything that is left over. There are a variety of flags that can be used to size the young generation:

-XX:NewRatio=*N*
    Set the ratio of the young generation to the old generation.

-XX:NewSize=*N*
    Set the initial size of the young generation.

`-XX:MaxNewSize=N`

Set the maximum size of the young generation.

`-XmnN`

Shorthand for setting both `NewSize` and `MaxNewSize` to the same value.

The young generation is first sized by the `NewRatio`, which has a default value of 2. Parameters that affect the sizing of heap spaces are generally specified as ratios; the value is used in an equation to determine the percentage of space affected. The `NewRatio` value is used in this formula:

```
Initial Young Gen Size = Initial Heap Size / (1 + NewRatio)
```

Plugging in the initial size of the heap and the `NewRatio` yields the value that becomes the setting for the young generation. By default, then, the young generation starts out at 33% of the initial heap size.

Alternately, the size of the young generation can be set explicitly by specifying the `NewSize` flag. If that option is set, it will take precedence over the value calculated from the `NewRatio`. There is no default for this flag (though `PrintFlagsFinal` will report a value of 1 MB). If the flag isn't set, the initial young generation size will be based on the `NewRatio` calculation.

As the heap expands, the young generation size will expand as well, up to the maximum size specified by the `MaxNewSize` flag. By default, that maximum is also set using the `NewRatio` value, though it is based on the maximum (rather than initial) heap size.

Tuning the young generation by specifying a range for its minimum and maximum sizes ends up being fairly difficult. When a heap size is fixed (by setting `-Xms` equal to `-Xmx`), it is usually preferable to use `-Xmn` to specify a fixed size for the young generation as well. If an application needs a dynamically sized heap and requires a larger (or smaller) young generation, then focus on setting the `NewRatio` value.

Quick Summary

1. Within the overall heap size, the sizes of the generations are controlled by how much space is allocated to the young generation.

2. The young generation will grow in tandem with the overall heap size, but it can also fluctuate as a percentage of the total heap (based on the initial and maximum size of the young generation).

Sizing Permgen and Metaspace

When the JVM loads classes, it must keep track of certain metadata about those classes. From the perspective of an end user, this is all just bookkeeping information. This data is held in a separate heap space. In Java 7, this is called the *permgen* (or permanent generation), and in Java 8, this is called the *metaspace*.

Permgen and metaspace are not exactly the same thing. In Java 7, permgen contains some miscellaneous objects that are unrelated to class data; these are moved into the regular heap in Java 8. Java 8 also fundamentally changes the kind of metadata that is held in this special region—though since end users don't know what that data is in the first place, that change doesn't really affect us. As end users, all we need to know is that permgen/metaspace holds a bunch of class-related data, and that there are certain circumstances where the size of that region needs to be tuned.

Note that permgen/metaspace does not hold the actual instance of the class (the Class objects), nor reflection objects (e.g., Method objects); those are held in the regular heap. Information in permgen/metaspace is really only used by the compiler and JVM runtime, and the data it holds is referred to as class metadata.

There isn't a good way to calculate in advance how much space a particular program needs for its permgen/metaspace. The size will be proportional to the number of classes it uses, so bigger applications will need bigger areas. One of the advantages to phasing out permgen is that the metaspace rarely needs to be sized—because (unlike permgen) metaspace will by default use as much space as it needs. Table 5-5 lists the default initial and maximum sizes for permgen and metaspace.

Table 5-5. Default sizes of permgen/metaspace

JVM	Default initial size	Default maximum permgen size	Default maximum metaspace size
32-bit client JVM	12 MB	64 MB	Unlimited
32-bit server JVM	16 MB	64 MB	Unlimited
64-bit JVM	20.75 MB	82 MB	Unlimited

These memory regions behave just like a separate instance of the regular heap. They are sized dynamically based on an initial size and will increase as needed to a maximum size. For permgen, the sizes are specified via these flags: -XX:PermSize=*N* and -XX:MaxPermSize=*N*. Metaspace is sized with these flags: -XX:MetaspaceSize=*N* and -XX:MaxMetaspaceSize=*N*.

Metaspace Too Big?

Because the default size of metaspace is unlimited, there is the possibility (particularly in a 32-bit JVM) that a Java 8 application can run out of memory by filling up metaspace. The Native Memory Tracking (NMT) tools discussed in Chapter 8 can help diagnose that case. If metaspace is growing too big, you can set the value of `MaxMetaspaceSize` lower—but then the application will eventually get an `OutOfMemoryError` when the metaspace fills up. Figuring out why the class metadata is too large is the real remedy in that case.

Resizing these regions requires a full GC, so it is an expensive operation. If there are a lot of full GCs during the startup of a program (as it is loading classes), it is often because permgen or metaspace is being resized, so increasing the initial size is a good idea to improve startup in that case. Java 7 applications that define a lot of classes should increase the maximum size as well. Application servers, for example, typically specify a maximum permgen size of 128 MB, 192 MB, or more.

Contrary to its name, data stored in permgen is not permanent (metaspace, then, is a much better name). In particular, classes can be eligible for GC just like anything else. This is a very common occurrence in an application server, which creates new classloaders every time an application is deployed (or redeployed). The old classloaders are then unreferenced and eligible for GC, as are any classes that they defined. In a long development cycle in an application server, it is not unusual to see full GCs triggered during deployment: permgen or metaspace has filled up with the new class information, but the old class metadata can be freed.

Heap dumps (see Chapter 7) can be used to diagnose what classloaders exist, which in turn can help determine if a classloader leak is filling up permgen (or metaspace). Otherwise, `jmap` can be used with the argument `-permstat` (in Java 7) or `-clstats` (in Java 8) to print out information about the classloaders. That particular command isn't the most stable, though, and it cannot be recommended.

1. The permanent generation or metaspace holds class metadata (not class data itself). It behaves like a separate heap.

2. For typical applications that do not load classes after startup, the initial size of this region can be based on its usage after all classes have been loaded. That will slightly speed up startup.

3. Application servers doing development (or any environment where classes are frequently redefined) will see an occasional full GC caused when permgen/metaspace fills up and old class metadata is discarded.

Controlling Parallelism

All GC algorithms except the serial collector use multiple threads. The number of these threads is controlled by the `-XX:ParallelGCThreads=N` flag. The value of this flag affects the number of threads used for the following operations:

- Collection of the young generation when using `-XX:+UseParallelGC`
- Collection of the old generation when using `-XX:+UseParallelOldGC`
- Collection of the young generation when using `-XX:+UseParNewGC`
- Collection of the young generation when using `-XX:+UseG1GC`
- Stop-the-world phases of CMS (though not full GCs)
- Stop-the-world phases of G1 (though not full GCs)

Because these GC operations stop the application threads from executing, the JVM attempts to use as many CPU resources as it can in order to minimize the pause time. By default, that means the JVM will run one thread for each CPU on a machine, up to eight. Once that threshold has been reached, the JVM only adds a new thread for every five-eighths of a CPU. So the total number of threads (where N is the number of CPUs) on a machine with more than eight CPUs is:

```
ParallelGCThreads = 8 + ((N - 8) * 5 / 8)
```

There are times when this number is too large. An application using a small heap (say, 1 GB) on a machine with eight CPUs will be slightly more efficient with four or six threads dividing up that heap. On a 128-CPU machine, 83 GC threads is too many for all but the largest heaps.

Additionally, if more than one JVM is running on the machine, it is a good idea to limit the total number of GC threads among all JVMs. When they run, the GC threads are quite efficient and each will consume 100% of a single CPU (this is why the average

CPU usage for the throughput collector was higher than expected in previous examples). In machines with eight or fewer CPUs, GC will consume 100% of the CPU on the machine. On machines with more CPUs and multiple JVMs, there will still be too many GC threads running in parallel.

Take the example of a 16-CPU machine running four JVMs; each JVM will have by default 13 GC threads. If all four JVMs execute GC at the same time, the machine will have 52 CPU-hungry threads contending for CPU time. That results in a fair amount of contention; it will be more efficient if each JVM is limited to four GC threads. Even though it may be unlikely for all four JVMs to perform a GC operation at the same time, one JVM executing GC with 13 threads means that the application threads in the remaining JVMs now have to compete for CPU resources on a machine where 13 of 16 CPUs are 100% busy executing GC tasks. Giving each JVM four GC threads provides a better balance in this case.

Note that this flag does not set the number of background threads used by CMS or G1 (though it does affect that). Details on that are given in the next chapter.

Quick Summary

1. The basic number of threads used by all GC algorithms is based on the number of CPUs on a machine.

2. When multiple JVMs are run on a single machine, that number will be too high and must be reduced.

Adaptive Sizing

The sizes of the heap, the generations, and the survivor spaces can vary during execution as the JVM attempts to find the optimal performance according to its policies and tunings.

This is a best-effort solution, and it relies on past performance: the assumption is that future GC cycles will look similar to the GC cycles in the recent past. That turns out to be a reasonable assumption for many workloads, and even if the allocation rate suddenly changes, the JVM will readapt its sizes based on the new information.

Adaptive sizing provides benefits in two important ways. First, it means that small applications don't need to worry about overspecifying the size of their heap. Consider the administrative command-line programs used to adjust the operations of things like an application server—those programs are usually very short-lived and use minimal memory resources. These applications will use 16 (or 64) MB of heap even though the default heap could potentially grow to 1 GB. Because of adaptive sizing, applications like that don't need to be specifically tuned; the platform defaults ensure that they will not use a large amount of memory.

Second, it means that many applications don't really need to worry about tuning their heap size at all—or if they need a larger heap than the platform default, they can just specify that larger heap and forget about the other details. The JVM can autotune the heap and generation sizes to use an optimal amount of memory given the GC algorithm's performance goals. Adaptive sizing is what allows that autotuning to work.

Still, doing the adjustment of the sizes takes a small amount of time—which occurs for the most part during a GC pause. If you have taken the time to finely tune GC parameters and the size constraints of the application's heap, adaptive sizing can be disabled. Disabling adaptive sizing is also useful for applications that go through markedly different phases, if you want to optimally tune GC for one of those phases.

At a global level, adaptive sizing is disabled by turning off the -XX:-UseAdaptiveSize Policy flag (which is true by default). With the exception of the survivor spaces (which are examined in detail in the next chapter), adaptive sizing is also effectively turned off if the minimum and maximum heap sizes are set to the same value, and the initial and maximum sizes of the new generation are set to the same value.

To see how the JVM is resizing the spaces in an application, set the -XX:+PrintAdapti veSizePolicy flag. When a GC is performed, the GC log will contain information detailing how the various generations were resized during a collection.

 Quick Summary

1. Adaptive sizing controls how the JVM alters the ratio of young generation to old generation within the heap.

2. Adaptive sizing should generally be kept enabled, since adjusting those generation sizes is how GC algorithms attempt to meet their pause time goals.

3. For finely tuned heaps, adaptive sizing can be disabled for a small performance boost.

GC Tools

Since GC is central to the performance of Java, there are many tools that monitor its performance.

The best way to see what effect GC has on the performance of an application is to become familiar with the GC log, which is a record of every GC operation during the program's execution.

The details in the GC log vary depending on the GC algorithm, but the basic management of the log is always the same. That management is covered here, and more details on the contents of the log are given in the algorithm-specific tuning sections in the next chapter.

There are multiple ways to enable the GC log: specifying either of the flags -verbose:gc or -XX:+PrintGC will create a simple GC log (the flags are aliases for each other, and by default the log is disabled). The -XX:+PrintGCDetails flag will create a log with much more information. This flag is recommended (it is also false by default); it is often too difficult to diagnose what is happening with GC using only the simple log. In conjunction with the detailed log, it is recommended to include -XX:+PrintGCTimeStamps or -XX:+PrintGCDateStamps, so that the time between GC operations can be determined. The difference in those two arguments is that the timestamps are relative to 0 (based on when the JVM starts), while the date stamps are an actual date string. That makes the date stamps ever-so-slightly less efficient as the dates are formatted, though it is an infrequent enough operation that its effect is unlikely to be noticed.

The GC log is written to standard output, though that location can be changed with the -Xloggc:*filename* flag. Using -Xloggc automatically enables the simple GC log unless PrintGCDetails has also been enabled. The amount of data that is kept in the GC log can be limited using log rotation; this is quite useful for a long-running server that might otherwise fill up its disk with logs over several months. Logfile rotation is controlled with these flags: -XX:+UseGCLogFileRotation -XX:NumberOfGCLogFiles=*N* -XX:GCLogFileSize=*N*. By default, UseGCLogFileRotation is disabled. When that flag is enabled, the default number of files is 0 (meaning unlimited), and the default logfile size is 0 (meaning unlimited). Hence, values must be specified for all these options in order for log rotation to work as expected. Note that a logfile size will be rounded up to 8 KB for values less than that.

You can parse and peruse the GC logfiles on your own, although there are several tools that do that. One of these is GC Histogram (*http://java.net/projects/gchisto*). GC Histogram reads in a GC log and provides several charts and tables about the data in that log. A summary of the overhead of GC produced by GC Histogram is shown in Figure 5-4.

	Num	Num (%)	Total GC (s...	Total GC (%)	Overhead (..	Avg (ms)	Sigma (ms)	Min (ms)	Max (ms)
All	474	100.00%	193.246	100.00%	41.29%	407.693	1,347.194	57.254	9,592.072
Young GC	457	96.41%	71.705	37.11%	15.32%	156.904	44.162	57.254	260.142
Full GC	17	3.59%	121.541	62.89%	25.97%	7,149.478	1,873.358	224.791	9,592.072

Figure 5-4. GC Histogram Pause Stats tab

In this particular case, the JVM is spending 41%(!) of its time performing GC, and the time to perform a full GC is more than 7 seconds. This is an application that definitely needs to improve its memory usage.

For real-time monitoring of the heap, use `jconsole`. The Memory panel of `jconsole` displays a real-time graph of the heap as shown in Figure 5-5.

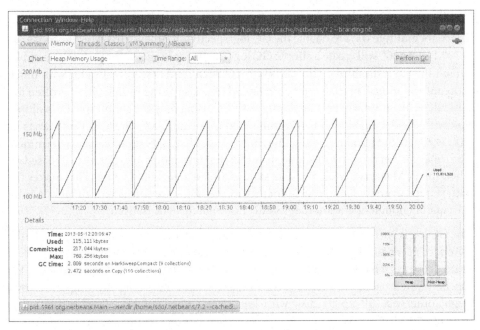

Figure 5-5. Real-time heap display

This particular view shows the entire heap, which is periodically cycling between using about 100 MB and 160 MB. `jconsole` can instead display only eden, or the survivor spaces, or the old generation, or the permanent generation. If I'd selected eden as the region to chart, it would have shown a similar pattern as eden fluctuated between 0 MB and 60 MB (and, as you can guess, that means if I'd charted the old generation, it would have been essentially a flat line at 100 MB).

For a scriptable solution, `jstat` is the tool of choice. `jstat` provides nine options to print different information about the heap; `jstat -options` will provide the full list. One useful option is `-gcutil`, which displays the time spent in GC as well as the percentage of each GC area that is currently filled. Other options to `jstat` will display the GC sizes in terms of KB.

Remember that `jstat` takes an optional argument—the number of milliseconds to repeat the command—so it can monitor over time the effect of GC in an application. Here is some sample output repeated every second:

```
% jstat -gcutil process_id 1000
  S0     S1     E      O      P      YGC    YGCT    FGC    FGCT    GCT
 51.71   0.00  99.12  60.00  99.93   98    1.985    8     2.397   4.382
  0.00  42.08   5.55  60.98  99.93   99    2.016    8     2.397   4.413
  0.00  42.08   6.32  60.98  99.93   99    2.016    8     2.397   4.413
  0.00  42.08  68.06  60.98  99.93   99    2.016    8     2.397   4.413
  0.00  42.08  82.27  60.98  99.93   99    2.016    8     2.397   4.413
  0.00  42.08  96.67  60.98  99.93   99    2.016    8     2.397   4.413
  0.00  42.08  99.30  60.98  99.93   99    2.016    8     2.397   4.413
 44.54   0.00   1.38  60.98  99.93  100    2.042    8     2.397   4.439
 44.54   0.00   1.91  60.98  99.93  100    2.042    8     2.397   4.439
```

When monitoring started, the program had already performed 98 collections of the young generation (YGC), which took a total of 1.985 seconds (YGCT). It had also performed eight full GCs (FGC) requiring 2.397 seconds (FGCT); hence the total time in GC (GCT) was 4.382 seconds.

All three sections of the young generation are displayed here: the two survivor spaces (S0 and S1) and eden (E). The monitoring started just as eden was filling up (99.12% full), so in the next second there was a young collection: eden reduced to 5.55% full, the survivor spaces switched places, and a small amount of memory was promoted to the old generation (O), which increased to using 60.98% of its space. As is typical, there is little or no change in the permanent generation (P) since all necessary classes have already been loaded by the application.

If you've forgotten to enable GC logging, this is a good substitute to watch how GC operates over time.

Quick Summary

1. GC logs are the key piece of data required to diagnose GC issues; they should be collected routinely (even on production servers).

2. A better GC logfile is obtained with the `PrintGCDetails` flag.

3. Programs to parse and understand GC logs are readily available; they are quite helpful in summarizing the data in the GC log.

4. `jstat` can provide good visibility into GC for a live program.

Summary

Performance of the garbage collector is one key feature to the overall performance of any Java application. For many applications, though, the only tuning required is to select the appropriate GC algorithm and, if needed, to increase the heap size of the application.

Adaptive sizing will then allow the JVM to autotune its behavior to provide good performance using the given heap.

More complex applications will require additional tuning, particularly for specific GC algorithms. If the simple GC settings in this chapter do not provide the performance an application requires, consult the tunings described in the next chapter.

## CHAPTER 6

Garbage Collection Algorithms

Chapter 5 examined the general behavior of all garbage collectors, including JVM flags that apply universally to all GC algorithms: how to select heap sizes, generation sizes, logging, and so on.

The basic tunings of garbage collection suffice for many circumstances. When they do not, it is time to examine the specific operation of the GC algorithm in use to determine how its parameters can be changed to minimize the impact of GC on the application.

The key information needed to tune an individual collector is the data from the GC log when that collector is enabled. This chapter starts, then, by looking at each algorithm from the perspective of its log output, which allows us to understand how the GC algorithm works and how it can be adjusted to work better. Each section then includes tuning information to achieve that better performance.

There are a few unusual cases that impact the performance of all GC algorithms: allocation of very large objects, objects that are neither short- nor long-lived, and so on. Those cases are covered at the end of this chapter.

Understanding the Throughput Collector

We'll start by looking at the individual garbage collectors, beginning with the throughput collector. The throughput collector has two basic operations: it collects the young generation, and it collects the old generation.

Figure 6-1 shows the heap before and after a young collection.

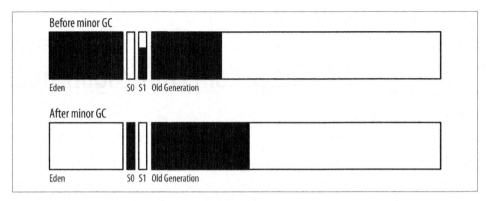

Figure 6-1. A throughput GC young collection

A young collection occurs when eden has filled up. The young collection moves all objects out of eden: some are moved to one of the survivor spaces (S0 in this diagram) and some are moved to the old generation, which now contains more objects. Many objects, of course, are discarded because they are no longer referenced.

In the `PrintGCDetails` GC log, a minor GC appears like this:

```
17.806: [GC [PSYoungGen: 227983K->14463K(264128K)]
            280122K->66610K(613696K), 0.0169320 secs]
            [Times: user=0.05 sys=0.00, real=0.02 secs]
```

This GC occurred 17.806 seconds after the program began. Objects in the young generation now occupy 14463 KB (14 MB, in the survivor space); before the GC, they occupied 227983 KB (227 MB). (Actually, 227893 KB is only 222 MB. For ease of discussion, I'll just truncate the KBs by 1000 in this chapter. Pretend I am a disk manufacturer.) The total size of the young generation at this point is 264 MB.

Meanwhile the overall occupancy of the heap (both young and old generations) decreased from 280 MB to 66 MB, and the size of the entire heap at this point in time was 613 MB. The operation took less than 0.02 seconds (the 0.02 seconds of real time at the end of the output is 0.0169320 seconds—the actual time—rounded). The program was charged for more CPU time than real time because the young collection was done by multiple threads (in this configuration, four threads).

Figure 6-2 shows the heap before and after a full GC.

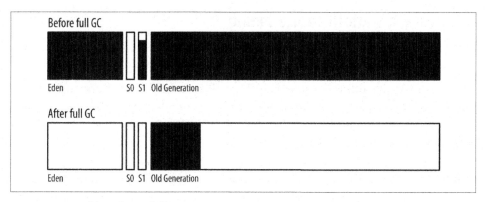

Figure 6-2. A throughput full GC

The old collection frees everything out of the young generation (including from the survivor spaces). The only objects that remain in the old generation are those which have active references, and all of those objects have been compacted so that the beginning of the old generation is occupied, and the remainder is free.

The GC log reports that operation like this:

```
64.546: [Full GC [PSYoungGen: 15808K->0K(339456K)]
        [ParOldGen: 457753K->392528K(554432K)] 473561K->392528K(893888K)
        [PSPermGen: 56728K->56728K(115392K)], 1.3367080 secs]
        [Times: user=4.44 sys=0.01, real=1.34 secs]
```

The young generation now occupies 0 bytes (and its size is 339 MB). The data in the old generation decreased from 457 MB to 392 MB, and hence the entire heap usage has decreased from 473 MB to 392 MB. The size of permgen is unchanged; it is not collected during most full GCs. (If permgen runs out of room, the JVM will run a full GC to collect pergmen, and you will see the size of permgen change—which is the only way to detect if permgen has been collected. Also, this example is from Java 7; the Java 8 output will include similar information on the metaspace.) Because there is substantially more work to do in a full GC, it has taken 1.3 seconds of real time, and 4.4 seconds of CPU time (again for four parallel threads).

Quick Summary

1. The throughput collector has two operations: minor collections and full GCs.

2. Timings taken from the GC log are a quick way to determine the overall impact of GC on an application using the throughput collector.

Adaptive and Static Heap Size Tuning

Tuning the throughput collector is all about pause times and striking a balance between the overall heap size and the sizes of the old and young generations.

There are two trade-offs to consider here. First, there is the classic programming trade-off of time versus space. A larger heap consumes more memory on the machine, and the benefit of consuming that memory is (at least to a certain extent) that the application will have a higher throughput.

The second trade-off concerns the length of time it takes to perform GC. The number of full GC pauses can be reduced by increasing the heap size, but that may have the perverse effect of increasing average response times because of the longer GC times. Similarly, full GC pauses can be shortened by allocating more of the heap to the young generation than to the old generation, but that in turn increases the frequency of the old GC collections.

The effect of these trade-offs is shown in Figure 6-3. This graph shows the maximum throughput of the stock servlet application running in a GlassFish instance with different heap sizes. With a small 256 MB heap, the application server is spending quite a lot of time in GC (36% of total time, in fact); the throughput is restricted as a result. As the heap size is increased, the throughput rapidly increases—until the heap size is set to 1,500 MB. After that, throughput increases less rapidly: the application isn't really GC-bound at that point (about 6% of time in GC). The law of diminishing returns has crept in here: the application can use additional memory to gain throughput, but the gains become more limited.

After a heap size of 4,500 MB, the throughput starts to decrease slightly. At that point, the application has reached the second trade-off: the additional memory has caused much longer GC cycles, and those longer cycles—even though they are less frequent—can impact the overall throughput.

The data in this graph was obtained by disabling adaptive sizing in the JVM; the minimum and maximum heap sizes were set to the same value. It is possible to run experiments on any application and determine the best sizes for the heap and for the generations, but it is often easier to let the JVM make those decisions (which is what usually happens, since adaptive sizing is enabled by default).

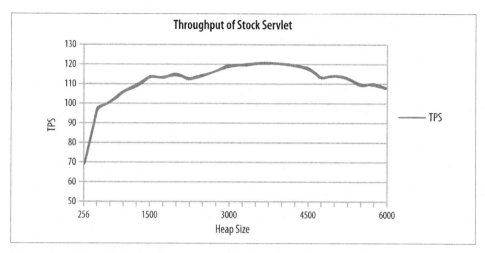

Figure 6-3. Throughput with various heap sizes

Adaptive sizing in the throughput collector will resize the heap (and the generations) in order to meet its pause time goals. Those goals are set with these flags: `-XX:MaxGCPauseMillis=N` and `-XX:GCTimeRatio=N`.

The `MaxGCPauseMillis` flag specifies the maximum pause time that the application is willing to tolerate. It might be tempting to set this to 0, or perhaps some very small value like 50 ms. Be aware that this goal applies to both minor and full GCs. If a very small value is used, the application will end up with a very small old generation: for example, one that can be cleaned in 50 ms. That will cause the JVM to perform very, very frequent full GCs, and performance will be dismal. So be realistic: set the value to something that can actually be achieved. By default, this flag is not set.

The `GCTimeRatio` flag specifies the amount of time you are willing for the application to spend in GC (compared to the amount of time its application-level threads should run). It is a ratio, so the value for *N* takes a little thought. The value is used in the following equation to determine the percentage of time the application threads should ideally run:

$$ThroughputGoal = 1 - \frac{1}{(1 + GCTimeRatio)}$$

The default value for `GCTimeRatio` is 99. Plugging that value into the equation yields 0.99, meaning that the goal is to spend 99% of time in application processing, and only 1% of time in GC. But don't be confused by how those numbers line up in the default case. A `GCTimeRatio` of 95 does not mean that GC should run up to 5% of the time: it means that GC should run up to 1.94% of the time.

I find it easier to decide what percentage of time I'd like the application to spend performing useful work (say, 95%), and then calculate the value of the GCTimeRatio from this equation:

$$GCTimeRatio = \frac{Throughput}{(1 - Throughput)}$$

For a throughput goal of 95% (0.95), this equation yields a GCTimeRatio of 19.

The JVM uses these two flags to set the size of the heap within the boundaries established by the initial (-Xms) and maximum (-Xmx) heap sizes. The MaxGCPauseMillis flag takes precedence: if it is set, the sizes of the young and old generation are adjusted until the pause time goal is met. Once that happens, the overall size of the heap is increased until the time ratio goal is met. Once both goals are met, the JVM will attempt to reduce the size of the heap so that it ends up with the smallest possible heap that meets these two goals.

Because the pause time goal is not set by default, the usual effect of automatic heap sizing is that the heap (and generation) sizes will increase until the GCTimeRatio goal is met. In practice, though, the default setting of that flag is quite optimistic. Your experience will vary, of course, but I am much more used to seeing applications that spend 3% to 6% of their time in GC and behave quite well. Sometimes I even work on applications in environments where memory is severely constrained; those applications end up spending 10% to 15% of their time in GC. GC has a substantial impact on the performance of those applications, but the overall performance goals are still met.

So the best setting will vary depending on the application goals. In the absence of other goals, I start with a time ratio of 19 (5% of time in GC).

Table 6-1 shows the effects of this dynamic tuning for an application that needs a small heap and does little GC (it is the stock servlet running in GlassFish where no session state is saved, and there are very few long-lived objects).

Table 6-1. Effect of dynamic GC tuning

GC settings	End heap size	Percent time in GC	OPS
Default	649 MB	0.9%	9.2
MaxGCPauseMillis=50ms	560 MB	1.0%	9.2
Xms=Xmx=2048m	2 GB	0.04%	9.2

By default, the heap will have a 64 MB minimum size and a 2 GB maximum size (since the machine has 8 GB of physical memory). In that case, the GCTimeRatio works just as expected: the heap dynamically resized to 649 MB, at which point the application was spending about 1% of total time in GC.

Setting the MaxGCPauseMillis flag in this case starts to reduce the size of the heap in order to meet that pause time goal. Because there is so little work for the garbage collector to perform in this example, it succeeds and can still spend only 1% of total time in GC, while maintaining the same throughput of 9.2 OPS.

Finally, notice that more isn't always better—a full 2 GB heap does mean that the application can spend less time in GC, but GC isn't the dominant performance factor here, so the throughput doesn't increase. As usual, spending time optimizing the wrong area of the application has not helped.

If the same application is changed so that the previous 50 requests for each user are saved in the session state, the garbage collector has to work harder. Table 6-2 shows the trade-offs in that situation.

Table 6-2. Effect of dynamic GC tuning

GC settings	End heap size	Percent time in GC	OPS
Default	1.7 GB	9.3%	8.4
MaxGCPauseMillis=50ms	588 MB	15.1%	7.9
Xms=Xmx=2048m	2 GB	5.1%	9.0
Xmx=3560M; MaxGCRatio=19	2.1 GB	8.8%	9.0

In a test that spends a significant amount of time in GC, things are different. The JVM will never be able to satisfy the 1% throughput goal in this test; it tries its best to accommodate the default goal and does a reasonable job, using 1.7 GB of space.

Things are worse when an unrealistic pause time goal is given. To achieve a 50 ms collection time, the heap is kept to 588 MB, but that means that GC now becomes excessively frequent. Consequently, the throughput has decreased significantly. In this scenario, the better performance comes from instructing the JVM to utilize the entire heap by setting both the initial and maximum sizes to 2 GB.

Finally, the last line of the table shows what happens when the heap is reasonably sized and we set a realistic time ratio goal of 5%. The JVM itself determined that approximately 2 GB was the optimal heap size, and it achieved the same throughput as the hand-tuned case.

 Quick Summary

1. Dynamic heap tuning is a good first step for heap sizing. For a wide set of applications, that will be all that is needed, and the dynamic settings will minimize the JVM's memory use.

2. It is possible to statically size the heap to get the maximum possible performance. The sizes the JVM determines for a reasonable set of performance goals are a good first start for that tuning.

Understanding the CMS Collector

CMS has three basic operations:

- CMS collects the young generation (stopping all application threads).
- CMS runs a concurrent cycle to clean data out of the old generation.
- If necessary, CMS performs a full GC.

A CMS collection of the young generation appears in Figure 6-4.

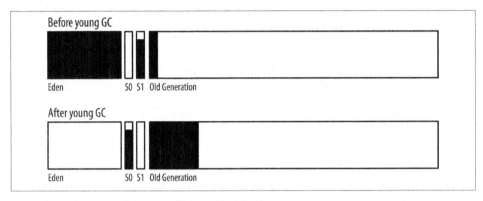

Figure 6-4. Young collection performed by CMS

A CMS young collection is very similar to a throughput young collection: data is moved from eden into one survivor space and into the old generation.

The GC log entry for CMS is also similar:

```
89.853: [GC 89.853: [ParNew: 629120K->69888K(629120K), 0.1218970 secs]
         1303940K->772142K(2027264K), 0.1220090 secs]
         [Times: user=0.42 sys=0.02, real=0.12 secs]
```

The size of the young generation is presently 629 MB; after collection, 69 MB of it remains (in a survivor space). Similarly, the size of the entire heap is 2,027 MB—772 MB of which is occupied after the collection. The entire process took 0.12 seconds, though the parallel GC threads racked up 0.42 seconds in CPU usage.

A concurrent cycle is shown in Figure 6-5.

The JVM starts a concurrent cycle based on the occupancy of the heap. When it is sufficiently full, the JVM starts background threads that cycle through the heap and remove objects. At the end of the cycle, the heap looks like the bottom row in this diagram. Notice that the old generation is not compacted: there are areas where objects are allocated, and free areas. When a young collection moves objects from eden into the old generation, the JVM will attempt to use those free areas to hold the objects.

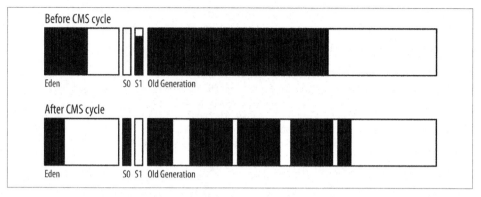

Figure 6-5. Concurrent collection performed by CMS

In the GC log, this cycle appears as a number of phases. Although a majority of the concurrent cycle uses background threads, some phases introduce short pauses where all application threads are stopped.

The concurrent cycle starts with an initial mark phase, which stops all the application threads:

```
89.976: [GC [1 CMS-initial-mark: 702254K(1398144K)]
            772530K(2027264K), 0.0830120 secs]
            [Times: user=0.08 sys=0.00, real=0.08 secs]
```

This phase is responsible for finding all the GC root objects in the heap. The first set of numbers shows that objects currently occupy 702 MB of 1,398 MB of the old generation, while the second set shows that the occupancy of the entire 2,027 MB heap is 772 MB. The application threads were stopped for a period of 0.08 seconds during this phase of the CMS cycle.

The next phase is the mark phase, and it does not stop the application threads. The phase is represented in the GC log by these lines:

```
90.059: [CMS-concurrent-mark-start]
90.887: [CMS-concurrent-mark: 0.823/0.828 secs]
            [Times: user=1.11 sys=0.00, real=0.83 secs]
```

The mark phase took 0.83 seconds (and 1.11 seconds of CPU time). Since it is just a marking phase, it hasn't done anything to the heap occupancy, and so no data is shown about that. If there were data, it would likely show a growth in the heap from objects allocated in the young generation during those 0.83 seconds, since the application threads have continued to execute.

Next comes a preclean phase, which also runs concurrently with the application threads:

```
90.887: [CMS-concurrent-preclean-start]
90.892: [CMS-concurrent-preclean: 0.005/0.005 secs]
          [Times: user=0.01 sys=0.00, real=0.01 secs]
```

The next phase is a remark phase, but it involves several operations:

```
90.892: [CMS-concurrent-abortable-preclean-start]
92.392: [GC 92.393: [ParNew: 629120K->69888K(629120K), 0.1289040 secs]
          1331374K->803967K(2027264K), 0.1290200 secs]
          [Times: user=0.44 sys=0.01, real=0.12 secs]
94.473: [CMS-concurrent-abortable-preclean: 3.451/3.581 secs]
          [Times: user=5.03 sys=0.03, real=3.58 secs]

94.474: [GC[YG occupancy: 466937 K (629120 K)]
        94.474: [Rescan (parallel) , 0.1850000 secs]
        94.659: [weak refs processing, 0.0000370 secs]
        94.659: [scrub string table, 0.0011530 secs]
        [1 CMS-remark: 734079K(1398144K)]
        1201017K(2027264K), 0.1863430 secs]
      [Times: user=0.60 sys=0.01, real=0.18 secs]
```

Wait, didn't CMS just execute a preclean phase? What's up with this abortable preclean phase?

The abortable preclean phase is used because the remark phase (which, strictly speaking, is the final entry in this output) is not concurrent—it will stop all the application threads. CMS wants to avoid the situation where a young generation collection occurs and is immediately followed by a remark phase, in which case the application threads would be stopped for two back-to-back pause operations. The goal here is to minimize pause lengths by preventing back-to-back pauses.

Hence, the abortable preclean phase waits until the young generation is about 50% full. In theory, that is halfway between young generation collections, giving CMS the best chance to avoid those back-to-back pauses. In this example, the abortable preclean phase starts at 90.8 seconds and waits about 1.5 seconds for the regular young collection to occur (at 92.392 seconds into the log). CMS uses past behavior to calculate when the next young collection is likely to occur—in this case, CMS calculated it would occur in about 4.2 seconds. So after 2.1 seconds (at 94.4 seconds), CMS ends the preclean phase (which it calls "aborting" the phase, even though that is the only way the phase is stopped). Then, finally, CMS executes the remark phase, which pauses the application threads for 0.18 seconds (the application threads were not paused during the abortable preclean phase).

Next comes another concurrent phase—the sweep phase:

```
94.661: [CMS-concurrent-sweep-start]
95.223: [GC 95.223: [ParNew: 629120K->69888K(629120K), 0.1322530 secs]
          999428K->472094K(2027264K), 0.1323690 secs]
          [Times: user=0.43 sys=0.00, real=0.13 secs]
```

```
95.474: [CMS-concurrent-sweep: 0.680/0.813 secs]
              [Times: user=1.45 sys=0.00, real=0.82 secs]
```

This phase took 0.82 seconds and ran concurrently with the application threads. It also happened to be interrupted by a young collection. This young collection had nothing to do with the sweep phase, but it is left in here as an example that the young collections can occur simultaneously with the old collection phases. In Figure 6-5, notice that the state of the young generation changed during the concurrent collection—there may have been an arbitrary number of young collections during the sweep phase (and there will have been at least one young collection because of the abortable preclean phase).

Next comes the concurrent reset phase:

```
95.474: [CMS-concurrent-reset-start]
95.479: [CMS-concurrent-reset: 0.005/0.005 secs]
              [Times: user=0.00 sys=0.00, real=0.00 secs]
```

That is the last of the concurrent phases; the CMS cycle is now complete, and the unreferenced objects found in the old generation are now free (resulting in the heap shown in Figure 6-5). Unfortunately, the log doesn't provide any information about how many objects were freed; the reset line doesn't give any information about the heap occupancy. To get an idea of that, look to the next young collection, which is:

```
98.049: [GC 98.049: [ParNew: 629120K->69888K(629120K), 0.1487040 secs]
              1031326K->504955K(2027264K), 0.1488730 secs]
```

Now compare the occupancy of the old generation at 89.853 seconds (before the CMS cycle began), which was roughly 703 MB (the entire heap occupied 772 MB at that point, which included 69 MB in the survivor space, so the old generation consumed the remaining 703 MB). In the collection at 98.049 seconds, the old generation occupies about 504 MB; the CMS cycle therefore cleaned up about 199 MB of memory.

If all goes well, these are the only cycles that CMS will run and the only log messages that will appear in the CMS GC log. But there are three more messages to look for, which indicate that CMS ran into a problem. The first is a concurrent mode failure:

```
267.006: [GC 267.006: [ParNew: 629120K->629120K(629120K), 0.0000200 secs]
              267.006: [CMS267.350: [CMS-concurrent-mark: 2.683/2.804 secs]
              [Times: user=4.81 sys=0.02, real=2.80 secs]
              (concurrent mode failure):
              1378132K->1366755K(1398144K), 5.6213320 secs]
              2007252K->1366755K(2027264K),
              [CMS Perm : 57231K->57222K(95548K)], 5.6215150 secs]
              [Times: user=5.63 sys=0.00, real=5.62 secs]
```

When a young collection occurs and there isn't enough room in the old generation to hold all the objects that are expected to be promoted, CMS executes what is essentially a full GC. All application threads are stopped, and the old generation is cleaned of any dead objects, reducing its occupancy to 1,366 MB—an operation which kept the application threads paused for a full 5.6 seconds. That operation is single-threaded, which is one reason it takes so long (and one reason why concurrent mode failures are worse as the heap grows).

The second problem occurs when there is enough room in the old generation to hold the promoted objects, but the free space is fragmented and so the promotion fails:

```
6043.903: [GC 6043.903:
         [ParNew (promotion failed): 614254K->629120K(629120K), 0.1619839 secs]
         6044.217: [CMS: 1342523K->1336533K(2027264K), 30.7884210 secs]
         2004251K->1336533K(1398144K),
         [CMS Perm : 57231K->57231K(95548K)], 28.1361340 secs]
         [Times: user=28.13 sys=0.38, real=28.13 secs]
```

Here, CMS started a young collection and assumed that there was enough free space to hold all the promoted objects (otherwise, it would have declared a concurrent mode failure). That assumption proved incorrect: CMS couldn't promote the objects because the old generation was fragmented (or, much less likely, because the amount of memory to be promoted was bigger than CMS expected).

As a result, in the middle of the young collection (when all threads were already stopped), CMS collected and compacted the entire old generation. The good news is that with the heap compacted, fragmentation issues have been solved (at least for a while). But that came with a hefty 28-second pause time. This time is much longer than when CMS had a concurrent mode failure because the entire heap was compacted; the concurrent mode failure simply freed objects in the heap. The heap at this point appears as it did at the end of the throughput collector's full GC (Figure 6-2): the young generation is completely empty, and the old generation has been compacted.

Finally, the CMS log may show a full GC without any of the usual concurrent GC messages:

```
279.803: [Full GC 279.803:
            [CMS: 88569K->68870K(1398144K), 0.6714090 secs]
            558070K->68870K(2027264K),
            [CMS Perm : 81919K->77654K(81920K)],
            0.6716570 secs]
```

This occurs when permgen has filled up and needs to be collected; notice that the size of the CMS Perm space has dropped. In Java 8, this can also occur if the metaspace needs to be resized. By default, CMS does not collect permgen (or the metaspace), so if it fills up, a full GC is needed to discard any unreferenced classes. The advanced tuning section for CMS shows how to overcome this issue.

Quick Summary

1. CMS has several GC operations, but the expected operations are minor GCs and concurrent cycles.
2. Concurrent mode failures and promotion failures in CMS are quite expensive; CMS should be tuned to avoid these as much as possible.
3. By default, CMS does not collect permgen.

Tuning to Solve Concurrent Mode Failures

The primary concern when tuning CMS is to make sure that there are no concurrent mode or promotion failures. As the CMS GC log showed, a concurrent mode failure occurs because CMS did not clean out the old generation fast enough: when it comes time to perform a collection in the young generation, CMS calculates that it doesn't have enough room to promote those objects to the old generation and instead collects the old generation first.

The old generation initially fills up by placing the objects right next to each other. When some amount of the old generation is filled (by default, 70%), the concurrent cycle begins and the background CMS thread(s) start scanning the old generation for garbage. At this point, a race is on: CMS must complete scanning the old generation and freeing objects before the remainder (30%) of the old generation fills up. If the concurrent cycle loses the race, CMS will experience a concurrent mode failure.

There are multiple ways to attempt to avoid this failure:

- Make the old generation larger, either by shifting the proportion of the new generation to the old generation, or by adding more heap space altogether.
- Run the background thread more often.
- Use more background threads.

Adaptive Sizing and CMS

CMS uses the MaxGCPauseMllis=*N* and GCTimeRatio=*N* settings to determine how large the heap and the generations should be.

One significant difference in the approach CMS takes is that the young generation is never resized unless a full GC occurs. Since the goal of CMS is to never have a full collection, this means a well-tuned CMS application will never resize its young generation.

> Concurrent mode failures can be frequent during program startup, as CMS adaptively sizes the heap and the permgen (or metaspace). It can be a good idea to start CMS with a larger initial heap size (and larger permgen/metaspace), which is a special case of making the heap larger to prevent those failures.

If more memory is available, the better solution is to increase the size of the heap. Otherwise, change the way the background threads operate.

Running the background thread more often

One way to let CMS win the race is to start the concurrent cycle sooner. If the concurrent cycle starts when 60% of the old generation is filled, CMS has a better chance of finishing than if the cycle starts when 70% of the old generation is filled. The easiest way to achieve that is to set both these flags: `-XX:CMSInitiatingOccupancyFraction=N` and `-XX:+UseCMSInitiatingOccupancyOnly`. Using both those flags also makes CMS easier to understand: if they are both set, then CMS determines when to start the background thread based only on the percentage of the old generation that is filled. By default, the `UseCMSInitiatingOccupancyOnly` flag is `false`, and CMS uses a more complex algorithm to determine when to start the background thread. If the background thread needs to be started earlier, better to start it the simplest way possible and set the `UseCMSInitiatingOccupancyOnly` flag to `true`.

Tuning the value of the `CMSInitiatingOccupancyFraction` may require a few iterations. If `UseCMSInitiatingOccupancyOnly` is enabled, then the default value for `CMSInitiatingOccupancyFraction` is 70: the CMS cycle starts when the old generation is 70% occupied.

A better value for that flag for a given application can be found in the GC log by figuring out when the failed CMS cycle started in the first place. Find the concurrent mode failure in the log, and then look back to when the most recent CMS cycle started. The CMS-initial-mark line will show how full the old generation was when the CMS cycle started:

```
89.976: [GC [1 CMS-initial-mark: 702254K(1398144K)]
            772530K(2027264K), 0.0830120 secs]
            [Times: user=0.08 sys=0.00, real=0.08 secs]
```

In this example, that works out to about 50% (702 MB out of 1,398 MB). That was not soon enough, so the `CMSInitiatingOccupancyFraction` needs to be set to something lower than 50. (Although the default value for that flag is 70, this example started the CMS threads when the old generation was 50% full because the `UseCMSInitiatingOccupancyOnly` flag was not set.)

The temptation here is just to set the value to 0 or some other small number so that the background CMS cycle runs all the time. That's usually discouraged, but as long as you are aware of the trade-offs being made, it may work out fine.

The first trade-off comes in CPU time: the CMS background thread(s) will run continually, and they consume a fair amount of CPU—each background CMS thread will consume 100% of a CPU. There will also be very short bursts when multiple CMS threads run and the total CPU on the box spikes as a result. If these threads are running needlessly, that wastes CPU resources.

On the other hand, it isn't necessarily a problem to use those CPU cycles. The background CMS threads have to run sometimes, even in the best case. Hence, the machine must always have enough CPU cycles available to run those CMS threads. So when sizing the machine, you must plan for that CPU usage.

Could those CPU cycles be used for something else when the CMS background thread isn't running? Not usually. If another application uses those cycles, it has no way of knowing when the CMS thread is running. As a result, the other application and the CMS thread will compete for CPU, which will make the CMS thread more likely to lose its race. Sophisticated operating system tuning can sometimes be used to run those competing applications with a priority that ensures the CMS thread takes precedence, but that can be tricky to get right. So yes, when CMS cycles run too frequently, far more CPU cycles are used, but those CPU cycles would otherwise just be idle.

The second trade-off is far more significant and has to do with pauses. As the GC log showed, certain phases of the CMS cycle stop all the application threads. The main reason CMS is used is to limit the effect of GC pauses, so running CMS more often than needed is counterproductive. The CMS pauses are generally much shorter than a young generation pause, and a particular application may not be sensitive to those additional pauses—it's a trade-off between the additional pauses and the reduced chance of a concurrent mode failure. But continually running the background GC pauses will likely lead to excessive overall pauses, which will in the end ultimately reduce the performance of the application.

Unless those trade-offs are acceptable, take care not to set the CMSInitiatingOccupan cyFraction higher than the amount of live data in the heap, plus at least 10% to 20%.

Adjusting the CMS background threads

Each CMS background thread will consume 100% of a CPU on a machine. If an application experiences a concurrent mode failure and there are extra CPU cycles available, the number of those background threads can be increased by setting the -XX:ConcGCThreads=N flag. By default, that value is set based on the value of the ParallelGCThreads flag:

```
ConcGCThreads = (3 + ParallelGCThreads) / 4
```

This calculation is performed using integer arithmetic, which means there will be one ConcGCThread for up to four ParallelGCThreads, two ConcGCThreads for between five and eight ParallelGCThreads, and so on.

The key to tuning this flag is whether there are available CPU cycles. If the number of ConcGCThreads is set too high, they will take CPU cycles away from the application threads; in effect, small pauses will be introduced into the program as the application threads wait for their chance to run on the CPU.

Alternately, on a system with lots of CPUs, the default value of ConcGCThreads may be too high. If concurrent mode failures are not occurring, the number of those threads can often be reduced in order to save CPU cycles.

Quick Summary

1. Avoiding concurrent mode failures is the key to achieving the best possible performance with CMS.
2. The simplest way to avoid those failures (when possible) is to increase the size of the heap.
3. Otherwise, the next step is to start the concurrent background threads sooner by adjusting the CMSInitiatingOccupancyFraction.
4. Tuning the number of background threads can also help.

Tuning CMS for Permgen

The example CMS GC log showed that a full GC occurred when permgen needed to be collected (and the same thing can happen if the metaspace needs to be resized). This will happen most frequently for developers who are continually (re)deploying applications to an application server, or to any other such application that frequently defines (and discards) classes.

By default, the CMS threads in Java 7 do not process permgen, so if permgen fills up, CMS executes a full GC to collect it. Alternately, the -XX:+CMSPermGenSweepingEnabled flag can be enabled (it is false by default), so that permgen is collected just like the old generation: by a set of background thread(s) concurrently sweeping permgen. Note that the trigger to perform this sweeping is independent of the old generation. CMS permgen collection occurs when the occupancy ratio of permgen hits the value specified by -XX:CMSInitiatingPermOccupancyFraction=N, which defaults to 80%.

Enabling permgen sweeping is only part of the story, though: to actually free the unreferenced classes, the flag -XX:+CMSClassUnloadingEnabled must be set. Otherwise, the CMS permgen sweeping will manage to free a few miscellaneous objects, but no class metadata will be freed. Since the bulk of the data in permgen is that class metadata, this flag should always be used when CMS permgen sweeping is enabled.

In Java 8, CMS does clean unloaded classes from the metaspace by default. If for some reason you wanted to disable that, unset the `-XX:-CMSClassUnloadingEnabled` flag (by default, it is `true`).

Incremental CMS

This chapter has continually stressed the fact that extra CPU is needed to run CMS effectively. What if you have only a single-CPU machine, but still need a low-pause collector? Or have multiple, but very busy, CPUs?

Incremental CMS Is Deprecated in Java 8

Incremental CMS (iCMS) is deprecated in Java 8—it still exists, but it may not be part of Java 9.

The main advantage to incremental CMS is that the background thread pauses periodically to allow application threads to run, making it usable on machines with limited CPUs. As multiple CPUs become the norm for all systems (even my phone has a quad-core chip), the rational for iCMS becomes less important.

On systems with limited CPU, consider the G1 collector instead—particularly since the background threads of G1 also will periodically pause during a background cycle, limiting the competition for the CPU.

In those cases, CMS can be set so that it operates incrementally, which means that when the background thread runs (and there should never be more than one such thread), it doesn't sweep through the entire heap at once. Having that background thread pause periodically will help overall throughput by making more CPU available to the application thread(s). When it does run, though, the application threads and the CMS thread will still compete for CPU cycles.

Incremental CMS is enabled by specifying the `-XX:+CMSIncrementalMode` flag. The rate at which the background thread yields to the application threads is controlled by changing the values of the `-XX:CMSIncrementalSafetyFactor=N`, `-XX:CMSIncrementalDutyCycleMin=N`, and `-XX:-CMSIncrementalPacing` flags.

Incremental CMS operates on the principle of a duty cycle, which governs how long the CMS background thread will scan the heap before yielding time to the application threads. At the operating system level, the background thread is already competing with (and will be time-sliced with) the application threads. These flags instead control how long the background thread will run before voluntarily stopping for a while to let the application threads run.

The duty cycle is calculated in terms of the length of time between collections of the young generation; by default, incremental CMS will be allowed to run for 20% of that time (at least to start, though CMS will adjust that value in order to try and keep pace with the amount of data promoted to the old generation). If that isn't long enough, concurrent mode failures (and full GCs) will occur; the goal here is to tune incremental CMS to avoid (or at least minimize) those GCs.

Start by increasing the `CMSIncrementalSafetyFactor`, which is the percent of time added to the default duty cycle. The default duty cycle value starts at 10%, and the safety factor is, by default, an additional 10% (yielding the default 20% initial duty cycle). To give the background thread more time to run, try increasing the safety factor (up to a maximum of 90—which will cause the incremental cycle to run 100% of the time).

Alternately, adjust the duty cycle directly by setting the `CMSIncrementalDutyCycleMin` value to a number greater than its default value (10). However, this value is subject to automatic adjustment by the JVM as it monitors the amount of data promoted to the old generation. So even if that number is increased, the JVM may decide on its own that the incremental CMS doesn't need to run that often, and hence it may decrease that value. If an application has bursts in its operation, that calculation will frequently be incorrect, and you will need to both set the duty cycle explicitly and disable the adjustment of that value by turning off the `CMSIncrementalDutyCycle` flag (which is `true` by default).

Quick Summary

1. Incremental CMS is useful when an application needs low pause times but is running on a machine with limited CPU resources.

2. Incremental CMS is controlled via a duty cycle; lengthening the duty cycle can help to prevent concurrent mode failures with CMS.

Understanding the G1 Collector

G1 is a concurrent collector that operates on discrete regions within the heap. Each region (there are by default around 2,048 of them) can belong to either the old or new generation, and the generational regions need not be contiguous. The idea behind having regions in the old generation is that when the concurrent background threads look for unreferenced objects, some regions will contain more garbage than other regions. The actual collection of a region still requires that application threads be stopped, but G1 can focus on the regions that are mostly garbage and only spend a little bit of time emptying those regions. This approach—clearing out only the mostly garbage regions—is what gives G1 its name: Garbage First.

That doesn't apply to the regions in the young generation: during a young GC, the entire young generation is either freed or promoted (to a survivor space or to the old generation). Still, the young generation is defined in terms of regions, in part because it makes resizing the generations much easier if the regions are predefined.

G1 has four main operations:

- A young collection
- A background, concurrent cycle
- A mixed collection
- If necessary, a full GC

We'll look at each of those in turn, starting with the G1 young collection shown in Figure 6-6.

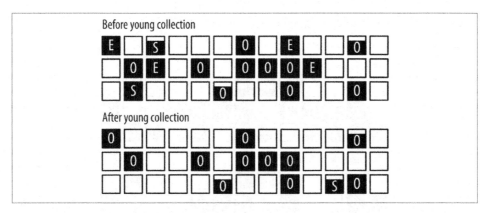

Figure 6-6. A G1 young collection

Each small square in this figure represents a G1 region. The data in each region is represented by the black area of the region, and the letter in each region identifies the generation to which the region belongs ([E]den, [O]ld generation, [S]urvivor space). Empty regions do not belong to a generation; G1 uses them arbitrarily for whichever generation it deems necessary.

The G1 young collection is triggered when eden fills up (in this case, after filling four regions). After the collection, there are no regions assigned to eden, since it is empty. There is at least one region assigned to the survivor space (partially filled in this example), and some data has moved into the old generation.

The GC log illustrates this collection a little differently in G1 than in other collectors. As usual, the example log was taken using `PrintGCDetails`, but the details in the log for G1 are more verbose. The examples show only a few of the important lines.

Here is the standard collection of the young generation:

```
23.430: [GC pause (young), 0.23094400 secs]
...
    [Eden: 1286M(1286M)->0B(1212M)
        Survivors: 78M->152M Heap: 1454M(4096M)->242M(4096M)]
    [Times: user=0.85 sys=0.05, real=0.23 secs]
```

Collection of the young generation took 0.23 seconds of real time, during which the GC threads consumed 0.85 seconds of CPU time. 1,286 MB of objects were moved out of eden (which was resized to 1,212 MB); 74 MB of that was moved to the survivor space (it increased in size from 78 M to 152 MB) and the rest were freed. We know they were freed by observing that the total heap occupancy decreased by 1,212 MB. In the general case, some objects from the survivor space might have been moved to the old generation, and if the survivor space were full, some objects from eden would have been promoted directly to the old generation—in those cases, the size of the old generation would increase.

A concurrent G1 cycle begins and ends as shown in Figure 6-7.

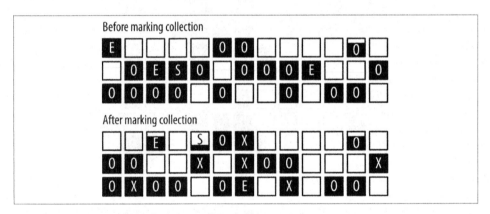

Figure 6-7. Concurrent collection performed by G1

The are three important things to observe in this diagram. First, the young generation has changed its occupancy: there will be at least one (and possibly more) young collections during the concurrent cycle. Hence, the eden regions before the marking cycle have been completely freed, and new eden regions have started to be allocated.

Second, some regions are now marked with an X. Those regions belong to the old generation (and note that they still contain data)—they are regions that the marking cycle has determined contain mostly garbage.

Finally, notice that the old generation (consisting of the regions marked with an O or an X) is actually more occupied after the cycle has completed. That's because the young generation collections that occurred during the marking cycle promoted data into the old generation. In addition, the marking cycle doesn't actually free any data in the old generation: it merely identifies regions that are mostly garbage. Data from those regions is freed in a later cycle.

The G1 concurrent cycle has several phases, some of which stop all application threads and some of which do not. The first phase is an initial-mark phase. That phase stops all application threads—partly because it also executes a young collection:

```
50.541: [GC pause (young) (initial-mark), 0.27767100 secs]
    [Eden: 1220M(1220M)->0B(1220M)
        Survivors: 144M->144M Heap: 3242M(4096M)->2093M(4096M)]
    [Times: user=1.02 sys=0.04, real=0.28 secs]
```

As in a regular young collection, the application threads were stopped (for 0.28 seconds), and the young generation was emptied (71 MB of data was moved from the young generation to the old generation). The initial-mark output announces that the background concurrent cycle has begun. Since the initial mark phase also requires all application threads to be stopped, G1 takes advantage of the young GC cycle to do that work. The impact of adding the initial mark phase to the young GC wasn't that large: it used 20% more CPU cycles than the previous collection, even though the pause was only slightly longer. (Fortunately, there were spare CPU cycles on the machine for the parallel G1 threads, or the pause would have been longer.)

Next, G1 scans the root region:

```
50.819: [GC concurrent-root-region-scan-start]
51.408: [GC concurrent-root-region-scan-end, 0.5890230]
```

This takes 0.58 seconds, but it doesn't stop the application threads; it only uses the background threads. However, this phase cannot be interrupted by a young collection, so having available CPU cycles for those background threads is crucial. If the young generation happens to fill up during the root region scanning, the young collection (which has stopped all the application threads) must wait for the root scanning to complete. In effect, this means a longer-than-usual pause to collect the young generation. That situation is shown in the GC log like this:

```
350.994: [GC pause (young)
        351.093: [GC concurrent-root-region-scan-end, 0.6100090]
        351.093: [GC concurrent-mark-start],
        0.37559600 secs]
```

The GC pause here starts before the end of the root region scanning, which (along with the interleaved output) indicates that it was waiting. The timestamps show that application threads waited about 100 ms—which is why the duration of the young GC pause is about 100 ms longer than the average duration of other pauses in this log. (If this occurs frequently, it is an indication that G1 needs to be better tuned, as discussed in the next section.)

After the root region scanning, G1 enters a concurrent marking phase. This happens completely in the background; a message is printed when it starts and ends:

```
111.382: [GC concurrent-mark-start]
....
120.905: [GC concurrent-mark-end, 9.5225160 sec]
```

Concurrent marking can be interrupted, so young collections may occur during this phase. The marking phase is followed by a remarking phase and a normal cleanup phase:

```
120.910: [GC remark 120.959:
        [GC ref-PRC, 0.0000890 secs], 0.0718990 secs]
        [Times: user=0.23 sys=0.01, real=0.08 secs]
120.985: [GC cleanup 3510M->3434M(4096M), 0.0111040 secs]
        [Times: user=0.04 sys=0.00, real=0.01 secs]
```

These phases stop the application threads, though usually for a quite short time. Next there is an additional cleanup phase that happens concurrently:

```
120.996: [GC concurrent-cleanup-start]
120.996: [GC concurrent-cleanup-end, 0.0004520]
```

And with that, the normal G1 cycle is complete—insofar as finding the garbage goes, at least. But very little has actually been freed yet. A little memory was reclaimed in the cleanup phase, but all G1 has really done at this point is to identify old regions that are mostly garbage and can be reclaimed (the ones marked with an X in Figure 6-7).

Now G1 executes a series of mixed GCs. They are called mixed because they perform the normal young collection, but they also collect some number of the marked regions from the background scan. The effect of a mixed GC is shown in Figure 6-8.

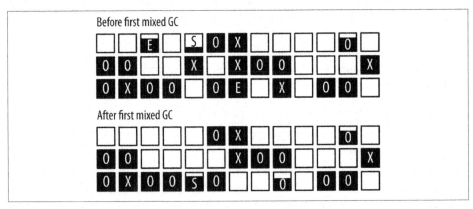

Figure 6-8. Mixed GC performed by G1

As is usual for a young collection, G1 has completely emptied eden and adjusted the survivor spaces. Additionally, two of the marked regions have been collected. Those regions were known to contain mostly garbage, and so a large part of them was freed.

Any live data in those regions was moved to another region (just as live data was moved from the young generation into regions in the old generation). This is why G1 ends up with a fragmented heap less often than CMS—moving the objects like this is compacting the heap as G1 goes along.

The mixed GC operation looks like this in the log:

```
79.826: [GC pause (mixed), 0.26161600 secs]
....
    [Eden: 1222M(1222M)->0B(1220M)
        Survivors: 142M->144M Heap: 3200M(4096M)->1964M(4096M)]
    [Times: user=1.01 sys=0.00, real=0.26 secs]
```

Notice that the entire heap usage has been reduced by more than just the 1,222 MB removed from eden. That difference (16 MB) seems small, but remember that some of the survivor space was promoted into the old generation at the same time; in addition, each mixed GC cleans up only a portion of the targeted old generation regions. As we continue, we'll see that it is important to make sure that the mixed GCs clean up enough memory to prevent future concurrent failures.

The mixed GC cycles will continue until (almost) all of the marked regions have been collected, at which point G1 will resume regular young GC cycles. Eventually, G1 will start another concurrent cycle to determine which regions should be freed next.

As with CMS, there are times when you'll observe a full GC in the log, which is an indication that more tuning (including, possibly, more heap space) will benefit the application performance. There are primarily four times when this is triggered:

Concurrent mode failure
G1 starts a marking cycle, but the old generation fills up before the cycle is completed. In that case, G1 aborts the marking cycle:

```
51.408: [GC concurrent-mark-start]
65.473: [Full GC 4095M->1395M(4096M), 6.1963770 secs]
 [Times: user=7.87 sys=0.00, real=6.20 secs]
71.669: [GC concurrent-mark-abort]
```

This failure means that heap size should be increased, or the G1 background processing must begin sooner, or the cycle must be tuned to run more quickly (e.g., by using additional background threads).

Promotion failure
G1 has completed a marking cycle and has started performing mixed GCs to clean up the old regions. Before it can clean enough space, too many objects are promoted from the young generation, and so the old generation still runs out of space. In the log, a full GC immediately follows a mixed GC:

```
2226.224: [GC pause (mixed)
        2226.440: [SoftReference, 0 refs, 0.0000060 secs]
        2226.441: [WeakReference, 0 refs, 0.0000020 secs]
```

```
        2226.441: [FinalReference, 0 refs, 0.0000010 secs]
        2226.441: [PhantomReference, 0 refs, 0.0000010 secs]
        2226.441: [JNI Weak Reference, 0.0000030 secs]
                (to-space exhausted), 0.2390040 secs]
    ....
    [Eden: 0.0B(400.0M)->0.0B(400.0M)
        Survivors: 0.0B->0.0B Heap: 2006.4M(2048.0M)->2006.4M(2048.0M)]
    [Times: user=1.70 sys=0.04, real=0.26 secs]
2226.510: [Full GC (Allocation Failure)
        2227.519: [SoftReference, 4329 refs, 0.0005520 secs]
        2227.520: [WeakReference, 12646 refs, 0.0010510 secs]
        2227.521: [FinalReference, 7538 refs, 0.0005660 secs]
        2227.521: [PhantomReference, 168 refs, 0.0000120 secs]
        2227.521: [JNI Weak Reference, 0.0000020 secs]
                2006M->907M(2048M), 4.1615450 secs]
    [Times: user=6.76 sys=0.01, real=4.16 secs]
```

This failure means the mixed collections need to happen more quickly; each young collection needs to process more regions in the old generation.

Evacuation failure

When performing a young collection, there isn't enough room in the survivor spaces and the old generation to hold all the surviving objects. This appears in the GC logs as a specific kind of young GC:

```
60.238: [GC pause (young) (to-space overflow), 0.41546900 secs]
```

This is an indication that the heap is largely full or fragmented. G1 will attempt to compensate for this, but you can expect this to end badly: G1 will resort to performing a full GC. The easy way to overcome this is to increase the heap size, though some possible solutions are given in "Advanced Tunings" on page 159.

Humongous allocation failure

Applications that allocate very large objects can trigger another kind of full GC in G1; see "G1 allocation of humongous objects" on page 169. There are no tools to diagnose that situation specifically from the standard GC log, though if a full GC occurs for no apparent reason, it is likely due to an issue with humongous allocations.

 Quick Summary

1. G1 has a number of cycles (and phases within the concurrent cycle). A well-tuned JVM running G1 should only experience young, mixed, and concurrent GC cycles.

2. Small pauses occur for some of the G1 concurrent phases.

3. G1 should be tuned if necessary to avoid full GC cycles.

Tuning G1

The major goal in tuning G1 is to make sure that there are no concurrent mode or evacuation failures that end up requiring a full GC. The techniques used to prevent a full GC can also be used when there are frequent young GCs that must wait for a root region scan to complete.

Secondarily, tuning can minimize the pauses that occur along the way.

These are the options to prevent a full GC:

- Increase the size of the old generation either by increasing the heap space overall or by adjusting the ratio between the generations.
- Increase the number of background threads (assuming there is sufficient CPU).
- Perform G1 background activities more frequently.
- Increase the amount of work done in mixed GC cycles.

There are a lot of tunings that can be applied here, but one of the goals of G1 is that it shouldn't have to be tuned that much. To that end, G1 is primarily tuned via a single flag: the same `-XX:MaxGCPauseMillis=N` flag that was used to tune the throughput collector.

When used with G1 (and unlike the throughput collector), that flag does have a default value: 200 ms. If pauses for any of the stop-the-world phases of G1 start to exceed that value, G1 will attempt to compensate—adjusting the young-to-old ratio, adjusting the heap size, starting the background processing sooner, changing the tenuring threshold, and (most significantly) processing more or fewer old generation regions during a mixed GC cycle.

The usual trade-off applies here: if that value is reduced, the young size will contract to meet the pause time goal, but more frequent young GCs will be performed. In addition, the number of old generation regions that can be collected during a mixed GC will decrease to meet the pause time goal, which increases the chances of a concurrent mode failure.

If setting a pause time goal does not prevent the full GCs from happening, these various aspects can be tuned individually. Tuning the heap sizes for G1 is accomplished in the same way as for other GC algorithms.

Tuning the G1 background threads

To have G1 win its race, try increasing the number of background marking threads (assuming there is sufficient CPU available on the machine).

Tuning the G1 threads is similar to tuning the CMS threads: the `ParallelGCThreads` option affects the number of threads used for phases when application threads are stopped, and the `ConcGCThreads` flag affects the number of threads used for concurrent phases. The default value for `ConcGCThreads` is different in G1, however. It is defined as:

```
ConcGCThreads = (ParallelGCThreads + 2) / 4
```

The arithmetic here is still integer-based; G1 simply increases that value one step later than CMS.

Tuning G1 to run more (or less) frequently

G1 can also win its race if it starts collecting earlier. The G1 cycle begins when the heap hits the occupancy ratio specified by `-XX:InitiatingHeapOccupancyPercent=N`, which has a default value of 45. Note that unlike CMS, that setting is based on the usage of the entire heap, not just the old generation.

The `InitiatingHeapOccupancyPercent` value is constant; G1 never changes that number as it attempts to meet its pause time goals. If that value is set too high, the application will end up performing full GCs because the concurrent phases don't have enough time to complete before the rest of the heap fills up. If that value is too small, the application will perform more background GC processing than it might otherwise. As was discussed for CMS, the CPU cycles to perform that background processing must be available anyway, so the extra CPU use isn't necessarily important. There can be a significant penalty here, though, because there will be more of the small pauses for those concurrent phases that stop the application threads. Those pauses can add up quickly, so performing background sweeping too frequently for G1 should be avoided. Check the size of the heap after a concurrent cycle, and make sure that the `InitiatingHeapOccupancyPercent` value is set higher than that.

Tuning G1 mixed GC cycles

After a concurrent cycle, G1 cannot begin a new concurrent cycle until all previously marked regions in the old generation have been collected. So another way to make G1 start a marking cycle earlier is to process more regions in a mixed GC cycle (so that there will end up being fewer mixed GC cycles).

The amount of work a mixed GC does is dependent on three factors. The first is how many regions were found to be mostly garbage in the first place. There is no way to directly affect that: a region is declared eligible for collection during a mixed GC if it is 35% garbage. (It is likely this value will become a tunable parameter at some point; the experimental name for the parameter (available in experiment builds of the open source code) is `-XX:G1MixedGCLiveThresholdPercent=N`.)

The second factor is the maximum number of mixed GC cycles over which G1 will process those regions, which is specified by the value of the flag -XX:G1MixedGCCount Target=N. The default value for that is 8; reducing that value can help overcome promotion failures (at the expense of longer pause times during the mixed GC cycle).

On the other hand, if mixed GC pause times are too long, that value can be increased so that less work is done during the mixed GC. Just be sure that increasing that number does not delay the next G1 concurrent cycle too long, or a concurrent mode failure may result.

Finally, the third factor is the maximum desired length of a GC pause (i.e., the value specified by MaxGCPauseMillis). The number of mixed cycles specified by the G1MixedGCCountTarget flag is an upper bound; if time is available within the pause target, G1 will collect more than one-eighth (or whatever value has been specified) of the marked old generation regions. Increasing the value of the MaxGCPauseMillis flag allows more old generation regions to be collected during each mixed GC, which in turn can allow G1 to begin the concurrent cycle sooner.

Quick Summary

1. G1 tuning should begin by setting a reasonable pause time target.
2. If full GCs are still an issue after that and the heap size cannot be increased, specific tunings can be applied for specific failures.
   a. To make the background threads run more frequently, adjust the InitiatingHeapOccupancyPercent.
   b. If additional CPU is available, adjust the number of threads via the ConcGCThreads flag.
   c. To prevent promotion failures, decrease the size of the G1MixedGCCountTarget.

Advanced Tunings

This section on tunings covers some fairly unusual situations. Even if those situations are not encountered frequently, many of the low-level details of the GC algorithms are explained in this section.

Tenuring and Survivor Spaces

When the young generation is collected, some objects will still be alive. This includes newly created objects that are destined to exist for a long time, but it also includes some objects that are otherwise short-lived. Consider the loop of BigDecimal calculations at the beginning of Chapter 5. If the JVM performs GC in the middle of that loop, some of those very-short-lived `BigDecimal` objects will be quite unlucky: they will have been just created and in use, so they can't be freed—but they aren't going to live long enough to justify moving them to the old generation.

This is the reason that the young generation is divided into two survivor spaces and eden. This setup allows objects to have some additional chances to be collected while still in the young generation, rather than being promoted into (and filling up) the old generation.

When the young generation is collected and the JVM finds an object that is still alive, that object is moved to a survivor space rather than to the old generation. During the first young generation collection, objects are moved from eden into survivor space 0. During the next collection, live objects are moved from both survivor space 0 and from eden into survivor space 1. At that point, eden and survivor space 0 are completely empty. The next collection moves live objects from survivor space 1 and eden into survivor space 0, and so on. (The survivor spaces are also referred to as the "to" and "from" spaces; during each collection, objects are moved out of the "from" space into the "to" space. "from" and "to" are simply pointers that switch between the two survivor spaces on every collection.)

Clearly this cannot continue forever, or nothing would ever be moved into the old generation. Objects are moved into the old generation in two circumstances. First, the survivor spaces are fairly small. When the target survivor space fills up during a young collection, any remaining live objects in eden are moved directly into the old generation. Second, there is a limit to the number of GC cycles during which an object can remain in the survivor spaces. That limit is called the tenuring threshold.

There are tunings to affect each of those situations. The survivor spaces take up part of the allocation for the young generation, and like other areas of the heap, the JVM sizes them dynamically. The initial size of the survivor spaces is determined by the `-XX:InitialSurvivorRatio=N` flag, which is used in this equation:

```
survivor_space_size = new_size / (initial_survivor_ratio + 2)
```

For the default initial survivor ratio of 8, each survivor space will occupy 10% of the young generation.

The JVM may increase the survivor spaces size to a maximum determined by the setting of the `-XX:MinSurvivorRatio=N` flag. That flag is used in this equation:

```
maximum_survivor_space_size = new_size / (min_survivor_ratio + 2)
```

By default, this value is 3, meaning the maximum size of a survivor space will be 20% of the young generation. Note again that the value is a ratio, so the minimum value of the ratio gives the maximum size of the survivor space. The name is hence a little counterintuitive.

To keep the survivor spaces at a fixed size, set the SurvivorRatio to the desired value and disable the UseAdaptiveSizePolicy flag (though remember that disabling adaptive sizing will apply to the old and new generations as well).

The JVM determines whether to increase or decrease the size of the survivor spaces (subject to the defined ratios) based on how full a survivor space is after a GC. The survivor spaces will be resized so that they are, by default, 50% full after a GC. That value can be changed with the -XX:TargetSurvivorRatio=N flag.

Finally, there is the question of how many GC cycles an object will remain ping-ponging between the survivor spaces before being moved into the old generation. That answer is determined by the tenuring threshold. The JVM continually calculates what it thinks the best tenuring threshold is. The threshold starts at the value specified by the -XX:InitialTenuringThreshold=N flag (the default is 7 for the throughput and G1 collectors, and 6 for CMS). The JVM will ultimately determine a threshold between 1 and the value specified by the -XX:MaxTenuringThreshold=N flag; for the throughput and G1 collectors, the default maximum threshold is 15, and for CMS it is 6.

Always and Never Tenure

The tenuring threshold will always take on some range between 1 and MaxTenuringThreshold. Even if the JVM is started with an initial tenuring threshold equal to the maximum tenuring threshold, the JVM may decrease that value.

There are two flags that can circumvent that behavior at either extreme. If you know that objects that survive a young collection will always be around for a long time, you can specify -XX:+AlwaysTenure (by default, false), which is essentially the same as setting the MaxTenuringThreshold to 0. This is a very, very rare situation; it means that objects will always be promoted to the old generation rather than stored in a survivor space.

The second flag is -XX:+NeverTenure (also false by default). This flag affects two things: it behaves as if the initial and max tenuring thresholds are infinity, and it prevents the JVM from adjusting that threshold down. In other words, as long as there is room in the survivor space, no object will ever be promoted to the old generation.

Given all that, which values might be tuned under which circumstances? It is helpful to look at the tenuring statistics, which can be added to the GC log by including the flag -XX:+PrintTenuringDistribution (which is false by default).

The most important thing to look for is whether the survivor spaces are so small that during a minor GC, objects are promoted directly from eden into the old generation. The reason to avoid that is short-lived objects will end up filling the old generation, causing full GCs to occur too frequently.

In GC logs taken with the throughput collector, the only hint for that condition is this line:

```
Desired survivor size 39059456 bytes, new threshold 1 (max 15)
        [PSYoungGen: 657856K->35712K(660864K)]
        1659879K->1073807K(2059008K), 0.0950040 secs]
        [Times: user=0.32 sys=0.00, real=0.09 secs]
```

The desired size for a single survivor space here is 39 MB out of a young generation of 660 MB: the JVM has calculated that the two survivor spaces should take up about 11% of the young generation. But the open question is whether that is large enough to prevent overflow. There is no definitive answer from this log, but the fact that the JVM has adjusted the tenuring threshold to 1 indicates that it has determined it is directly promoting most objects to the old generation anyway, so it has minimized the tenuring threshold. This application is probably promoting directly to the old generation without fully using the survivor spaces.

When G1 or CMS is used, more informative output is obtained:

```
Desired survivor size 35782656 bytes, new threshold 2 (max 6)
- age   1:   33291392 bytes,   33291392 total
- age   2:    4098176 bytes,   37389568 total
```

The desired survivor space is similar to the last example—35 MB—but the output also shows the size of all the objects in the survivor space. With 37 MB of data to promote, the survivor space is indeed overflowing.

Whether or not this situation can be improved upon is very dependent on the application. If the objects are going to live longer than a few more GC cycles, they will eventually end up in the old generation anyway, so adjusting the survivor spaces and tenuring threshold won't really help. But if the objects would go away after just a few more GC cycles, then some performance can be gained by arranging for the survivor spaces to be more efficient.

If the size of the survivor spaces is increased (by decreasing the survivor ratio), then memory is taken away from the eden section of the young generation. That is where the objects actually are allocated, meaning fewer objects can be allocated before incurring a minor GC. So that option is usually not recommended.

Another possibility is to increase the size of the young generation. That can be counterproductive in this situation: objects might be promoted less often into the old generation, but since the old generation is smaller, the application may do full GCs more often.

If the size of the heap can be increased altogether, then both the young generation and the survivor spaces can get more memory, which will be the best solution. A good process is to increase the heap size (or at least the young generation size) and to decrease the survivor ratio. That will increase the size of the survivor spaces more than it will increase the size of eden. The application should end up having roughly the same number of young collections as before. It should have fewer full GCs, though, since fewer objects will be promoted into the old generation (again, assuming that the objects will no longer be live after a few more GC cycles).

If the sizes of the survivor spaces have been adjusted so that they never overflow, then objects will only be promoted to the old generation after the MaxTenuringThreshold is reached. That value can be increased to keep the objects in the survivor spaces for a few more young GC cycles. But be aware that if the tenuring threshold is increased and objects stay in the survivor space longer, there will be less room in the survivor space during future young collections: it is then more likely that the survivor space will overflow and start promoting directly into the old generation again.

Quick Summary

1. Survivor spaces are designed to allow objects (particularly just-allocated objects) to remain in the young generation for a few GC cycles. This increases the probability the object will be freed before it is promoted to the old generation.

2. If the survivor spaces are too small, objects will promoted directly into the old generation, which in turn causes more old GC cycles.

3. The best way to handle that situation is to increase the size of the heap (or at least the young generation) and allow the JVM to handle the survivor spaces.

4. In rare cases, adjusting the tenuring threshold or survivor space sizes can prevent promotion of objects into the old generation.

Allocating Large Objects

This section describes in detail how the JVM allocates objects. This is interesting background information, and it is important to applications that frequently create a significant number of large objects. In this context, "large" is a relative term; it depends, as we'll see, on the size of a TLAB within the JVM.

TLAB sizing is a consideration for all GC algorithms, and G1 has an additional consideration for very large objects (again, a relative term—but for a 2 GB heap, objects larger than 512 MB). The effects of very large objects on G1 can be very important— TLAB sizing (to overcome somewhat large objects when using any collector) is fairly unusual, but G1 region sizing (to overcome very large objects when using G1) is more common.

Thread-local allocation buffers

Chapter 5 discusses how objects are allocated within eden; this allows for faster allocation (particularly for objects that are quickly discarded).

It turns out that one reason allocation in eden is so fast is that each thread has a dedicated region where it allocates objects—a TLAB. When objects are allocated directly in a shared space, some synchronization is required to manage the free-space pointers within in that space. By setting up each thread with its own dedicated allocation area, the thread needn't perform any synchronization when allocating objects. (This is a variation of how thread-local variables can prevent lock contention [see Chapter 9].)

Usually, the use of TLABs is transparent to developers and end users: TLABs are enabled by default, and the JVM manages their sizes and how they are used. The important thing to realize about TLABs is that they have a small size, so large objects cannot be allocated within a TLAB. Large objects must be allocated directly from the heap, which requires extra time because of the synchronization.

As a TLAB becomes full, objects of a certain size can no longer be allocated in it. At this point, the JVM has a choice. One option is to "retire" the TLAB and allocate a new one for the thread. Since the TLAB is just a section within eden, the retired TLAB will be cleaned at the next young collection and can be reused subsequently. Alternately, the JVM can allocate the object directly on the heap and keep the existing TLAB (at least until the thread allocates additional objects into the TLAB). Consider the case where a TLAB is 100 KB, and 75 KB has already been allocated. If a new 30 KB allocation is needed, the TLAB can be retired, which wastes 25 KB of eden space. Or the 30 KB object can be allocated directly from the heap, and the thread can hope that the next object that is allocated will fit in the 25 KB of space that is still free within the TLAB.

There are parameters to control this (which are discussed later in this section), but the key is that the size of the TLAB is crucial. By default, the size of a TLAB is based on three things: the number of threads in the application, the size of eden, and the allocation rate of threads.

Hence two types of applications may benefit from tuning the TLAB parameters: applications that allocate a lot of large objects, and applications that have a relatively large number of threads compared to the size of eden. By default, TLABs are enabled; they can be disabled by specifying -XX:-UseTLAB, although they give such a performance boost that disabling them is always a bad idea.

Since the calculation of the TLAB size is based in part on the allocation rate of the threads, it is impossible to definitively predict the best TLAB size for an application. What can be done instead is to monitor the TLAB allocation to see if any allocations occur outside of the TLABs. If a significant number of allocations occur outside of TLABs, then there are two choices: reduce the size of the object being allocated, or adjust the TLAB sizing parameters.

Monitoring the TLAB allocation is another case where Java Flight Recorder is much more powerful than other tools. Figure 6-9 shows a sample of the TLAB allocation screen from a JFR recording.

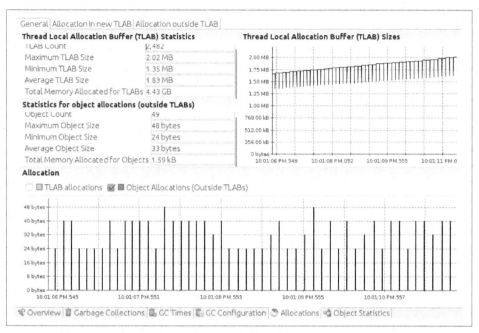

Figure 6-9. View of TLABs in Java Flight Recorder

In the 5 seconds selected in this recording, 49 objects were allocated outside of TLABs; the maximum size of those objects was 48 bytes. Since the minimum TLAB size is 1.35 MB, we know that these objects were allocated on the heap only because the TLAB was full at the time of allocation: they were not allocated directly in the heap because of their size. That is typical immediately before a young GC occurs (as eden—and hence the TLABs carved out of eden—becomes full).

The total allocation in this period is 1.59 KB; neither the number of allocations nor the size in this example are a cause for concern. There will always be some object allocated outside of TLABs, particularly as eden approaches a young collection. Compare that example to Figure 6-10, which shows a great deal of allocation occurring outside of the TLABs.

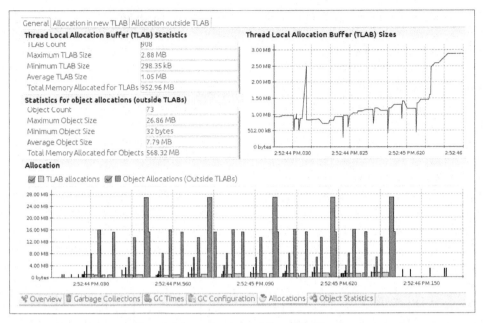

Figure 6-10. Excessive allocation occurring outside of TLABs

The total memory allocated inside TLABs during this recording is 952.96 MB, and the total memory allocated for objects outside of TLABs is 568.32 MB. This is a case where either changing the application to use smaller objects, or tuning the JVM to allocate those objects in larger TLABs, can have a beneficial effect. Note that there are other tabs here that can display the actual objects that were allocated out of the TLAB; we can even arrange to get the stacks from when those objects were allocated. If there is a problem with TLAB allocation, JFR will pinpoint it very quickly.

In the open source version of the JVM (without JFR), the best thing to do is monitor the TLAB allocation by adding the -XX:+PrintTLAB flag to the command line. Then, at every young collection, the GC log will contain two kinds of line: a line for each thread describing the TLAB usage for that thread, and a summary line describing the overall TLAB usage of the JVM.

The per-thread line looks like this:

```
TLAB: gc thread: 0x00007f3c10b8f800 [id: 18519] desired_size: 221KB
    slow allocs: 8  refill waste: 3536B alloc: 0.01613    11058KB
    refills: 73 waste  0.1% gc: 10368B slow: 2112B fast: 0B
```

The gc in this output means that the line was printed during GC; the thread itself is a regular application thread. The size of this thread's TLAB is 221 KB. Since the last young collection, it allocated eight objects from the heap (slow allocs); that was 1.6% (0.01613) of the total amount of allocation done by this thread, and it amounted to

11,058 KB. 0.1% of the TLAB was "wasted," which comes from three things: 10,336 bytes were free in the TLAB when the current GC cycle started; 2,112 bytes were free in other (retired) TLABs, and 0 bytes were allocated via a special "fast" allocator.

After the TLAB data for each thread has been printed, the JVM provides a line of summary data:

```
TLAB totals: thrds: 66  refills: 3234 max: 105
        slow allocs: 406 max 14 waste:  1.1% gc: 7519856B
        max: 211464B slow: 120016B max: 4808B fast: 0B max: 0B
```

In this case, 66 threads performed some sort of allocation since the last young collection. Among those threads, they refilled their TLABs 3,234 times; the most any particular thread refilled its TLAB was 105. Overall there were 406 allocations to the heap (with a maximum of 14 done by one thread), and 1.1% of the TLABs were wasted from the free space in retired TLABs.

In the per-thread data, if threads show a large number of allocations outside of TLABs, consider resizing them.

Sizing TLABs

Applications that spend a lot of time allocating objects outside of TLABs will benefit from changes that can move the allocation to a TLAB. If there are only a few specific object types that are always allocated outside of a TLAB, then programmatic changes are the best solution.

Otherwise—or if programmatic changes are not possible—you can attempt to resize the TLABs to fit the application use case. Because the TLAB size is based on the size of eden, adjusting the new size parameters will automatically increase the size of the TLABs.

The size of the TLABs can be set explicitly using the flag -XX:TLABSize=*N* (the default value, 0, means to use the dynamic calculation previously described). That flag sets only the initial size of the TLABs; to prevent resizing at each GC, add -XX:-ResizeTLAB (the default for that flag is true on most common platforms). This is the easiest (and, frankly, the only really useful) option for exploring the performance of adjusting the TLABs.

When a new object does not fit in the current TLAB (but would fit within a new, empty TLAB), the JVM has a decision to make: whether to allocate the object in the heap, or whether to retire the current TLAB and allocate a new one. That decision is based on several parameters. In the TLAB logging output, the refill waste value gives the current threshold for that decision: if the TLAB cannot accommodate a new object that is larger than that value, then the new object will be allocated in the heap. If the object in question is smaller than that value, the TLAB will be retired.

That value is dynamic, but it begins by default at 1% of the TLAB size—or, specifically, at the value specified by -XX:TLABWasteTargetPercent=N. As each allocation is done outside the heap, that value is increased by the value of -XX:TLABWasteIncrement=N (the default is 4). This prevents a thread from reaching the threshold in the TLAB and continually allocating objects in the heap: as the target percentage increases, the chances of the TLAB being retired also increases. Adjusting the TLABWasteTargetPercent value also adjusts the size of the TLAB, so while it is possible to play with this value, its effect is not always predictable.

Finally, when TLAB resizing is in effect, the minimum size of a TLAB can be specified with -XX:MinTLABSize=N (the default is 2 KB). The maximum size of a TLAB is slightly less than 1 GB (the maximum space that can be occupied by an array of integers, rounded down for object alignment purposes) and cannot be changed.

Quick Summary

1. Applications that allocate a lot of large objects may need to tune the TLABs (though often using smaller objects in the application is a better approach).

Humongous objects

Objects that are allocated outside a TLAB are still allocated within eden when possible. If the object cannot fit within eden, then it must be allocated directly in the old generation. That prevents the normal GC lifecycle for that object, so if it is short-lived, GC is negatively affected. There's little to do in that case other than change the application so that it doesn't need those short-lived huge objects.

Humongous objects are treated differently in G1, however: G1 will allocate them in the old generation if they are bigger than a G1 region. So applications that use a lot of humongous objects in G1 may need special tuning to compensate for that.

G1 region sizes

G1 divides the heap into a number of regions, each of which has a fixed size. The region size is not dynamic; it is determined at startup based on the minimum size of the heap (the value of Xms). The minimum region size is 1 MB. If the minimum heap size is greater than 2 GB, the size of the regions will be set according to this formula (using log base 2):

```
region_size = 1 << log(Initial Heap Size / 2048);
```

In short, the region size is the smallest power of 2 such that there are close to 2,048 regions when the initial heap size is divided. There are some minimum and maximum constraints in use here too; the region size is always at least 1 MB and never more than 32 MB. Table 6-3 sorts out all the possibilities.

Table 6-3. Default G1 region sizes

Heap size	Default G1 region size
Less than 4 GB	1 MB
Between 4 GB and 8 GB	2 MB
Between 8 GB and 16 GB	4 MB
Between 16 GB and 32 GB	8 MB
Between 32 GB and 64 GB	16 MB
Larger than 64 GB	32 MB

The size of a G1 region can be set with the `-XX:G1HeapRegionSize=N` flag (the default for which is nominally 0, meaning to use the dynamic value just described). The value given here should be a power of 2 (e.g., 1 MB or 2 MB); otherwise it is rounded down to the nearest power of 2.

G1 Region Sizes and Large Heaps

Normally the G1 region size needs to be tuned only to handle humongous object allocation, but there is one other case where it might need to be tuned.

Consider an application that specifies a very large heap range, e.g., `-Xms2G -Xmx32G`. In that case, the region size will be 1 MB. When the heap is fully expanded, there will be 32,000 G1 regions. That is a lot of separate regions to process; the G1 algorithm is designed around the idea that the number of regions is closer to 2,048. Increasing the size of the G1 region will make G1 a little more efficient in this example; select a value so that there will be close to 2,048 regions at the expected heap size.

G1 allocation of humongous objects

If the G1 region size is 1 MB and a program allocates an array of 2 million bytes, the array will not fit within a single G1 region. But these humongous objects must be allocated in contiguous G1 regions. If the G1 region size is 1 MB, then to allocate a 3.1 MB array, G1 must find four contiguous regions within the old generation in which to allocate the array. (The rest of the last region will remain empty, wasting 0.9 MB of space.) This defeats the way G1 normally performs compaction, which is to free arbitrary regions based on how full they are. Often, G1 will have to perform a full GC in order to find contiguous regions.

Because the humongous object is allocated directly in the old generation, it cannot be freed during a young collection. So if the object is short-lived, this also defeats the generational design of the collector. The humongous object will be collected during the concurrent G1 cycle. On the bright side, the humongous object can be freed quickly since it is the only object in the regions it occupies. Humongous objects are freed during the cleanup phase of the concurrent cycle (rather than during a mixed GC).

Increasing the size of a G1 region so that all objects the program will allocate can fit within a single G1 region can make G1 more efficient.

To determine if humongous object allocation is causing the full GCs in a particular application, the GC log must have adaptive size policy logging enabled. When the application allocates a humongous object, G1 will first attempt to start a concurrent cycle:

```
5.349: [G1Ergonomics (Concurrent Cycles) request concurrent cycle initiation,
    reason: occupancy higher than threshold, occupancy: 483393536 bytes,
    allocation request: 524304 bytes, threshold: 483183810 bytes (45.00 %),
    source: concurrent humongous allocation]
...
5.350: [GC pause (young) (initial-mark) 0.349: [G1Ergonomics
    (CSet Construction) start choosing CSet, _pending_cards:
    1624, predicted base time: 19.74 ms, remaining time: 180.26 ms,
    target pause time: 200.00 ms]
```

This indicates that the humongous allocation occurred, triggering a concurrent G1 cycle. In this entry, the allocation succeeded without other effects on GC (G1 happened to find the needed contiguous regions).

If no contiguous regions are found, G1 will run a full GC:

```
25.270: [G1Ergonomics (Heap Sizing) attempt heap expansion,
    reason: allocation request failed, allocation request: 48 bytes]
25.270: [G1Ergonomics (Heap Sizing) expand the heap,
    requested expansion amount: 1048576 bytes,
    attempted expansion amount: 1048576 bytes]
25.270: [G1Ergonomics (Heap Sizing) did not expand the heap,
    reason: heap expansion operation failed]
25.270: [Full GC 1535M->1521M(3072M), 1.0358230 secs]
    [Eden: 0.0B(153.0M)->0.0B(153.0M)
     Survivors: 0.0B->0.0B Heap: 1535.9M(3072.0M)->1521.3M(3072.0M)]
    [Times: user=5.24 sys=0.00, real=1.04 secs]
```

Because the heap could not be expanded to accommodate the new humongous object, G1 had to perform a full GC to compact the heap in order to provide the contiguous regions needed to fulfill the request, Without the additional logging provided by enabling PrintAdaptiveSizePolicy, the standard G1 GC log does not provide enough information to diagnose this situation.

To prevent this full GC, first determine the size of the humongous objects that are causing the issue (that value is in the log above: 524,304 bytes in this example). A better next step is to reduce the size of those objects rather than tune the JVM around them. If that is not possible, calculate the region size that will be needed to accommodate those objects. G1 considers an object to be humongous if it will fill more than 50% of a region. Hence, if the object in question is 524,304 bytes, the G1 region size needs to be at least 1.1 MB. Since G1 regions are always a power of 2, the G1 region size must be set to 2 MB in order for those objects to be allocated in a standard G1 region.

Quick Summary

1. G1 regions are sized in powers of 2, starting at 1 MB.

2. Heaps that have a very different maximum size than initial size will have too many G1 regions; the G1 region size should be increased in that case.

3. Applications that allocate objects larger than half the size of a G1 region should increase the G1 region size, so that the objects can fit within a G1 region. An application must allocate an object that is at least 512 KB for this to apply (since the smallest G1 region is 1 MB).

AggressiveHeap

The AggressiveHeap flag (by default, false), was introduced in an early version of Java as an attempt to make it easier to easily set a variety of command-line arguments—arguments that would be appropriate for a very large machine with a lot of memory running a single JVM. It applies only to 64-bit JVMs.

Although the flag has been carried forward since those versions and is still present, it is no longer recommended (though it is not yet officially deprecated). The problem with this flag is that it hides the actual tunings it adopts, making it quite hard to figure out what the JVM is actually setting. Some of the values it sets are now set ergonomically based on better information about the machine running the JVM, so there are actually cases where enabling this flag hurts performance. I have often seen command lines that include this flag and then later override values that it sets. (For the record, that works: later values in the command line currently override earlier values. That behavior is not guaranteed.)

Table 6-4 lists all the tunings that are automatically set when the AggressiveHeap flag is enabled.

Table 6-4. Tunings enabled with AggressiveHeap

Flag	Value
Xmx	The minimum of half of all memory, or all memory: 160 MB
Xms	The same as Xmx
NewSize	3/8ths of whatever was set as Xmx
UseLargePages	true
ResizeTLAB	false
TLABSize	256 KB
UseParallelGC	true
ParallelGCThreads	Same as current default
YoungPLABSize	256 KB (default is 4 KB)
OldPLABSize	8 KB (default is 1 KB)
CompilationPolicyChoice	0 (the current default)
ThresholdTolerance	100 (default is 10)
ScavengeBeforeFullGC	false (default is true)
BindGCTaskThreadsToCPUs	true (default is false)

Those last six flags are obscure enough that I have not discussed them elsewhere in this book. Briefly, they cover these areas:

PLAB sizing
> PLABs are promotion-local allocation buffers—these are per-thread regions used during scavenging the generations in a GC. Each thread can promote into a specific PLAB, negating the need for synchronization (analogous to the way TLABs work).

Compilation policies
> The JVM ships with some alternate JIT compilation algorithms. The current default algorithm was, at one time, somewhat experimental, but this is now the recommended policy.

Disabling young GCs before full GCs
> Setting `ScavengeBeforeFullGC` to `false` means that when a full GC occurs, the JVM will not perform a young GC before a full GC. That is usually a bad thing, since it means that garbage objects in the young generation (which are eligible for collection) can prevent objects in the old generation from being collected. Clearly there is (or was) a point in time when that setting made sense (at least for certain benchmarks), but the general recommendation is not to change that flag.

Binding GC threads to CPUs
> Setting the last flag in that list means that each parallel GC thread is bound to a particular CPU (using OS-specific calls). In limited circumstances—when the GC threads are the only thing running on the machine, and heaps are very large—that

makes sense. In the general case, it is better if GC threads can run on any available CPU.

As with all tunings, your mileage may vary, and if you carefully test the AggressiveHeap flag and find that it improves performance, then by all means use it. Just be aware of what it is doing behind the scenes, and realize that whenever the JVM is upgraded, the relative benefit of this flag will need to be reevaluated.

Quick Summary

1. The AggressiveHeap flag is a legacy attempt to set a number of heap parameters to values that make sense for a single JVM running on a very large machine.

2. Values set by this flag are not adjusted as JVM technology improves, so its usefulness in the long run is dubious (even though it still is often used).

Full Control Over Heap Size

"Sizing the Heap" on page 119 discussed the default values for the initial minimum and maximum size of the heap. Those values are dependent on the amount of memory on the machine as well as the JVM in use, and the data presented there had a number of corner cases to it. If you're curious about the full details about how the default heap size is actually calculated, this section will explain the details. Those details include some very low-level tuning flags; in certain circumstances, it might be more convenient to adjust the way those calculations are done (rather than simply setting the heap size). This might be the case if, for example, you want to run multiple JVMs with a common (but adjusted) set of ergonomic heap sizes. For the most part, the real goal of this section is to complete the explanation of how those default values are chosen.

The default sizes are based on the amount of memory on a machine, which can be set with the -XX:MaxRAM=N flag. Normally, that value is calculated by the JVM by inspecting the amount of memory on the machine. However, the JVM limits MaxRAM to 1 GB for the client compiler, 4 GB for 32-bit server compilers, and 128 GB for 64-bit compilers. The maximum heap size is one-quarter of MaxRAM. This is why the default heap size can vary: if the physical memory on a machine is less than MaxRAM, the default heap size is one-quarter of that. But even if hundreds of gigabytes of RAM are available, the most the JVM will use by default is 32 GB: one-quarter of 128 GB.

The default maximum heap calculation is actually this:

```
Default Xmx = MaxRAM / MaxRAMFraction
```

Hence, the default maximum heap can also be set by adjusting the value of the -XX:MaxRAMFraction=N flag, which defaults to 4. Finally, just to keep things interesting, the -XX:ErgoHeapSizeLimit=N flag can also be set to a maximum default value that the JVM should use. That value is 0 by default (meaning to ignore it); otherwise, that limit is used if it is smaller than MaxRAM / MaxRAMFraction.

On the other hand, on a machine with a very small amount of physical memory, the JVM wants to be sure it leaves enough memory for the operating system. This is why the JVM will limit the maximum heap to 96 MB or less on machines with only 192 MB of memory. That calculation is based on the value of the -XX:MinRAMFraction=N flag, which defaults to 2:

```
if ((96 MB * MinRAMFraction) > Physical Memory) {
    Default Xmx = Physical Memory / MinRAMFraction;
}
```

The initial heap size choice is similar, though it has fewer complications. The initial heap size value is determined like this:

```
Default Xms =  MaxRAM / InitialRAMFraction
```

As can be concluded from the default minimum heap sizes, the default value of the InitialRAMFraction flag is 64. The one caveat here occurs if that value is less than 5 MB—or, strictly speaking, less than the values specified by -XX:OldSize=N (which defaults to 4 MB) plus -XX:NewSize=N (which defaults to 1 MB). In that case, the sum of the old and new sizes is used as the initial heap size.

Quick Summary

1. The calculations for the default initial and maximum heap sizes are fairly straightforward on most machines.

2. Around the edges, these calculations can be quite involved.

Summary

The past two chapters have spent a lot of time delving into the deep details of how GC (and its various algorithms) work. If GC is taking longer than you'd like, knowing how all of that works should aid you in taking the necessary steps to improve things.

Now that we understand all the details, let's take a step back to determine an approach to choosing and tuning a garbage collector. Here's a quick set of questions to ask yourself to help put everything in context:

Can your application tolerate some full GC pauses?
    If so, then the throughput collector will likely offer the best performance, while using less CPU and a smaller heap than other collectors. If not, then choose a concurrent collector—for smaller heaps, either CMS or G1. For larger heaps, G1.

Are you getting the performance you need with the default settings?
> Try the default settings first. As GC technology matures, the ergonomic (automatic) tuning gets better all the time.

> If you're not getting the performance you need, make sure that GC is your problem. Look at the GC logs and see how much time you're spending in GC and how frequently the long pauses occur. For a busy application, if you're spending 3% or less time in GC, you're not going to get a lot out of tuning (though you can always try and reduce outliers if that is your goal).

Are the pause times that you have somewhat close to your goal?
> If they are, then adjusting the maximum pause time may be all you need. If they aren't, then you need to do something else. If the pause times are too large but your throughput is OK, you can reduce the size of the young generation (and for full GC pauses, the old generation); you'll get more, but shorter, pauses.

Is throughput lagging even though GC pause times are short?
> You need to increase the size of the heap (or at least the young generation).

> More isn't always better: bigger heaps lead to longer pause times. Even with a concurrent collector, a bigger heap means a bigger young generation by default, so you'll see longer pause times for young collections. But if you can, increase the heap size, or at least the relative sizes of the generations.

Are you using a concurrent collector and seeing full GCs due to concurrent-mode failures?
> If you have available CPU, try increasing the number of concurrent GC threads or starting the background sweep sooner by adjusting the `InitiatingHeapOccupancyPercent`. For G1, the concurrent cycle won't start if there are pending mixed GCs; try reducing the mixed GC count target.

Are you using a concurrent collector and seeing full GCs due to promotion failures?
> In CMS, a promotion failure indicates that the heap is fragmented. There is little to do about that; using a larger heap and/or performing the background sweep sooner can help in some cases. It may be better to try G1 instead. In G1, an evacuation failure (to-space overflow) indicates essentially the same thing, but the fragmentation can be solved if G1 performs its background sweeping sooner and mixed GCs faster. Try increasing the number of concurrent G1 threads, adjusting the `InitiatingHeapOccupancyPercent`, or reducing the mixed GC count target.

## CHAPTER 7

Heap Memory Best Practices

Chapters 5 and 6 discussed the details of how to tune the garbage collector so that it has as little effect on a program as possible. Tuning the garbage collector is important, but often better performance gains can be made by utilizing better programming practices. This chapter discusses some of the best-practice approaches to using heap memory in Java.

There are two conflicting goals here. The first general rule is to create objects sparingly and to discard them as quickly as possible. Using less memory is the best way to improve the efficiency of the garbage collector. On the other hand, frequently re-creating some kinds of objects can lead to worse overall performance (even if GC performance improves). If those objects are instead reused, programs can see substantial performance gains. There are a variety of ways in which objects can be reused, including thread-local variables, special object references, and object pools. Reusing objects means they will be long-lived and impact the garbage collector, but when they are reused judiciously, overall performance will improve.

This chapter discusses both approaches and the trade-offs between them. First, though, we'll look into tools for understanding what is happening inside the heap.

Heap Analysis

GC logs and the tools discussed in Chapter 5 are great at understanding the impact GC has on an application, but for additional visibility, we must look into the heap itself. The tools discussed in this section provide insight into the objects that the application is currently using.

Most of the time, these tools operate only on live objects in the heap—objects that will be reclaimed during the next full GC cycle are not included in the tools' output. In some cases, tools accomplish that by forcing a full GC, so the application behavior can be affected after the tool is used. In other cases, the tools walk through the heap and report live data without freeing objects along the way. In either case, though, the tools require some amount of time and machine resources; they are generally not useful during measurement of a program's execution.

Heap Histograms

Reducing memory use is an important goal, but as with most performance topics, it helps to target efforts to maximize the available benefits. Later in this chapter, I'll show an example around lazily initializing a Calendar object. That will save 640 bytes in the heap, but if the application only ever initializes one such object, there will not be a measurable difference in performance. Analysis must be performed to know which kinds of objects are consuming large amounts of memory.

The easiest way to do that is via a heap histogram. Histograms are a quick way to look at the number of objects within an application without doing a full heap dump (since heap dumps can take a while to analyze, and they consume a large amount of disk space). If a few particular object types are responsible for creating memory pressure in an application, a heap histogram is a quick way to find that.

Heap histograms can be obtained by using jcmd (here with process ID 8898):

```
% jcmd 8898 GC.class_histogram
8898:

 num     #instances         #bytes  class name
----------------------------------------------
   1:        789087       31563480  java.math.BigDecimal
   2:        237997       22617192  [C
   3:        137371       20696640  <constMethodKlass>
   4:        137371       18695208  <methodKlass>
   5:         13456       15654944  <constantPoolKlass>
   6:         13456       10331560  <instanceKlassKlass>
   7:         37059        9238848  [B
   8:         10621        8363392  <constantPoolCacheKlass>
```

In a heap histogram, Klass-related objects are often near the top; those are the metadata objects from loading the classes. It is also quite common to see character arrays ([C) and String objects near the top, as these are the most commonly created Java objects. Byte arrays ([B) and object arrays ([Ljava.lang.Object;) are also quite common, since classloaders store their data in those structures. (If you're unfamiliar with the syntax here, it comes from the way the Java Native Interface (JNI) identifies object types; see the JNI reference documentation for more details.)

In this example (which comes from running a variation of the sample stock servlet in an application server), the inclusion of the BigDecimal class is something to pursue: we know the sample code produces a lot of transient BigDecimal objects, but having so many stay around in the heap is not what we might ordinarily expect. The output from

`GC.class_histogram` includes only live objects, though the command does not force a full GC.

Similar output is available by running this command:

```
% jmap -histo process_id
```

The output from `jmap` includes objects that are eligible to be collected (dead objects). To force a full GC prior to seeing the histogram, run this command instead:

```
% jmap -histo:live process_id
```

Histograms are quite small, so gathering one for every test in an automated system can be quite helpful. Still, because they take a few seconds to obtain, they should not be taken during a performance measurement steady state.

Heap Dumps

Histograms are great at identifying issues caused by allocating too many instances of one or two particular classes, but for deeper analysis, a heap dump is required. There are many tools that can look at heap dumps, and most of them can connect to a live program to generate the dump. It is often easier to generate the dump from the command line, which can be done with either of the following commands:

```
% jcmd process_id GC.heap_dump /path/to/heap_dump.hprof
```

or

```
% jmap -dump:live,file=/path/to/heap_dump.hprof process_id
```

Including the `live` option in `jmap` will force a full GC to occur before the heap is dumped. That is the default for `jcmd`, though if for some reason you want those other (dead) objects included, you can specify `-all` at the end of the `jcmd` command line.

Either command creates a file named *heap_dump.hprof* in the given directory; a number of tools can then be used to open that file. Three of the most common are:

jhat

This is the original heap analyzer tool; it reads the heap dump and runs a small HTTP server that lets you look at the dump through a series of web page links.

jvisualvm

The monitor tab of `jvisualvm` can take a heap dump from a running program or open a previously produced heap dump. From there you can browse through the heap, examining the largest retained objects and executing arbitrary queries against the heap.

mat

The open source EclipseLink Memory Analyzer Tool (`mat`) can load one or more heap dumps and perform analysis on them. It can produce reports that suggest where problems are likely to be found, and it too can be used to browse through the heap and execute SQL-like queries into the heap.

The first-pass analysis of a heap generally involves retained memory. The retained memory of an object is the amount of memory that would be freed if the object itself were eligible to be collected. In Figure 7-1, the retained memory of the String Trio object includes the memory occupied by that object as well as the memory occupied by the Sally and David objects. It does not include the memory used by the Michael object, since that object has another reference and won't be eligible for GC if the String Trio is freed.

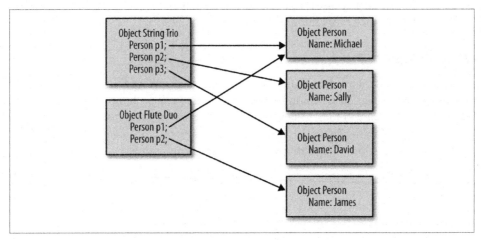

Figure 7-1. Object graph of retained memory

Shallow, Retained, and Deep Object Sizes

Two other useful terms for memory analysis are shallow and deep. The shallow size of an object is the size of the object itself. If the object contains a reference to another object, the 4 or 8 bytes of the reference is included, but the size of the target object is not included.

The deep size of an object includes the size of those objects. The difference between the deep size of an object and the retained memory of an object lies in objects that are otherwise shared. In Figure 7-1, the deep size of the Flute Duo object includes the space consumed by the Michael object, whereas the retained size of the Flute Duo object does not.

Objects that retain a large amount of heap space are often called the dominators of the heap. If the heap analysis tool shows that there are a few objects that dominate the bulk of the heap, then things are easy: all you need to do is create fewer of them, retain them for a shorter period of time, simplify their object graph, or make them smaller. That may be easier said than done, but at least the analysis is simple.

More commonly, some detective work will be necessary because the program is likely sharing objects. Like the Michael object in the previous figure, those shared objects are not counted in the retained set of any other object, since freeing one individual object will not free the shared object. Also, the largest retained sizes are often classloaders over which you have little control. As an extreme example, Figure 7-2 shows the top retained objects of a heap from a version of the stock servlet running in GlassFish that caches items strongly in the user's session and weakly in a global hashmap (so that the cached items have multiple references).

Class Name	Shallow Heap	▼ Retained Heap	Percentage
⟫ <Regex>	<Numeric>	<Numeric>	<Numeric>
▶ ☐ org.apache.felix.bundlerepository.impl.LocalRepositoryImpl @ 0x77	32	6,537,744	0.43%
▶ ☒ org.apache.felix.framework.BundleWiringImpl$BundleClassLoader	96	5,446,344	0.36%
▶ ☐ org.jvnet.hk2.osgiadapter.OSGiModulesRegistryImpl @ 0x77d3fc6a0	64	4,894,168	0.32%
▶ ☐ com.sun.tools.javac.file.ZipFileIndex @ 0x7827d5fa0	88	2,384,344	0.16%
▶ ☒ org.apache.felix.framework.BundleWiringImpl$BundleClassLoader	96	1,453,056	0.10%
▶ ☐ net.sdo.stockimpl.StockPriceHistoryImpl @ 0x7c018c868	48	1,357,544	0.09%
▶ ☐ com.sun.tools.javac.file.ZipFileIndex @ 0x78301f4c0	88	1,346,072	0.09%
▶ ☐ net.sdo.stockimpl.StockPriceHistoryImpl @ 0x7a27a59a0	48	1,334,664	0.09%
▶ ☒ org.apache.felix.framework.BundleWiringImpl$BundleClassLoader	96	1,331,296	0.09%
▶ ☐ net.sdo.stockimpl.StockPriceHistoryImpl @ 0x788769d38	48	1,328,368	0.09%
▶ ☐ net.sdo.stockimpl.StockPriceHistoryImpl @ 0x7acfd9098	48	1,327,776	0.09%
▶ ☐ net.sdo.stockimpl.StockPriceHistoryImpl @ 0x79d051d88	48	1,322,528	0.09%
▶ ☐ net.sdo.stockimpl.StockPriceHistoryImpl @ 0x7a71fe2b8	48	1,321,344	0.09%
▶ ☐ net.sdo.stockimpl.StockPriceHistoryImpl @ 0x7c32cada0	48	1,319,480	0.09%
Σ. Total: 14 of 70,584 entries; 70,570 more			

Figure 7-2. Retained Memory view in Memory Analyzer

The heap has some 1.4 GB of objects in it (that value doesn't appear on this tab). Even so, the largest set of objects that is referenced singly is only 6 MB (and is, unsurprisingly, part of GlassFish's OSGi classloading framework). Looking at the objects that directly retain the largest amount of memory isn't going to solve the memory issues.

In this example, there are multiple instances of StockPriceHistoryImpl objects in this list, each of which retains a fair amount of memory. It can be deduced from the amount of memory consumed by those objects that they are the issue. In the general case, though, objects might be shared in such a way that looking at the retained heap won't show anything obvious.

The histogram of objects is a useful second step (see Figure 7-3).

Class Name	Objects	▼ Shallow Heap	Retained Heap
🔧 <Regex>	<Numeric>	<Numeric>	<Numeric>
⊙ java.math.BigDecimal	12,920,067	516,802,680	517,429,776
⊙ java.util.TreeMap$Entry	7,255,390	290,215,600	1,450,796,576
⊙ net.sdo.stockimpl.StockPriceImpl	7,240,530	289,621,200	980,225,584
⊙ java.util.Date	7,244,268	173,862,432	174,077,552
⊙ net.sdo.stockimpl.StockPricePK	7,240,530	173,772,720	173,799,360
⊙ char[]	266,992	25,934,280	25,934,280
⊙ java.lang.String	255,336	6,128,064	30,780,696
⊙ java.util.HashMap$Entry[]	59,102	5,050,328	30,515,800
⊙ java.util.HashMap$Entry	151,237	4,839,584	30,295,176
⊙ java.util.LinkedHashMap$Entry	72,786	2,911,440	6,298,496
⊙ com.sun.tools.javac.file.ZipFileIndex$Entry	44,416	2,131,968	6,049,552
⊙ java.lang.Object[]	31,328	1,930,928	23,857,992
⊙ java.util.HashMap	34,114	1,910,384	29,772,824
⊙ java.lang.reflect.Method	21,579	1,726,320	3,714,040
Σ. Total: 14 of 12,007 entries; 11,993 more	43,446,283	1,517,322,152	

Figure 7-3. Histogram view in Memory Analyzer

The histogram aggregates objects of the same type, and in this example it is much more apparent that the 1.4 GB of memory retained by the seven million TreeMap$Entry objects is the key here. Even without knowing what is going on in the program, it is straightforward enough to use the Memory Analyzer's facility to trace those objects to see what is holding onto them.

Heap analysis tools provide a way to find the GC roots of a particular object (or set of objects in this case)—though jumping directly to the GC roots isn't necessarily helpful. The GC roots are the system objects that hold some static, global reference that (through a long chain of other objects) refers to the object in question. Typically these come from the static variables of a class loaded on the system or bootstrap classpath. This includes the Thread class and all active threads; threads retain objects either through their thread-local variables or through references via their target Runnable object (or, in the case of a subclass of the Thread class, any other references the subclass has).

In some cases, knowing the GC roots of a target object is helpful, but if the object has multiple references, it will have many GC roots. The references here are a tree structure in reverse. Say that there are two objects referring to a particular TreeMap$Entry object. Each of those objects may be referred to by two other objects, each of which may be referred to by three other objects, and so on. The explosion of references as the roots are traced back means that there are likely multiple GC roots for any given object.

Instead, it can be more fruitful to play detective and find the lowest point in the object graph where the target object is shared. This is done by examining the objects and their incoming references, and tracing those incoming references until the duplicate path is identified. In this case, references to the StockPriceHistoryImpl objects held in the tree map have two referents: the ConcurrentHashMap, which holds attribute data for the session, and the WeakHashMap, which holds the global cache.

In Figure 7-4, the back traces are expanded enough to show only a little data about the two of them. The way to conclude that it is the session data is to continue to expand the ConcurrentHashMap path until it becomes clear that path is the session data. A similar logic applies to the path for the WeakHashMap.

Class Name	Shallow Heap	Retained Heap
i Overview | Histogram | list_objects [selection of 'BigDecimal'] -inbound | list_objects [selection of 'StockPriceHistoryImpl @ 0x...		
<Regex>	<Numeric>	<Numeric>
▼ net.sdo.stockimpl.StockPriceHistoryImpl @ 0x7d7ac7b88	48	1,304,496
▼ [27] java.lang.Object[100] @ 0x7850bcf50	416	416
▼ elementData java.util.ArrayList @ 0x7850bcf38	24	440
▶ value java.util.concurrent.ConcurrentHashMap$Hash	32	472
▼ referent java.lang.ref.WeakReference @ 0x7d7ca2e08	32	32
▼ key java.util.HashMap$Entry @ 0x7d7ca2e28	32	64
▶ [1178] java.util.HashMap$Entry[2048] @ 0x7bdb59500	8,208	79,248
Σ Total: 2 entries		

Figure 7-4. Back traces of object references in Memory Analyzer

The object types used in this example made the analysis a little easier than is often the case. If the primary data in this application had been modeled as String objects instead of BigDecimal objects, and stored in HashMap objects instead of TreeMap objects, things would have been more difficult. There are hundreds of thousands of other strings, and tens of thousands of other HashMap objects in the heap dump. Finding paths to the interesting objects, then, takes some patience. As a general rule of thumb, start with collection objects (e.g., HashMap) rather than the entries (e.g., HashMap$Entry), and look for the biggest collections.

Quick Summary

1. Knowing which objects are consuming memory is the first step in knowing which objects to optimize in your code.

2. Histograms are a quick and easy way to identify memory issues caused by creating too many objects of a certain type.

3. Heap dump analysis is the most powerful technique to track down memory usage, though it requires some patience and effort to be utilized well.

Out of Memory Errors

The JVM throws an out of memory error under these circumstances:

- No native memory is available for the JVM.
- The permgen (in Java 7 and earlier) or metaspace (in Java 8) is out of memory.
- The Java heap itself is out of memory: the application has too many live objects for the given heap size.
- The JVM is spending too much time performing GC.

The last two cases—involving the Java heap itself—are more common, but don't automatically conclude from an out of memory error that the heap is the problem. It is necessary to look at why the out of memory error occurred (that reason is part of the output of the exception).

Out of native memory

The first case in this list—no native memory available for the JVM—occurs for reasons unrelated to the heap at all. In a 32-bit JVM, the maximum size of a process is 4 GB (3 GB on some versions of Windows, and about 3.5 GB on some older versions of Linux). Specifying a very large heap—say, 3.8 GB—brings the application size dangerously close to that limit. Even in a 64-bit JVM, the operating system may not have sufficient virtual memory for whatever the JVM requests.

This topic is addressed more fully in Chapter 8. Be aware that if the message for the out of memory error discusses allocation of native memory, then heap tuning isn't the answer: you need to look into whatever native memory issue is mentioned in the error. For example, the following message tells you that the native memory for thread stacks is exhausted:

```
Exception in thread "main" java.lang.OutOfMemoryError:
unable to create new native thread
```

Out of permgen or metaspace memory

This memory error is also not associated with the heap—it occurs because the permgen (in Java 7) or the metaspace native memory (in Java 8) is full. The root cause can be two things: the first is simply that the application uses more classes than can fit in the default perm space; the solution to that is to increase the size of permgen (see "Sizing Permgen and Metaspace" on page 124). (As in Chapter 5, the discussion in this section refers to permgen for simplicity; the same issues can occur with the Java 8 class metaspace if its maximum size is set.)

The second case is trickier: it involves a classloader memory leak. This occurs most frequently in a Java EE application server. Each application that is deployed to an app server runs in its own classloader (that provides isolation, so that classes from one application are not shared with—and do not interfere with—classes from another application). In development, each time the application is changed, it must be redeployed: a new classloader is created to load the new classes, and the old classloader is allowed to go out of scope. Once the classloader goes out of scope, the class metadata can be collected.

If the old classloader does not go out of scope, then the class metadata cannot be freed, and eventually permgen will fill up and throw an out of memory error. In this case, increasing the size of permgen will help, but ultimately that will simply postpone the error.

If this situation occurs in an app server environment, there is little to do but contact the app server vendor and get them to fix the leak. If you are writing your own application that creates and discards lots of classloaders, then take care to make sure the class loaders themselves are discarded correctly (in particular, make sure that no thread sets its context classloader to one of the temporary classloaders). To debug this situation, the heap dump analysis just described is quite helpful: in the histogram, find all the instances of the ClassLoader class, and trace their GC roots to see what is holding onto them.

The key to recognizing this situation is again the full-text output of the out of memory error. In Java 8, if the metaspace is full the error text will appear like this:

```
Exception in thread "main" java.lang.OutOfMemoryError: Metaspace
```

Similarly in Java 7:

```
Exception in thread "main" java.lang.OutOfMemoryError: PermGen space
```

Out of heap memory

When the heap itself is actually out of memory, the error message appears like this:

```
Exception in thread "main" java.lang.OutOfMemoryError: Java heap space
```

The common cases where an out of memory condition is triggered by a lack of heap space are similar to the permgen case. The application may simply need more heap space: the number of live objects that it is holding onto cannot fit in the heap space configured for it. Or, the application may have a memory leak: it continues to allocate additional objects without allowing other objects to go out of scope. In the first case, increasing the heap size will solve the issue; in the second case, increasing the heap size will merely postpone the error.

In either case, heap dump analysis is necessary to find out what is consuming the most memory; the focus can then be on reducing the number (or size) of those objects. If the application has a memory leak, then take successive heap dumps a few minutes apart and compare them. mat has that functionality built into it: if two heap dumps are open, then mat has an option to calculate the difference in the histograms between the two heaps.

Automatic Heap Dumps

Out of memory errors can occur unpredictably, making it difficult to know when to get a heap dump. There are several JVM flags that can help.

`-XX:+HeapDumpOnOutOfMemoryError`
> Turning on this flag (which is `false` by default) will cause the JVM to create a heap dump whenever an out of memory error is thrown.

`-XX:HeapDumpPath=<path>`
> This specifies the location where the heap dump will be written; the default is *java_pid<pid>.hprof* in the application's current working directory. The path can specify either a directory (in which case the default file name is used), or the name of the actual file to produce.

`-XX:+HeapDumpAfterFullGC`
> This generates a heap dump after running a full GC.

`-XX:+HeapDumpBeforeFullGC`
> This generates a heap dump before running a full GC.

In the case where multiple heap dumps are generated (e.g., because multiple full GCs occur), a sequence number is appended to the heap dump filename.

Try turning on these flags if the application unpredictably throws an out of memory error due to the heap space, and you need the heap dump at that point to analyze why the failure occurred.

Figure 7-5 shows the classic case of a Java memory leak caused by a collection class (in this case, a HashMap). (Collection classes are the most frequent cause of a memory leak: the application inserts items into the collection and never frees them.) This is a comparison histogram view: it displays the difference in the number of objects in two different heap dumps. For example, there are 19,744 more Integer objects that occur in the target heap dump compared to its baseline.

The best way to overcome this situation is to change the application logic such that items are proactively discarded from the collection when they are no longer needed. Alternatively, a collection that uses weak or soft references can automatically discard the items when nothing else in the application is referencing them, but those collections come with a cost (as is discussed later in this chapter).

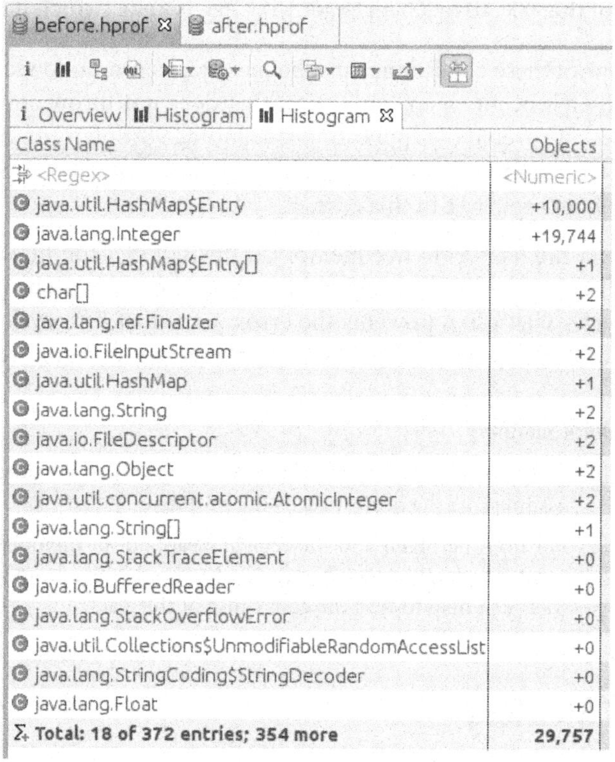

Figure 7-5. Histogram comparison

GC overhead limit reached

The final case where the JVM throws an out of memory error is when it determines that is it spending too much time performing GC:

```
Exception in thread "main" java.lang.OutOfMemoryError: GC overhead limit exceeded
```

This error is thrown when all of the following conditions are met:

1. The amount of time spent in full GCs exceeds the value specified by the -XX:GCTimeLimit=*N* flag. The default value is 98 (i.e., if 98% of the time is spent in GC).

2. The amount of memory reclaimed by a full GC is less than the value specified by the -XX:GCHeapFreeLimit=*N* flag. The default value for this is 2, meaning that if less than 2% of the heap is freed during the full GC, this condition is met.

3. The above two conditions have held true for five consecutive full GC cycles (that value is not tunable).

4. The value of the -XX:+UseGCOverheadLimit flag is true (which it is by default).

Note that all four of these conditions must be met. It is common to see more than five consecutive full GCs occur in an application that does not throw an out of memory error. That is because even if the application is spending 98% of its time performing full GCs, it may be freeing more than 2% of the heap during each GC. Consider increasing the value of GCHeapFreeLimit in that case.

Note that as a last-ditch effort to free memory, if the first two conditions hold for four consecutive full GC cycles, then all soft references in the JVM will be freed before the fifth full GC cycle. That often prevents the error, since that fifth cycle will likely free more than 2% of the heap (assuming that the application uses soft references).

Quick Summary

1. Out of memory errors are thrown for a variety of reasons; do not assume that the heap space is the problem.

2. For both permgen and the regular heap, out of memory errors most frequently occur because of memory leaks; heap analysis tools can help to find the root cause of the leak.

Using Less Memory

The first approach to using memory more efficiently in Java is to use less heap memory. That statement should be unsurprising: using less memory means the heap will fill up less often, requiring fewer GC cycles. The effect can multiply: fewer collections of the young generation means the tenuring age of an object is increased less often—meaning that the object is less likely to be promoted into the old generation. Hence, the number of full GC cycles (or concurrent GC cycles) will be reduced. And if those full GC cycles can clear up more memory, then they will also occur less frequently.

This section investigates three ways to use less memory: reducing object size, lazy initialization of objects, and using canonical objects.

Reducing Object Size

Objects occupy a certain amount of heap memory, so the simplest way to use less memory is to make objects smaller. Given the memory constraints on the machine running your program, it may not be possible to increase the heap size by 10%, but a 20% reduction of half the objects in the heap can achieve the same goal.

The size of an object can be decreased by (obviously) reducing the number of instance variables it holds and (less obviously) by reducing the size of those variables. Table 7-1 gives the size of an instance variable of all Java types.

Table 7-1. Size of Java instance variables

Type	Size
byte	1
char	2
short	2
int	4
float	4
long	8
double	8
reference	4 on 32-bit JVMs and 64-bit JVMs with heaps of less than 32 GB; 8 on 64-bit JVMs with large heaps[a]

[a] See "Compressed oops" on page 234 for more details.

The reference type here is the reference to any kind of Java object—instances of classes or arrays. That space is the storage only for the reference itself. The size of an object that contains references to other objects varies depending on whether we want to consider the shallow, deep, or retained size of the object, but that size also includes some invisible object header fields. For a regular object, the size of the header fields is 8 bytes on a 32-bit JVM and 16 bytes on a 64-bit JVM (regardless of heap size). For an array, the size of the header fields is 16 bytes on a 32-bit JVM or a 64-bit JVM with a heap of less than 32 GB, and 24 bytes otherwise.

For example, consider these class definitions:

```java
public class A {
    private int i;
}

public class B {
    private int i;
    private Locale l = Locale.US;
}

public class C {
    private int i;
    private ConcurrentHashMap chm = new ConcurrentHashMap();
}
```

The actual sizes of a single instance of these objects (on a 64-bit Java 7 JVM with a heap size of less than 32 GB) is given in Table 7-2.

Table 7-2. Sizes of simple objects

	Shallow size	Deep size	Retained size
A	16	16	16
B	24	216	24
C	24	200	200

In class B, defining the `Locale` reference adds 8 bytes to the object size, but at least in that example, the actual `Locale` object is shared among other classes. If the `Locale` object is never actually needed by the class, including that instance variable will waste only the additional bytes for the reference. Still, those bytes add up if the application creates a lot of instances of class B.

On the other hand, defining and creating a `ConcurrentHashMap` consumed additional bytes for the object reference, plus an additional 200 bytes for the hashmap object. If the hashmap is never used, instances of class C are quite wasteful.

Defining only required instance variables is one way to save space in an object. The less obvious case involves using smaller data types. If a class needs to keep track of one of eight possible states, it can do so using a `byte` rather than an `int`—potentially saving 3 bytes. Using `float` instead of `double`, `int` instead of `long`, and so on can help to save memory, particularly in classes that are frequently instantiated. As discussed in Chapter 12, using appropriately sized collections (or using simple instance variables instead of collections) achieves similar savings.

Object Alignment and Object Sizes

The classes mentioned in Table 7-2 all contain an extra integer field that was not referenced in the discussion. Why is that there?

In truth, that variable served the purpose of making the discussion of those classes easier to follow: class B contained 8 more bytes than class A, which is what we'd expect (and which made the point more clearly).

That glossed over an important detail: object sizes are always padded so that they are a multiple of 8 bytes. Without the definition of `i` in class A, instances of A still consume 16 bytes—the 4 bytes are just used for padding the object size to a multiple of 8, rather than being used to holding the reference to `i`. Without the definition of `i`, instances of class B would consume only 16 bytes—the same as A, even though B has that extra object reference. That padding is also why an instance of B is 8 bytes larger than an instance of A even though it contains only one additional (4-byte) reference.

The JVM will also pad objects that have an uneven number of bytes so that arrays of that object fit neatly along whatever address boundaries are optimal for the underlying architecture.

> So eliminating some instance fields or reducing some field sizes in an object may or may not yield a benefit, but there is no reason not to do it.

Eliminating instance fields in an object can help make the object smaller, but there is a gray area here: what about object fields that hold the result of a calculation based on pieces of data? This is the classic computer science trade-off of time versus space: is it better to spend the memory (space) to store the value, or better to spend the time (CPU cycles) to calculate the value as needed? In Java, though, the trade-off applies to CPU time as well, since the additional memory can cause GC to consume more CPU cycles.

The hashcode for a String, for example, is calculated by summing an equation involving each character of the string; it is somewhat time-consuming to calculate. Hence, the String class stores that value in an instance variable so that the hashcode need only be calculated once: in the end, reusing that value will almost always produce better performance than any memory savings from not storing it. On the other hand, the toString() method of most classes does not cache the string representation of the object in an instance variable, which would consume memory both for the instance variable and the string it references. Instead, the time required to calculate a new string will usually give better performance than the memory required to keep the string reference around. (It is also the case that the hash value for a String is used quite frequently, and the toString() representation of an object is often used quite rarely.)

This case is definitely a your-mileage-may-vary situation, and the point along the time/space continuum where it makes sense to switch between using the memory to cache a value and recalculating the value will depend on many factors. If reducing GC is the goal, then the balance will swing more to recalculating.

 Quick Summary

1. Reducing object sizes can often improve the efficiency of GC.
2. The size of an object is not always immediately apparent: objects are padded to fit on 8-byte boundaries, and object reference sizes are different between 32- and 64-bit JVMs.
3. Even null instance variables consume space within object classes.

Lazy Initialization

Much of the time, the decision about whether a particular instance variable is needed is not as black-and-white as the previous section suggests. A particular class may need a Calendar object only 10% of the time, but Calendar objects are expensive to create, and it definitely makes sense to keep that object around rather than re-create it on demand. This is a case where lazy initialization can help.

So far, this discussion has assumed that instance variables are initialized eagerly. A class that needs to use a `Calendar` object (and that doesn't need to be thread-safe) might look something like this:

```
public class CalDateInitialization {
    private Calendar calendar = Calendar.getInstance();
    private DateFormat df = DateFormat.getDateInstance();

    private void report(Writer w) {
        w.write("On " + df.format(calendar.getTime()) + ": " + this);
    }
}
```

To initialize the fields lazily instead, there is a small trade-off in terms of computation performance—the code must test the state of the variable each time the code is executed:

```
public class CalDateInitialization {
    private Calendar calendar;
    private DateFormat df;

    private void report(Writer w) {
        if (calendar == null) {
            calendar = Calendar.getInstance();
            df = DateFormat.getDateInstance();
        }
        w.write("On " + df.format(calendar.getTime()) + ": " + this);
    }
}
```

Lazy initialization is best used when the operation in question is only infrequently used: if the operation is commonly used, then no memory will actually be saved (since it will always be allocated), and there will be that slight performance penalty on a common operation.

Lazy Initialization Runtime Performance

The usual performance penalty for checking whether lazily initialized variables have been initialized may not always exist. Consider this example from the JDK's `ArrayList` class. That class maintains an array of the elements it stores, and prior to JDK 7u40, pseudocode for the class looked like this:

```
public class ArrayList {
    private Object[] elementData = new Object[16];
    int index = 0;
    public void add(Object o) {
        ensureCapacity();
        elementData[index++] = o;
```

```
        }
        private void ensureCapacity() {
            if (index == elementData.length) {
                ...reallocate array and copy old data in...
            }
        }
    }
```

In JDK 7u40, this class was changed so that the elementData array is initialized lazily. But because the ensureCapacity() method already needed to check the array size, the common methods of the class didn't suffer a performance penalty: the code to check for initialization is the same as the code to check whether the array size needs to be increased. The new code uses a static, shared, 0-length array so that performance is the same:

```
public class ArrayList {
    private static final Object[] EMPTY_ELEMENTDATA = {} ;
    private Object[] elementData = EMPTY_ELEMENTDATA;
}
```

That means the ensureCapacity() method can be (essentially) unchanged, since the index and elementData.length will both start at 0.

When the code involved must be thread-safe, lazy initialization becomes more complicated. As a first step, it is easiest simply to add traditional synchronization:

```
public class CalDateInitialization {
    private Calendar calendar;
    private DateFormat df;

    private synchronized void report(Writer w) {
        if (calendar == null) {
            calendar = Calendar.getInstance();
            df = DateFormat.getDateInstance();
        }
        w.write("On " + df.format(calendar.getTime()) + ": " + this);
    }
}
```

Introducing synchronization into the solution opens up the possibility that the synchronization will become a performance bottleneck. That case should be rare. The performance benefit from lazy initialization only occurs when the object in question will only rarely initialize those fields—since if it usually initializes those fields, then no memory has actually been saved. So synchronization becomes a bottleneck for lazily initialized fields when an infrequently used code path is suddenly subject to use by a lot of threads simultaneously. That case is not inconceivable, but it isn't the most common case either.

Solving that synchronization bottleneck can only happen if the lazily initialized variables are themselves thread-safe. DateFormat objects are not thread-safe, so in the current example, it doesn't really matter if the lock includes the `Calendar` object: if the lazily initialized objects are suddenly used heavily, the required synchronization around the `DateFormat` object will be an issue no matter what. The thread-safe code would have to look like this:

```
public class CalDateInitialization {
    private Calendar calendar;
    private DateFormat df;

    private void report(Writer w) {
        unsychronizedCalendarInit();
        synchronized(df) {
            w.write("On " + df.format(calendar.getTime()) + ": " + this);
        }
    }
}
```

Lazy initialization that involves an instance variable that is not thread-safe can always synchronize around that variable (e.g., using the `synchronized` version of the method shown previously).

Consider a somewhat different example, where a large `ConcurrentHashMap` is lazily initialized:

```
public class CHMInitialization {
    private ConcurrentHashMap chm;

    public void doOperation() {
        synchronized(this) {
            if (chm == null) {
                chm = new ConcurrentHashMap();
                ... code to populate the map ...
            }
        }
        ...use the chm...
    }
}
```

Because the `ConcurrentHashMap` can be safely accessed by multiple threads, the extra synchronization in this example is one of the infrequent cases where properly used lazy initialization could introduce a synchronization bottleneck. (Such a bottleneck should still be rare, though; if access to the hashmap is that frequent, consider if anything is really saved by initializing it lazily.) The bottleneck is solved using the double-checked locking idiom:

```
public class CHMInitialization {
    private volatile ConcurrentHashMap instanceChm;

    public void doOperation() {
        ConcurrentHashMap chm = instanceChm;
        if (chm == null) {
```

```
            synchronized(this) {
                chm = instanceChm;
                if (chm == null) {
                    chm = new ConcurrentHashMap();
                    ... code to populate the map
                    instanceChm = chm;
                }
            }
            ...use the chm...
        }
    }
}
```

There are some important threading issues here: the instance variable must be declared `volatile`, and there is a slight performance benefit in assigning the instance variable to a local variable. More details of that are given in Chapter 9; in the occasional case where lazy initialization of threaded code makes sense, this is the design pattern to follow.

Eager deinitialization

The corollary to lazily initializing variables is eagerly deinitializing them by setting their value to `null`. That allows the object in question to be collected more quickly by the garbage collector. While that sounds like a good thing in theory, it is really useful only in limited circumstances.

A variable that is a candidate for lazy initialization might seem like a candidate for eager deinitialization: in the examples above, the `Calendar` and `DateFormat` objects could be set to `null` upon completion of the `report()` method. However, if the variable isn't going to be used in subsequent invocations of the method (or elsewhere in the class), there is no reason to make it an instance variable in the first place: simply create the local variable in the method, and when the method completes, the local variable will fall out of scope and the garbage collector can free it.

The common exception to the rule about not needing to eagerly deinitialize variables occurs with classes like those in the Java collection framework: classes that hold references to data for a long time, and then are informed that the data in question is no longer needed. Consider the implementation of the `remove()` method in the `ArrayList` class of the JDK (some code simplified):

```
public E remove(int index) {
    E oldValue = elementData(index);
    int numMoved = size - index - 1;
    if (numMoved > 0)
        System.arraycopy(elementData, index+1,
                         elementData, index, numMoved);
    elementData[--size] = null; // clear to let GC do its work
    return oldValue;
}
```

The code comment about GC appears in the (otherwise sparsely commented) JDK source itself: setting the value of a variable to null like that is an unusual enough operation that some explanation is needed. In this case, trace through what happens when the last element of the array is removed. The number of items remaining in the array—the size instance variable—is decremented. Say that size is decremented from 5 to 4. Now whatever is stored in elementData[4] cannot be accessed: it is beyond the valid size of the array.

elementData[4] is, in this case, a stale reference. The elementData array is probably going to remain active for a long time, and so anything that it no longer needs to reference needs to be actively set to null.

This notion of stale references is the key: if a long-lived class caches and then discards object references, care must be taken to avoid stale references. Otherwise, explicitly setting an object reference to null will offer little performance benefit.

Quick Summary

1. Use lazy initialization only when the common code paths will leave variables uninitialized.

2. Lazy initialization of thread-safe code is unusual but can often piggyback on existing synchronization.

3. Use double-checked locking for lazy initialization of code using thread-safe objects.

Immutable and Canonical Objects

In Java, many object types are immutable. This includes objects that have a corresponding primitive type—Integer, Double, Boolean, and so on—as well as other numeric-based types, like BigDecimal. The most common Java object, of course, is the immutable String. From a program design perspective, it is often a good idea for custom classes to represent immutable objects as well.

When these objects are quickly created and discarded, they have a small effect on young collections; as we saw in Chapter 5, that impact is limited. But as is true of any object, if a large number of immutable objects are promoted to the old generation, performance can suffer.

Hence, there is no reason to avoid designing and using immutable objects, even if it may seem a little counterproductive that these objects cannot be changed and must be re-created. But one optimization that is often possible when handling these objects is to avoid creating duplicate copies of the same object.

The best example of this is the `Boolean` class. In any Java application, there need ever be only two instances of the `Boolean` class: one for true, and one for false. Unfortunately, the `Boolean` class is badly designed. Because it has a `public` constructor, applications can create as many of these objects as they like, even though they are all exactly the same as one of the two canonical `Boolean` objects. A better design would have been for the `Boolean` class to have only a private constructor, and static methods to return either `Boolean.TRUE` or `Boolean.FALSE` based on their parameter. If such a model can be followed for your own immutable classes, you can prevent them from contributing to the heap usage of your application. (Hopefully it is obvious that you should never create a `Boolean` object; you should just use `Boolean.TRUE` or `Boolean.FALSE` as necessary.)

These singular representations of immutable objects are known as the canonical version of the object.

Creating canonical objects

Even if the universe of objects for a particular class is practically limitless, using canonical values can often save memory. The JDK provides a facility to do this for the most-common immutable object: strings can call the `intern()` method to find a canonical version of the string. More details of string interning are examined in the next section, but for now we'll look at how to accomplish the same thing for custom classes.

To canonicalize an object, create a map that stores the canonical version of the object. In order to prevent a memory leak, make sure that the objects in the map are weakly referenced. The skeleton of such a class looks like this:

```
public class ImmutableObject {
    private static  WeakHashMap<ImmutableObject, ImmutableObject>
        map = new WeakHashMap();

    public ImmutableObject canonicalVersion(ImmutableObject io) {
        synchronized(map) {
            ImmutableObject canonicalVersion = map.get(io);
            if (canonicalVersion == null) {
                map.put(io, new WeakReference(io));
                canonicalVersion = io;
            }
            return canonicalVersion;
        }
    }
}
```

In a threaded environment, the synchronization here can potentially become a bottleneck. There is no easy solution for that if you stick to JDK classes, since they do not provide a concurrent hashmap for weak references. However, there have been proposals to add a `CustomConcurrentHashMap` to the JDK (originally as part of Java Specification

Request, or JSR, 166), and you can find various third-party implementations of such a class.

Quick Summary

1. Objects that are immutable offer the possibility of special lifecycle management: canonicalization.

2. Eliminating duplicate copies of immutable objects via canonicalization can greatly decrease the amount of heap an application uses.

String Interning

Strings are, far and away, the most common Java object; your application's heap is almost certainly filled with them.

If a large number of those strings are the same, then a large part of the heap is wasted. Since strings are immutable, there is never any reason to have more than one string representing the same sequence of characters. Programming being what it is, though, it can be hard to know if you are creating duplicate strings.

Knowing if you have a large number of duplicate strings requires some heap analysis. One way to do that is to load a heap dump in the Eclipse Memory Analyzer, calculate the retained size for all the `String` objects, and list those objects sorted by their maximum retained size. Figure 7-6 shows such a heap dump. It seems likely that the first three strings are the same, and that interning them would save 650 KB of memory. (The strings can be inspected in the tool for verification.) The same is true of the fourth and fifth strings, the seventh though ninth strings, and so on—except of course the lower in the list, the less memory that is saved by interning the string.

This is a case where interning those particular strings is advantageous; retaining only the canonical version of the string can save all the memory allocated by those duplicate cases. That could be done with a variant of the canonicalization example in the previous section, but the `String` class provides its own method to perform canonicalization: the `intern()` method.

Like most optimizations, interning strings shouldn't be done arbitrarily, but it can be effective if there are lots of duplicate strings occupying a significant portion of the heap. One caveat about interning too many strings is that the table of interned strings—which is held in native memory—is a fixed-size hashtable. In releases prior to Java 7u40, the default size of the table is 1,009 buckets; on average, then, it can be expected to hold about 500 strings before there are collisions due to chaining. In 64-bit versions of Java 7u40 and later, the default size is 60,013.

Class Name	Shallow Heap	▼ Retained He
🔆 <Regex>	<Numeric>	<Numeric>
▶ 🔲 java.lang.String @ 0x703bd42d8	24	328,592
▶ 🔲 java.lang.String @ 0x702208118	24	328,592
▶ 🔲 java.lang.String @ 0x701a37578	24	328,592
▶ 🔲 java.lang.String @ 0x70242a4c0	24	53,208
▶ 🔲 java.lang.String @ 0x701d847c8	24	53,208
▶ 🔲 java.lang.String @ 0x7032542c8	24	40,600
▶ 🔲 java.lang.String @ 0x703b2ae08	24	37,168
▶ 🔲 java.lang.String @ 0x70213a7b8	24	37,168
▶ 🔲 java.lang.String @ 0x70135d758	24	37,168
▶ 🔲 java.lang.String @ 0x700066bd8	24	32,112
▶ 🔲 java.lang.String @ 0x7021e3d78	24	26,224
▶ 🔲 java.lang.String @ 0x700f7e450	24	26,224
▶ 🔲 java.lang.String @ 0x702294c50	24	23,632
▶ 🔲 java.lang.String @ 0x701dde1c8	24	23,632
Σ₊ **Total: 14 of 236,646 entries; 236,632 more**		

Figure 7-6. Memory retained by String objects

Fixed-Size Hashtables

If you're not familiar with the basic structure of hashtables and hashmaps, you may be wondering what is meant by a fixed-size hashtable (particularly since the Java implementations of those classes are not of fixed size).

Conceptually, a hashtable contains an array that can hold some number of entries (each element in the array is called a *bucket*). When something is stored in a hashtable, it is stored in the array position determined by the object's hash value modulus the number of buckets. It is quite possible for two objects with different hash values to map to the same bucket in this scheme, so each bucket is really a linked list of all the stored items that map to that bucket. When two objects map to the same bucket, it is called a collision.

As more and more objects are inserted into this table, there are more and more collisions; more items get stored into each linked list. Finding an item then becomes a matter of searching through a linked list. That can be very slow, particularly as the list gets longer.

The way around this is to size the hashtable so that it has more buckets (and, as a result, fewer collisions). Many implementations do that dynamically; in fact, that is the way the Java Hashtable and HashMap classes work.

But other implementations—like the one internal to the JVM being discussed here—cannot resize themselves; the size of their array is fixed when the map is created.

Starting in Java 7, the size of this table can be set when the JVM starts by using the flag -XX:StringTableSize=N (which defaults to 1,009 or 60,013 as previously mentioned). If an application will intern a lot of strings, this number should be increased. The string intern table will operate most efficiently if that value is a prime number.

The performance of the intern() method is dominated by how well the string table size is tuned. As an example, Table 7-3 shows the total time to create and intern 10 million randomly created strings under various scenarios:

Table 7-3. Time to intern 10 million strings

Tuning	Time
String table size 1009	2.3 hours
String table size 1 million	30.4 seconds
String table size 10 million	25.2 seconds
Custom method	26.4 seconds

Note the very severe penalty for the improperly sized string intern table. Once the table is sized according to the expected data, performance is drastically improved.

For that last test case, instead of using the intern() method, I used the sample canonicalVersion() method shown previously and implemented with a CustomConcurrentHashMap class (from a prerelease version of JSR 166) with weak keys and values. That didn't help performance against a well-tuned string intern table, but the advantage with the custom implementation is that I didn't need to tune the size of that custom map at all. The CustomConcurrentHashMap was given an initial size of 1,009, and it resized itself dynamically as needed. That had a small penalty against the best-tuned string table size, but it was far easier to run. (In that case, though, the code had to call the canonicalVersion() method of the custom class; this isn't a simple replacement for the intern() method.)

To see how the string table is performing, run your application with the -XX:+PrintStringTableStatistics argument (this flag requires JDK 7u6 or later and is false by default). When the JVM exits, it will print out a table like this:

```
StringTable statistics:
Number of buckets      :    1009
Average bucket size    :    3008
Variance of bucket size :   2870
Std. dev. of bucket size:     54
Maximum bucket size    :    3186
```

This command also displays information about the symbol table, but the string table is what interests us here. (The symbol table is used to hold some class information. JDK 8 has an experimental flag to adjust the size of that table, but it is not generally tunable.) In this case, there are 3,035,072 interned strings (since there are 1,009 buckets with an average of 3,008 strings per bucket). Ideally, the average bucket size should be 0 or 1. The size won't ever actually be 0—just less than 0.5, but the calculation is done using integer arithmetic, so it might be rounded down in the report. If the averages are larger than 1, increase the string table size.

The number of interned strings an application has allocated (and their total size) can also be obtained using the `jmap` command (this also requires JDK 7u6 or later):

```
% jmap -heap process_id
... other output ...
36361 interned Strings occupying 3247040 bytes.
```

The penalty for setting the size of the string table too high is minimal: each bucket takes only 4 or 8 bytes (depending on whether you have a 32- or 64-bit JVM), so having a few thousand more entries than optimal is a one-time cost of a few kilobytes of native (not heap) memory.

String Interning and Equals

On the topic of interning strings, what about using the `intern()` method to make the program run faster, since interned strings can be compared via the == operator? That is a popular thought, though in most cases it turns out to be a myth. The `String.equals()` method is pretty fast. It starts by knowing that unequal-length strings are never equal, though if the strings have equal length, it must scan the string and compare all the characters (at least until it finds that the strings do not match). Comparing strings via the == operation is undeniably faster, but the cost of interning the string must also be taken into consideration. That requires (among other things) calculating the string's hashcode, which means scanning the entire string and performing an operation on each of its characters (just as the `equals()` method must do).

The only time a benefit in string comparison can be expected from using the `intern()` method is if an application performs a lot of repeated comparisons on a set of strings of the same length. If *both* strings have been previously interned, then the == comparison is faster; the cost of calling the `intern()` method needn't be counted more than once. But in the general case, the costs are mostly the same.

Quick Summary

1. Applications that reuse the same strings a lot will benefit by interning those strings.

2. Applications that intern many strings may need to adjust the size of the string intern table (unless they are running on a 64-bit server JVM starting in Java 7u40).

Object Lifecycle Management

The second broad topic of memory management discussed in this chapter is object lifecycle management. For the most part, Java attempts to minimize the effort developers must put into managing the lifecycle of objects: the developer creates the objects when needed, and when they are no longer needed, the objects fall out of scope and are freed by the garbage collector.

There are times when this normal lifecycle is not optimal. Some objects are expensive to create, and managing the lifecycle of those objects will improve the efficiency of an application, even at the expense of requiring some additional work by the garbage collector. This section explores when and how the normal lifecycle of objects should be changed, either by reusing the objects, or by maintaining special references to them.

Object Reuse

There are two ways by which object reuse is commonly achieved: object pools and thread-local variables. GC engineers around the world are now groaning, since either of these techniques hampers the efficiency of GC. Object pooling in particular is widely disliked in GC circles for that reason, though for that matter, object pools are also widely disliked in development circles for many other reasons.

At one level, the reason for this position seems obvious: objects that are reused stay around for a long time in the heap. If there are a lot of objects in the heap, then there is less room to create new objects, and hence GC operations will occur more frequently. But that is only part of the story.

As we saw in Chapter 6, when an object is created it is allocated in eden. It will spend a few young GC cycles shuffling back and forth between the survivor spaces, before finally it gets promoted to the old generation. Each time the (recently or) newly created pooled object is processed, the GC algorithm must perform some work to copy it and adjust references to it until it finally makes it into the old generation.

Although that seems like it might be the end of it, once the object is promoted to the old generation, it can cause even more performance problems. The length of time it takes to perform a full GC is proportional to the number of objects that are still alive in the old generation. The amount of live data is more important even than the size of the heap; it is faster to process a 3 GB old generation with few surviving objects than to process a 1 GB old generation where 75% of the objects survive.

GC Efficiency

Just how much does the amount of live data in the heap affect GC times? The answer can be more than an order of magnitude.

Here's the output of a GC log from a test on my standard four-core Linux system using a 4 GB heap (of which 1 GB is the fixed size for the new generation):

```
[Full GC [PSYoungGen: 786432K->786431K(917504K)]
        [ParOldGen: 3145727K->3145727K(3145728K)]
        3932159K->3932159K(4063232K)
        [PSPermGen: 2349K->2349K(21248K)], 0.5432730 secs]
        [Times: user=1.72 sys=0.01, real=0.54 secs]
...
[Full GC [PSYoungGen: 786432K->0K(917504K)]
        [ParOldGen: 3145727K->210K(3145728K)]
        3932159K->210K(4063232K)
        [PSPermGen: 2349K->2349K(21248K)], 0.0687770 secs]
        [Times: user=0.08 sys=0.00, real=0.07 secs]
...
[Full GC [PSYoungGen: 349567K->349567K(699072K)]
        [ParOldGen: 3145727K->3145727K(3145728K)]
        3495295K->3495295K(3844800K)
        [PSPermGen: 2349K->2349K(21248K)], 0.7228880 secs]
        [Times: user=2.41 sys=0.01, real=0.73 secs]
```

Notice that middle output: the application cleared most references to things in the old generation, and hence the data in the old generation after the GC was only 210 KB. That operation took a mere 70 ms. In the other cases, most of the data in the heap is still live; the full GC operations, which removed very little data from the heap, took between 540 ms and 730 ms. And fortunately, there are four GC threads running in this test. On a single-core system, the short GC in this example took 80 ms, and the long GC required 2,410 ms (more than 30 times longer).

Using a concurrent collector and avoiding full GCs doesn't make the situation that much better, since the time required by the marking phases of the concurrent collectors similarly depends on the amount of still-live data. And for CMS in particular, the objects in a pool are likely to be promoted at different times, increasing the chance of a concurrent failure due to fragmentation. Overall, the longer objects are kept in the heap, the less efficient GC will be.

So: object reuse is bad. Now we can discuss how and when to reuse objects.

The JDK provides some common object pools: the thread pool, which is discussed in Chapter 9, and soft references. Soft references, which are discussed later in this section, are essentially a big pool of reusable objects. Java EE, meanwhile, depends on object pools for connections to databases and other resources, and the entire lifecycle of Enterprise Java Beans is built around the notion of an object pool.

The situation is similar for thread-local values; the JDK is filled with classes that use thread-local variables to avoid reallocating certain kinds of objects.

Clearly, even Java experts understand the need for object reuse in some circumstances.

The reason for reusing objects is that many objects are quite expensive to initialize, and reusing them is more efficient than the trade-off in increased GC time. That is certainly true of things like the JDBC connection pool: creating the network connection, and possibly logging in and establishing a database session, is quite expensive. Object pooling in that case is a big performance win. Threads are pooled to save the time associated with creating a thread; random number generators are supplied as thread-local variables to save the time require to seed them; and so on.

One feature these examples share is that it takes a long time to initialize the object. In Java, object *allocation* is quite fast and inexpensive (and arguments against object reuse tend to focus on that part of the equation). Object *initialization* performance depends on the object. You should only consider reusing objects with a very high initialization cost, and only then if the cost of initializing those objects is one of the dominant operations in your program.

Another feature these examples share is that the number of shared objects tends to be small, which minimizes their impact on GC operations: there aren't enough of them to slow down those GC cycles. Having a few objects in a pool isn't going to affect the GC efficiency too much; filling the heap with pooled objects will slow down GC significantly.

Here are just some examples of where (and why) the JDK and Java EE reuse objects:

Thread pools
 Threads are expensive to initialize.

JDBC pools
 Database connections are expensive to initialize.

EJB pools
 EJBs can be expensive to initialize (see Chapter 10).

Large arrays
 Java requires that when an array is allocated, all individual elements in the array must be initialized to some default value (`null`, `0`, or `false` as appropriate). This can be quite time-consuming for large arrays.

Native NIO buffers
 Allocating a direct `java.nio.Buffer` (that is, a buffer returned from calling the `allocateDirect()` method) is an expensive operation regardless of the size of the

buffer. It is better to create one large buffer and manage the buffers from that by slicing off portions as required, and return them to be reused by future operations.

Security classes
Instances of MessageDigest, Signature, and other security algorithms are expensive to initialize. The Apache-based XML code uses thread-local variables to save these instances.

String encoder and decoder objects
Various classes in the JDK create and reuse these objects. For the most part, these are also soft references, as we'll see in the next section.

StringBuilder *helpers*
The BigDecimal class reuses a StringBuilder object when calculating intermediate results.

Random number generators
Instances of either the Random and—especially—SecureRandom classes are expensive to seed.

Names obtained from DNS lookups
Network lookups are expensive.

ZIP encoders and decoders
In an interesting twist, these are not particularly expensive to initialize. They are, however, quite expensive to free, because they rely on object finalization to ensure that the native memory they use is also freed. See "Finalizers and final references" on page 216 for more details.

There are some differences in performance between the two options (object pools and thread-local variables) being discussed here; let's look at those in more detail.

Object pools

Object pools are disliked for many reasons, only some of which have to do with their performance. They can be difficult to size correctly, and they place the burden of object management back on the programmer: rather than simply letting an object go out of scope, the programmer must remember to return the object to the pool.

The focus here, though, is on the performance of an object pool, which is subject to the following:

GC impact
As we've seen, holding lots of objects reduces (sometimes quite drastically) the efficiency of GC.

Synchronization

Pools of objects are inevitably synchronized, and if the objects are frequently re-moved and replaced, the pool can have a lot of contention. The result is that access to the pool can become slower than initializing a new object.

Throttling

This performance impact of pools can be beneficial: pools allow access to scarce resources to be throttled. As discussed in Chapter 2, if you attempt to increase load on a system beyond what it can handle, performance will decrease. This is one reason thread pools are important. If too many threads run simultaneously, the CPUs will be overwhelmed and performance will degrade (an example of that is shown in Chapter 9).

This principle applies to remote system access as well, and is frequently seen with JDBC connections. If more JDBC connections are made to a database than it can handle, performance of the database will degrade. In these situations, it is better to throttle the number of resources (e.g., JDBC connections) by capping the size of the pool—even if it means that threads in the application must wait for a free resource.

Thread-local variables

There are different performance trade-offs when reusing objects by storing them as thread-local variables:

Lifecycle management

Thread-local variables are much easier and less expensive to manage than objects in a pool. Both techniques require you to obtain the initial object: you check it out of the pool, or you call the `get()` method on the thread-local object. But object pools require that you return the object when you are done with it (else no one else can use it); thread-local objects are always available within the thread and needn't be explicitly returned.

Cardinality

Thread-local variables usually end up with a one-to-one correspondence between the number of threads and the number of saved (reused) objects. That isn't strictly the case. The thread's copy of the variable isn't created until the first time the thread uses it, so it is possible that there are fewer saved objects than threads. But there cannot be any more saved objects than threads, and much of the time it ends up being the same number.

On the other hand, an object pool may be sized arbitrarily. If a servlet sometimes needs one JDBC connection and sometimes needs two, the JDBC pool can be sized accordingly (with, say, 12 connections for 8 threads). Thread-local variables cannot do this effectively; nor can they throttle access to a resource (unless the number of threads itself serves as the throttle).

Synchronization

Thread-local variables need no synchronization since they can only be used within a single thread; the thread-local get() method is relatively fast. (This wasn't always the case; in early versions of Java, obtaining a thread-local variable was quite expensive. If you shied away from thread-local variables because of bad performance in the past, reconsider their use in current versions of Java.)

Synchronization brings up an interesting point, because the performance benefit of thread-local objects is often couched in terms of saving synchronization costs (rather than in the savings from reusing an object). For example, Java 7 introduced a ThreadLocalRandom class; that class (rather than a single Random instance) is used in the sample stock applications. Otherwise, many of the examples throughout the book would encounter a synchronization bottleneck on the next() method of the single Random object. Using a thread-local object is a good way to avoid synchronization bottlenecks, since only one thread can ever use that object.

However, that synchronization problem would have been solved just as easily if the examples had simply created a new instance of the Random class each time one was needed. Solving the synchronization problem that way would not have helped the overall performance, though: it is quite expensive to initialize a Random object, and continually creating instances of that class would have had worse performance than the synchronization bottleneck from many threads sharing one instance of the class.

Better performance comes from using the ThreadLocalRandom class, as is shown in Table 7-4. This example uses the batching stock application, and either creates a new instance of a Random object or reuses a ThreadLocalRandom for each stock.

Table 7-4. Effect of ThreadLocalRandom on stock calculations

Number of stocks	Allocate new Random	Reuse ThreadLocalRandom
1	0.174 seconds	0.175 seconds
10	0.258 seconds	0.236 seconds
100	0.564 seconds	0.49 seconds
1,000	2.308 seconds	1.916 seconds
10,000	17.32 seconds	13.55 seconds

The lesson here—and in general for object reuse—is that when initialization of objects takes a long time, don't be afraid to explore object pooling or thread-local variables to reuse those expensive-to-create objects. As always, though, strike a balance: large object pools of generic classes will most certainly lead to more performance issues than they solve. Leave these techniques to classes that are expensive to initialize, and when the number of the reused objects will be small.

Quick Summary

1. Object reuse is discouraged as a general-purpose operation but may be appropriate for small groups of objects that are expensive to initialize.

2. There are trade-offs between reusing an object via an object pool or using a thread-local variable. In general, thread-local variables are easier to work with, assuming that a one-to-one correspondence between threads and reusable objects is desired.

Weak, Soft, and Other References

Weak and soft references in Java also allow objects to be reused, though as developers, we don't always think of it in those terms. These kinds of references—which I will generally refer to as indefinite references—are more frequently used to cache the result of a long calculation or a database lookup rather than to reuse a simple object. For example, in the stock servlet, an indirect reference could be used to cache the result of the getHistory() method (which entails either a lengthy calculation or a long database call). That result is just an object, and when it is cached via an indefinite reference, we are simply reusing the object because it is otherwise expensive to initialize.

A Note on Terminology

Discussing weak and soft references can be confusing because so much of the terminology uses similar words. Here's a quick primer on that terminology:

Reference
> A reference (or object reference) is any kind of reference: strong, weak, soft, and so on. An ordinary instance variable that refers to an object is a strong reference.

Indefinite reference
> This is the term I use to distinguish between a strong reference and other, special kinds of references (e.g., soft or weak). An indefinite reference is actually an instance of an object (e.g., an instance of the SoftReference class).

Referent
> Indefinite references work by embedding another reference (almost always a strong reference) within an instance of the indefinite reference class. The encapsulated object is called the referent.

Still, to many programmers this "feels" different. In fact, even the terminology reflects that: no one speaks of "caching" a thread for reuse, but we will explore the reuse of indefinite references in terms of caching the result of database operations.

The advantage to an indefinite reference over an object pool or a thread-local variable is that indefinite references will be (eventually) reclaimed by the garbage collector. If an object pool contains the last 10,000 stock lookups that have been performed and the heap starts running low, the application is out of luck: whatever heap space remains after those 10,000 elements are stored is all the remaining heap the application can use. If those lookups are stored via indefinite references, the JVM can free up some space (depending on the type of reference), giving better GC throughput.

The disadvantage is that indefinite references have a slightly greater effect on the efficiency of the garbage collector. Figure 7-7 shows a side-by-side comparison of the memory used without and with an indefinite reference (in this case, a soft reference).

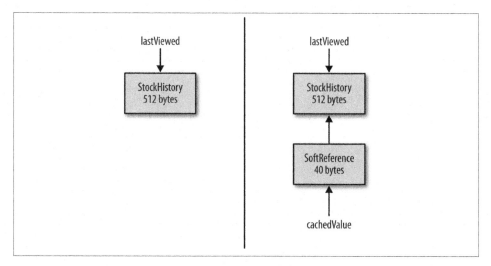

Figure 7-7. Memory allocated by indefinite reference

The object being cached occupies 512 bytes. On the left, that's all the memory consumed (absent the memory for the instance variable pointing to the object). On the right, the object is being cached inside a SoftReference object, which adds 40 additional bytes of memory consumption. Indefinite references are just like any other object: they consume memory, and other things (the cachedValue variable on the righthand side of the diagram) reference them strongly.

So the first impact on the garbage collector is that indefinite references cause the application to use more memory. A bigger impact on the garbage collector is that it takes at least two GC cycles for the indefinite reference object to be reclaimed by the garbage collector.

Figure 7-8 shows what happens when a referent is no longer strongly referenced (i.e., the lastViewed variable has been set to null). If there are no references to the Stock History object, it is freed during the next GC. So the left side of the diagram now consumes 0 bytes.

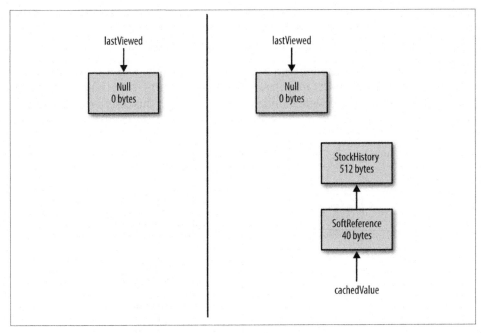

Figure 7-8. Indefinite references retain memory through GC cycles

On the righthand side of the diagram, memory is still consumed. The exact point at which the referent gets freed varies by the type of the indefinite reference, but for now let's take the case of a soft reference. The referent will stick around until the JVM decides that the object has not been used recently enough. When that happens, the first GC cycle frees the referent—but not the indefinite reference object itself. The application ends up with the memory state shown in Figure 7-9.

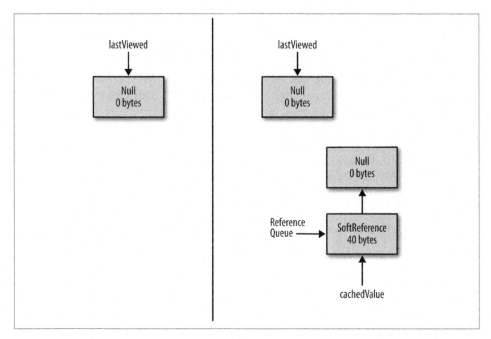

Figure 7-9. Indefinite references are not cleared immediately

The indefinite reference object itself now has (at least) two strong references to it: the original strong reference(s) created by the application, and a new strong reference (created by the JVM) on a reference queue. All of these strong references must be cleared before the indefinite reference object itself can be reclaimed by the garbage collector.

Typically this cleanup is done by whatever code is processing the reference queue. That code will get notified that there is a new object on the queue and immediately remove all strong references to that object. Then, during the next GC cycle, the indefinite reference object will get freed. In the worst case, that reference queue will not be processed immediately, and there can be many GC cycles before everything is cleaned up. Even in the best case, though, the indefinite reference has to go through two GC cycles before it is freed.

Depending on the type of indefinite reference, there are some important variations to this general algorithm, but all indefinite references have this penalty to some degree.

Soft references

Soft references are used when the object in question has a good chance of being reused in the future, but you want to let the garbage collector reclaim the object if it hasn't been used very recently (a calculation that also takes into consideration how much memory the heap has available). Soft references are essentially one large, least recently used (LRU) object pool. The key to getting good performance from them is to make sure that they are cleared on a timely basis.

Here is an example. The stock servlet can set up a global cache of stock histories keyed by their symbol (or symbol and date). When a request comes in for the stock history of TPKS from 6/1/13 to 8/31/13, the cache can be consulted to see if the result from a similar request is already there.

The reason to cache that data is that requests tend to come in for certain items more often than for others. If TPKS is the most requested stock, it can be expected to remain in the soft reference cache. On the other hand, a lone request for KENG will live in the cache for a while but eventually be reclaimed. This also accounts for requests over time: a cluster of requests for DNLD can reuse the result from the first request. As users realize that DNLD is a bad investment, those cached items will eventually age out of the heap.

When, exactly, is a soft reference freed? First the referent must not be strongly referenced elsewhere. If the soft reference is the only remaining reference to its referent, the referent is freed during the next GC cycle only if the soft reference has not recently been accessed. Specifically, the equation functions like this pseudocode:

```
long ms = SoftRefLRUPolicyMSPerMB * AmountOfFreeMemoryInMB;
if (now - last_access_to_reference > ms)
    free the reference
```

There are two key values here. The first is set by the `-XX:SoftRefLRUPolicyMSPerMB=N` flag, which has a default value of 1,000.

The second value is the amount of free memory in the heap (once the GC cycle has completed). Since the heap is sized dynamically, the JVM has two choices when it calculates how much memory in the heap is free: the free memory in the heap at its current size, or the free memory in the heap if it were to expand to its maximum capacity. The choice of those values is determined by the compiler in use. The client compiler bases that value on the available memory in the current heap, while the server compiler uses the maximum possible size of the heap.

So how does that all work? Take the example of a JVM using the server compiler and a 4 GB heap. After a full GC (or a concurrent cycle), the heap might be 50% occupied; the free heap is therefore 2 GB. The default value of `SoftRefLRUPolicyMSPerMB` (1,000) means that any soft reference that has not been used for the past 2,048 seconds (2,048,000 ms) will be cleared: the free heap is 2,048 (in megabytes), which is multiplied by 1,000:

```
long ms = 2048000; // 1000 * 2048
if (System.currentTimeMillis() - last_access_to_reference_in_ms > ms)
    free the reference
```

If the 4 GB heap is 75% occupied, objects not accessed in the last 1,024 seconds are reclaimed, and so on.

To reclaim soft references more frequently, decrease the value of the `SoftRefLRU PolicyMSPerMB` flag. Setting that value to 500 means that a JVM with a 4 GB heap that is 75% full will reclaim objects not accessed in the past 512 seconds.

Tuning this flag is often necessary if the heap fills up quickly with soft references. Say that the heap has 2 GB free and the application starts to create soft references. If it creates 1.7 GB of soft references in less than 2,048 seconds (roughly 34 minutes), none of those soft references will be eligible to be reclaimed. There will be only 300 MB of space left in the heap for other objects; GC will occur quite frequently as a result (yielding very bad overall performance).

If the JVM completely runs out of memory or starts thrashing too severely, it will clear all soft references, since the alternative would be to throw an `OutOfMemoryError`. Not throwing the error is good, but indiscriminately throwing away all the cached results is probably not ideal. Hence, another time to lower the `SoftRefLRUPolicyMSPerMB` value is when the reference processing GC logs indicates that a very large number of soft references are being cleared unexpectedly. As discussed in "GC overhead limit reached" on page 187, that will only occur after four consecutive full GC cycles (and only if other factors apply).

On the other side of the spectrum, a long-running application can consider raising that value if two conditions are met:

- There is a lot of free heap available.
- The soft references are infrequently accessed.

That is a quite unusual situation. It is similar to a situation discussed about setting GC policies: you may think that if the soft reference policy value is increased that you are telling the JVM to discard soft references only as a last resort. That is true, but you've also told the JVM not to leave any headroom in the heap for normal operations, and you are quite likely to end up spending too much time in GC instead.

The caution, then, is not to use too many soft references, since they can easily fill up the entire heap. This caution is even stronger than the caution against creating an object pool with too many instances: soft references work well when the number of objects is not too large. Otherwise, consider a more traditional object pool with a bounded size, implemented as an LRU cache.

Weak references

Weak references should be used when the referent in question will be used by several threads simultaneously. Otherwise, the weak reference is too likely to be reclaimed by the garbage collector: objects that are only weakly referenced are reclaimed at every GC cycle.

What that means is that weak references never get into the state shown (for soft references) in Figure 7-8. When the strong references are removed, the weak reference is immediately freed. Hence the program state moves directly from Figure 7-7 to Figure 7-9.

The interesting effect here, though, is where the weak reference ends up in the heap. Reference objects are just like other Java objects: they are created in the young generation and eventually promoted to the old generation. If the referent of the weak reference is freed while the weak reference itself is still in the young generation, the weak reference will be freed quickly (at the next minor GC). (This assumes that the reference queue is quickly processed for the object in question.) If the referent remains around long enough for the weak reference to be promoted into the old generation, then the weak reference will not be freed until the next concurrent or full GC cycle.

Using the cache of the stock servlet as an example, let's say we know that if a particular user accesses TPKS during her session, she is almost always likely to access it again. It makes sense to keep the values for that stock as a strong reference in the user's HTTP session: it will always be there for her, and as soon as she logs out, the HTTP session is cleared and the memory reclaimed.

Now when another user comes along and needs data for TPKS, how will they find it? Since the object is in memory somewhere, we don't want to look it up again, but the servlet code can't search the session data for other users to find it. So in addition to keeping a strong reference to the TPKS data in the first user's HTTP session, it makes sense to keep a weak reference to that data in a global cache. Now the second user will be able to find the TPKS data—assuming that the first user has not logged out and cleared her session. (This is the scenario used in the heap analysis section of this chapter where the data had two references and wasn't easily found by looking at objects with the largest retained memory.)

This is what is meant by simultaneous access. It is as if we are saying to the JVM: "Hey, as long as someone else is interested in this object, let me know where it is, but if they no longer need it, throw it away and I will re-create it myself." Compare that to a soft reference, which essentially says: "Hey, try and keep this around as long as there is enough memory and as long as it seems that someone is occasionally accessing it."

Not understanding this distinction is the most frequent performance issue that occurs when using weak references. Don't make the mistake of thinking that a weak reference is just like a soft reference except that it is freed more quickly: a softly referenced object will be available for (usually) minutes or even hours, but a weakly referenced object will be available only for as long as its referent is still around (subject to the next GC cycle clearing it).

Indefinite References and Collections

Collection classes are frequently the source of memory leaks in Java: an application puts objects into (for example) a HashMap object and never removes them. Over time, the hashmap grows ever larger, consuming the heap.

One way developers like to handle this situation is with a collection class that holds indefinite references. The JDK provides two such classes: WeakHashMap and WeakIdentityMap. Custom collection classes based on soft (and other) references are available from many third-party sources (including sample implementations of JSR 166, such as the one used for the examples of how to create and store canonical objects).

Using these classes is convenient, but be aware that they have two costs. First, as discussed throughout this section, indefinite references can have a negative effect on the garbage collector. Second, the class itself must periodically perform an operation to clear all the unreferenced data in the collection (i.e., that class is responsible for processing the reference queue of the indefinite references it stores).

The WeakHashMap, class, for instance, uses weak references for its keys. When the weakly referenced key is no longer available, the WeakHashMap code must clear out the value in the map that used to be associated with that key. That operation is carried out every time the map is referenced: the reference queue for the weak key is processed, and the value associated with any key on the reference queue is removed from the map.

There are two performance implications to that. The first is that the weak reference and its associated value won't actually be freed until the map is used again. So if the map is used infrequently, it means that the memory associated with the map won't be freed as quickly as desired.

Second, it means that the performance of operations on the map are unpredictable. Normally, operations on a hashmap are quite fast; that's why the hashmap is so popular. The operation on a WeakHashMap immediately after a GC will have to process the reference queue; that operation no longer has a fixed, short time. So even if the keys are freed somewhat infrequently, performance will be difficult to predict. Worse, if the keys in the map are freed quite frequently, the performance of the WeakHashMap can be quite bad.

Collections based on indefinite references can be useful, but they should be approached with caution. If it is feasible, have the application manage the collection itself.

Finalizers and final references

Every Java class has a finalize() method inherited from the Object class; that method can used to clean up data once the object is eligible for GC. That sounds like a nice feature, and it is required in a few circumstances. In practice, it turns out to be a bad idea, and you should try very hard not to use this method.

Finalizers are bad for functional reasons, and they are also bad for performance. Finalizers are actually a special case of an indefinite reference: the JVM uses a private reference class (java.lang.ref.Finalizer, which in turn is a java.lang.ref.Final Reference) to keep track of objects that have defined a finalize() method. When an object that has a finalize() method is allocated, the JVM allocates two objects: the object itself, and a Finalizer reference that uses the object as its referent.

As with other indefinite references, it takes at least two GC cycles before the indefinite reference object can be freed. However, the penalty here is much greater than with other indefinite reference types. When the referent of a soft or weak reference is eligible for GC, the referent itself is immediately freed; that leads to the memory use previously shown in Figure 7-9. The weak or soft reference is placed on the reference queue, but the reference object no longer refers to anything (that is, its get() method returns null rather than the original referent). In the case of soft and weak references, the two-cycle penalty for GC applies only to the reference object itself (and not the referent).

This is not the case for final references. The implementation of the Finalizer class must have access to the referent in order to call the referent's finalize() method, so the referent cannot be freed when the finalizer reference is placed on its reference queue. When the referent of a finalizer becomes eligible for collection, the program state is reflected by Figure 7-10.

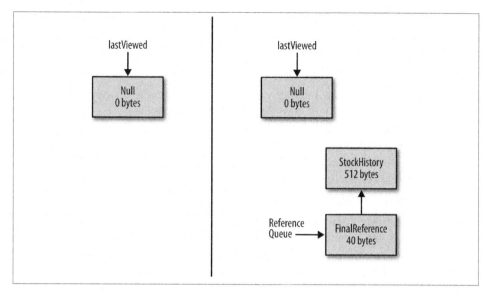

Figure 7-10. Finalizer references retain more memory

When the reference queue processes the finalizer, the Finalizer object (as usual) will be removed from the queue and then eligible for collection. Only then will the referent also be freed. This is why finalizers have a much greater performance effect on GC than other indefinite references—the memory consumed by the referent can be much more significant than the memory consumed by the indefinite reference object.

This leads to the functional problem with finalizers, which is that the finalize() method can inadvertently create a new strong reference to the referent. That again causes a GC performance penalty: now the referent won't be freed until it is no longer strongly referenced again. And functionally it creates a big problem, because the next time the referent is eligible to be collected, its finalize() method won't be called, and the expected cleanup of the referent won't happen. This kind of error is reason enough why finalizers should be used as seldom as possible.

Unfortunately, finalizers are unavoidable in certain circumstances. The JDK, for example, uses a finalizer in its classes that manipulate ZIP files, because opening a ZIP file uses some native code that allocates native memory. That memory is freed when the ZIP file is closed, but what happens if the developer forgets to call the close() method? The finalizer can ensure that the close() method has been called, even if the developer forgets that.

As a rule, then, if you are in a situation where a finalizer is unavoidable, make sure that the memory accessed by the object is kept to a minimum.

There is an alternative to using finalizers that avoids at least some of these problems—and in particular, it allows the referent to be freed during normal GC operations. This is accomplished by simply using another kind of indefinite reference rather than implicitly using a `Finalizer` reference.

It is sometimes recommended to use yet another indefinite reference type for this: the `PhantomReference` class. That's a good choice, because the reference object will be cleaned up relatively quickly once the referent is no longer strongly referenced, and while debugging, the purpose of the reference is clear. Still, the same goal can be achieved with a weak reference (plus, the weak reference can be used in more places). And in certain circumstances, a soft reference could be used if the caching semantics of the soft reference match the need of the application.

To create a substitute finalizer, you must create a subclass of the indefinite reference class to hold any information that needs to be cleaned up after the referent has been collected. Then you perform the cleanup in a method of the reference object (as opposed to defining a `finalize()` method in the referent class).

```
private static class CleanupFinalizer extends WeakReference {

    private static ReferenceQueue<CleanupFinalizer> finRefQueue;
    private static HashSet<CleanupFinalizer> pendingRefs = new HashSet<>();

    private boolean closed = false;

    public CleanupFinalizer(Object o) {
        super(o, finRefQueue);
        allocateNative();
        pendingRefs.add(this);
    }

    public void setClosed() {
        closed = true;
        doNativeCleanup();
    }

    public void cleanup() {
        if (!closed) {
            doNativeCleanup();
        }
    }

    private native void allocateNative();
    private native void doNativeCleanup();
}
```

Here is the outline of such a class, which uses a weak reference. The constructor here allocates some native resource. Under normal usage, the `setClosed()` method is expected to be called; that will clean up the native memory.

However, the weak reference is also placed on a reference queue. When the reference is pulled from the queue, it can check to make sure the native memory has been cleaned up (and clean it if it has not).

Processing of the reference queue happens in a daemon thread:

```
static {
    finRefQueue = new ReferenceQueue<>();
    Runnable r = new Runnable() {
        public void run() {
            CleanupFinalizer fr;
            while (true) {
                try {
                    fr = (CleanupFinalizer) finRefQueue.remove();
                    fr.cleanup();
                    pendingRefs.remove(fr);
                } catch (Exception ex) {
                    Logger.getLogger(
                            CleanupFinalizer.class.getName()).
                            log(Level.SEVERE, null, ex);
                }
            }
        }
    };
    Thread t = new Thread(r);
    t.setDaemon(true);
    t.start();
}
```

All of that is in a `private static` inner class hidden from the developer using the actual class, which looks like this:

```
public class CleanupExample {
    private CleanupFinalizer cf;
    private HashMap data = new HashMap();

    public CleanupExample() {
        cf = new CleanupFinalizer(this);
    }

    ...methods to put things into the hashmap...

    public void close() {
        data = null;
        cf.setClosed();
    }
}
```

Developers construct this object just as they would any other object. They are told to call the `close()` method, which will clean up the native memory—but if they don't, it's OK. The weak reference still exists behind the scenes, so the `CleanupFinalizer` class has its own chance to clean up that memory when the inner class processes the weak reference.

The one tricky part of this example is the need for the `pendingRefs` set of weak references. Without that, the weak references themselves will be collected before there is the chance to put them onto the reference queue.

This example overcomes two limitations of the traditional finalizer: it offers better performance, because the memory associated with the referent object (the `data` hashmap in this case) is released as soon as the referent is collected (rather than doing that in the `finalizer()` method). And there is no way for the referent object to be resurrected in the cleanup code, since it has already been collected.

Still, other objections that apply to the use of finalizers apply to this code as well: you can't ensure the garbage collector will ever get around to freeing the referent, nor that the reference queue thread will ever process any particular object on the queue. If there are a large number of these objects, processing that reference queue will be quite expensive. Like all indefinite references, this example should still be used sparingly.

The Finalizer Queue

The finalizer queue is the reference queue used to process the `Finalizer` references when the referent is eligible for GC.

When performing heap dump analysis, it is often convenient to make sure that there are no objects on the finalizer queue: those objects are about to be freed anyway, so eliminating them from the heap dump will make it easier to see what else is occurring in the heap. You can cause the finalizer queue to be processed by executing this command:

```
% jcmd process_id GC.run_finalization
```

To monitor the finalizer queue to see if it might be an issue for an application, look for its size (which is updated in real time) on the VM Summary tab of `jconsole`. Scripts can gather that information by running this command:

```
% jmap -finalizerinfo process_id
```

Quick Summary

1. Indefinite (soft, weak, phantom, and final) references alter the ordinary lifecycle of Java objects, allowing them to be reused in ways that may be more GC-friendly than pools or thread-local variables.

2. Weak references should be used when an application is interested in an object only if that object is strongly referenced elsewhere in the application.

3. Soft references hold onto objects for (possibly) long periods of time, providing a simple GC-friendly LRU cache.

4. Indefinite references consume their own memory and hold onto memory of other objects for long periods of time; they should be used sparingly.

Summary

Fast Java programs depend crucially on memory management. Tuning GC is important, but to obtain maximum performance, memory must be utilized effectively within applications.

Current hardware trends tend to dissuade developers from thinking about memory: if my laptop has 16 GB of memory, how concerned need I be with an object that has an extra, unused 8-byte object reference? And we forget that the normal time/space trade-off of programming can swing to a time/space-and-time trade-off: using too much space in the heap can make things slower by requiring more GC. In Java, managing the heap is still important.

Much of that management centers around when and how to use special memory techniques: object pools, thread-local variables, and indefinite references. Judicious use of these techniques can vastly improve the performance of an application, but overuse of them can just as easily degrade performance. In limited quantities—when the number of objects in question is small and bounded—the use of these memory techniques can be quite effective.

## CHAPTER 8

Native Memory Best Practices

The heap is the largest consumer of memory in a Java application, but the JVM will allocate and use a large amount of native memory. And while Chapter 7 discussed ways to efficiently manage the heap from a programmatic point of view, the configuration of the heap and how it interacts with the native memory of the operating system is another important factor in the overall performance of an application.

This chapter discusses these aspects of native (or operating system) memory. We start with a discussion of the entire memory use of the JVM, with a goal of understanding how to monitor that usage for performance issues. Then we'll discuss various ways to tune the JVM and operating system for optimal memory use.

Footprint

The heap (usually) accounts for the largest amount of memory used by the JVM, but the JVM also uses memory for its internal operations. This nonheap memory is native memory. Native memory can also be allocated in applications (via JNI calls to `malloc()` and similar methods, or when using New I/O, or NIO). The total of native and heap memory used by the JVM yields the total footprint of an application.

From the point of view of the operating system, this total footprint is the key to performance. If enough physical memory to contain the entire total footprint of an application is not available, performance may begin to suffer. The operative word here is "may." There are parts of native memory that are really only used during startup (for instance, the memory associated to load the JAR files in the classpath), and if that memory is swapped out, it won't necessarily be noticed. Some of the native memory used by one Java process is shared with other Java processes on the system, and some smaller part is shared with other kinds of processes on the system. For the most part, though, for optimal performance you want to be sure that the total footprint of all Java processes does not exceed the physical memory of the machine (plus you want to leave some memory available for other applications).

Measuring Footprint

To measure the total footprint of a process, you need to use an operating-system-specific tool. In Unix-based systems, programs like `top` and `ps` can show you that data at a basic level; on Windows, you can use `perfmon` or `VMMap`. No matter which tool and platform are used, you need to look at the actual allocated memory (as opposed to the reserved memory) of the process.

The distinction between allocated and reserved memory comes about as a result of the way the JVM (and all programs) manage memory. Consider a heap that is specified with the parameters `-Xms512m -Xmx2048m`. The heap starts by using 512 MB, and it will be resized as needed to meet the GC goals of the application.

That concept is the essential difference between committed (or allocated) memory and reserved memory (sometimes called the virtual size of a process). The JVM must tell the operating system that it might need as much as 2 GB of memory for the heap, so that memory is reserved: the operating system promises that when the JVM attempts to allocate additional memory when it increases the size of the heap, that memory will be available.

Still, only 512 MB of that memory is actually allocated initially, and that 512 MB is all of the memory that actually is being used (for the heap). That (actually allocated) memory is known as the committed memory. The amount of committed memory will fluctuate as the heap resizes; in particular, as the heap size increases, the committed memory correspondingly increases.

***

Is Over-Reserving a Problem?

When we look at performance, only committed memory really matters: there is never a performance problem from reserving too much memory.

However, sometimes you want to make sure that the JVM does not reserve too much memory. This is particularly true for 32-bit JVMs. Since the maximum process size of a 32-bit application is 4 GB (or less, depending on the operating system), over-reserving memory can be an issue. A JVM that reserves 3.5 GB of memory for the heap is left with only 0.5 GB of native memory for its stacks, code cache, and so on. It doesn't matter if the heap only expands to commit 1 GB of memory: because of the 3.5 GB reservation, the amount of memory for other operations is limited to 0.5 GB.

64-bit JVMs aren't limited that way by the process size, but they are limited by the total amount of virtual memory on the machine. Say that you have a small server with 4 GB of physical memory and 10 GB of virtual memory and start a JVM with a maximum

***

heap size of 6 GB. That will reserve 6 GB of virtual memory (plus more for nonheap memory sections). Regardless of how large that heap actually grows (and the memory that is actually committed), a second JVM will only be able to reserve less than 4 GB of memory on that machine.

All things being equal, it's convenient to oversize JVM structures and let the JVM optimally use that memory. But it isn't always feasible.

This difference applies to almost all significant memory that the JVM allocates. The code cache grows from an initial to a maximum value as more code gets compiled. Permgen or metaspace is allocated separately and grows between its initial (committed) size and its maximum (reserved) size.

One exception to this is thread stacks. Every time the JVM creates a thread, the OS allocates some native memory to hold that thread's stack, committing more memory to the process (until the thread exits, at least). Thread stacks, though, are fully allocated when they are created.

In Unix systems, the actual footprint of an application can be estimated by the resident set size (RSS) of the process as reported by various OS tools. That value is a good estimate of the amount of committed memory a process is using, though it is inexact in two ways. First, the few pages that are shared at the OS level between JVM and other processes (that is, the text portions of shared libraries) are counted in the RSS of each process. Second, a process may have committed more memory than it actually paged in at any moment. Still, tracking the RSS of a process is a good first-pass way to monitor the total memory use. On more recent Linux kernels, the PSS is a refinement of the RSS that removes the data shared by other programs.

On Windows systems, the equivalent idea is called the working set of an application, which is what is reported by the task manager.

Minimizing Footprint

To minimize the footprint used by the JVM, limit the amount of memory used by the following:

Heap

The heap is the biggest chunk of memory, though surprisingly it may take up only 50% to 60% of the total footprint. Using a smaller maximum heap (or setting the GC tuning parameters such that the heap never fully expands) limits the program's footprint.

Thread stacks

Thread stacks are quite large, particularly for a 64-bit JVM. See Chapter 9 for ways to limit the amount of memory consumed by thread stacks.

Code cache

The code cache uses native memory to hold compiled code. As discussed in Chapter 4, this can be tuned (though performance will suffer if all the code cannot be compiled due to space limitations).

Direct byte buffers

These are discussed in the next section.

Native NIO Buffers

Developers can allocate native memory via JNI calls, but NIO byte buffers will also allocate native memory if they are created via the `allocateDirect()` method. Native byte buffers are quite important from a performance perspective, since they allow native code and Java code to share data without copying it. The most common example here is buffers that are used for filesystem and socket operations. Writing data to a native NIO buffer and then sending that data to the channel (e.g., the file or socket) requires no copying of data between the JVM and the C library used to transmit the data. If a heap byte buffer is used instead, contents of the buffer must be copied by the JVM.

The `allocateDirect()` method call is quite expensive; direct byte buffers should be reused as much as possible. The ideal situation is when threads are independent and each can keep a direct byte buffer as a thread-local variable. That can sometimes use too much native memory if there are many threads that need buffers of variable sizes, since eventually each thread will end up with a buffer at the maximum possible size. For that kind of situation—or when thread-local buffers don't fit the application design—an object pool of direct byte buffers may be more useful.

Byte buffers can also be managed by slicing them. The application can allocate one very large direct byte buffer, and individual requests can allocate a portion out of that buffer using the `slice()` method of the `ByteBuffer` class. This solution can become unwieldy when the slices are not always the same size: the original byte buffer can then become fragmented in the same way the heap becomes fragmented when allocating and freeing objects of different sizes. Unlike the heap, however, the individual slices of a byte buffer cannot be compacted, so this solution really works well only when all the slices are a uniform size.

From a tuning perspective, the one thing to realize with any of these programming models is that the amount of direct byte buffer space that an application can allocate can be limited by the JVM. The total amount of memory that can be allocated for direct byte buffers is specified by setting the `-XX:MaxDirectMemorySize=N` flag. Starting in Java 7, the default value for this flag is 0, which means there is no limit (subject to the address space size and any operating system limits on the process). That flag can be set to limit the direct byte buffer use of an application (and to provide compatibility with previous releases of Java, where the limit was 64 MB).

Quick Summary

1. The total footprint of the JVM has a significant effect on its performance, particularly if physical memory on the machine is constrained. Footprint is another aspect of performance tests that should be commonly monitored.

2. From a tuning perspective, the footprint of the JVM can be limited in the amount of native memory it uses for direct byte buffers, thread stack sizes, and the code cache (as well as the heap).

Native Memory Tracking

Beginning in Java 8, the JVM allows some visibility into how it allocates native memory when using this option: -XX:NativeMemoryTracking=*off*|*summary*|*detail*. By default, Native Memory Tracking (NMT) is off. If the summary or detail mode is enabled, you can get the native memory information at any time from jcmd:

```
% jcmd process_id VM.native_memory summary
```

If the JVM is started with the argument -XX:+PrintNMTStatistics (by default, false), the JVM will print out information about the allocation when the program exits.

Here is the summary output from a JVM running with a 512 MB initial heap size and a 4 GB maximum heap size:

```
Native Memory Tracking:

  Total:  reserved=4787210KB,  committed=1857677KB
```

Although the JVM has made memory reservations totaling 4.7 GB, it has used much less than that: only 1.8 GB total. This is fairly typical (and one reason not to pay particular attention to the virtual size of the process displayed in OS tools, since that reflects only the memory reservations).

This memory usage breaks down as follows:

```
-              Java Heap (reserved=4296704KB, committed=1470428KB)
                        (mmap: reserved=4296704KB, committed=1470428KB)
```

The heap itself is (unsurprisingly) the largest part of the reserved memory at 4 GB. But the dynamic sizing of the heap meant it grew only to 1.4 GB.

```
-              Class (reserved=65817KB, committed=60065KB)
                     (classes #19378)
                     (malloc=6425KB, #14245)
                     (mmap: reserved=59392KB, committed=53640KB)
```

This is the native memory used to hold class metadata. Again, note that the JVM has reserved more memory than it actually used to hold the 19,378 classes in the program.

```
-              Thread (reserved=84455KB, committed=84455KB)
                      (thread #77)
                      (stack: reserved=79156KB, committed=79156KB)
                      (malloc=243KB, #314)
                      (arena=5056KB, #154)
```

Seventy-seven thread stacks were allocated at about 1 MB each.

```
-              Code (reserved=102581KB, committed=15221KB)
                      (malloc=2741KB, #4520)
                      (mmap: reserved=99840KB, committed=12480KB)
```

This is the JIT code cache: 19,378 classes is not very many, so just a small section of the code cache is committed.

```
-              GC (reserved=183268KB, committed=173156KB)
                      (malloc=5768KB, #110)
                      (mmap: reserved=177500KB, committed=167388KB)
```

These are areas outside the heap that GC algorithms use for their processing.

```
-              Compiler (reserved=162KB, committed=162KB)
                      (malloc=63KB, #229)
                      (arena=99KB, #3)
```

Similarly, this area is used by the compiler for its operations, apart from the resulting code placed in the code cache.

```
-              Symbol (reserved=12093KB, committed=12093KB)
                      (malloc=10039KB, #110773)
                      (arena=2054KB, #1)
```

Interned String references and symbol table references are held here.

```
-              Memory Tracking (reserved=22466KB, committed=22466KB)
                      (malloc=22466KB, #1872)
```

NMT itself needs some space for its operation.

Detailed Memory Tracking Information

If the JVM is started with -XX:NativeMemoryTracking=detail, then jcmd (with a final detail argument) will provide very detailed information about the native memory allocation. That includes a map of the entire memory space, which includes lines like this:

```
0x00000006c0000000 - 0x00000007c0000000] reserved 4194304KB for Java Heap
        from [ReservedSpace::initialize(unsigned long, unsigned long,
                          bool, char*, unsigned long, bool)+0xc2]
        [0x00000006c0000000 - 0x00000006fb100000] committed 967680KB
            from [PSVirtualSpace::expand_by(unsigned long)+0x53]
        [0x000000076ab00000 - 0x00000007c0000000] committed 1397760KB
            from [PSVirtualSpace::expand_by(unsigned long)+0x53]
```

The 4 GB of heap space was reserved in the `initialize()` function, with two allocations from that actually made in the `expand_by()` function.

That kind of information is repeated for the entire process space. It provides really interesting clues if you are a JVM engineer, but for the rest of us, the summary information is useful enough.

NMT provides two keys pieces of information:

Total committed size

The total committed size of the process is the actual amount of physical memory that the process will consume. This is close to the RSS (or working set) of the application, but those OS-provided measurements don't include any memory that has been committed but paged out of the process. In fact, if the RSS of the process is less than the committed memory, that is often an indication that the OS is having difficulty fitting all of the JVM in physical memory.

Individual committed sizes

When it is time to tune maximum values—of the heap, the code cache, and the metaspace—it is helpful to know how much of that memory the JVM is actually using. Overallocating those areas usually leads only to harmless memory reservations, though in those cases where the reserved memory is important, NMT can help to track down where those maximum sizes can be trimmed.

NMT over time

NMT also allows you to track how memory allocations occur over time. After the JVM is started with NMT enabled, you can establish a baseline for memory usage with this command:

```
% jcmd process_id VM.native_memory baseline
```

That causes the JVM to mark its current memory allocations. Later, you can compare the current memory usage to that mark:

```
% jcmd process_id VM.native_memory summary.diff
Native Memory Tracking:

Total:  reserved=5896078KB  -3655KB, committed=2358357KB -448047KB

-            Java Heap (reserved=4194304KB, committed=1920512KB -444927KB)
                     (mmap: reserved=4194304KB, committed=1920512KB -444927KB)
....
```

In this case, the JVM has reserved 5.8 GB of memory and is presently using 2.3 GB. That committed size is 448 MB less than when the baseline was established. Similarly, the committed memory used by the heap has declined by 444 MB (and the rest of the output could be inspected to see where else the memory use declined to account for the remaining 4 MB).

This is a very useful technique to examine the footprint of the JVM over time.

Quick Summary

1. Available in Java 8, Native Memory Tracking (NMT) provides details about the native memory usage of the JVM. From an operating system perspective, that includes the JVM heap (which to the OS is just a section of native memory).

2. The summary mode of NMT is sufficient for most analysis, and allows you to determine how much memory the JVM has committed (and what that memory is used for).

JVM Tunings for the Operating System

There are several tunings that the JVM can use to improve the way in which it uses OS memory.

Large Pages

Discussions about memory allocation and swapping occur in terms of pages. A page is a unit of memory by which operating systems manage physical memory. It is the minimum unit of allocation for the operating system: when 1 byte is allocated, the operating system must allocate an entire page. Further allocations for that program come from that same page until it is filled, at which point a new page is allocated.

The operating system allocates many more pages than can fit in physical memory, which is why there is paging: pages of the address space are moved to and from swap space (or other storage depending on what the page contains). This means there must be some mapping between these pages and where they are currently stored in the computer's RAM. Those mappings are handled in two different ways. All page mappings are held in a global page table (which the OS can scan to find a particular mapping), and the most frequently used mappings are held in translation lookaside buffers (TLBs). TLBs are held in a fast cache, so accessing pages through a TLB entry is much faster than accessing it through the the page table.

Machines have a limited number of TLB entries, so it becomes important to maximize the hit rate on TLB entries (it functions as a least recently used cache). Since each entry represents a page of memory, it is often advantageous to increase the page size used by an application. If each page represents more memory, fewer TLB entries are required to encompass the entire program, and it is more likely that a page will be found in the TLB when required. This is true in general for any program, and so is also true in specific for things like Java application servers or other Java programs with even a moderately sized heap.

Java supports this with the `-XX:+UseLargePages` option. The default value of this flag varies depending on the operating system configuration. On Windows, large pages must be enabled in the OS. In Windows terms, this means giving individual users the ability to lock pages into memory, which is possible only on server versions of Windows. Even so, the JVM on Windows defaults to using regular pages unless the `UseLargePages` flag is explicitly enabled.

On Linux, the `UseLargePages` flags is not enabled by default, and the OS must also be configured to support large pages.

On Solaris, no OS configuration is required, and large pages are enabled by default.

If the `UseLargePages` flag is enabled on a system that does not support large pages, no warning is given and the JVM uses regular pages. If the `UseLargePages` flag is enabled on a system that does support large pages, but for which no large pages are available (either because they are already all in use or because the operating system is misconfigured), the JVM will print a warning.

Linux huge (large) pages

Linux refers to large pages as huge pages. The configuration of huge pages on Linux varies somewhat from release to release; for the most accurate instructions, consult the documentation for your release. But the general procedure for Linux 5 is this:

1. Determine which huge page sizes the kernel supports. The size is based on the computer's processor and the boot parameters given when the kernel has started, but the most common value is 2 MB:

   ```
   # grep Hugepagesize /proc/meminfo
   Hugepagesize:    2048 kB
   ```

2. Figure out how many huge pages are needed. If a JVM will allocate a 4 GB heap and the system has 2 MB huge pages, 2,048 huge pages will be needed for that heap. The number of huge pages that can be used is defined globally in the Linux kernel, so repeat this process for all the JVMs that will run (plus any other programs that will use huge pages). You should overestimate this value by 10% to account for other nonheap uses of huge pages (so the example here uses 2,200 huge pages).

3. Write out that value to the operating system (so it takes effect immediately):

   ```
   # echo 2200 > /proc/sys/vm/nr_hugepages
   ```

4. Save that value in */etc/sysctl.conf* so that it is preserved after rebooting:

   ```
   sys.nr_hugepages=2200
   ```

5. On many versions of Linux, the amount of huge page memory that a user can allocate is limited. Edit the */etc/security/limits.conf* file and add `memlock` entries for the user running your JVMs (e.g., in the example, the user `appuser`):

```
appuser soft    memlock         4613734400
appuser hard    memlock         4613734400
```

If the *limits.conf* file is modified, the user must log in again for the value to take effect. At this point, the JVM should be able to allocate the necessary huge pages. To verify that it works, run the following command:

```
# java -Xms4G -Xmx4G -XX:+UseLargePages -version
java version "1.7.0_17"
Java(TM) SE Runtime Environment (build 1.7.0_17-b02)
Java HotSpot(TM) 64-Bit Server VM (build 23.7-b01, mixed mode)
```

Successful completion of that command indicates that the huge pages are configured correctly. If the huge page memory configuration is not correct, a warning will be given:

```
Java HotSpot(TM) 64-Bit Server VM warning:
Failed to reserve shared memory (errno = 22).
```

Linux transparent huge pages

Linux kernels starting with version 2.6.32 support transparent huge pages, which obviate the need for the configuration described above. Transparent large pages must still be enabled for Java, which is done by changing the contents of */sys/kernel/mm/transparent_hugepage/enabled*:

```
# cat /sys/kernel/mm/transparent_hugepage/enabled
always [madvise] never
# echo always > /sys/kernel/mm/transparent_hugepage/enabled
# cat /sys/kernel/mm/transparent_hugepage/enabled
[always] madvise never
```

The default value in that file (shown in the output for the first command) is `madvise`—huge pages are used only for programs that explicitly advise the kernel they will be using huge pages. The JVM does not issue that advisory, so the default value must be set to `always` (by issuing the second command). Be aware this affects the JVM and any other programs run on the system; they will all run with huge pages.

If transparent large pages are enabled, do not specify the `UseLargePages` flag. If that flag is explicitly set, the JVM will return to using traditional huge pages if they are configured, or standard pages if traditional huge pages are not configured. If the flag is left to its default value, then the transparent huge pages will be used (if they have been configured).

Windows large pages

Windows large pages can only be enabled on server-based Windows versions. Exact instructions for Windows 7 are given here; there will be some variations between releases.

1. Start the Microsoft Management Center. Press the Start button and in the Search box, type mmc.

2. If the lefthand panel does not display a Local Computer Policy icon, select "Add/ Remove Snap-in" from the File menu and add the Group Policy Object Editor. If that option is not available, then the version of Windows in use does not support large pages.

3. In the lefthand panel, expand Local Computer Policy → Computer Configuration → Windows Settings → Security Settings → Local Policies and click on the User Rights Assignment folder.

4. In the righthand panel, double-click on "Lock pages in memory."

5. In the pop up, add the user or group.

6. Click OK.

7. Quit the MMC.

8. Reboot.

At this point, the JVM should be able to allocate the necessary large pages. To verify that it works, run the following command:

```
# java -Xms4G -Xmx4G -XX:+UseLargePages -version
java version "1.7.0_17"
Java(TM) SE Runtime Environment (build 1.7.0_17-b02)
Java HotSpot(TM) 64-Bit Server VM (build 23.7-b01, mixed mode)
```

If the command completes successfully like that, large pages are set up correctly. If the large memory configuration is incorrect, a warning is given:

```
Java HotSpot(TM) Server VM warning: JVM cannot use large page memory
because it does not have enough privilege to lock pages in memory.
```

Remember that the command will not print an error on a Windows system (such as "home" versions) that does not support large pages: once the JVM finds out that large pages are not supported on the OS, it sets the UseLargePages flag to false, regardless of the command-line setting.

Large page sizes

On most Linux and Windows systems, the OS uses 2 MB large pages, but that number can vary depending on the operating system configuration.

Strictly speaking, it is the processor that defines the possible page sizes. Most current Intel and SPARC processors support a number of possible page sizes: 4 KB, 8 KB, 2 MB, 256 MB, and so on. However, the operating system determines which page sizes can actually be allocated. On Solaris, all processor page sizes are supported, and the JVM is free to allocate pages of any size. On Linux kernels (at least as of this writing), you can specify which processor-supported large page size should be used when the kernel is booted, but that is the only large page size an application can actually allocate. On Windows, the large page size is fixed (again, at least for now) at 2 MB.

To support Solaris, Java allows the size of the large pages it allocates to be set via the -XX:LargePageSizeInBytes=N flag. By default, that flag is set to 0, which means that the JVM should choose a processor-specific large page size.

That flag can be set on all platforms, and there is never any indication that the specified page size was or was not used. On a Linux system where you are allocating a very large heap, you might think you should specify -XX:LargePageSizeInBytes=256M to get the best chance of getting TLB cache hits. You can do that, and the JVM won't complain, but it will still allocate only 2 MB pages (or whatever page size the kernel is set to support). In fact, it is possible to specify page sizes that don't make any sense at all, like -XX:LargePageSizeInBytes=11111. Because that page size is unavailable, the JVM will simply use the default large page size for the platform.

So—for now at least—this flag is really useful only on Solaris. On Solaris, choose a different page size to use larger pages than the default (which is 4 MB on SPARC processors). On systems with a large amount of memory, this will increase the number of pages that will fit in the TLB cache and improve performance. To find the available page sizes on Solaris, use the pagesize -a command.

Quick Summary

1. Using large pages will usually measurably speed up applications.
2. Large page support must be explicitly enabled in most operating systems.

Compressed oops

Chapter 4 mentioned that the performance of a 32-bit JVM is anywhere from 5% to 20% faster than the performance of a 64-bit JVM for the same task. This assumes, of course, that the application can fit in a 32-bit process space, which limits the size of the heap to less than 4 GB. (In practical terms, this often means less than 3.5 GB, since the JVM needs some native memory space, and on certain versions of Windows, the limit is 3 GB.)

This performance gap is because of the 64-bit object references. The main reason for this is 64-bit references take up twice the space (8 bytes) in the heap as 32-bit references (4 bytes). That leads to more GC cycles, since there is now less room in the heap for other data.

The JVM can compensate for that additional memory by using compressed oops. "oop" stands for ordinary object pointer: oops are the handles the JVM uses as object references. When oops are only 32 bits long, they can reference only 4 GB of memory (2^{32}), which is why a 32-bit JVM is limited to a 4 GB heap size. (The same restriction applies at the operating system level, which is why any 32-bit process is limited to 4GB of address space.) When oops are 64 bits long, they can reference terabytes of memory.

There is a middle ground here: what if there were 35-bit oops? Then the pointer could reference 32 GB of memory (2^{35}) and still take up less space in the heap than 64-bit references. The problem is that there aren't 35-bit registers in which to store such references. Instead, though, the JVM can assume that the last 3 bits of the reference are all 0. Now every reference can be stored in 32 bits in the heap. When the reference is stored into a 64-bit register, the JVM can shift it left by 3 bits (adding three zeros at the end). When the reference is saved from a register, the JVM can right-shift it by 3 bits, discarding the zeros at the end.

This leaves the JVM with pointers that can reference 32 GB of memory while using only 32 bits in the heap. However it also means that the JVM cannot access any object at an address that isn't divisible by 8, since any address from a compressed oop ends with three zeros. The first possible oop is 0x1, which when shifted becomes 0x8. The next oop is 0x2, which when shifted becomes 0x10 (16). Objects must therefore be located on an 8-byte boundary.

It turns out that objects are already aligned on an 8-byte boundary in the JVM (in both the 32- and 64-bit versions); this is the optimal alignment for most processors. So nothing is lost by using compressed oops. If the first object in the JVM is stored at location 0 and occupies 57 bytes, then the next object will be stored at location 64—wasting 7 bytes that cannot be allocated. That memory trade-off is worthwhile (and will occur whether compressed oops are used or not), because the object can be accessed faster given that 8-byte alignment.

But that is the reason that the JVM doesn't try to emulate a 36-bit reference that could access 64 GB of memory. In that case, objects would have to be aligned on a 16-byte boundary, and the savings from storing the compressed pointer in the heap would be outweighed by the amount of memory that would be wasted in between the memory-aligned objects.

This has two implications. First, for heaps that are between 4 GB and 32 GB, use compressed oops. Compressed oops are enabled using the -XX:+UseCompressedOops flag; in Java 7 and later versions, they are enabled by default whenever the maximum heap size is less than 32 GB. (In "Reducing Object Size" on page 188, it was noted that the size of an object reference on a 64-bit JVM with a 32 GB heap is 4 bytes—which is the default case since compressed oops are enabled by default.)

Second, a program that uses a 31 GB heap and compressed oops will usually be faster than a program that uses a 33 GB heap. Although the 33 GB heap is larger, the extra space used by the pointers in that heap means that the larger heap will perform more frequent GC cycles and have worse performance.

Hence, it is better to use heaps that are less than 32 GB, or heaps that are at least a few GB larger than 32 GB. Once extra memory is added to the heap to make up for the space used by the uncompressed references, the number of GC cycles will be reduced. There is no hard rule there for how much memory is needed before the GC impact of the uncompressed oops is ameliorated—but given that 20% of an average heap might be used for object references, planning on at least 38 GB is a good start.

Quick Summary

1. Compressed oops are enabled by default whenever they are most useful.

2. A 31 GB heap using compressed oops will often outperform slightly larger heaps that are too big to use compressed oops.

Summary

Although the Java heap is the memory region that gets the most attention, the entire footprint of the JVM is crucial to its performance, particularly in relation to the operating system. The tools discussed in this chapter allow you to track that footprint over time (and, crucially, to focus on the committed memory of the JVM rather than the reserved memory).

Certain ways that the JVM uses OS memory—particularly large pages—can also be tuned to improve performance. Long-running JVMs will almost always benefit by using large pages, particularly if they have large heaps.

## CHAPTER 9

Threading and Synchronization Performance

From its first days, some of Java's appeal has been because it is multithreaded. Even in the days before multicore and multi-CPU systems were the norm, the ability to easily write threaded programs in Java has been considered one of its hallmark features.

In performance terms, the appeal is obvious: if two CPUs are available, then an application might be able to do twice as much work, or the same amount of work twice as fast. This assumes that the task can be broken into discrete segments, since Java is not an autoparallelizing language that will figure out the algorithmic parts. Fortunately, computing today is often about discrete tasks: a server handling simultaneous requests from discrete clients, a batch job performing the same operation on a series of data, mathematical algorithms that break into constituent parts, and so on.

This chapter explores how to get the maximum performance out of Java threading and synchronization facilities.

Thread Pools and ThreadPoolExecutors

Threads can be managed by custom code in Java, or applications can utilize a thread pool. Java EE application servers are built around the notion of one or more thread pools to handle requests: each servlet call into the server is handled by a (potentially different) thread from the pool. Similarly, other applications can use Java's ThreadPoolExecutor to execute tasks in parallel.

In fact, some Java EE application servers use instances of the ThreadPoolExecutor class to manage their tasks, though many have written their own thread pools (if only because they predate the addition of ThreadPoolExecutor to the Java API). Although the implementation of the pools in these cases might differ, the basic concepts are the same, and both are discussed in this section.

The key factor in using a thread pool is that tuning the size of the pool is crucial to getting the best performance. Thread pool performance varies depending on basic choices about thread pool size, and under certain circumstances an oversized thread pool will be quite detrimental to performance.

All thread pools work in essentially the same way: there is a queue to which tasks are submitted. (There can be more than one queue but the concept is the same.) Then some number of threads picks up tasks from the queue and executes them. The result of the task can be sent back to the client (e.g., in the case of an application server), stored in a database, stored in some internal data structure, or whatever. But after finishing the task, the thread returns to the task queue to retrieve another job to execute (and if there are no more tasks to perform, the thread waits for a task).

Thread pools have a minimum and maximum number of threads. The minimum number of threads is kept around, waiting for tasks to be assigned to them. Because creating a thread is a fairly expensive operation, this speeds up the overall operation when a task is submitted: it is expected that an already-existing thread can pick it up. On the other hand, threads require some system resources—including some native memory for their stacks—and having too many idle threads can consume resources that could be used by other processes. The maximum number of threads also serves as a necessary throttle, preventing too many tasks from executing at once.

The ThreadPoolExecutor and related classes refer to the minimum number of threads as the *core pool size*, while most application servers use some term similar to minimum (e.g., MinThreads). Don't let the terminology confuse you: they are the same concept. However, there are key differences in the way a ThreadPoolExecutor determines when to resize a pool and the way in which most Java EE application servers determine when to resize a pool. Those differences will be explored later in this section. For now, consider the simplest case of the ThreadPoolExecutor, which is also the way most Java EE application servers work: if there is a task to be executed, and all current threads are busy executing another task, a new thread is started (until the maximum number of threads has been created).

Setting the Maximum Number of Threads

Let's address the maximum number of threads first: what is the optimal maximum number of threads for a given workload on given hardware? There is no simple answer to this; it depends on characteristics of the workload and the hardware on which it is run. In particular, the optimal number of threads depends on how often each individual task will block.

For the sake of discussion, assume there are four CPUs that are available to the JVM. It doesn't matter if there are only four CPUs on the system, or if there are 128 hardware threads but you want to utilize only 4 of them: the goal is to maximize the CPU usage of those four CPUs.

Clearly, then, the maximum number of threads must be set to at least four. Granted, there are threads in the JVM doing things other than processing these tasks, but these threads will almost never need an entire CPU. One exception is if a concurrent mode garbage collector is being used as discussed in Chapter 5—the background threads there must have enough CPU to operate, lest they fall behind in processing the heap.

Does it help to have more than four threads? This is where the characteristics of the workload come into play. Take the simple case where the tasks are all compute-bound: they don't make external network calls (e.g., to a database), nor do they have significant contention on an internal lock. The stock price history batch program is such an application (when using a mock entity manager): the data on the entities can be calculated completely in parallel.

Table 9-1 shows the performance of calculating the history of 10,000 mock stock entities using a thread pool set to use the given number of threads on a machine with four CPUs. With only a single thread in the pool, 255.6 seconds are needed to calculate the data set; with four threads, only 77 seconds are required. After that, a little more time is needed as additional threads are added.

Table 9-1. Time required to calculate 10,000 mock price histories

Number of threads	Seconds required	Percent of baseline
1	255.6	100%
2	134.8	52.7%
4	77.0	30.1%
8	81.7	31.9%
15	85.6	33.5%

If the tasks in the application were completely parallel, then the "Percent of baseline" column would show 50% for two threads and 25% for four threads. Such completely linear scaling is impossible to come by for a number of reasons: if nothing else, the threads must coordinate among themselves to pick a task from the run queue (and in general, there is usually more synchronization among the threads). By the time four threads are used, the system is consuming 100% of available CPU, and although the machine may not be running any other user-level applications, there are various system-level processes that will kick in and use some CPU, preventing the JVM from utilizing all 100% of the cycles.

Still, this application is doing a good job of scaling, and even if the number of threads in the pool is overestimated, there is only a slight penalty to pay.

In other circumstances, though, that penalty can be larger. In the servlet version of the stock history calculator, having too many threads has a bigger effect, as is shown in Table 9-2. The application server is configured here to have the given number of threads, and a load generator is sending 20 simultaneous requests to the server.

Table 9-2. Operations per second for mock stock prices through a servlet

Number of threads	Operations per second	Percent of baseline
4	77.43	100%
8	75.93	98.8%
16	71.65	92.5%
32	69.34	89.5%
64	60.44	78.1%

Given that the application server has four available CPUs, maximum throughput is achieved with that many threads in the pool.

Chapter 1 discussed the need to determine where the bottleneck is when investigating performance issues. In this example, the bottleneck is clearly the CPU: at four CPUs, the CPU is 100% utilized. Still, the penalty for adding more threads in this case is somewhat minimal, at least until there are eight times too many threads.

But what if the bottleneck is elsewhere? This example is also somewhat unusual in that the tasks are completely CPU-bound: they do no I/O. Typically, the threads might be expected to make calls to a database, or write their output somewhere, or even rendezvous with some other resource. In that case, the CPU won't necessarily be the bottleneck: that external resource might be.

When that is the case, adding threads to the thread pool is quite detrimental. Although I said (only somewhat tongue-in-cheek) in Chapter 1 that the database is always the bottleneck, the bottleneck can be any external resource.

As an example, consider the stock servlet with the roles reversed: what if the goal is to make optimal use of the load generator machine (which, after all, is simply running a threaded Java program)?

In typical usage, if the servlet application is run in an application server with four CPUs and has only a single client requesting data, then the application server will be about 25% busy, and the client machine will be almost idle. If the load is increased to four concurrent clients, then the application server will be 100% busy, and the client machine will be perhaps only 20% busy.

Looking only at the client, it is easy to conclude that because the client has a lot of excess CPU, it should be possible to add more threads to the client and improve its scaling. Table 9-3 shows how wrong that assumption is: when additional threads are added into the client, performance is drastically affected.

Table 9-3. Average response time for calculating mock stock price histories

Number of client threads	Average response time	Percent of baseline
1	0.05 seconds	100%
2	0.05 seconds	100%
4	0.05 seconds	100%
6	0.076 seconds	152%
8	0.104 seconds	208%
16	0.212 seconds	424%
32	0.437 seconds	874%
64	0.909 seconds	1818%

Once the application server is the bottleneck in this example (i.e., at four client threads), adding load into the server is quite harmful—even by adding just a few threads on the client side.

This example may seem somewhat contrived. Who would add more client threads when the server is already CPU-bound? But the reason I've used this example is simply because it is easy to understand and uses only Java programs. That means you can run it yourself to understand how it works, without having to set up database connections and schemas and whatnot.

The point is that the same principle holds here for an application server that is sending database requests to machine that is CPU- or I/O-bound. You might look only at the application server CPU, see that is it well below 100% and that it has additional requests to process, and assume that increasing the number of application server threads is a good idea. That would lead to a big surprise, because increasing the number of threads in that situation will actually decrease the total throughput (and possibly quite significantly), just as it did in the Java-only example.

This is another reason why it is quite important to know where the actual bottleneck in a system is: if load is increased into the bottleneck, performance will decrease significantly. Conversely, if load into the current bottleneck is reduced, performance will likely increase.

This is also why self-tuning of thread pools is quite difficult. Thread pools usually have some visibility into the amount of work that they have pending, and perhaps even how much CPU the machine has available—but they usually have no visibility into other aspects of the entire environment in which they are executing. Hence, adding threads when work is pending—a key feature of many self-tuning thread pools (as well as certain configurations of the ThreadPoolExecutor)—is often exactly the wrong thing to do.

Unfortunately, this is also why setting the maximum size of a thread pool is often more art than science. In the real world, a self-tuning thread pool may get you 80% to 90% of the possible performance of the system under test, and overestimating the number of threads needed in a pool may exact only a small penalty. But when things go wrong with this sizing, they can go wrong in a very big way. Adequate testing in this regard is, unfortunately, still a key requirement.

Setting the Minimum Number of Threads

Once the maximum number of threads in a thread pool has been determined, it's time to determine the minimum number of threads needed. To cut to the chase, in almost all cases, set the minimum number of threads to the same value as the maximum.

The argument for setting the minimum number of threads to some other value (e.g., 1) is that it prevents the system from creating too many threads, which saves on system resources. It is true that each thread requires a certain amount of memory, particularly for its stack (which is discussed later in this chapter). Again, though, following one of the general rules from Chapter 2, the system needs to be sized to handle the maximum expected throughput, at which point it will need to create all those threads. If the system can't handle the maximum number of threads, then choosing a small minimum number of threads doesn't really help: if the system does hit the condition that requires the maximum number of threads (and which it cannot handle), the system will certainly be in the weeds. Better to create all the threads that might eventually be needed and ensure that the system can handle the maximum expected load.

On the other hand, the downside to specifying a minimum number of threads is fairly minimal. That downside occurs the first time there are multiple tasks to execute: then the pool will need to create a new thread. Creating threads is detrimental to performance —which is why thread pools are needed in the first place—but this one-time cost for creating the thread is likely to be unnoticed in performance testing (as long as it then remains in the pool).

In a batch application, it does not matter whether the thread is allocated when the pool is created (which is what will occur if you set the minimum and maximum number of threads to the same value) or whether the thread is allocated on demand: the time to execute the application will be the same. In other applications, the new threads are likely allocated during the warm-up period (and again the total time to allocate the threads is the same); the effect on the performance of an application will be negligible. Even if the thread creation occurs during the measurement cycle, as long as the thread creation is limited, it will likely not be noticed.

One other tuning that applies here is the idle time for a thread. Say that the pool is sized with a minimum of one thread and a maximum of four. Now suppose there is usually one thread executing a task, and then the application starts a cycle where every 15 seconds, the workload has on average two tasks to execute. The first time through that cycle, the pool will create the second thread—and now it makes sense for that second thread to stay in the pool for at least some period of time. You want to avoid the situation where that second thread is created, finishes its task in 5 seconds, is idle for 5 seconds, and then exits—since 5 seconds later, a second thread will be needed for the next task. In general, once a thread is created in a pool for a minimum size, it should stick around for at least a few minutes to handle any spike in load. To the extent that you have a good model of the arrival rate, you can base the idle time on that. Otherwise, plan on the idle time being measured in minutes, at least anywhere from 10 to 30.

Keeping idle threads around usually has little impact on an application. Usually, the thread object itself doesn't take a very large amount of heap space. The exception to that rule is if the thread holds onto a large amount of thread-local storage, or if a large amount of memory is referenced through the thread's runnable object. In either of those cases, freeing a thread can offer significant savings in terms of the live data left in the heap (which in turn affects the efficiency of GC).

These cases are unusual for thread pools, however. When a thread in a pool is idle, it should not be referencing any runnable object anymore (if it is, there is a bug some-where). Depending on the pool implementation, the thread-local variables may remain in place—but while thread-local variables can be an effective way to promote object reuse in certain circumstances (see Chapter 7), the total amount of memory those thread-local objects occupy should be limited.

One important exception to this rule is for thread pools that can grow to be very large (and hence run on a very large machine). Take an example where the task queue for a thread pool is expected to average 20 tasks; 20 is then a good minimum size for the pool. Now say the pool is running on a very large machine, and that it is designed to handle a spike of 2,000 tasks. Keeping 2,000 idle threads around in this pool will affect its performance when it is running only the 20 tasks—the throughput of this pool may be as much as 50% when it contains 1,980 idle threads, as opposed to when it has only the core 20 busy threads. Thread pools don't usually encounter sizing issues like that, but when they do, that's a good time to make sure they have a good minimum value.

Thread Pool Task Sizes

The tasks pending for a thread pool are held on some sort of queue or list; when a thread in the pool can execute a task, it pulls a task from the queue. This can lead to an imbal-ance: it is possible for the number of tasks on the queue to grow very large. If the queue is too large, then tasks in the queue will have to wait a long time until the tasks in front of them have completed execution. Imagine a web server that is overloaded: if a task is added to the queue and isn't executed for 3 seconds, the user has likely moved on to another page.

As a result, thread pools typically limit the size of the queue of pending tasks. The ThreadPoolExecutor does this in various ways depending on the data structure it is configured with (more on that in the next section); application servers usually have some tuning parameter to adjust this value.

Like the maximum size of the thread pool, there is no universal rule regarding how this value should be tuned. An application server with 30,000 items in its queue and four available CPUs can clear the queue in 6 minutes if it takes only 50 ms to execute a task (assuming no new tasks arrive during that time). That might be acceptable, but if each task requires 1 second to execute, it will take 2 hours to clear the queue. Once again, measuring your actual application is the only way to be sure of what value will give you the performance you require.

In any case, when the queue limit is reached, attempts to add a task to the queue will fail. A ThreadPoolExecutor has a rejectedExecution method that handles that case (by default, it throws a RejectedExecutionException). Application servers will return some error to the user: either an HTTP status code of 500 (for an internal error), or—in the best case—the web application will catch the error and display a reasonable explanation to the user.

Sizing a ThreadPoolExecutor

The general behavior for a thread pool is that it starts with a minimum number of threads, and if a task arrives when all existing threads are busy, a new thread is started (up to the maximum number of threads) and the task is executed immediately. Otherwise, the task is queued, unless there is some large number of pending tasks already, in which case the task is rejected. While that is the canonical behavior of a thread pool, the ThreadPoolExecutor can behave somewhat differently.

The ThreadPoolExecutor decides when to start a new thread based on the type of queue used to hold the tasks. There are three possibilities.

A SynchronousQueue
> When the executor uses a SynchronousQueue, the thread pool behaves as expected with respect to the number of threads: new tasks will start a new thread if all existing threads are busy and if the pool has less than the number of maximum threads. However, this queue has no way to hold pending tasks: if a task arrives, and the maximum number of threads is already busy, the task is always rejected. So this choice is good for managing a small number of tasks, but otherwise may be unsuitable. The documentation for this class suggests specifying a very large number for the maximum thread size—which may be OK if the tasks are completely CPU-bound, but as we've seen may be counterproductive in other situations. On the other hand, if you need a thread pool where the number of threads is easy to tune, this is the better choice.

Unbounded queues
> When the executor uses an unbounded queue (such as a LinkedBlockedingQueue), no task will ever by rejected (since the queue size is unlimited). In this case, the executor will only use at most the number of threads specified by the core (i.e.,

minimum) thread pool size: the maximum pool size is ignored. If the core and maximum pool size are the same value, this choice comes closest to the operation of a traditional thread pool configured with a fixed number of threads.

Bounded queues

Executors that use a bounded queue (e.g., an `ArrayBlockingQueue`) employ a quite complicated algorithm to determine when to start a new thread. For example, say that the pool's core size is 4, its maximum size is 8, and the maximum size of the `ArrayBlockingQueue` is 10. As tasks arrive and are placed in the queue, the pool will run a maximum of 4 threads (the core pool size). Even if the queue completely fills up—so that it is holding 10 pending tasks—the executor will only utilize 4 threads.

An additional thread will only be started when the queue is full, and a new task is added to the queue. Instead of rejecting the task (since the queue is full), the executor starts a new thread. That new thread runs the first task on the queue, making room for the pending task to be added to the queue.

In this example, the only way the pool will end up with 8 threads (its specified maximum) is if there are 7 tasks in progress, 10 tasks in the queue, and a new task is added to the queue.

The idea behind this algorithm is that the pool will operate with only the core threads (four) most of the time, even if a moderate number of tasks are in the queue waiting to be run. That allows the pool to act as a throttle (which is advantageous). If the backlog of requests becomes too great, the pool then attempts to run more threads to clear out the backlog (subject to a second throttle, the maximum number of threads).

If there are no external bottlenecks in the system and there are available CPU cycles, then everything here works out: adding the new threads will process the queue faster and likely bring it back to its desired size. So cases where this algorithm is appropriate can certainly be constructed.

On the other hand, this algorithm has no idea why the queue size has suddenly increased. If it is due to an external backlog, then adding more threads is the wrong thing to do. If the pool is running on a machine that is CPU-bound, adding more threads is the wrong thing to do. Adding threads will only make sense if the backlog occurred because additional load came into the system (e.g., more clients started making an HTTP request). (Yet if that is the case, why wait to add threads until the queue size has reached some bound? If the additional resources are available to utilize additional threads, then adding them sooner will improve the overall performance of the system.)

There are many arguments for and against each of these choices, but when attempting to maximize performance, this is a time to apply the KISS principle: keep it simple, stupid. Specify that the ThreadPoolExecutor has the same number of core and maximum threads and utilize a LinkedBlockingQueue to hold the pending tasks (if an unbounded task list is appropriate), or an ArrayBlockingQueue (if a bounded task list is appropriate).

Quick Summary

1. Thread pools are one case where object pooling is a good thing: threads are expensive to initialize, and a thread pool allows the number of threads on a system to be easily throttled.

2. Thread pools must be carefully tuned. Blindly adding new threads into a pool can, in some circumstances, have a detrimental effect on performance.

3. Using simpler options for a ThreadPoolExecutor will usually provide the best (and most predictable) performance.

The ForkJoinPool

Java 7 introduces a new thread pool: the ForkJoinPool class. This class looks just like any other thread pool; like the ThreadPoolExecutor class, it implements the Executor and ExecutorService interfaces. When those interfaces are used, the ForkJoinPool uses an internal unbounded list of tasks that will be run by the number of threads specified in its constructor (or the number of CPUs on the machine if the no-args constructor is used).

The ForkJoinPool class is designed to work with divide-and-conquer algorithms: those where a task can be recursively broken into subsets. The subsets can then be processed in parallel, and then the results from each subset are merged into a single result. The classic example of this is the quicksort sorting algorithm.

The important point about divide-and-conquer algorithms is that they create a lot of tasks that must be managed by relatively few threads. Say that we want to sort an array of 10 million elements. We start by creating separate tasks to perform three operations: sort the subarray containing the first 5 million elements, sort the subarray containing the second 5 million elements, and then merge the two subarrays.

The sorting of the 5 million element arrays is similarly accomplished by sorting subarrays of 2.5 million elements and merging those arrays. This recursion continues until at some point (e.g., when the subarray has 10 elements), it is more efficient to use insertion sort on the array and sort it directly. Figure 9-1 shows how that all works out.

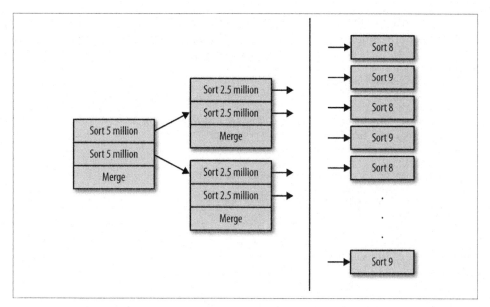

Figure 9-1. Tasks in a recursive quicksort

In the end, there will be more than 1 million tasks to sort the leaf arrays (each of which will be smaller than 10 elements—the point at which sorting them directly makes sense). (The actual value for that varies by implementation; 10 is just used for illustration here. Current versions of Java use insertion sort when the array size is less than 47 elements.) More than 500,000 tasks are needed to merge those sorted arrays, 250,000 tasks to merge the next set of sorted arrays, and so on. In the end, there will be 2,097,151 tasks.

The larger point here is that none of the tasks can complete until the tasks that they have spawned have also completed. The tasks directly sorting arrays of less than 10 elements must be completed first, and then tasks can merge the two small arrays that they created, and so on: everything is merged up the chain until the entire array is merged into its final, sorted value.

It isn't possible to perform that algorithm efficiently using a `ThreadPoolExecutor`, because a parent task must wait for its child tasks to complete. A thread inside a `ThreadPoolExecutor` cannot add another task to the queue and then wait for it to finish: once the thread is waiting, it cannot be used to execute one of the subtasks. The `ForkJoinPool`, on the other hand, allows its threads to create new tasks and then suspend their current task. While the task is suspended, the thread can execute other pending tasks.

Let's take a simple example: say that we have an array of doubles, and the goal is to count the number of values in the array that are less than 0.5. It's trivial simply to scan the array sequentially (and possibly advantageous, as we'll see later in this section)—but for now, it is instructive to divide the array into subarrays and scan them in parallel (emulating the more complex quicksort and other divide-and-conquer algorithms). Here's an outline of the code to achieve that with a ForkJoinPool:

```java
public class ForkJoinTest {
    private double[] d;

    private class ForkJoinTask extends RecursiveTask<Integer> {
        private int first;
        private int last;

        public ForkJoinTask(int first, int last) {
            this.first = first;
            this.last = last;
        }

        protected Integer compute() {
            int subCount;
            if (last - first < 10) {
                subCount = 0;
                for (int i = first; i <= last; i++) {
                    if (d[i] < 0.5)
                        subCount++;
                }
            }
            else {
                int mid = (first + last) >>> 1;
                ForkJoinTask left = new ForkJoinTask(first, mid);
                left.fork();
                ForkJoinTask right = new ForkJoinTask(mid + 1, last);
                right.fork();
                subCount = left.join();
                subCount += right.join();
            }
            return subCount;
        }
    }

    public static void main(String[] args) {
        d = createArrayOfRandomDoubles();
        int n = new ForkJoinPool().invoke(new ForkJoinTask(0, 9999999));
        System.out.println("Found " + n + " values");
    }
}
```

The fork() and join() methods here are the key: we'd be hard-pressed to implement this sort of recursion without those methods (which are not available in the tasks executed by a ThreadPoolExecutor). Those methods use a series of internal, per-thread queues to manipulate the tasks and switch threads from executing one task to executing another. The details of that are transparent to the developer, though if you're interested in algorithms, the code makes fascinating reading. Our focus here is on the performance: what trade-offs are there between the `ForkJoinPool` and `ThreadPoolExecutor` classes?

First and foremost is that the suspension implemented by the fork/join paradigm allows all the tasks to be executed by only a few threads. Counting the double values in an array of 10 million elements using this example code creates more than 2 million tasks, but those tasks are easily executed by only a few threads (even one, if that makes sense for the machine running the test). Running a similar algorithm using a `ThreadPoolExecutor` would require more than 2 million threads, since each thread would have to wait for its subtasks to complete, and those subtasks could only complete if there were additional threads available in the pool. So the fork/join suspension allows us to use algorithms that we otherwise could not, which is a performance win.

However, while divide-and-conquer techniques are very powerful, overusing them can yield worse performance. In the counting example, a single thread can scan and count the array, though that won't necessarily be as fast as running the fork/join algorithm in parallel. However, it would be easy enough to partition the array into chunks and use a `ThreadPoolExecutor` to have multiple threads scan the array:

```java
public class ThreadPoolTest {
    private double[] d;

    private class ThreadPoolExecutorTask implements Callable<Integer> {
        private int first;
        private int last;

        public ThreadPoolExecutorTask(int first, int last) {
            this.first = first;
            this.last = last;
        }

        public Integer call() {
            int subCount = 0;
            for (int i = first; i <= last; i++) {
                if (d[i] < 0.5) {
                    subCount++;
                }
            }
            return subCount;
        }
    }

    public static void main(String[] args) {
        d = createArrayOfRandomDoubles();
        ThreadPoolExecutor tpe = new ThreadPoolExecutor(4, 4,
                                     Long.MAX_VALUE,
                                     TimeUnit.SECONDS,
                                     new LinkedBlockingQueue());
        Future[] f = new Future[4];
        int size = d.length / 4;
```

```
    for (int i = 0; i < 3; i++) {
        f[i] = tpe.submit(
                    new ThreadPoolExecutorTask(i * size, (i + 1) * size - 1);
    }
    f[3] = tpe.submit(new ThreadPoolExecutorTask(3 * size, d.length - 1);
    int n = 0;
    for (int i = 0; i < 4; i++) {
        n += f.get();
    }
    System.out.println("Found " + n + " values");
    }
}
```

On a four-CPU machine, this code will fully utilize all available CPUs, processing the array in parallel while avoiding creating and queuing the 2 million tasks used by the fork/join example. The performance is predictably faster, as Table 9-4 shows.

Table 9-4. Time to count an array of 100 million elements

Number of threads	ForkJoinPool	ThreadPoolExecutor
1	3.2 seconds	0.31 seconds
4	1.9 seconds	0.15 seconds

This test is from a four-CPU machine with a 4 GB fixed-size heap. The test using a ThreadPoolExecutor required no GC at all, but each ForkJoinPool test spent about 1.2 seconds in GC. That is a significant contribution to the performance difference, but it isn't the entire story: the overhead of creating and managing the task objects hampers the performance of the ForkJoinPool. When a similar alternative is available, it is likely to be faster—at least in this simple case.

An additional feature of the ForkJoinPool is that it implements work-stealing. That's basically an implementation detail; it means that each thread in the pool has its own queue of tasks it has forked. Threads will preferentially work on tasks from their own queue, but if that queue is empty they will steal tasks from the queues of other threads. The upshot is that even if one of the 2 million tasks takes a long time to execute, other threads in the ForkJoinPool can complete any and all of the remaining tasks. The same is not true of the ThreadPoolExecutor: if one of its tasks requires a long time, the other threads cannot pick up additional work.

The example code started by simply counting elements in the array that are less than 0.5. What if, in addition, the code calculated a new value for the double array to store? A nonsensical (but CPU-intensive) implementation could execute this code:

```
for (int i = first; i <= last; i++) {
    if (d[i] < 0.5) {
        subCount++;
    }
    for (int j = 0; j < d.length - i; j++) {
        for (int k = 0; k < 100; k++) {
```

```
        dummy = j * k + i; // dummy is volatile, so multiple writes occur
        d[i] = dummy;
    }
  }
}
```

Because the outer loop (indexed by j) is based on the position of the element in the array, the calculation requires a length of time proportional to the element position: calculating the value for d[0] will take a very long time, while calculating the value for d[d.length - 1] will take relatively little time.

Now the simple partitioning of the ThreadPoolExecutor test will be at a disadvantage. The thread calculating the first partition of the array will take a very long time to complete: much longer than the time spent by the fourth thread operating on the last partition. Once that fourth thread is finished, it will remain idle: everything must wait for the first thread to complete its long task.

The granularity of the 2 million tasks in the ForkJoinPool means that although one thread will get stuck doing the very long calculations on the first 10 elements in the array, the remaining threads will still have work to perform, and the CPU will be kept busy during most of the test. That difference is shown in Table 9-5.

Table 9-5. Time to process an array of 10,000 elements

Number of threads	ForkJoinPool	ThreadPoolExecutor
1	54.5 seconds	53.3 seconds
4	16.6 seconds	24.2 seconds

When there is a single thread in the pool, the computation takes essentially the same amount of time. That makes sense: the number of calculations is the same regardless of the pool implementation, and since those calculations are never done in parallel, they can be expected to take the same amount of time (though there is still some small overhead for creating the 2 million tasks). But when the pool contains four threads, the granularity of the tasks in the ForkJoinPool gives it a decided advantage: it is able to keep the CPUs busy for almost the entire duration of the test.

This situation is called "unbalanced," because some tasks take longer than others (and hence the tasks in the previous example are called balanced). In general, this leads to the recommendation that using a ThreadPoolExecutor with partitioning will give better performance when the tasks are balanced, and a ForkJoinPool will give better performance when the tasks are unbalanced.

There is a more subtle performance recommendation here as well: carefully consider the point at which the recursion for the fork/join paradigm should end. In this example, I've arbitrarily chosen it to end when the array size is less than 10. If I'd stopped the recursion when the array size was 2.5 million, then the fork/join test (specifically for the balanced code processing a 10-million element array on a four-CPU machine) would have created only four tasks, and its performance would have been essentially the same as that of the ThreadPoolExecutor.

On the other hand, continuing the recursion in the unbalanced test gives even better performance for that case, even though it creates yet more tasks—some representative data points for that are shown in Table 9-6.

Table 9-6. Time to process an array of 10,000 elements

Target size of leaf array	ForkJoinPool
20	17.8 seconds
10	16.6 seconds
5	15.6 seconds
1	16.8 seconds

Automatic Parallelization

Java 8 introduces the ability for Java to automatically parallelize certain kinds of code. This parallelization relies on the use of the ForkJoinPool class. Java 8 adds one new feature to that class: a common pool that can be used by any ForkJoinTask that is not explicitly submitted to a specified pool. The common pool is a static element of the ForkJoinPool class, and by default it is sized to the number of processors on the target machine.

This parallelization occurs in many new methods of the Arrays class: methods to sort an array using parallel quicksorting, methods to operate on each individual element of an array, and so on. It is also used within the Java 8 streams feature, which allows for operations (either sequential or parallel) to be performed on each element in a collection. Some basic performance implications of streams are discussed in Chapter 12; in this section, we'll look at how streams can automatically be processed in parallel.

Given a collection containing a series of integers, the following code will calculate the stock price history for the symbol corresponding to the given integer:

```
Stream<Integer> stream = arrayList.parallelStream();
stream.forEach(a -> {
    String symbol = StockPriceUtils.makeSymbol(a);
    StockPriceHistory sph = new StockPriceHistoryImpl(symbol, startDate,
                                    endDate, entityManager);
});
```

This code will calculate the mock price histories in parallel: the forEach() method will create a task for each element in the array list, and each task will be processed by the common ForkJoinTask pool. That is functionally equivalent to the test at the beginning of this chapter, where a thread pool was used to calculate the histories in parallel (though this code is much easier to write than dealing with the thread pool explicitly).

Sizing the common `ForkJoinTask` pool is as important as sizing any other thread pool. By default, the common pool will have as many threads as the target machines has CPUs. If you are running multiple JVMs on the same machine, limiting that number makes sense so that the JVMs do not compete for CPU against each other. Similarly, if servlet code will execute a parallel task and you want to make sure that CPU is available for other tasks, consider lowering the size of the common pool. Or if tasks in the common pool will block waiting for I/O or other data, the common pool size might need to be increased.

The size can be set by specifying the system property `-Djava.util.concurrent.Fork JoinPool.common.parallelism=N`.

Earlier in this chapter, Table 9-1 showed the effect on the performance of the parallel stock history calculations when the pool had various sizes. Table 9-7 compares that data to the `forEach()` construct using the common `ForkJoinPool` (with the `parallelism` system property set to the given value).

Table 9-7. Time required to calculate 10,000 mock price histories

Number of threads	ThreadPoolExecutor	ForkJoinPool
1	255.6 seconds	135.4 seconds
2	134.8 seconds	110.2 seconds
4	77.0 seconds	96.5 seconds
8	81.7 seconds	84.0 seconds
15	85.6 seconds	84.6 seconds

By default, the common pool will have four threads (on this four-CPU machine), so the third line in the table is the common case. The results for a common pool size of one and two are exactly the sort of result that should give a performance engineer fits: they seem to be completely out of line, and when a test is out of line like that, the most common reason is a testing error. In this case, however, it turns out that the `forEach()` method does something tricky: it uses both the thread executing the statement and the threads in the common pool to process the data coming from the stream. Even though the common pool in the first test is configured to have a single thread, two threads are used to calculate the result. (Consequently, the time for a `ThreadPoolExecutor` with two threads and a `ForkJoinPool` with one thread is essentially the same.)

If you need to tune the size of the common pool when using parallel stream constructs and other autoparallel features, consider decreasing the desired value by one.

Thread Synchronization

In a perfect world—or in examples for a book—it is relatively easy for threads to avoid the need for synchronization. In the real world, things are not necessarily so easy.

Synchronization and Java Concurrent Utilities

In this section, when the term *synchronization* is used, it means code that is within a block where access to a set of variables appears serialized: only a single thread at a time can access the memory. This includes code blocks protected by the `synchronized` keyword. It also means code that is protected by an instance of the `java.util.concurrent.lock.Lock` class, and code within the `java.util.concurrent` and `java.util.concurrent.atomic` packages.

Strictly speaking, the atomic classes do not use synchronization, at least in CPU programming terms. Atomic classes utilize a "Compare and Swap" (CAS) CPU instruction, while synchronization requires exclusive access to a resource. Threads that utilize CAS instructions will not block when simultaneously accessing the same resource, while a thread that needs a synchronization lock will block if another thread holds that resource.

There are performance trade-offs between the two approaches (which are discussed later in this section). However, even though CAS instructions are lockless and non-blocking, they still exhibit most of the behavior of blocking constructs: their end result makes it appear to the developer that threads can only access the protected memory serially.

Costs of Synchronization

Synchronized areas of code affect performance in two ways. First, the amount of time an application spends in a synchronized block affects the scalability of an application.

Second, obtaining the synchronization lock requires some CPU cycles and hence affects performance.

Synchronization and scalability

First things first: when an application is split up to run on multiple threads, the speedup it sees is defined by an equation known as Amdahl's law:

$$Speedup = \frac{1}{(1 - P) + \dfrac{P}{N}}$$

P is the amount of the program that is run in parallel, and N is the number of threads utilized (assuming that each thread always has available CPU). So if 20% of the code exists in serialized blocks (meaning that P is 80%), with eight available CPUs the code can be expected to run (only) 3.33 times faster.

One key fact about this equation is that as P decreases—that is, as more code is located within serialized blocks—the performance benefit of having multiple threads also decreases. That is why limiting the amount of code that lies in the serialized block is so important. In this example, with eight CPUs available we might have hoped for an eight times increase in speed. When only 20% of the code is within a serialized block, the benefit of having multiple threads was reduced by over 50% (i.e., the increase was only 3.3 times).

Costs of locking objects

Aside from its impact on scalability, there are two basic costs to the operation of synchronization itself.

First, there is the cost of obtaining the synchronization lock. If a lock is uncontended —meaning that two threads are not attempting to access the lock at the same time— then this cost is quite minimal. There is a slight difference here between the synchronized keyword and CAS instructions. Uncontended synchronized locks are known as uninflated locks, and the cost of obtaining an uninflated lock is on the order of a few hundred nanoseconds. Uncontended CAS code will see an even smaller performance penalty. (See Chapter 12 for an example of the difference.)

Contended constructs are more expensive. When a second thread attempts to access a synchronized lock, the lock becomes (predictably) inflated. This cost is fixed; the same amount of code is executed whether there are 2 or 20 threads attempting to access the same lock. (All 20 threads must execute the locking code, of course, so the cost does increase based on the number of threads—the point is that it is fixed on a per-thread basis).

The cost for a contended operation in code using CAS instructions is unpredictable. CAS primitives are based on an optimistic strategy: the thread sets a value, executes some code, and then makes sure that the initial value has not changed. If it has, then the CAS-based code must execute the code again. In the worst case, this means that two threads could run into an infinite loop as each modifies the CAS-protected value, only to see that the other thread has modified it simultaneously. In practice, two threads are not going to get into an infinite loop like that, but as the number of threads contending for the CAS-based value increase, the number of retries increases. (If the operations here are read-only, then CAS-based protection is not affected by contended access. For example, any number of threads may call the AtomicLong.get() method on the same object at the same time without paying any penalty for contention. This is another significant advantage to using CAS-based utilities.)

The second cost of synchronization is specific to Java and depends on the Java Memory Model. Java, unlike languages such as C++ and C, has a strict guarantee about the memory semantics around synchronization, and the guarantee applies to CAS-based protection, to traditional synchronization, and to the volatile keyword.

Uses of volatile in Examples

The Java Memory Model has subtly influenced two other examples in this book. Chapter 2 discussed the problems in writing a microbenchmark; the ultimate solution there required a volatile variable to store the result of each loop iteration:

```java
public class MicroBenchmark {
    private volatile double answer;
    public static void main(String[] args) {
        long then = System.currentTimeMills();
        for (int i = 0; i < nLoops; i++) {
            answer = compute(randomValue[i]);
        }
        long now = System.currentTimeMills();
        System.out.println("Elapsed time: " + (now - then));
    }
}
```

As the compiler optimized the code, it could unroll the loop, yielding the following pseudocode:

```java
for (int i = 0; i < nLoops; i += 4) {
    answer = compute(randomValue[i]);
    answer = compute(randomValue[i + 1]);
    answer = compute(randomValue[i + 2]);
    answer = compute(randomValue[i + 3]);
}
```

If the JVM stored the value of answer in a register, it could notice that the register is written multiple times without being read (since other threads cannot read the register), and as a result optimize away all the loop calculations except for the final one. Defining answer as volatile ensures that the JVM must store the calculation of each loop as it is made. The JVM cannot optimize those calculations out, since it can never know if another thread will come along and read the value out of main memory.

Similarly, the double-checked locking example in Chapter 7 required the use of a volatile variable:

```
private volatile ConcurrentHashMap instanceChm;
...
public void doOperation() {
    ConcurrentHashMap chm = instanceChm;
    if (chm == null) {
        synchronized(this) {
            chm = instanceChm;
            if (chm == null) {
                chm = new ConcurrentHashMap();
                ... code to populate the map
                instanceChm = chm;
            }
        }
    }
    ...use the chm...
}
```

The volatile keyword accomplishes two things in this example. First, note that the hashmap is initialized using a local variable first, and only the final (fully initialized) value is assigned to the instanceChm variable. If the code populating the hashmap were using the instance variable directly, a second thread could see a partially populated map. And second, it ensures that when the map is completely initialized, other threads will immediately see that value stored into the instanceChm variable.

The purpose of synchronization is to protect access to values in memory—that is, to variables. As discussed in Chapter 4, variables may be temporarily stored in registers, which is much more efficient than directly accessing them in main memory. Register values are not visible to other threads; the thread that modifies a value in a register must at some point flush that register to main memory so that other threads can see the value. The point when the register values must be flushed is dictated by thread synchronization.

The actual semantics can get fairly complicated, but the easiest way to think of this is that when a thread leaves a synchronized block, it must flush any modified variables to main memory. That means other threads that enter the synchronized block will see the most recently updated values. Similarly, CAS-based protection ensures that variables modified during their operation are flushed to main memory, and a variable marked volatile is always consistently updated in main memory whenever it is changed.

In Chapter 1, I mentioned that you should learn to avoid nonperformant code constructs in Java, even if it seems like that might be "prematurely optimizing" your code (it isn't). An interesting case of that—and a real-world example—comes from this loop:

```
Vector v;
for (int i = 0; i < v.size(); i++) {
    process(v.get(i));
}
```

In production, this loop was found to be taking a surprising amount of time, and the logical assumption was that the process() method was the culprit. But it wasn't that, nor was the issue the size() and get() method calls themselves (which had been inlined by the compiler). The get() and size() methods of the Vector class are synchronized, and it turned out that the register flushing required by all those calls was a huge performance problem.

This isn't ideal code for other reasons. In particular, the state of the vector can change between the time a thread calls the size() method and the time it calls the get() method. If a second thread removes the last element from the vector in between the two calls made by the first thread, the get() method will throw an ArrayIndexOutOfBoundsException. Quite apart from the semantic issues in the code, the fine-grained synchronization was a bad choice here.

One way to avoid that is to wrap lots of successive, fine-grained synchronization calls within a synchronized block:

```
synchronized(v) {
    for (int i = 0; i < v.size(); i++) {
        process(v.get(i));
    }
}
```

That doesn't work well if the process() method takes a long time to execute, since the vector can no longer be processed in parallel. Alternately it may be necessary to copy and partition the vector so that its elements can be processed in parallel within the copies, while other threads can still modify the original vector.

The effect of register flushing is also dependent on the kind of processor the program is running on; processors that have a lot of registers for threads will require more flushing than simpler processors. In fact, this code executed for a long time without problems in thousands of environments. It became an issue only when it was tried on a large SPARC-based machine with a large number of registers per thread.

Does that mean you are unlikely to see issues around register flushing in smaller environments? Perhaps. But just as multicore CPUs have become the norm for simple laptops, more complex CPUs with more caching and registers are also becoming more commonplace, which will expose hidden performance issues like this.

Quick Summary

1. Thread synchronization has two performance costs: it limits the scalability of an application, and there is a cost in obtaining locks.

2. The memory semantics of synchronization, CAS-based utilities, and the volatile keyword can have a large performance impact, particularly on large machines with many registers.

Avoiding Synchronization

If synchronization can be avoided altogether, then locking penalties will not affect the application's performance. There are two general approaches to achieve that.

The first approach is to use different objects in each thread so that access to the objects will be uncontended. Many Java objects are synchronized to make them thread-safe but don't necessarily need to be shared. The Random class falls into that category; Chapter 12 shows an example within the JDK where the thread-local technique was used to develop a new class to avoid the synchronization in that class.

On the flip side, many Java objects are expensive to create or use a substantial amount of memory. Take, for example, the NumberFormat class: instances of that class are not thread-safe, and the internationalization required to create an instance makes constructing new objects quite expensive. A program could get by with a single, shared global NumberFormat instance, but access to that shared object would need to be synchronized.

Instead, a better pattern is to use a ThreadLocal object:

```
public class Thermometer {
    private static ThreadLocal<NumberFormat> nfLocal = new ThreadLocal<>() {
        public NumberFormat initialValue() {
            NumberFormat nf = NumberFormat.getInstance();
            nf.setMinumumIntegerDigits(2);
            return nf;
        }
    }
    public String toString() {
        NumberFormat nf = nfLocal.get();
        nf.format(...);
    }
}
```

By using a thread-local variable, the total number of objects is limited (minimizing the effect on GC), and each object will never be subject to thread contention.

The second way to avoid synchronization is to use CAS-based alternatives. In some sense this isn't avoiding synchronization as much as solving the problem differently. But in this context, reducing the penalty for synchronization, it works out to have the same effect.

The difference in performance between CAS-based protections and traditional synchronization seems like the ideal case to employ a microbenchmark: it should be trivial to write code that compares a CAS-based operation with a traditional synchronized method. For example, the JDK provides a simple way to keep a counter using CAS-based protection: the AtomicLong and similar classes. A microbenchmark could then compare code that uses CAS-based protection to traditional synchronization. For example, consider the following:

```
AtomicLong al = new AtomicLong(0);
public long doOperation() {
    return al.getAndIncrement();
}
```

That code could be compared to this:

```
private volatile long al = 0;
public synchronized doOperation() {
    return al++;
}
```

This turns out to be impossible to measure with a microbenchmark. If there is a single thread (so there is no possibility of contention), then the microbenchmark using this code can produce a reasonable estimate of the cost of using the two approaches in an uncontended environment (and the result of that test is cited in Chapter 12). But that doesn't provide any information about what happens in a contended environment (and if the code won't ever be contended, then it doesn't need to be thread-safe in the first place).

In a microbenchmark built around these code snippets that is run with only two threads, there will be an enormous amount of contention on the shared resource. That isn't realistic either: in a real application, it is quite unlikely that two threads will always be accessing the shared resource simultaneously. Adding more threads simply adds more unrealistic contention to the equation.

Contention and volatile Variables

Developers sometimes think of using volatile variables to reduce synchronization and hence reduce contention in their applications. It turns out that simultaneous writes to volatile variables are quite slow.

Earlier in this chapter, the example using the ForkJoinPool contained a loop designed to consume a lot of CPU cycles by writing nonsense values to a volatile variable:

```
    for (int j = 0; j < d.length - i; j++) {
        for (int k = 0; k < 100; k++) {
            dummy = j * k + i; // dummy is volatile, so multiple writes occur
            d[i] = dummy;
        }
    }
```

dummy is defined as an instance variable within the class defining this code, and although there are four threads simultaneously executing in the example, they are operating on different instances of the class. Hence, there is no contention around using the dummy variable, and the test in the example completed in 16 seconds.

Change the definition of dummy to a static, however, and things change. Now there are multiple threads accessing that volatile variable at the same time, and the same test requires 209 seconds.

As discussed in Chapter 2, microbenchmarks tend to greatly overstate the effect of synchronization bottlenecks on the test in question. This discussion hopefully elucidates that point. A much more realistic picture of the trade-off will be obtained if the code in this section is used in an actual application.

In the general case, the following guidelines apply to the performance of CAS-based utilities compared to traditional synchronization:

- If access to a resource is uncontended, then CAS-based protection will be slightly faster than traditional synchronization (though no protection at all will be slightly faster still).

- If access to a resource is lightly or moderately contended, CAS-based protection will be faster (often much faster) than traditional synchronization.

- As access to the resource becomes heavily contended, traditional synchronization will at some point become the more efficient choice. In practice, this occurs only on very large machines running a large number of threads.

- CAS-based protection is not subject to contention when values are read and not written.

Java 8 and Contended Atomic Classes

Classes in the java.util.concurrent.atomic package use CAS-based primitives instead of traditional synchronization. As a result, performance of those classes (for example, the AtomicLong class) tends to be faster than writing a synchronized method to increment a long variable—at least until the contention for the CAS primitive becomes too high.

Java 8 introduces a number of classes to address this: atomic adders and accumulators (for example, the `LongAdder` class). These classes are more scalable than the traditional atomic classes. When multiple threads update a `LongAdder`, the class can hold the updates separately for each thread. That means the threads needn't wait for each other to complete their operation; instead, the values are stored in (essentially) an array and each thread can return quickly. Later, the values will be added or accumulated when some thread attempts to retrieve the current value.

Under little or no contention, the value is accumulated as the program runs, and the behavior of the adder will be the same as that of the traditional atomic class. Under severe contention, the updates will be much faster, though the instance will start to use more memory to store the array of values. Retrieval of a value in that case will also be slightly slower since it must process all the pending updates in the array. Still, under very contended conditions, these new classes will perform even better than their atomic counterparts.

In the end, there is no substitute for extensive testing under the actual production conditions where the code will run: only then can a definite statement be made as to which implementation of a particular method is better. Even in that case, the definite statement applies only to those conditions.

Quick Summary

1. Avoiding contention for synchronized objects is a useful way to mitigate their performance impact.

2. Thread-local variables are never subject to contention; they are ideal for holding synchronized objects that don't actually need to be shared between threads.

3. CAS-based utilities are a way to avoid traditional synchronization for objects that do need to be shared.

False Sharing

One little-discussed performance implication of synchronization involves false sharing. That used to be a fairly obscure artifact of threaded programs, but as multicore machines become the norm—and as other, more obvious, synchronization performance issues are addressed—false sharing is an increasingly important issue.

False sharing occurs because of the way in which CPUs handle their cache. Consider the data in this simple class:

```
public class DataHolder {
    public volatile long l1;
    public volatile long l2;
```

```
        public volatile long l3;
        public volatile long l4;
    }
```

Each of the long values here is stored in memory adjacent to one another; for example, l1 could be stored at memory location 0xF20. Then l2 would be stored in memory at 0xF28, l3 at 0xF2C, and so on. When it comes time for the program to operate on l2, it will load a relatively large amount of memory—for example, 128 bytes from location 0xF00 to 0xF80—into a cache line on one of the cores of (one of) the CPU(s). A second thread that wants to operate on l3 will load that same chunk of memory into a cache line on a different core.

Loading nearby values like that makes sense in most cases: if the application accesses one particular instance variable in an object, it is likely to access nearby instance variables. If they are already loaded into the core's cache, then that memory access is very, very fast—a big performance win.

The downside to this scheme is that whenever the program updates a value in its local cache, that core must notify all the other cores that the memory in question has been changed. Those other cores must invalidate their cache lines and reload that data from memory.

Let's see what happens if the DataHolder class is heavily used by multiple threads:

```
public class ContendedTest extends Thread {
    private static class DataHolder {
        private volatile long l1 = 0;
        private volatile long l2 = 0;
        private volatile long l3 = 0;
        private volatile long l4 = 0;
    }
    private static DataHolder dh = new DataHolder();
    private static long nLoops;

    public ContendedTest(Runnable r) {
        super(r);
    }

    public static void main(String[] args) throws Exception {
        nLoops = Long.parseLong(args[0]);
        ContendedTest[] tests = new ContendedTest[4];
        tests[0] = new ContendedTest(() -> {
                for (long i = 0; i < nLoops; i++) {
                    dh.l1 += i;
                }
        });
        tests[1] = new ContendedTest(() -> {
                for (long i = 0; i < nLoops; i++) {
                    dh.l2 += i;
                }
```

```
        });
        //...similar for 2 and 3...
        long then = System.currentTimeMillis();
        for (ContendedTest ct : tests) {
            ct.start();
        }
        for (ContendedTest ct : tests) {
            ct.join();
        }
        long now = System.currentTimeMillis();
        System.out.println("Duration: " + (now - then) + " ms");
    }
}
```

There are four separate threads here, and they are not sharing any variables: each is accessing only a single member of the `DataHolder` class. From a synchronization standpoint, there is no contention, and we might reasonably expect that this code would execute in the same amount of time regardless of whether it runs one thread or four threads (given a four-core machine).

It doesn't turn out that way—when one particular thread writes the `volatile` value in its loop, the cache line for every other thread will get invalidated, and the memory values must be reloaded. Table 9-8 shows the result: performance gets worse as more threads are added.

Table 9-8. Time to sum 1,000,000 values with false sharing

Number of threads	Elapsed time
1	7.1 seconds
2	52.1 seconds
3	91.0 seconds
4	128.3 seconds

Strictly speaking, false sharing does not have to involve synchronized (or `volatile`) variables: whenever any data value in the CPU cache is written, other caches that hold the same data range must be invalidated. However, remember that the Java memory model requires that the data must be written to main memory only at the end of a synchronization primitive (including CAS and `volatile` constructs). So that is the situation where it will be encountered most frequently. If, in this example, the `long` variables are not `volatile`, then the compiler will hold the values in registers, and the test will execute in about 7.1 seconds regardless of the number of threads involved.

This is obviously an extreme example, but it brings up the question of how false sharing can be detected and corrected. Unfortunately, the answer is murky and incomplete. Nothing in the standard set of tools discussed in Chapter 3 addresses false sharing, since it requires very specific knowledge about the architecture of a processor.

If you are lucky, the vendor of the target processor for your application will have a tool that can be used to diagnose false sharing. Intel, for example, has a program called VTune that can be used to help detect false sharing by inspecting cache miss events. Certain native profilers can provide information about the number of clock cycles per instruction (CPI) for a given line of code; a high CPI for a simple instruction within a loop can indicate that the code is waiting to reload the target memory into the CPU cache.

Otherwise, detecting false sharing requires some intuition and experimentation. If an ordinary profile indicates a particular loop is taking a surprising amount of time, inspect the loop for the possibility that multiple threads may be accessing unshared variables within the loop. (In the realm of performance tuning as an art rather than a science, even the Intel VTune manual says that the "primary means of avoiding false sharing is through code inspection.")

Preventing false sharing requires some code changes. The ideal situation is when the variables involved can be written less frequently. In the example above, the calculation could take place using local variables, and only the end result is written back to the DataHolder variable. The very small number of writes that ensues are unlikely to create contention for the cache lines, and they won't have a performance impact even if all four threads update their results at the same time at the end of the loop.

A second possibility involves padding the variables so that they won't be loaded on the same cache line. If the target CPU has a 128-byte cache, then padding like this may work (but also, it may not):

```
public class DataHolder {
    public volatile long l1;
    pubilc long[] dummy1 = new long[128 / 8];
    public volatile long l2;
    pubilc long[] dummy2 = new long[128 / 8];
    public volatile long l3;
    pubilc long[] dummy3 = new long[128 / 8];
    public volatile long l4;
}
```

Using arrays like that is unlikely to work, because the JVM will probably rearrange the layout of those instance variables so that all the arrays are next to each other, and then all the long variables will still be next to each other. Using primitive values to pad the structure is more likely to work, though it can be impractical because of the number of variables required.

There are other issues when using padding to prevent false sharing. The size of the padding is hard to predict, since different CPUs will have different cache sizes. And the padding obviously adds significant size to the instances in question, which will have an impact on the garbage collector (depending, of course, on the number of instances required). Still, absent an algorithmic solution, padding of the data can sometimes offer significant advantages.

The @Contended Annotation

One of the new features of Java 8 is the ability to reduce cache contention on specified fields (JEP 142). This is achieved by using a new annotation (@sun.misc.Contended) to mark variables that should be automatically padded by the JVM.

The package that this annotation belongs to is significant: although this is a JDK Enhancement Proposal (JEP) feature, it is intended for use primarily by the JVM itself. There is no guarantee that the annotation will carry forward into future releases (nor that its behavior will remain the same).

If you are unable to solve false sharing through any other means, consider using this annotation. One benefit is that, since the JVM understands the architecture of the CPU it is running on, it can automatically figure out the size of the required padding—though when AMD (or whoever) comes out with a new processor with a new cache line size, older versions of the JVM will have to guess what the necessary size is. Like all padding solutions, though, using this annotation greatly expands the size of the target instance, so use great caution as to where it is applied.

By default, the JVM ignores this annotation except within classes in the JDK. To enable application code to use the annotation, include the -XX:-RestrictContended flag, which by default is true (meaning that the annotation is restricted to JDK classes). On the other hand, to disable the automatic padding that occurs in the JDK, set the -XX:-EnableContended flag, which by default is true. This will lead to reductions in the size of the Thread and ConcurrentHashMap classes.

Quick Summary

1. False sharing can have significant performance impact on code that frequently modifies volatile variables or exits synchronized blocks.

2. False sharing is difficult to detect. When a loop seems to be taking too long to occur, inspect the code to see if it matches the pattern where false sharing can occur.

3. False sharing is best avoided by moving the data to local variables and storing them later. Alternately, padding can sometimes be used to move the conflicting variables to different cache lines.

JVM Thread Tunings

The JVM has a few miscellaneous tunings that affect the performance of threads and synchronization.

Tuning Thread Stack Sizes

When space is at a premium, the memory used by threads can be adjusted. Each thread has a native stack, which is where the OS stores the call stack information of the thread (e.g., the fact that the main() method has called the calculate() method, which has called the add() method).

The default thread stack size for different versions of the JVM is shown in Table 9-9. As a general rule, many applications can actually run with a 128 KB stack size in a 32-bit JVM, and a 256 KB stack size in a 64-bit JVM. The potential downside to setting this value too small is that a thread with an extremely large call stack will throw a StackOverflowError.

Table 9-9. Default stack size for various JVMs

Operating system	32-bit	64-bit
Linux	320 KB	1 MB
Mac OS	N/A	1 MB
Solaris Sparc	512 KB	1 MB
Solaris X86	320 KB	1 MB
Windows	320 KB	1 MB

In a 64-bit JVM, there is usually no reason to set this value unless the machine is quite strained for physical memory and the smaller stack size will prevent applications from running out of native memory. On the other hand, using a smaller (e.g., 128 KB) stack size on a 32-bit JVM is often a good idea, as it frees up memory in the process size and allows the JVM to utilize a larger heap.

Out of Native Memory

One time an OutOfMemoryError can occur is when there isn't enough native memory to create the thread. This can indicate one of three things:

1. In a 32-bit JVM, the process is at its 4 GB (or less, depending on the OS) maximum size.

2. The system has actually run out of virtual memory.

3. On Unix-style systems, the user has already created (between all programs she is running) the maximum number of processes configured for her login. Individual threads are considered a process in that regard.

Reducing the stack size can overcome the first two issues, but it will have no effect on the third. Unfortunately, there is no way to tell from the JVM error which of these three cases applies, but consider any of these causes when this error is encountered.

To change the stack size for a thread, use the -Xss=*N* flag (e.g., -Xss=256k).

 Quick Summary

1. Thread stack sizes can be reduced on machines where memory is scarce.

2. Thread stack sizes can be reduced on 32-bit JVMs to allow the heap to consume slightly more memory within the 4 GB process size limit.

Biased Locking

When locks are contended, the JVM (and operating system) have choices about how the lock should be allocated. The lock can be granted fairly, meaning that each thread will be given the lock in a round-robin fashion. Alternately, the lock can be biased toward the thread that most recently accessed the lock.

The theory behind biased locking is that if a thread recently used a lock, the processor's cache is more likely to still contain data the thread will need the next time it executes code protected by that same lock. If the thread is given priority for reobtaining the lock, the probability of cache hits increases. When this works out, performance is improved. But because biased locking requires some bookkeeping, it can sometimes be worse for performance.

In particular, applications that use a thread pool—including most application servers —often perform worse when biased locking is in effect. In that programming model, different threads are equally likely to access the contended locks. For these kind of applications, a small performance improvement can be obtained by disabling biased locking using the -XX:-UseBiasedLocking option. Biased locking is enabled by default.

Lock Spinning

The JVM has two options for handling a synchronized lock that is contended. The thread that is blocked from accessing the lock can enter a busy loop, where it executes a few instructions and then checks the lock again, or the thread can be placed in a queue somewhere and notified when the lock is available (making the CPU available for other threads).

If the contended lock is held for a short period of time, then the busy loop (known as thread spinning) is much faster than the alternative. If the contended lock is held for a long period of time, then it is better for the second thread to wait for a notification, which allows a third thread to use the CPU.

The JVM will find a reasonable balance between these two cases, self-adjusting the amount it spins before relegating a thread to a queue to be notified. There are parameters to tune the spinning, but most of them are experimental, and all of them are subject to change, even within minor update releases.

The only reasonable way to affect how the JVM treats spinning locks is something that should be done in all cases anyway: make the synchronized blocks as short as possible. That limits the amount of nonproductive spinning and makes it less likely that the thread will need to be placed in the notify queue.

The UseSpinning Flag

Previous versions of Java supported a flag to enable or disable spin locks: `-XX:+UseSpinning`. In Java 7 and beyond, that flag no longer has any effect: the use of spin locks cannot be disabled. For backward compatibility, that flag is still accepted in Java 7 command lines up through 7u40, but it is a no-op. Somewhat oddly, the default value for that flag is reported to be `false`, even through spinning is always in effect.

Beginning in Java 7u40 (and in Java 8), that flag is no longer supported, and use of the flag will generate an error.

Thread Priorities

Each Java thread has a developer-defined priority, which is a hint to the operating system about how important the program thinks the particular thread is. If you have different threads doing different tasks, you might think you could use the thread priority to improve the performance of certain tasks at the expense of other tasks running on a lower-priority thread. Unfortunately, it doesn't quite work like that.

Operating systems calculate a "current" priority for every thread running on a machine. The current priority takes into account the Java-assigned priority, but it also includes many other factors, the most important of which is how long it has been since the thread last ran. This ensures that all threads will have an opportunity to run at some point. Regardless of its priority, no thread will "starve" waiting for access to the CPU.

The balance between these two factors varies among operating systems. On Unix-based systems, the calculation of the overall priority is dominated by the amount of time it has been since the thread has last run—the Java-level priority of a thread has very little effect. On Windows, threads with a higher Java priority tend to run more than threads with a lower priority, but even low-priority threads get a fair amount of CPU time.

In either case, you cannot depend on the priority of a thread to affect its performance. If some tasks are more important than other tasks, application logic must be used to prioritize them.

One way this can be done (to some extent) is to assign the tasks to different thread pools and change the size of those pools. An example of that appears in Chapter 10.

Monitoring Threads and Locks

When analyzing an application's performance for the efficiency of threading and synchronization, there are two things to look for: the overall number of threads (to make sure it is neither too high nor too low), and the amount of time threads spend waiting for a lock or other resource.

Thread Visibility

Virtually every JVM monitoring tool provides information about the number of threads (and what they are doing). Interactive tools like `jconsole` show the state of threads within the JVM. On the `jconsole` Threads panel, you can watch in real time as the number of threads increases and decreases during the execution of your program. Figure 9-2 shows an example.

At one point in time, the application (NetBeans) was using a maximum of 45 threads. There was a burst at the beginning of the graph where it was using up to 38, but it settled on using between 30 and 31. `jconsole` can also print an individual thread stack; as the figure shows, the Java2D Disposer thread is presently waiting on a reference queue lock.

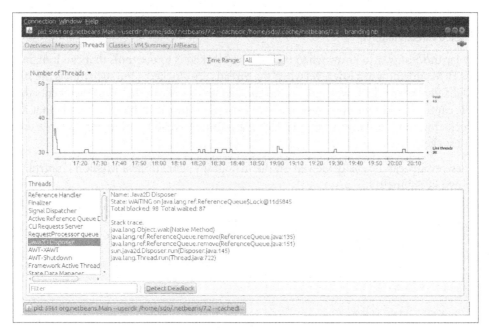

Figure 9-2. View of live threads in JConsole

Blocked Thread Visibility

Real-time thread monitoring is useful for a very high-level picture of what threads are running in the application, but it doesn't really provide any data on what those threads are doing. Determining where the threads are spending CPU cycles requires the use of a profiler, as discussed in Chapter 3. Profilers provide great visibility into what threads are executing, and they are generally sophisticated enough to guide you to areas in the code where better algorithms and code choices can speed up overall execution.

It is more difficult to diagnose threads that are blocked, although that information is often more important in the overall execution of an application—particularly if that code is running on a multi-CPU system and is not utilizing all the available CPU. There are three approaches to performing this diagnosis. One approach is again to use a profiler, since most profiling tools will provide a timeline of thread execution that allows you to see the points in time when a thread was blocked. An example of that is also given in Chapter 3.

Blocked threads and JFR

By far the best way to know when threads are blocked is to use tools that can look into the JVM and know at a low level when the threads are blocked. One such tool is the Java Flight Recorder, which was introduced in Chapter 3. We can drill into the events that JFR captures and look for those that are causing a thread to block (threads that are blocked waiting to acquire a monitor, or are waiting to read or, more rarely, write data to a socket).

These events can be easily viewed on the histogram panel of Java Mission Control, as shown in Figure 9-3.

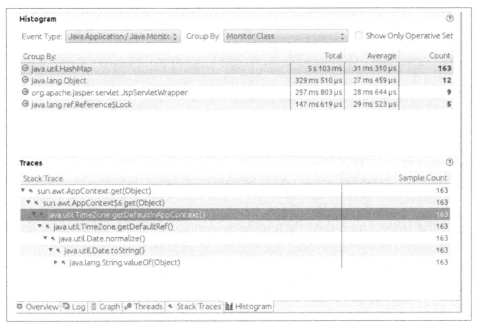

Figure 9-3. Threads blocked by a monitor in JFR

In this sample, the lock associated with the HashMap in the sun.awt.AppContext.get() method was contended 163 times (over 66 seconds), causing an average 31 ms increase in the response time of the request being measured. The stack trace points out that the contention stems from the way the JSP is writing a java.util.Date object. To improve the scalability of this code, a thread-local date formatter could be used instead of simply calling the date's toString() method.

This process—choosing the blocking event from the histogram and examining the calling code—works for any kind of blocking event; it is made possible by the tight integration of the tool with the JVM.

Blocked threads and JStack

If a commercial version of the JVM is not available, one alternative is to take a lot of thread stacks from the program and examine those. jstack, jcmd, and other tools can provide information about the state of every thread in a VM, including whether the thread is running, waiting for a lock, waiting for I/O, and so on. This can be quite useful for determining what's going on in an application, as long as too much is not expected from the output.

The first caveat in looking at thread stacks is that the JVM can only dump a thread's stack at certain locations (safepoints). Second, stacks are dumped for each thread one at a time, so it is possible to get conflicting information from them: two threads can show up holding the same lock, or a thread can show up waiting for a lock that no other thread holds.

A JStack Profiler

It is tempting to think you can take multiple stack dumps in rapid succession and use that data as a quick-and-dirty profiler. After all, sampling profilers work in essentially the same way: they periodically probe the stack a thread is executing and extrapolate how much time is spent in methods based on that. But between safepoints and inconsistent snapshots, this doesn't work out too well; you can sometimes get a very high-level overview of the expensive methods in your application by looking at thread stacks, but a real profiler will give far more accurate information.

Thread stacks can show how significantly threads are blocked (since a thread that is blocked is already at a safepoint). If successive thread dumps show a large number of threads blocked on a lock, then you can conclude that the lock in question has significant contention. If successive thread dumps show a large number of threads blocked waiting for I/O, then you can conclude that whatever I/O they are reading needs to be tuned (e.g., if they are making a database call, the SQL they are executing needs to be tuned, or the database itself needs to be tuned).

The online examples for this book have a rudimentary parser for jstack output that can summarize the state of all threads from one or more thread dumps. A problem with jstack output is that it can change from release to release, so developing a robust parser can be difficult. There is no guarantee that the parser in the online examples won't need to be tweaked for your particular JVM.

The basic output of the jstack parser looks like this:

```
% jstack pid > jstack.out
% java ParseJStack jstack.out
[Partial output...]
Threads in start Running
    8 threads in java.lang.Throwable.getStackTraceElement(Native
Total Running Threads: 8

Threads in state Blocked by Locks
    41 threads running in
        com.sun.enterprise.loader.EJBClassLoader.getResourceAsStream
        (EJBClassLoader.java:801)
Total Blocked by Locks Threads: 41

Threads in state Waiting for notify
    39 threads running in
        com.sun.enterprise.web.connector.grizzly.LinkedListPipeline.getTask
        (LinkedListPipeline.java:294)
    18 threads running in System Thread
Total Waiting for notify Threads: 74

Threads in state Waiting for I/O read
    14 threads running in com.acme.MyServlet.doGet(MyServlet.java:603)
Total Waiting for I/O read Threads: 14
```

The parser aggregates all the threads and shows how many are in various states. Eight threads are currently running (they happen to be doing a stack trace—a quite expensive operation which is better to avoid).

Forty-one threads are blocked by a lock. The method reported is the first non-JDK method in the stack trace, which in this example is the GlassFish method EJBClassLoader.getResourceAsStream(). The next step would be to consult the stack trace and search for that method and see what resource the thread is blocked on.

In this example, all the threads were blocked waiting to read the same JAR file, and the stack trace for those threads showed that all the calls came from instantiating a new SAX parser. As discussed in Chapter 10, the SAX parser can be defined dynamically by listing the resource in the manifest file of the application's JAR files, which means that the JDK must search the entire class path for those entries until it finds the one the application wants to use (or until it doesn't find anything and falls back to the system parser). Since reading the JAR file requires a synchronization lock, all those threads trying to create a parser end up contending for the same lock, which is greatly hampering the application's throughput. (This is why Chapter 10 recommends setting the -Djavax.xml.pars ers.SAXParserFactory property to avoid those lookups.)

The larger point here is that a lot of blocked threads is a problem affecting performance. Whatever the cause of the blocking is, changes need to be made to the configuration or application to avoid it.

What about the threads that are waiting for notification? Those threads are waiting for something else to happen. Often they are in a pool waiting for notification that a task is ready (e.g., the getTask() method in the output above is waiting for a request). System threads are doing things like RMI distributed GC, or JMX monitoring—they appear in the jstack output as threads that have only JDK classes in their stack. These conditions do not necessarily indicate a performance problem; it is normal for them to be waiting for a notification.

Another problem creeps up in the threads waiting for I/O read: these are doing a blocking I/O call (usually the socketRead0() method). This is also hampering throughput: the thread is waiting for a backend resource to answer its request. That's the time to start looking into the performance of the database or other backend resource.

 Quick Summary

1. Basic visibility into the threads of a system provides an overview of the number of threads running.

2. For performance analysis, the important facet of thread visibility is when threads are blocked on a resource or on I/O.

3. Java Flight Recorder provides an easy way to examine the events that caused a thread to block.

4. jstack provides some level of visibility into the resources threads are blocked on.

Summary

Understanding how threads operate can yield important performance benefits. Thread performance, though, is not so much about tuning—there are relatively few JVM flags to tweak, and those few flags have limited effects.

Instead, good thread performance is about following best-practice guidelines for managing the number of threads and for limiting the effects of synchronization. With the help of appropriate profiling and lock analysis tools, applications can be examined and modified so that threading and locking issues do not negatively affect performance.

## CHAPTER 10

Java Enterprise Edition Performance

This chapter focuses on using Java EE (specifically, Java EE 6 and 7). It covers JSPs, servlets, and EJB 3.0 Session Beans—though not EJB 3.0 Entity Beans (Java Persistence API entities), since they are not specifically a Java EE technology (they are discussed in depth in Chapter 11).

Basic Web Container Performance

The heart of a Java EE application server is the performance of its web container, which handles HTTP requests via basic servlets and JSP pages.

Here are the basic ways to improve performance of the web container. The details of how these changes are made vary depending on the Java EE implementation, but the concepts apply to any server.

Produce less output
> Producing less output will speed up the time it takes your web page to get to the browser.

Produce less whitespace
> In servlet code, don't put whitespace in calls to the `PrintWriter`; that whitespace takes time to transmit over the network (and, for that matter, to process in the code, but the network time is more important). This means you should call the `print()` method in preference to the `println()` method, but it primarily means not writing tabs or spaces to reflect the structure of the HTML. It is true that someone who views the source of the web page won't see its structure, though they can always use an XML or HTML editor if they're really interested in that. That applies to an in-house QA or performance group too: certainly it makes my job easier when debugging a web page if the source reflects the structure of the page. But in the end, I'll put up with loading the source into a formatting editor in order to improve the application's response time. Most application servers can trim the whitespace out

of JSPs automatically; for example, in Tomcat (and open source Java EE servers based on Tomcat), there is a `trimSpaces` directive that will trim out any leading and trailing whitespace from JSP pages. That allows the JSP pages to be developed and maintained with correct (for humans, at least) indentation, but without paying the penalty for transmitting all that needless whitespace over the network.

Combine CSS and JavaScript resources

As a developer, it makes sense to keep CSS resources in separate files; they are easier to maintain that way. The same is true of JavaScript routines. But when it comes time to serve up those resources, it is much more efficient to send one larger file rather than several smaller files. There is no Java EE standard for this, nor is there a way to do it automatically in most application servers. But there are several development tools that can help you combine those resources.

Compress the output

From the perspective of the user sitting at her browser, the longest time in executing a web request is often the time required to send the HTML back from the server. This is something that is frequently missed in performance testing, since performance testing between clients (emulating browsers) and servers often occurs over fast local-area networks. Your actual users might be on a "fast" broadband network, but that network is still an order of magnitude slower than the LAN between the machines in your lab. Most application servers have a mechanism to compress the data sent to the browser: the HTML data is compressed and sent to the browser with a content type of `zip` or `gzip`. This is done only if the original request indicates that the browser supports compression. All modern browsers support that feature. Enabling compression requires more CPU cycles on the server, but the smaller amount of data usually takes less time to traverse the network, yielding a net improvement. However, unlike the other optimizations discussed in this section, it is not universally an improvement; examples later in this section show that when compression is enabled on a LAN, performance may decrease. The same is true for an application that sends very small pages (though most application servers will allow output to be compressed only if it is larger than some specified size).

Don't use dynamic JSP compilation

By default, most Java EE application servers will allow a JSP page to be changed on the fly: the JSP file can be edited in place (wherever it is deployed), and those changes will be reflected the next time the page is visited. That's quite useful when a new JSP is being developed, but in production it slows down the server, since every time the JSP is accessed, the server must check the last modified date on its file to see if the JSP needs to be reloaded. This tunable is often called development mode, and it should be off in production and for performance testing.

Should You Pre-encode Strings?

Application servers spend a lot of time doing character conversion: converting from Java `String` objects (which are stored in UTF-16 format) to whatever bytes the client is expecting. Many of these strings are always the same. The HTML strings in a web page don't usually change based on the data (and if they do, they are still drawn from a constant set of strings).

Should these strings be pre-encoded into a byte array so that the byte array can be reused? The answer depends on the application server and application.

The HTML strings in JSP pages are written by the application server. Whether or not those strings are pre-encoded depends on the server; some servers offer this ability as an option, and some do it automatically.

In a servlet, those strings can be pre-encoded and sent to the network using the `write()` method of a `ServletOutputStream` rather than using the `print()` method of a `PrintWriter`. Dynamic data, though, still needs to go through the `print()` method so that it is correctly encoded for the target. (You can figure out the target encoding from the headers and encode the string yourself, but that is relatively error prone.)

There are important differences in the way application servers implement those output interfaces and where the application server is buffering data within them. In some servers, mixing calls between the servlet output stream and its companion print writer causes network buffers to be flushed frequently. Frequent flushing of the buffers is very expensive in terms of performance—more expensive than re-encoding the data would be. Similarly, encoding a large block of data is usually not much more expensive than encoding a small block of data: setting up the call to the encoders is what is expensive in the first place. Hence, frequent calls to the encoder for small pieces of dynamic data interleaved with calls to send the pre-encoded byte arrays may slow down an application: the many calls to the encoder will take longer to execute than one call to encode everything (including the static data).

There are cases where the pre-encoding in your code can help. But it is definitely a your-mileage-may-vary situation.

These optimizations can make a significant difference in real-world (as opposed to laboratory) performance. Table 10-1 shows the kind of results that might be expected. Tests were run using the long-output form of the stock history servlet, retrieving data for a 10-year period. This results in an uncompressed, untrimmed HTML page of about 100 KB. To minimize the effect of bandwidth considerations, the test ran only a single user with a 100 ms think time and measured the average response time for requests. In the LAN case, tests were run over a local network with a 100 MB switch connecting components; in the broadband case, tests were run over my home machine's cable modem (where I average 30 Mb per second download speed). The WAN case uses the public WiFi connection in my local coffee shop—the speed of which is fairly unreliable (the table shows the average of samples over a 4-hour period).

Table 10-1. Effect of optimizations on web output size

Optimization applied	ART on LAN	ART on broadband	ART on public WiFi
None	20 ms	26 ms	1003 ms
Whitespace removed	20 ms	10 ms	43 ms
Output compressed	30 ms	5 ms	17 ms

This highlights the importance of testing in the environment where the application will actually be deployed. If only the lab test were used to inform tuning choices, 80% of performance would have been left on the table. Although the nonlaboratory tests in this case were run to a remote application server (using a public cloud service), hardware-based emulators can simulate such connectivity in a lab environment, allowing control over all the machines involved. (The cloud service machine is faster than the LAN machine as well; the numbers between machines are not directly comparable.)

Quick Summary

1. Test Java EE applications on the network infrastructure(s) where they will actually be used.

2. External networks are still relatively slow. Limiting the amount of data an application writes will be a big performance win.

HTTP Session State

There are two important performance tips regarding HTTP session state.

HTTP session state memory

Pay attention to the way that HTTP session state is managed in an application. HTTP session data is usually long-lived, so it is quite easy to fill the heap up with session state data. That leads to the usual issues when GC needs to run too frequently. (In addition, recall from Chapter 7 that the more live data that exists in the heap, the longer each individual GC takes.)

This is best dealt with at an application level: think carefully before deciding to store something in the HTTP session. If the data can be easily re-created, it is probably best left out of the session state. Also be aware of how long the session state is kept around. This value is stored in the *web.xml* file for an application and defaults to 30 minutes:

```
<session-timeout>30</session-timeout>
```

That's a long time to keep session data around—is a user really expected to return after a 29-minute absence? Reducing that value can definitely mitigate the heap impact of having too much session data.

This is an area where the implementation of the Java EE application server can help. Although the session data must be available for 30 minutes (or whatever value is specified), the data doesn't necessarily have to remain in the Java heap. The application server can move the session data (by serializing it) to disk or a remote cache—say, maybe after 10 minutes of idle time. That frees up space within the application server's heap and still fulfills the contract with the application to save the state for 30 minutes. If the user does come back after 29 minutes, her first request might take a little longer as the state is read back from disk, but overall performance of the application server will have been better in the meantime.

This is also an important principle to keep in mind while testing: what is the realistic expectation for session management among the users of the application? Do they log in once in the morning and use that session all day? Do they come and go frequently, leaving lots of abandoned sessions on the server? Something in between? Whatever the answer is, make sure that testing scenario reflects the expected use of the session. Otherwise, the production server will be ill-tuned, since its heap will be utilized in a completely different way than the performance tests measured.

Load generators have different ways of managing sessions, but in general there will be an option to start a new session at certain points of the testing (which is accomplished by closing the socket connection to the server and discarding all previous cookies). In the tests throughout this book using fhb, a single session is maintained throughout each test for each client thread. (fhb doesn't actually have an option to create new sessions anyway, though a custom driver written in faban can do so.)

Highly available HTTP session state

If an application server is tested in a highly available (HA) configuration, then you must also pay attention to how the server replicates the session state data. The application server has the choice to replicate the entire session state on every request, or to replicate only the data that has changed. It should come as no surprise that the second option is almost always the more performant one. Once again, this is a feature that is supported by most application servers but that is set in a vendor-specific way. Consult the app server documentation regarding how to replicate on an attribute basis.

However, for this solution to work, developers must follow guidelines about how session state is handled. In particular, the application server cannot keep track of changes to objects that are already stored in the session. If an object is retrieved from a session and then changed, the setAttribute() method must be called to let the application server know that the value of the object has changed:

```
HttpSession session = request.getSession(true);
ArrayList<StockPriceHistory> al =
    (ArrayList<StockPriceHistory>) session.getAttribute("saveHistory");
al.add(...some data...);
session.setAttribute("saveHistory", al);
```

That final call to setAttribute() is not required in a single (nonreplicated) server: the array list is already in the session state. If that call is omitted and all future requests for this session return to this server, everything will work correctly.

If that call is omitted, the session is replicated to a backup server, and a request is then processed by the backup server, the application may find that the data in the array list has not been changed. This is because the application server "optimized" its session state handling by copying only changed data to the backup server. Absent a call to the setAttribute() method, the application server had no idea that the array list was changed, and so did not replicate it again after the above code was executed.

This is a somewhat murky area of the Java EE specification. The spec does not mandate that the setAttribute() method be called in this case, but that convention is used by virtually every Java EE application server that supports high availability. For some application servers, that is the only way session replication works. Others allow you to configure how data is replicated—including replicating all the session state data on every call, so that an application that did not call the setAttribute() method would still function correctly. That works functionally, but the performance will be much worse than if the app server could replicate only the changed attributes.

The moral of the story: call the setAttribute() method whenever you change the value of an object stored in the session state, and make sure that your application server is configured to replicate only changed data.

 Quick Summary

1. Session state can have a major impact on the performance of an application server.

2. To reduce the effect of session state on the garbage collector, keep as little data in the session state as possible, and expire the session as soon as possible.

3. Look into app server-specific tunings to move stale session data out of the heap.

4. When using high availability, make sure to configure the application server to replicate only attributes that have changed.

Thread Pools

Thread pools are covered in depth in Chapter 9. Java EE servers make extensive use of such pools; everything that chapter says about properly sizing the thread pool applies to application servers.

Application servers typically have more than one thread pool. One thread pool is commonly used to handle servlet requests, another handles remote EJB requests, and a third might handle Java Message Service (JMS) requests. Some application servers also allow multiple pools to be used for each kind of traffic: for example, servlet requests to different URLs or calls to different remote EJBs can be handled by separate thread pools.

Separate thread pools allow limited prioritization of different traffic within the application server. Take the case of an application server that is running on a machine with four CPUs; assume that its HTTP thread pool has 12 threads and its EJB thread pool has 4. All threads will compete for the CPU, but when all threads are busy, a servlet request will be three times more likely than an EJB request to get access to the CPU. In effect, the servlet is given a 3x priority.

There are limitations to this. The separate pools cannot be set so that an EJB request would run only if there were no servlet requests pending. As long as there are threads in the EJB thread pool, those threads will compete equally for the CPU, no matter how busy the servlet thread pool is.

Similarly, care should be taken not to throttle a particular pool below the amount of work expected when the server is otherwise idle. If the JMS pool is sized to have only three threads on the four-CPU machine, then it won't use all of the available CPU if there are only JMS requests to process. To compensate for that, the size of all pools can be increased proportionally, but then you run the risk of oversaturating the machine by trying to run too many threads.

Hence, this kind of tuning is quite delicate and depends on having a good model of the traffic into your application server. It is used to get that last few percentage points of performance from your application.

Enterprise Java Session Beans

This section looks into the performance of EJB 3.0 session beans. Java EE containers manage the lifecycle of an EJB in a very specific way; the guidelines in this section can help make sure that lifecycle management doesn't impact the application's performance.

Tuning EJB Pools

EJBs are stored in object pools because they can be quite expensive to construct (and destroy). Without pooling, a call to an EJB would involve these steps:

- Create the EJB object

- Process annotations and inject any resource dependencies into the new EJB

- Call any method annotated with `@PostConstruct`

- For stateful beans, call any method annotated with `@Init`, or call the `ejbCreate()` method

- Execute the business method

- Call any method annotated with `@PreRemove`

- For stateful beans, call the `remove()` method

When the EJB is obtained from a pool, only the business method needs to be executed —the other six steps can be skipped. Though object pooling is not necessarily useful in the general case (see Chapter 7), this is one case where the expense of initializing an object makes pooling worthwhile.

The Cost of EJB Object Pooling

EJB pools provide a good idea of the relative benefits of object pools, since a Java EE application server can be tested with differently sized EJB pools to measure the difference in performance between objects obtained from the pool and objects created on demand.

In this example, I used the GlassFish 4.0 application server with the standard stock history servlet. The stateless bean in that application has virtually no initialization overhead. It does have a `@PostConstruct` method, but that method is empty.

The `@PostConstruct` method is typically used for initializing resources; for example, it could perform a (relatively expensive) Java Naming and Directory Interface (JNDI) lookup. To emulate that, I changed the stock servlet's `@PostConstruct` method to `sleep` so it can mimic the time that would otherwise be required to execute some initialization code.

Table 10-2 shows the response time from simulating 64 clients hitting that application with different EJB pool sizes and sleep times in the `@PostConstruct` method.

Table 10-2. Effect of object pools on EJB response time

Size of EJB pool	Time to initialize	Average response time
1	0 ms	0.37 seconds
64	0 ms	0.37 seconds
1	25 ms	0.40 seconds
64	25 ms	0.37 seconds
1	50 ms	0.42 seconds
64	50 ms	0.37 seconds

With no initialization time, there is no benefit in having an EJB pool. But when initialization takes 25 ms or 50 ms and the pool has a size of 1—meaning it must create a new EJB object for each invocation—there is a predictable penalty in the average response time.

Since there are only 64 (small) objects in the EJB pool, the pool is unlikely to introduce any GC penalty here. This is another key feature of a successful object pool: when it makes sense to use one, keep it small.

This performance benefit only accrues if there is an available EJB object in the application server's pool, so the application server must be tuned to support the expected number of EJBs an application will simultaneously use. If an application uses an EJB and there are no pooled instances, the application server will go through the entire lifecycle of creating, initializing, using, and destroying the EJB object.

The number of objects an application needs depends, of course, on how the application is used. A typical starting point is to make sure that there are as many objects in the EJB pool as there are worker threads in the application server, since it is common that each request will need at most one EJB. Note that EJB pools are per type: if an application has two EJB classes, the application server will use two pools (each of which can be sized to the number of threads in the pool).

Application servers differ in the way EJB pools are tuned, but the common case is that there is a global (or default) configuration for each EJB pool, and individual EJBs that need a different configuration can override that (often in their deployment descriptors). For instance, in the GlassFish application server, the EJB container uses a default of 32 EJB instances in each pool, and the size of an individual bean's pool can be set with this stanza in the *sun-ejb-jar.xml* file:

```
<bean-pool>
  <steady-pool-size>8</steady-pool-size>
  <resize-quantity>2</resize-quantity>
  <max-pool-size>64</max-pool-size>
  <pool-idle-timeout-in-seconds>300</pool-idle-timeout-in-seconds>
</bean-pool>
```

This doubles the maximum size of the bean's EJB pool to 64.

The penalty for creating an EJB pool size that is too big is not usually very large. Unused instances in the pool will mean that GC will be slightly less efficient, but the pool sizes in general should be so small that the unused instances don't have a significant impact. The exception is if the bean holds onto a lot of memory, in which case the GC penalty starts to grow. However, as can be deduced from the above XML stanza, the common way for an application server to manage the pool is to have a steady size in addition to a maximum size. In the example above, if traffic comes in such that at most 10 instances of this EJB (e.g., from 10 simultaneous requests) are used, only 10 EJB instances will ever be created—the pool will never begin to approach its maximum of 64.

If there is a brief traffic spike, the pool might create those 64 instances, but as the traffic wanes, those additional EJBs will be idle. Once they are idle for 300 seconds, they will be destroyed and their memory eligible for GC. This minimizes the effect of the pool on GC.

Hence, be more concerned about tuning the steady size of EJB pools than the maximum size.

Quick Summary

1. EJB pools are a classic example of object pooling: they are effectively pooled because they can be expensive to initialize, and because there are relatively few of them.

2. EJB pools generally have a steady and maximum size. Both values should be tuned for a particular environment, but the steady size is more important to minimize long-term effects on the garbage collector.

Tuning EJB Caches

There is another consideration for stateful session beans, which is that they are subject to passivation: in order to save memory, the application server can choose to serialize the state of the bean and save it to disk. This is a severe performance penalty and in most cases is best avoided.

Or, frankly, I would recommend that it should be avoided in almost all cases. The usual argument for passivation is the scenario where the session is idle for hours or days at a time. When the user does come back (days later), you want her to find her state intact. The problem with that scenario is it assumes the EJB session is the only important state. Usually, though, the EJB is associated with an HTTP session, and keeping that session for days is not recommended. If the application server has a nonstandard feature to store the HTTP session to disk, then a configuration where both the HTTP session and EJB session data are passivated at the same time (and for the same duration) may make sense. Even then, though, there is likely an additional external state as well. (What if the user has in his shopping cart an item that is no longer available?)

If long-lived state is required, you'll usually need to bypass the normal Java EE state mechanisms.

Stateful beans that are assigned to a session are not held in the EJB pool; they are held in the EJB cache. Hence, the EJB cache must be tuned so that it is large enough to hold the maximum number of sessions expected to be active simultaneously in an application. Otherwise, the sessions that have been least recently used will be passivated. Again, accomplishing this is different in different application servers. GlassFish sets a default value for the cache size of 512, and the value can be overridden globally in the domain configuration, or on a per-EJB basis in the *sun-ejb-jar.xml* file.

Quick Summary

1. EJB caches are used only for stateful session beans while they are associated with an HTTP session.

2. EJB caches should be tuned large enough to prevent passivation.

Monitoring EJB Pools

Just how do you know what values to use for the size of the EJB pools and caches? One way is to make an educated guess based on knowledge of how the application works in conjunction with its expected load. But the only way actually to know if too many EJBs are being created (or too many stateful session beans are being passivated) is to use the monitoring facilities of the application server.

Figure 10-1 shows an example of how the monitoring is accomplished in GlassFish. In this case, the number of EJBs destroyed is not zero, indicating that some EJBs were created and then destroyed because there was no available bean in the pool for that operation. Accordingly, the number of EJBs created is greater than the maximum pool size (which in this case was four). That is an indication that the EJB pool is undersized.

Monitor (5 Statistics)	
▽ EJB Pool Statistics : StockPriceHi	
Name	**Value**
NumThreadsWaiting	0count
JmsMaxMessagesLoad	0 count
TotalBeansDestroyed	70 count
NumBeansInPool	4count
TotalBeansCreated	74 count

Figure 10-1. Sample EJB pool monitoring

It is important to monitor statistics like this in order to understand the performance of applications, but be aware the monitoring itself imposes some cost. In this case, I set the GlassFish monitoring level for the EJB container to HIGH to generate those statistics, and the total throughput dropped by about 5%. That's a small price to pay for some visibility into an application, but for application servers that offer configurable monitoring, pay attention to what you need and configure monitoring accordingly. In the case of Glass-Fish, configuring the monitoring level to LOW has a negligible impact—that monitoring can be used for most operations, and monitoring can be dynamically set to HIGH when more information is required.

Local and Remote Instances

EJBs can be accessed via local or remote interfaces. In the canonical Java EE deployment, EJBs are accessed through servlets, and the servlet has the choice of using the local or remote interface to access the EJB. If the EJB is on another system, then of course the remote interface must be used, but if the EJB is colocated with the servlet (which is the more common deployment topology), the servlet should always use a local interface to access the EJB.

That may seem obvious, since a remote interface implies a network call. But that isn't the reason—when the servlet and remote EJB are deployed in the same application server, most servers are smart enough to bypass the network call and just invoke the EJB method through normal method calls.

The reason to prefer local interfaces is the way in which the two interfaces handle their arguments. Arguments that are passed to (or returned from) a local EJB follow normal Java semantics: primitives are passed by value and objects are passed by reference. (Or, strictly speaking, the object handle is still passed by value, but references through the object make it appear that the object is passed by reference.)

Arguments that are passed to (or returned from) a remote EJB must always be passed by value. That is the only possible semantic over a network: the sender serializes the object and transmits the byte stream, while the receiver deserializes the byte stream to reconstitute the object. Even when the server optimizes the local call by avoiding the network, it is not allowed to bypass the serialization/deserialization step. (Most servers will realize when the object in question is immutable—a String, or a primitive value—and skip the serialization of those objects. But that isn't possible in the general case.) No matter how well written the server is, using a remote EJB interface within the server will always be slower than using a local one.

Java EE offers other deployment scenarios. For example, the servlet and EJBs can be deployed in different tiers, and remote EJBs can be accessed from an ordinary application via their remote interface. There are often business or functional reasons that dictate the topology; for example, if the EJBs access corporate databases, you may want to run them on machines that are behind a separate firewall from the servlet container. Those reasons trump performance considerations. But from the strict perspective of performance, colocating EJBs with whatever is accessing them and using local interfaces will always be faster than using a remote protocol.

Speaking of protocols, all remote EJBs must support the IIOP (CORBA) protocol. That is great for interoperability, particular with other programs that are not written in Java. Java EE server vendors are also allowed to use any other protocol, including proprietary ones, for remote access. Those proprietary protocols are invariably faster than CORBA (that is the reason the server vendors developed them in the first place). So when remote EJB calls must be used (and when interoperability is not a concern), explore the options for access protocols provided by the application server vendor.

Quick Summary

Remote interfaces impose a performance burden when calling EJBs, even within the same server.

XML and JSON Processing

When Java EE application servers host servlet-based applications to display their output in a browser, the data returned to the user is almost always HTML. This chapter has covered some best practices of how to exchange that data.

Application servers are also used to exchange data with other programs, particularly via HTTP. Java EE supports different kinds of HTTP-based data transfer: full-blown web service calls using the JAX-WS stack, RESTful calls using JAX-RS, and even simpler roll-your-own HTTP calls. The common feature of these APIs is that they utilize a text-based data transfer (based on either XML or JSON). Although they are quite different in their data representation, XML and JSON are similar in terms of how they are processed in Java, and the performance considerations of that processing are similar.

This is not meant to minimize the important functional differences between the two representations. As always, the choice of which representation to utilize should be based on algorithmic and programmatic factors rather than (solely) on their performance characteristics. If interoperability with another system is the goal, then the choice is dictated by that defined interface. In a complex program, dealing with traditional Java objects is often much easier than walking through document trees; in that case, JAXB (and hence XML) is the better option, at least for the time being: Java EE 7 only mandates support for JSON-P via JSR 353 (which supplies standard parsing and document model features). At the time of this writing, the JSON-B JSR (which will supply JAXB-like features for JSON) has not yet been approved (but will likely be a future technology).

There are other important functional differences between XML and JSON as well. So while this section makes some performance comparisons, the real goal here is to understand how to get the best possible performance out of whichever representation is chosen, rather than to drive a choice that might not be optimal for a particular environment.

Data Size

"Basic Web Container Performance" on page 277 showed the effect of the size of data on overall performance. In a distributed network environment, that size is always important. In that regard, JSON is widely considered to be smaller than XML, though that difference is typically small. In the tests for this section, I used the XML and JSON returned from requesting the 20 most popular items from eBay. The XML in that example is 23,031 bytes, while the JSON is smaller at only 16,078 bytes. The JSON data has no whitespace at all, making it difficult for a human to read, which makes sense—human readability isn't the goal. But oddly, the XML data is well structured, with lots of whitespace; it could be trimmed to 20,556 bytes. Still, that's a 25% difference, which occurs mostly because of the XML closing tags. In general, those closing tags will always make the XML output larger. Interestingly, there are a number of websites that automatically convert XML to JSON. These tend to take a naive approach; the JSON output will usually be larger than the XML data, mostly because human-readable JSON output has lots of whitespace, and a lot of unneeded structure.

Sample Data Payloads

The sample data used throughout this section comes from eBay. Like many companies, eBay provides interfaces for developers to leverage in their own applications. As is also typical, the data can be retrieved in either XML or JSON format.

The data retrieved is a list of the 20 best-selling items on eBay. A reduced sample of the XML data looks like this:

```
<xml version="1.0" encoding="UTF-8"?>
  <FindPopularItemsResponse xmlns="urn:ebay:apis:eBLBaseComponents"
      xmlns:xsi="http://www.w3.org/2001/XMLSchema-instance"
      xsi:schemaLocation="urn:ebay:apis:eBLBaseComponents docs/xsd/ebay.xsd">
  <Timestamp>2013-03-29T01:57:46.530Z</Timestamp>
  <Ack>Success</Ack>
  <Build>E815_CORE_APILW2_15855352_R1</Build>
  <Version>815</Version>
  <ItemArray>
   <Item>
     <ItemID>140356481394</ItemID>
     ...roughly 17 individual attributes for an item
   </Item>
   ... 19 other items in identical structure ...
  </ItemArray>
</FindPopularItemsResponse>
```

The JSON data is similar (though it has no whitespace, which has been added here for readability):

```
{"Timestamp":"2013-03-29T02:17:14.898Z",
 "Ack":"Success",
 "Build":"E815_CORE_APILW2_15855352_R1",
 "Version":"815",
 "ItemArray":{
    "Item":[{"ItemID":"140356481394", ... 17 individual attributes ... }],
    ... 19 other items in identical structure ...
 },
}
```

Whichever representation is used, both greatly benefit from enabling compression as they are transferred. In fact, once the data is compressed, the sizes are much closer: 3,471 bytes for the compressed JSON data and 3,742 for the compressed XML file. That makes the size difference less important, and the time to transmit the smaller compressed data will show the same benefit as transferring any other compressed HTTP data.

Quick Summary

Like HTML data, programmatic data will greatly benefit from reducing whitespace and being compressed.

An Overview of Parsing and Marshalling

Given a series of XML or JSON strings, a program must convert those strings into data suitable for processing by Java. This is called either marshalling or parsing, depending on the context and the resulting output. The reverse—producing XML or JSON strings from other data—is called unmarshalling.

There are four general techniques to handle the data:

Token parsers

A parser goes through the tokens of the input data and calls back methods on an object as it discovers tokens.

Pull parsers

The input data is associated with a parser and the program asks for (or pulls) a series of tokens from the parser.

Document models

The input data is converted to a document-style object that the application can then walk through as it looks for pieces of data.

Object representations

The input data is converted to one or more Java objects using a set of predefined classes that reflect the structure of the data (e.g., there will be a predefined `Person` class for data that represents an individual).

These techniques are listed in rough order of slowest to fastest, but again the functional differences between them are more important than their performance differences. There isn't a great deal of functional difference between the first two: either parser is adaptable to most algorithms that need only to scan through the data once and pull out information. But simple scanning is all a parser can do. Parsers are not ideally suited for data that must be accessed in random order, or examined more than once. To handle those situations, a program using only a simple parser would need to build some internal data structure, which is a simple matter of programming. But the document and Java object models already provide structured data, which may be easier than defining new structures on your own.

This, in fact, is the real difference between using a parser and using a data marshaller. The first two items in the list are pure parsers, and it is up to the application logic to handle the data as the parser provides it. The second two are data marshallers: they must use a parser to process the data, but they provide a data representation that more complex programs can use in their logic.

So the primary choice regarding which technique to use is determined by how the application needs to be written. If a program needs to make one simple pass through the data, then simply using the fastest parser will suffice. Directly using a parser is also appropriate if the data is to be saved in a simple, application-defined structure; for example, the prices for the items in the sample data could be saved to an `ArrayList`, which would be easy for other application logic to process.

Using a document model is more appropriate when the format of the data is important. If the format of the data must be preserved, then a document format is very easy: the data can be read into the document format, altered in some way, and then the document format can simply be written to a new data stream.

For ultimate flexibility, an object model provides Java-language level representation of the data. The data can be manipulated in the familiar terms of objects and their attributes. The added complexity in the marshalling is (mostly) transparent to the developer and may make that part of the application a little slower, but the productivity improvement in working with the code can offset that issue.

The goal of the examples used in this section is to take the 20-item XML or JSON document and save the item IDs into an array list. For some tests, only the first 10 items are needed. This emulates something often found in the real world—web interfaces often return more data than is actually needed. As a design consideration for a web service, that's a good thing: the setup for the call takes some time, and it is better to have fewer remote calls (even if they retrieve too much data) than to make many fine-grained remote calls.

While all the examples show this common operation, the point is not to compare their performance directly on only that part of the task. Rather, each example will show how to perform the operation most efficiently within the chosen framework, since the choice of the framework will be driven by reasons other than the pure parsing and/or marshalling performance.

Quick Summary

1. There are many ways for Java EE applications to process programmatic data.

2. As these techniques provide more functionality to developers, the cost of the data processing itself will increase. Don't let that dissuade you from choosing the right paradigm for handling the data in your application.

Choosing a Parser

All programmatic data must be parsed. Whether applications use a parser directly, or indirectly by using a marshalling framework, the choice of the parser is important in the overall performance of the data operations.

Pull parsers

From a developer's perspective, it is usually easiest to use a pull parser. In the XML world, these are known as StAX (Streaming API for XML) parsers. JSON-P provides only a pull parser.

Pull parsers operate by retrieving data from the stream on demand. The basic pull parser for the tests in this section has this loop as its main logic:

```
XMLStreamReader reader = staxFactory.createXMLStreamReader(ins);
while (reader.hasNext()) {
    reader.next();
    int state = reader.getEventType();
    switch (state) {
        case XMLStreamConstants.START_ELEMENT:
            String s = reader.getLocalName();
            if (ITEM_ID.equals(s)) {
                isItemID = true;
            }
            break;
        case XMLStreamConstants.CHARACTERS:
            if (isItemID) {
                String id = reader.getText();
```

```
            isItemID = false;
            if (addItemId(id)) {
                return;
            }
        }
        break;
    default:
        break;
    }
}
```

The parser returns a series of tokens. In the example most tokens are just discarded. When a start token is found, the code checks to see if the token is an item ID. If it is, then the next character token will be the ID the application wants to save. The ID is saved via the `addItemId()` method, which returns `true` if the desired number of IDs have been stored. When that happens, the loop can just return and not process the remaining data in the input stream.

Conceptually, the JSON parser works exactly the same way; only some of the API calls have changed:

```
while (parser.hasNext()) {
    Event event = parser.next();
    switch (event) {
        case KEY_NAME:
            String s = parser.getString();
            if (ITEM_ID.equals(s)) {
                isItemID = true;
            }
            break;
        case VALUE_STRING:
            if (isItemID) {
                if (addItemId(parser.getString())) {
                    return;
                }
                isItemID = false;
            }
            continue;
        default:
            continue;
    }
}
```

Processing only the necessary data here gives a predictable performance benefit. Table 10-3 shows the average time in milliseconds to parse the sample document assuming parsing stops after 10 items, and to process the entire document. Stopping after finding 10 items does not save 50% of the time (because there are other sections of the document that still get parsed), but the difference is still significant.

Table 10-3. Performance of pull parsers

Items processed	XML parser	JSON parser
10	143 ms	68 ms
20	265 ms	146 ms

Push parsers (SAX)

The standard XML parser is a SAX (Simple API for XML) parser. The SAX parser is a push parser: it reads the data and when it finds a token, it executes a callback to some class that is expected to handle the token. The parsing logic for the test remains the same, but the logic now appears in callback methods defined in a class:

```
protected class CustomizedInnerHandler extends DefaultHandler {
    public void startElement(String space, String name,
                String raw, Attributes atts) {
        if (name.length() == 0)
            name = raw;
        if (name.equalsIgnoreCase(ITEM_ID))
            isItemID = true;
    }

    public void characters(char[] ch, int start,
                int length) throws SAXDoneException {
        if (isItemID) {
            String s = new String(ch, start, length);
            isItemID = false;
            if (addItemId(s)) {
                throw new SAXDoneException("Done");
            }
        }
    }
}
```

The only difference in the program logic here is that an exception must be thrown to signal that parsing is completed, since that's the only way the XML push parsing framework can detect that parsing should stop. The application-defined `SAXDoneException` is the class this example defines for that case. In general any kind of `SAXException` can be thrown; this example uses a subclass so that the rest of the program logic can differentiate between an actual error and the signal that processing should stop.

SAX parsers tend to be faster than StAX parsers, though the performance difference is slight—the choice of which parser to use should be made based on which model is easiest to use in development. Table 10-4 shows the difference in processing time between the push and pull parsers.

Table 10-4. Performance of push parsers

Items processed	XML StAX parser	XML SAX parser
10	143 ms	132 ms
20	265 ms	231 ms

There is no corresponding push parser model for JSON-P.

Alternate parsing implementations and parser factories

The XML and JSON specifications define a standard interface for parsers. The JDK provides a reference implementation of the XML parser, and the JSON-P project (*http:// jsonp.java.net*) provides a reference implementation of the JSON parser. Applications can use any arbitrary parser (as long as it implements the desired interfaces, of course).

Parsers are obtained via a parser factory. Using a different parser implementation is a matter of configuring the parser factory to return an instance of the desired parser (rather than the default parser). There are a few performance implications around this:

- Factory instantiation is expensive: make sure the factory is reused via a global (or at least a thread-local) reference.
- The configuration of the factory can be achieved in different ways, some of which (including the default mechanism) can be quite suboptimal from a performance standpoint.
- Different parser implementations may be faster than the default ones.

Reusing Factories and Parsers

XML and JSON parser factories are expensive to create. Fortunately the factories are thread-safe, so it is easy to store the factory in a global static variable and reuse the factory as needed.

In general, the actual parsers cannot be reused, nor are they thread-safe. Parsers, therefore, are usually created on demand.

One advantage of the SAX parser is that it allows the parser object to be reused. In order to reuse the parser, call its `reset()` method in between parser invocations. The parser is still not thread-safe, however, so make sure to limit its reuse to within a single thread at a time.

Let's look at those points in order.

In these tests, the data stream is parsed 1 million times in order to find the average parsing speed (after a warm-up period of 10,000 parses). The example code needs to make sure it constructs the factory only once, which is done in an initialization method called at the beginning of the test. The actual parser for each test is then retrieved via the factory on demand. Hence the SAX test contains this code:

```
SAXParserFactory spf;
// Called once on program initialization
protected void engineInit(RunParams rp) throws IOException {
    spf = SAXParserFactory.newInstance();
}
// Called each iteration
protected XMLReader getReader() Throws SAXException {
    return spf.newSAXParser().getXMLReader();
}
```

The StAX parser looks similar, though the factory (of type XMLInputFactory) is returned from calling the XMLFactory.newInstance() method, and the reader is returned from calling the createStreamReader() method. For JSON, the corresponding calls are the Json.createParserFactory() and createParser() methods.

To use a different parser implementation, we must start with a different factory, so that the call to the factory returns the desired implementation. This brings us to the second point about factory configuration: make sure the factory to use is optimally specified.

XML factories are specified by setting a property in one of three ways. The property used in the discussion here (javax.xml.stream.XMLInputFactory) is the property for the default StAX parser. To override the default SAX parser, the property in question is javax.xml.parsers.SAXParserFactory.

In order to determine which factory is in use, the following options are searched in order:

1. Use the factory specified by the system property -Djavax.xml.stream.XMLInput Factory=my.factory.class.

2. Use the factory specified in the file called called *jaxp.properties* in the *JAVA/jre/lib* directory. The factory is specified by a line like this:

    javax.xml.stream.XMLInputFactory=my.factory.class

3. Search the classpath for a file called *META-INF/services/javax.xml.stream.XMLInputFactory*. The file should contain the single line my.factory.class.

4. Use a JDK-defined default factory.

The third option can have a significant performance penalty, particularly in an environment where there is a very lengthy classpath. To see if an alternate implementation has been specified, each entry in the classpath must be scanned for the appropriate file in the *META-INF/services* directory. That search is repeated every time a factory is created, so if the classloader does not cache the lookup of that resource (and most classloaders do not), instantiating factories will be very expensive.

It is much better to use one of the first two options to configure your application. The options in the list work in order; once the factory is found, searching stops.

The downside of those first two options is that they apply globally to all code in the application server. If two different EE applications are deployed to the same server and each requires a different parser factory, the server must rely on the (potentially slow) classpath technique.

The way that the parser factory is found affects even the default factory: the JDK can't know to use the default factory until it searches the classpath. Hence, even if you want to use the default factory, you should configure the global system property or Java Runtime Environment (JRE) property file to point to the default implementation. Otherwise, the default factory (choice 4 in the list) won't be used until the expensive search in step 3 has been made.

For JSON, the configuration is a slightly different: the only way to specify an alternate implementation is to create one using the *META-INF/services* route, specifying a file with the name *javax.json.spi.JsonProvider* that contains the classname of the new JSON implementation. There is (unfortunately) no way to circumvent searching the entire classpath when looking for a JSON factory.

The final performance consideration in choosing a parser is the performance of the alternate implementation. This section can only give a snapshot of the performance of some implementations; don't necessarily take the results at face value. The point is that there will always be different parser implementations. In terms of performance, different implementations will likely leapfrog each other's performance. At some point, alternate parsers will be faster than the reference implementations (possibly until new releases of the JDK or JSON-P reference implementation come along and leapfrog the alternate implementation).

At the time of this writing, for example, the alternate Woodstox parser (*http://wood stox.codehaus.org/*) provides a slightly faster implementation of the StAX parser than what ships with JDK 7 and 8 (see Table 10-5).

Table 10-5. Performance of alternate StAX parsers

Items processed	JDK StAX parser	Woodstox StAX parser
10	143 ms	125 ms
20	265 ms	237 ms

The JSON situation is more muddled. As I write this, the JSON-P specification has just been made final, and there are no JSR 353–compatible alternate implementations of

JSON parsers. There are other parsers for JSON, and it is only a matter of time until at least some of them conform to the JSR 353 API.

This is a fluid situation, so it may be a good idea to look for alternate JSON implementations and see if they offer better performance. One (currently noncompliant) implementation is the Jackson JSON processor (*https://github.com/FasterXML/jackson*), which already implements a basic pull parser (just not the exact API calls of JSR 353). See Table 10-6.

Table 10-6. Performance of alternate JSON parsers

Items processed	Java EE JSON parser	Jackson JSON parser
10	68 ms	40 ms
20	146 ms	74 ms

This is a usual situation for new JSR reference implementations; just as the JDK 7 XML parser is much faster than previous versions, new JSON-P parsers can be expected to show large performance gains as well. (In fact, the numbers in this section are using the 1.0.2 version of the reference JSON parser, which is about 65% faster on this test than the initial 1.0 implementation.)

Quick Summary

1. Choosing the right parser can have a big impact on the performance of an application.

2. Push parsers tend to be faster than pull parsers.

3. The algorithm used to find the factory for a parser can be quite time-consuming; if possible, bypass the services implementation and specify a factory directly via a system property.

4. At any point in time, the winner of the fastest parser implementation race may be different. Seek out alternate parsers when appropriate.

XML Validation

XML data can optionally be validated against a schema. This allows the parser to reject a document that isn't well formed—meaning one that is missing some required information, or one that contains some unexpected information. "Well formed" is used here in terms of the *content* of the document; if the document has a syntax error (e.g., content not within an XML tag, or a missing XML closing tag, etc.), then all parsers will reject the document.

This validation is one benefit XML has over JSON. You can supply your own validation logic when parsing JSON documents, but with XML, the parser can perform the validation for you. That benefit is not without cost in terms of performance.

XML validation is done against one more more schema or DTD files. Although validating against DTDs is faster, XML schemas are more flexible, and their use now predominates in the XML world. One thing that makes schemas slower than DTDs is that schemas are usually specified in different files. So the first thing that can be done to reduce the penalty for validation is to consolidate the schema files: the more schema files that need to be processed, the more expensive validation is. There is a trade-off here between the maintainability of the separate files and the performance gain involved. Unfortunately, schema files are not easy to combine (e.g., as CSS or JavaScript files are), since they maintain different namespaces.

The location from which schema files are loaded can be a significant source of performance issues. If a schema or DTD must be repeatedly loaded from the network, performance will suffer. Ideally, the schema files should be delivered along with the application code so that the schema(s) can be loaded from the local filesystem.

For normal validation with SAX, the code simply sets some properties on the SAX parser factory (this procedure applies only to SAX parsers; StAX parsers can validate against DTD files, but not schemas, unless they use a `Validator` object as discussed later in this section):

```
SAXParserFactory spf = SAXParserFactory.newInstance();
spf.setValidating(true);
spf.setNamepsaceAware(true);
SAXParser parser = spf.newSAXParser();
// Note: above lines can be executed once to create a parser. If
// reusing a parser, instead call parser.reset() and then set its
// properties
parser.setProperty(JAXPConstants.JAXP_SCHEMA_LANGUAGE,
        XMLConstants.W3C_XML_SCHEMA_NS_URI);
XMLReader xr = parser.getXMLReader();
xr.setErrorHandler(new MyCustomErrorHandler());
```

The default for the parser is for it to be nonvalidating, so the first call needed is to the `setValidating()` method. Then a property must be set to tell the parser which language to validate against—in this case, the W3C XML schema language (e.g., XSD files). Finally, all validating parsers must set an error handler.

This processing—the default way to process the XML document—will reread the schema each time a new document is parsed, even if the parser itself is being reused. For additional performance, consider reusing schemas.

Reusing schemas provides an important benefit even when the schema is loaded from the filesystem. When loaded, the schema must itself be parsed and processed (it is an XML document, after all). Saving the results of this processing it and reusing it will give a big boost to XML processing. This is particularly true in the most common use case: that the application receives and processes thousands of XML documents, all of which conform to the same (set of) schema(s).

There are two options for reusing a schema. The first option (which works only for the SAX parser) is to create schema objects and associate them with the parser factory:

```
SchemaFactory sf = SchemaFactory.newInstance(
        XMLConstants.W3C_XML_SCHEMA_NS_URI);
StreamSource ss = new StreamSource(rp.getSchemaFileName());
Schema schema = sf.newSchema(new Source[]{ss});
SAXParserFactory spf = SAXParserFactory.newInstance();
spf.setValidating(false);
spf.setNamespaceAware(true);
spf.setSchema(schema);
parser = spf.newSAXParser();
```

Note that the setValidating() method is called with a parameter of false in this case. The setSchema() and setValidating() methods are mutually exclusive ways of performing schema validation.

The second option for reusing schema objects is to use an instance of the Validator class. That allows parsing to be separated from validation, so the two operations can be performed at different times. When used with the StAX parser, this also allows validation to be performed during parsing by embedding a special reader into the validation stream.

To use a Validator, first create that special reader. The logic of the reader is the same as before: it looks for the itemID start element and saves those IDs when they are found. However, it must do this by acting as a delegate to a default StAX stream reader:

```
private class MyXMLStreamReader extends StreamReaderDelegate() {
    XMLStreamReader reader;
    public MyXMLStreamReader(XMLStreamReader xsr) {
        reader = xsr;
    }

    public int next() throws XMLStreamException {
        int state = super.next();
        switch (state) {
            case XMLStreamConstants.START_ELEMENT:
                ...process the start element looking for Item ID...
                break;
            case XMLStreamConstants.CHARACTERS:
                ...if item id, save the characters.
                break;
        }
        return state;
    }
}
```

Next, associate this reader with the input stream that the `Validator` object will use:

```
SchemaFactory sf = SchemaFactory.newInstance(
        XMLConstants.W3C_XML_SCHEMA_NS_URI);
StreamSource ss = new StreamSource(rp.getSchemaFileName());
Schema schema = sf.newSchema(new Source[]{ss});
XMLInputFactory staxFactory = XMLInputFactory.newInstance();
staxFactory.setProperty (XMLInputFactory.IS_VALIDATING, Boolean.FALSE);
XMLStreamReader xsr = staxFactory.createXMLStreamReader(ins);
XMLStreamReader reader = new MyXMLStreamReader(xsr);
Validator validator = schema.newValidator();
validator.validate(new StAXSource(new StaxSource(reader)));
```

The `validate()` method, while performing regular validation, will also call the stream reader delegate, which will parse the desired information from the input data (essentially, as a side effect of validation).

One downside to this approach is that processing cannot be cleanly terminated once the 10 items have been read. The code can still throw an exception from the `next()` method and catch that exception later—just as was previously done for the `SAXDoneException`. The problem is that the default schema listener will print out an error message during processing when the exception is thrown.

Table 10-7 shows the effect of all these operations. Compared to simple (nonvalidating) parsing, parsing with the default validation incurs a large penalty. Reusing the schema makes up some of that penalty and gives us the assurance that the XML document in question is well formed, but validation always carries a significant price.

Table 10-7. Performance of validation of an XML document

Parsing mode	SAX	StAX
No validation	231 ms	265 ms
Default validation	730 ms	N/A
Schema reuse	649 ms	1392 ms

Quick Summary

1. When schema validation is functionally important, make sure to use it; just be aware that it will add a significant performance penalty to parsing the data.

2. Always reuse schemas to minimize the effect of validation.

Document Models

Building a Document Object Model (DOM) or JSON object is a relatively simple series of calls. The object itself is created with an underlying parser, so it is important to configure the parser for optimal performance (in the case of DOM, the StAX parser is used by default).

DOM objects are created with a `DocumentBuilder` object that is retrieved from the `DocumentBuilderFactory`. The default document builder factory is specified via the `javax.xml.parsers.DocumentBuilderFactory` property (or the *META-INF/services* file of that name). Just as it is important to configure a property for optimal performance when creating a parser, it is important to configure that system property for optimal performance when creating document builders.

Like SAX parsers, `DocumentBuilder` objects can be reused as long as their `reset()` method is called in between uses.

JSON objects are created with a `JsonReader` object that is retrieved from the `Json` object directly (by calling the `Json.createReader()` method) or from a `JsonReaderFactory` object (by calling the `Json.createJsonReaderFactory()` method). The reader factory can be configured via a `Map` of properties, although the JSR 353 RI does not presently support any configuration options. `JsonReader` objects are not reusable.

DOMs are expensive to create compared to simply parsing the corresponding data, as shown in Table 10-8.

Table 10-8. Performance of DOM parsing

Time required to	XML	JSON
Parse data	265 ms	146 ms
Build document	348 ms	197 ms

The time to build the document includes parsing time, plus the time to create the document object structure—so it can be inferred from this table that the time to create the structure is roughly 33% of the total time for XML, and 25% of the total time of JSON. More complicated documents may show a larger percentage of time spent building the document model.

The previous parsing tests were sometimes only interested in the first 10 items. If the object representation similarly should contain only the first 10 items, then there are two choices. First, the object can be created, and then various methods can be used to walk through the object and discard any undesired items. That is the only option for JSON objects.

DOM objects can set up a filtering parser using DOM level 3 attributes. This first requires that a parsing filter be created:

```
private class InputFilter implements LSParserFilter {
    private boolean done = false;
    private boolean itemCountReached;
```

```
    public short acceptNode(Node node) {
        if (itemCountReached) {
            String s = node.getNodeName();
            if ("ItemArray".equals(s)) {
                return NodeFilter.FILTER_ACCEPT;
            }
            if (done) {
                return NodeFilter.FILTER_SKIP;
            }
            // This is the </Item> element
            // the last thing we need
            if ("Item".equals(s)) {
                done = true;
            }
        }
        return NodeFilter.FILTER_ACCEPT;
    }

    public int getWhatToShow() {
        return NodeFilter.SHOW_ALL;
    }

    public short startElement(Element element) {
        if (itemCountReached) {
            return NodeFilter.FILTER_ACCEPT;
        }
        String s = element.getTagName();
        if (ITEM_ID.equals(element.getTagName())) {
            if (addItemId(element.getNodeValue())) {
                itemCountReached = true;
            }
        }
        return NodeFilter.FILTER_ACCEPT;
    }
}
```

The parsing filter is called twice for each element: the startElement() method is called when parsing of an element begins, and the acceptNode() method is called when parsing of an element is finished. If the element in question should not be represented in the final DOM document, one of those methods should return FILTER_SKIP. In this case, the startElement() method is used to keep track of how many items have been processed, and the acceptNode() method is used to determine whether the entire element should be skipped or not. Note that the code must also keep track of the ending <Item> tag so as not to skip that. Also notice that only elements of type ItemArray are skipped; the XML document has other elements in it that should not be skipped.

To set up the input filter, the following code is used:

```
System.setProperty(DOMImplementationRegistry.PROPERTY,
        "com.sun.org.apache.xerces.internal.dom.DOMImplementationSourceImpl");
DOMImplementationRegistry registry =
```

```
                DOMImplementationRegistry.newInstance();
DOMImplementation domImpl = registry.getDOMImplementation("LS 3.0");
domLS = (DOMImplementationLS) domImpl;
LSParser lsp = domLS.createLSParser(DOMImplementationLS.MODE_SYNCHRONOUS,
                "http://www.w3.org/2001/XMLSchema");
lsp.setFilter(new InputFilter());
LSInput lsi = domLS.createLSInput();
lsi.setByteStream(is);
Document doc = lsp.parse(lsi);
```

In the end, a `Document` object is created, just as it would have been without filtering the input—but in this case, the resulting document is much smaller. That is the point of filtering: the actual parsing and filtering will take much longer to produce a filtered document than a document that contains all the original data. Because the document occupies less memory, it is a useful technique if the document will be long-lived (or if there are many such documents in use), since it reduces pressure on the garbage collector.

Table 10-9 shows the difference for parsing speeds of the usual XML file when constructing a DOM object representing only half (10) of the items.

Table 10-9. Effect of filtering a DOM document

	Standard DOM	Filtering DOM
Time to create DOM	348 ms	417 ms
Size of DOM	101,440 bytes	58,824 bytes

Quick Summary

1. DOM and `JsonObject` models of data are more powerful to work with than simple parsers, but the time to construct the model can be significant.

2. Filtering data out of the model will take even more time than constructing the default model, but that can still be worthwhile for long-lived or very large documents.

Java Object Models

The final option in handling textual data is to create a set of Java classes that correspond to the data being parsed. There are JSR proposals for doing this in JSON, but no standard. For XML, this is accomplished using JAXB.

JAXB uses an underlying StAX parser, so configuring the best StAX parser for your platform will help JAXB performance. The Java objects created via JAXB come from creating an `Unmarshaller` object:

```
JAXBContext jc = JAXBContext.newInstance("net.sdo.jaxb");
Unmarshaller u = jc.createUnmarshaller();
```

The JAXBContext is expensive to create. Fortunately, it is thread-safe: a single global context can be created and reused (and shared among threads). Unmarshaller objects are not thread-safe; a new one must be created for each thread. However, the Unmarshaller object can be reused, so keeping one in a thread-local variable (or keeping a pool of them) will help performance when processing lots of documents.

Creating objects via JAXB is more expensive than either parsing or creating a DOM document. The trade-off is that using those objects is much faster than walking through a document (not to mention that using the objects is a simple matter of writing regular Java code, instead of the convoluted API used to access documents). In addition, writing out the XML that a set of JAXB documents represents is much faster than writing out the XML from a document. Table 10-10 shows the performance differences for the sample 20-item document.

Table 10-10. JAXB marshalling and unmarshalling performance

	Marshall	Unmarshall
DOM	348 ms	298 ms
JAXB	414 ms	232 ms

Filtering XML and JAX-WS

As always, you might be interested in processing only a portion of the XML data even when using JAXB. Normally, JAX-WS will translate all the XML into JAXB-created Java objects. That's great from an ease-of-use perspective; it makes the application code much easier to write and maintain. But if access is needed only to a portion of the XML, all that JAXB processing may be too expensive, and all those JAXB objects may consume too much heap.

In this case, the XML data should be sent as an attachment to the SOAP message (using a MIME type of *application/xml*). The attachments are not translated into JAXB objects, and you can use either a filtering DOM builder or a simple StAX parser to process only that part of the document you are interested in.

Quick Summary

1. For XML documents, producing Java objects via JAXB yields the simplest programming model for accessing and using the data.

2. Creating the JAXB objects will be more expensive than creating a DOM object model.

3. Writing out XML data from JAXB objects will be faster than writing out a DOM object.

Object Serialization

XML, JSON, and similar text-based formats are useful for exchanging data between different kinds of systems. Between Java processes, data is typically exchanged by sending the serialized state of an object. Although it is used extensively throughout Java, serialization has two important considerations in Java EE:

- EJB calls between Java EE servers—remote EJB calls—use serialization to exchange data.

- HTTP session state is saved via object serialization, which enables HTTP sessions to be highly available.

The JDK provides a default mechanism to serialize objects that implement either the `Serializable` or `Externalizable` interface. The serialization performance of practically every object imaginable can be improved from the default serialization code, but this is definitely one of those times when it would be unwise to perform that optimization prematurely. The special code to serialize and deserialize the object will take a fair amount of time to write, and the code will be harder to maintain than code that uses default serialization. Serialization code can also be a little tricky to write correctly, so attempting to optimize it increases the risk of producing incorrect code.

Transient Fields

In general, the way to improve object serialization cost is to serialize less data. This is done by marking fields as `transient`, in which case they are not serialized by default. Then the class can supply special `writeObject()` and `readObject()` methods to handle that data. If the data isn't needed, then it is sufficient simply to mark it as `transient`.

Overriding Default Serialization

The `writeObject()` and `readObject()` methods allow complete control over how data is serialized. With great control comes great responsibility: it's easy to get this wrong.

To get an idea of why serialization optimizations are tricky, take the case of a simple `Point` object that represents a location:

```java
public class Point implements Serializable {
    private int x;
    private int y;
    ...
}
```

On my machine, 100,000 of these objects can be serialized in 133 ms, and deserialized in 741 ms. But even as simple as that object is, it could—if very, very hard pressed for performance—be improved:

```java
public class Point implements Serializable {
    private transient int x;
    private transient int y;
    ....
    private void writeObject(ObjectOutputStream oos) throws IOException {
        oos.defaultWriteObject();
        oos.writeInt(x);
        oos.writeInt(y);
    }
    private void readObject(ObjectInputStream ois)
                            throws IOException, ClassNotFoundException {
        ois.defaultReadObject();
        x = ois.readInt();
        y = ois.readInt();
    }
}
```

Serializing 100,000 of these objects on my machine still takes 132 ms, but deserializing them takes only 468 ms—a 30% improvement. If deserializing a simple object is what takes a significant portion of time in a program, then it might make sense to optimize it like this. Be aware, however, that it makes the code harder to maintain as fields are added, moved, and so on.

So far, though, the code is more complex but is still functionally correct (and faster). But beware of using this technique in the general case:

```java
public class TripHistory implements Serializable {
    private transient Point[] airportsVisited;
    ....
    // THIS CODE IS NOT FUNCTIONALLY CORRECT
    private void writeObject(ObjectOutputStream oos) throws IOException {
        oos.defaultWriteObject();
        oos.writeInt(airportsVisited.length);
        for (int i = 0; i < airportsVisited.length; i++) {
            oos.writeInt(airportsVisited[i].getX());
            oos.writeInt(airportsVisited[i].getY());
        }
    }
}
```

```
    private void readObject(ObjectInputStream ois)
                            throws IOException, ClassNotFoundException {
        ois.defaultReadObject();
        int length = ois.readInt();
        airportsVisited = new Point[length];
        for (int i = 0; i < length; i++) {
            airportsVisited[i] = new Point(ois.readInt(), ois.readInt());
        }
    }
}
```

Here, the `airportsVisited` field is an array of all the airports I've ever flown to or from, in the order in which I visited them. So certain airports, like JFK, appear frequently in the array; SYD appears only once (so far).

Because it is expensive to write object references, this code would certainly perform faster than the default serialization mechanism for that array: an array of 100,000 `Point` objects takes 4.7 seconds to serialize on my machine and 6.9 seconds to deserialize. Using the above "optimization," it takes only 2 seconds to serialize and 1.7 seconds to deserialize.

This code, however, is incorrect. The references in the array that specify the location of JFK all started out referring to the same object. That means when I discover that the location represented in that data is incorrect, the single JFK reference can be changed, and all objects in the array will reflect that change (since they are references to the same object).

When the array is deserialized by the above code, those JFK references end up as separate, different objects. Now when one of those objects is changed, only that object is changed, and it ends up with different data than the remaining objects that refer to JFK.

This is a very important principle to keep in mind, because optimizing serialization is often about performing special handling for object references. Done correctly, that can greatly increase the performance of serialization code. Done incorrectly, it can introduce quite subtle bugs.

With that in mind, let's explore the serialization of the `StockPriceHistory` class to see how serialization optimizations can be made. The fields in that class include the following:

```
public class StockPriceHistoryImpl implements StockPriceHistory {
    private String symbol;
    protected SortedMap<Date, StockPrice> prices = new TreeMap<>();
    protected Date firstDate;
    protected Date lastDate;
    protected boolean needsCalc = true;
    protected BigDecimal highPrice;
    protected BigDecimal lowPrice;
    protected BigDecimal averagePrice;
    protected BigDecimal stdDev;
```

```
        private Map<BigDecimal, ArrayList<Date>> histogram;
        ....
        public StockPriceHistoryImpl(String s, Date firstDate, Date lastDate) {
            prices = ....
        }
    }
```

When the history for a stock is constructed for a given symbol s, the object creates and stores a sorted map of prices keyed by date of all the prices between start and end. The code also saves the firstDate and the lastDate. The constructor doesn't fill in any other fields; they are initialized lazily. When a getter on any of those fields is called, the getter checks if needsCalc is true. If it is, it calculates the appropriate values for the remaining fields if necessary (all at once).

This calculation includes creating the histogram, which records how many days the stock closed at a particular price. The histogram contains the same data (in terms of BigDecimal and Date objects) as is found in the prices map; it is just a different way of looking at the data.

Because all of the lazily initialized fields can be calculated from the prices array, they can all be marked transient, and no special work is required to serialize or deserialize them. The example is easy in this case because the code was already doing lazy initialization of the fields; it can repeat that lazy initialization when receiving the data. Even if the code eagerly initialized these fields, it could still mark any calculated fields transient and recalculate their values in the readObject() method of the class.

Note too that this preserves the object relationship between the prices and histogram objects: when the histogram is recalculated, it will just insert existing objects into the new map.

This kind of optimization is almost always a good thing, but there are cases when it can actually hurt performance. Table 10-11 shows the time it takes to serialize and deserialize this case where the histogram object is transient versus nontransient, as well as the size of the serialized data for each case.

Table 10-11. Time to serialize and deserialize objects with transient fields

Object	Serialization time	Deserialization time	Size of data
No transient fields	12.8 seconds	11.9 seconds	46,969 bytes
Transient histogram	11.5 seconds	10.1 seconds	40,910 bytes

So far, the example saves about 15% of the total time to serialize and deserialize the object. But this test has not actually re-created the histogram object on the receiving side: that object will be created when the receiving code first accesses it.

There are times that the histogram object will not be needed: the client may only be interested in the prices on particular days, and not the histogram. That is where the more unusual case comes in: if the histogram will always be needed, and if it takes more than 3.1 seconds to calculate all the histograms in this test, then the case with the lazily initialized fields will actually have a net performance decrease.

In this case, calculating the histogram does not fall into that category—it is a very fast operation. In general, it may be hard to find a case where recalculating a piece of data is more expensive than serializing and deserializing that data. But it is something to consider as code is optimized.

This test is not actually transmitting data; the data is written to and read from preallocated byte arrays, so that it measures only the time for serialization and deserialization. Still, notice that making the histogram field transient has also saved about 13% in the size of the data. That will be quite important if the data is to be transmitted via a network.

Compressing Serialized Data

This leads to a third way that serialization performance of code can be improved: compress the serialized data so that it is faster to transmit over a slow network. In the stock history class, that is done by compressing the prices map during serialization:

```
public class StockPriceHistoryCompress
        implements StockPriceHistory, Serializable {

    private byte[] zippedPrices;
    private transient SortedMap<Date, StockPrice> prices;

    private void writeObject(ObjectOutputStream out)
                throws IOException {
        if (zippedPrices == null) {
            makeZippedPrices();
        }
        out.defaultWriteObject();
    }

    private void readObject(ObjectInputStream in)
                throws IOException, ClassNotFoundException {
        in.defaultReadObject();
        unzipPrices();
    }

    protected void makeZippedPrices() throws IOException {
        ByteArrayOutputStream baos = new ByteArrayOutputStream();
        GZIPOutputStream zip = new GZIPOutputStream(baos);
        ObjectOutputStream oos = new ObjectOutputStream(
                new BufferedOutputStream(zip));
        oos.writeObject(prices);
        oos.close();
        zip.close();
        zippedPrices = baos.toByteArray();
    }
```

```
protected void unzipPrices()
            throws IOException, ClassNotFoundException {
    ByteArrayInputStream bais = new ByteArrayInputStream(zippedPrices);
    GZIPInputStream zip = new GZIPInputStream(bais);
    ObjectInputStream ois = new ObjectInputStream(
            new BufferedInputStream(zip));
    prices = (SortedMap<Date, StockPrice>) ois.readObject();
    ois.close();
    zip.close();
    }
}
```

The `zipPrices()` method serializes the map of prices to a byte array and saves the resulting bytes, which are then serialized normally in the `writeObject()` method when it calls the `defaultWriteObject()` method. (In fact, as long as the serialization is being customized, it will be ever-so-slightly better to make the `zippedPrices` array transient, and write out its length and bytes directly. But this example code is a little clearer, and simpler is better.) On deserialization, the reverse operation is performed.

If the goal is to serialize to a byte stream (as in the original sample code), this is a losing proposition. That isn't surprising; the time required to compress the bytes is much longer than the time to write them to a local byte array. Those times are shown in Table 10-12.

Table 10-12. Time to serialize and deserialize 10,000 objects with compression

Use case	Serialization time	Deserialization time	Size of data
No compression	12.1 seconds	8.0 seconds	41,170 bytes
Compression/decompression	26.8 seconds	12.7 seconds	5,849 bytes
Compression only	26.8 seconds	0.494 seconds	5,849 bytes

The most interesting point about this table is the last line. In that test, the data is compressed before sending, but the `unzipPrices()` method isn't called in the `readObject()` method. Instead, it is called when needed, which will be the first time the client calls the `getPrice()` method. Absent that call, there are only a few `BigDecimal` objects to deserialize, which is quite fast.

It is quite possible in this example that the client will never need the actual prices: the client may only need to call the `getHighPrice()` and similar methods to retrieve aggregate information about the data. As long as those methods are all that is needed, a lot of time can be saved by lazily decompressing the `prices` information. This lazy decompression is also quite useful if the object in question is being persisted (e.g., if it is HTTP session state that is being stored as a backup copy in case the application server fails). Lazily decompressing the data saves both CPU time (from skipping the decompression) and memory (since the compressed data takes up less space).

So even if the application runs on a local, high-speed network—and particularly if the goal is to save memory rather than time—compressing data for serialization and then lazily decompressing it can be quite useful.

If the point of the serialization is to transfer data over the network, then the compression will win any time there is data savings. Table 10-13 performs the same serialization for the 10,000 stock objects, but this time it transmits the data to another process. The other process is either on the same machine, or on a machine accessed via my broadband connection.

Table 10-13. Network transfer time for 10,000 objects

Object	Same machine	Broadband WAN
No compression	30.1 seconds	150.1 seconds
Compression/decompression	41.3 seconds	54.3 seconds
Compression only	28.0 seconds	44.1 seconds

The fastest possible network communication is between two processes on the same machine—that communication doesn't go onto the network at all, though it does send data through the operating system interfaces. Even in that case, compressing the data and lazily decompressing it has resulted in the fastest performance (at least for this test —a smaller data amount may still show a regression). And the order of magnitude difference in the amount of data has made a (predictably) large difference in the total time once a slower network is involved.

Keeping Track of Duplicate Objects

This section began with an example of how not to serialize data that contains object references, lest the object references be compromised when the data is deserialized. However, one of the more powerful optimizations possible in the writeObject() method is to not write out duplicate object references. In the case of the StockPriceHistoryImpl class, that means not writing out the duplicate references of the prices map. Because the example uses a standard JDK class for that map, we don't have to worry about that: the JDK classes are already written to optimally serialize their data. Still, it is instructive to look into how those classes perform their optimizations in order to understand what is possible.

In the StockPriceHistoryImpl class, the key structure is a TreeMap. A simplified version of that map appears in Figure 10-2. With default serialization, the JVM would write out the primitive data fields for node A; then it would recursively call the writeObject() method for node B (and then for node C). The code for node B would write out its primitive data fields, and then recursively write out the data for its parent field.

But wait a minute—that `parent` field is node A, which has already been written. The object serialization code is smart enough to realize that: it doesn't rewrite the data for node A. Instead, it simply adds an object reference to the previously written data.

Keeping track of that set of previously written objects, as well as all that recursion, adds a small performance hit to object serialization. However, as demonstrated in the example with an array of `Point` objects, it can't be avoided: code must keep track of the previously written objects and reconstitute the correct object references. However, it is possible to perform smart optimizations by suppressing object references that can be easily re-created when the object is deserialized.

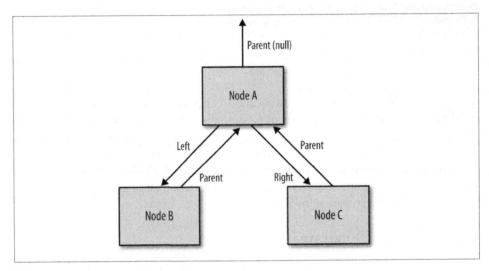

Figure 10-2. Simple TreeMap structure

Different collection classes handle this differently. The `TreeMap` class, for example, simply iterates through the tree and writes only the keys and values; serialization discards all information about the relationship between the keys (i.e., their sort order). When the data has been deserialized, the `readObject()` method then re-sorts the data to produce a tree. Although sorting the objects again sounds like it would be expensive, it is not: that process is about 20% faster on a set of 10,000 stock objects than using the default object serialization, which chases all the object references.

The `TreeMap` class also benefits from this optimization because it can write out fewer objects. A node (or in JDK language, an `Entry`) within a map contains two objects: the key and the value. Because the map cannot contain two identical nodes, the serialization code doesn't need to worry about preserving object references to nodes. In this case, it can skip writing the node object itself, and simply write the key and value objects directly. So the `writeObject()` method ends up looking something like this (syntax adapted for ease of reading):

```
private void writeObject(ObjectOutputStream oos) throws IOException {
    ....
    for (Map.Entry<K,V> e : entrySet()) {
        oos.writeObject(e.getKey());
        oos.writeObject(e.getValue());
    }
    ....
}
```

This looks very much like the code that didn't work for the `Point` example. The difference in this case is that the code is still writing objects where those objects can be the same. A `TreeMap` cannot have two nodes that are the same, so there is no need to write out node references. The `TreeMap` *can* have two values that are the same, so the values must be written out as object references.

This brings us full circle: as I stated at the beginning of this section, getting object serialization optimizations correct can be tricky. But when object serialization is a significant bottleneck in an application, optimizing it correctly can offer important benefits.

What About Externalizable?

This section has not talked about another approach to optimizing object serialization, which is to implement the `Externalizable` interface rather than the `Serializable` interface.

The practical difference between these two interfaces is how they handle nontransient fields. The `Serializable` interface writes out nontransient fields when the `writeObject()` method calls the `defaultWriteObject()` method. The `Externalizable` interface has no such method. An `Externalizable` class must explicitly write out all fields, transient or not, that it is interested in transmitting.

Even if all the fields in an object are transient, it is better to implement the `Serializable` interface and call the `defaultWriteObject()` method. That path leads to code that is much easier to maintain as fields are added to (and deleted from) the code. And there is no inherent benefit to the `Externalizable` interface from a performance point of view: in the end, what matters is the amount of data that is written.

1. Serialization of data, particularly within Java EE, can be a big performance bottleneck.

2. Marking instance variables `transient` will make serialization faster and reduce the amount of data to be transmitted. Both of those are usually big performance wins, unless re-creating the data on the receiver takes a very long time.

3. Other optimizations via the `writeObject()` and `readObject()` methods can significantly speed up serialization. Approach them with caution, since it is easy to make a mistake and introduce a subtle bug.

4. Compressing serialized data is often beneficial, even if the data will not travel across a slow network.

Java EE Networking APIs

The data exchange techniques that we have just examined—XML parsing, JSON processing, and object serialization—have their uses within a variety of applications, but one of their primary uses is within one of the Java EE networking APIs: JAX-WS, JAX-RS, and IIOP/RMI.

These are very different protocols with very different features. Their feature sets are the primary determinant of why and when you would use each of them. There are endless debates, for example, about whether JAX-RS is faster than JAX-WS, but those debates of necessity assume a common denominator application that can be written in either framework. If certain security features are required, then the choice will be JAX-WS, regardless of its performance relative to JAX-RS. If an application must talk to an existing server that exports an IIOP interface, then that dictates the choice.

As a set, though, the networking APIs have similar performance challenges to overcome. This section discusses some of those challenges and addresses how to meet them.

Sizing Data Transfers

The primary factor driving performance of these technologies is their data exchange, which is one reason this chapter spent a lot of time looking into that. The amount of data transfer should be minimized, whether by compression, or pruning of documents, or some other technique.

On the other hand, setting up a network call in the first place has measurable overhead. When designing a network interface, the interface should be "coarse"—that is, it is better to return lots of data in one call, so as to minimize the total number of network calls that the client must make. That principle is at odds with the objective to reduce the amount of data being exchanged; some balance must be struck here.

This balance can be observed if we test the average response time for a RESTful web service based on the stock history class. The service can be designed to return either just the basic data (high, low, average, and standard deviation) for the period, or to return the basic data plus all the individual daily data points.

If it is known ahead of time how the client will use the data, then it is easy to know exactly which data to return. However, that isn't always possible. In this example, say that the client requests a 5-year history for a stock, and the client application will initially just present a summary of that data to the user. What happens if the user wants to drill into that data and look at individual daily points? Should all the data be returned to the client in the first call, so that no further network calls are needed to drill into the data? Should only the summary data be returned, and if the user wants to drill into the data for year 3, the program must make another call to get the daily data for that year? Should that second call get the entire 5-year history even though the user right now is only looking at the third year?

To figure out a strategy here, consider the time for returning all the data compared to the time for making multiple network calls. Table 10-14 shows the average response time for retrieving data under various scenarios:

1. The client requests 1 year of data.
2. The client requests a 1-year summary.
3. The client requests 5 years of data.
4. The client makes two requests: a summary request, and a drill-down request for a specific date.
5. The client makes 10 requests: a summary request plus 9 drill-down requests for a specific date.

My broadband Internet connection was used for these tests; as always, the speed of the network will have a large effect on the times reported (see Table 10-14).

Table 10-14. Average response time for RESTful scenarios

Scenario	Average response time	Size of data
1-year data	90 ms	30 KB
1-year summary	30 ms	60 bytes
5-year data	300 ms	186 KB
2 summary requests	60 ms	2 calls; 60 bytes each
10 summary requests	280 ms	10 calls; 60 bytes each

The time to retrieve a full year's worth of data is not particularly longer than retrieving just the summary data, and if the user is expected to need three individual pieces of that data, returning the entire set of data at once is always better.

The 5-year summary is a little different: it takes much longer to marshall and transmit that data, so the user would need to make 11 drill-down requests before the total time approaches parity.

The times in this example include time to marshall the JSON data being returned from the RESTful service, and that time is dependent on the number of years the data represents. But requests could come in from multiple clients for the same set of data, in which case previously marshalled data could be reused. If the marshalled string is already calculated, then the inflection points in the trade-off are quite different, as shown in Table 10-15.

Table 10-15. Average response time for RESTful scenarios (cached response)

Scenario	Average response time
1-year data	50 ms
1-year summary	30 ms
5-year data	90 ms
2 summary requests	60 ms
10 summary requests	270 ms

The overhead in making the call remains constant, so there is little difference in the response time for the summary cases. The 1- and 5-year full scenarios are left with only the time to transmit the data, which is significantly less than the previous case where the data needed to be calculated and marshalled. In general, this case can afford to return a lot of possibly unneeded data to the client without much performance penalty.

Networking Isn't What It Used to Be

Not to sound too much like an old crank, but I used to connect to remote networks via a 300-baud modem. (Fortunately, I did not have to walk 5 miles to school through 4-foot snow drifts.) There is an inherent bias in that situation against making too many network calls.

Today, I will sit at my browser, and every time I type a few characters, it will make a remote call to a Google server, which will respond with a small amount of text to aid me in my searches. Google has calculated that if this can be done in 200 ms or less, I won't notice the lag time.

As networks get faster and faster, the trade-offs I've discussed in this section may seem less and less important. On the other hand, my smartphone is lucky if it gets a fast 3G signal much of the time, and a few times a year, I'm fortunate enough to be in the middle of the ocean connecting to the Internet via satellite. Throwing faster hardware (or networks) at applications always helps performance, but don't take that as a substitute for performant designs. If the application can detect that it is on a fast network and make quick, fine-grained network calls, then that is a great optional feature to include. Just make sure that the application can work well no matter where it is deployed.

Summary

The performance of Java EE applications is dependent on several factors. As always, the quality of the application code is paramount, and because they use so many external resources, performance bottlenecks in a application server are often outside of the Java layer.

Within an application server, much of the performance depends on factors that are not unique to Java EE—notably thread performance, object pools, and networking performance. In an application server, the most important factor is the amount of data it transmits or processes—whether that data is simple HTML, XML payloads, serialized object states, JSON payloads, or what have you. The practices outlined in this chapter should help you make the most of the resources available to an application server.

## CHAPTER 11

Database Performance Best Practices

This chapter investigates the performance of Java-driven database applications. Applications that access a database are subject to non-Java performance issues: if a database is I/O-bound, or if it is executing SQL queries that require full table scans because an index is missing, no amount of Java tuning or application coding is going to solve the performance issues. When dealing with database technologies, be prepared to learn (from another source) about how to tune and program the database.

This is not to say that the performance of an application that uses a database is insensitive to things under the control of the JVM and the Java technologies that are used. Rather, for good performance it is necessary to ensure that both the database and the application are correctly tuned and executing the best possible code.

Sample Database

The examples in this chapter use a sample database set up to store the data for 128 stock entities for the period of one year. During the year, there are 261 business days.

Prices for the individual stocks are held in a table called STOCKPRICE, which has a primary key of the stock symbol and the date. There are 33,408 rows in that table (128*261).

Each stock has a set of five associated options, which are also priced daily. The STOCK-OPTIONPRICE table holds that data with a primary key of the symbol, the date, and an integer representing the option number. There are 167,040 rows in that table (128*261*5).

JDBC

This chapter covers database performance from the perspective of JPA—the Java Persistence API, version 2.0. However, JPA uses JDBC under the covers, and many developers still write applications directly to the JDBC APIs—so it is important to look at the most important performance aspects of JDBC also. Even for applications that use JPA (or some other database framework), understanding JDBC performance will help get better performance out of the framework.

JDBC Drivers

The JDBC driver is the most important factor in the performance of database applications. Databases come with their own set of JDBC drivers, and alternate JDBC drivers are available for most popular databases. Frequently, the justification for these alternate drivers is that they offer better performance.

I can't adjudicate the performance claims of all database drivers, but here are some things to consider when evaluating different drivers.

Where work is performed

JDBC drivers can be written to perform more work within the Java application (the database client) or to perform more work on the database server. The best example of this is the thin and thick drivers for Oracle databases. The thin driver is written to have a fairly small footprint within the Java application: it relies on the database server to do more processing. The thick driver is just the opposite: it offloads work from the database at the expense of requiring more processing and more memory on the Java client. That kind of trade-off is possible in most databases.

There are competing claims as to which model gives the better performance. The truth is that neither model offers an inherent advantage—the driver that will offer the best performance depends on the specifics of the environment in which it is run. Consider the case where an application host is a small, two-core machine connecting to a huge, well-tuned database. The CPU of the application host is likely to become saturated well before any significant load is placed on the database. A thin-style driver will give the better performance in that case. Conversely, an enterprise that has 100 departments accessing a single HR database will see the best performance if database resources are preserved and the clients deploy a thick-style driver.

This is a reason to be suspicious of any performance claims when it comes to JDBC drivers: it is quite easy to pick a driver that is well suited to a particular environment and show that it is superior to some other vendor's driver that performs badly on the exact same setup. As always, test in your own environment, and make sure that environment mirrors what you will deploy on.

The JDBC driver type

JDBC drivers come in four types (1–4). The driver types in wide use today are type 2 (which uses native code), and type 4 (which is pure Java).

Type 1 drivers provide a bridge between ODBC and JBDC. If an application must talk to an ODBC database, then it must use this driver. Type 1 drivers generally have quite bad performance; given a choice to avoid ODBC, you should.

Type 3 drivers are, like type 4 drivers, written purely in Java, but they are designed for a specific architecture where some piece of middleware (sometimes, though usually not, an application server) provides an intermediary translation. In this architecture, a JDBC client (usually a standalone program, though conceivably an application server) sends JDBC protocol to the middleware, which translates the requests into a database-specific protocol and forwards the request to the database (and performs the reverse translation for the response).

There are some situations where this architecture is required: the middleware can sit in the network demilitarized zone (DMZ) and provide some additional security for connections to the database. From a performance standpoint, there are potential advantages and disadvantages. The middleware is free to cache database information, which offloads the database (making it faster) and returns data to the client sooner (decreasing the latency of the request). Without that caching, however, performance will suffer, as two round-trip network requests are now required to perform a database operation. In the ideal case, those will balance out (or the caching will be even faster).

As a practical situation, though, this architecture has not really been widely adopted. (As always, things are subject to change. Oracle, for example, supplies a JDBC driver for its Distributed Remote Connection Pool [DRCP] implementation. Strictly speaking, that is a type 3 driver, though it is the same driver JAR file as the usual type 4 JDBC driver, and the type 3/type 4 dichotomy is transparent to end users.) It is generally easier to put the application server itself in the middle tier (including in the DMZ if needed). The application server can then perform the database operations, but it needn't provide a JDBC interface to clients: it is better off providing servlet interfaces, web service interfaces, and so on—isolating the client from any knowledge of the database.

That leaves type 2 and 4 drivers, neither of which has an inherent performance advantage over the other. Type 2 drivers can suffer from JNI overhead, but a well-written type 2 driver can overcome that. Don't conflate the driver type (2 or 4) with whether the driver is considered "thick" or "thin," as discussed in the previous section. It is true that type 2 drivers tend to be thick and type 4 drivers tend to be thin, but that is not a requirement. In the end, whether a type 2 or type 4 driver is better depends on the environment and the specific drivers in question. There is really no a priori way to know which will perform better.

Quick Summary

1. Spend time evaluating the best JDBC driver for the application.
2. The best driver will often vary depending on the specific deployment. The same application may be better with one JDBC driver in one deployment and a different JDBC driver in a different deployment.
3. If there is a choice, avoid ODBC and type 1 JDBC drivers.

Prepared Statements and Statement Pooling

In most circumstances, code should use a `PreparedStatement` rather than a `Statement` for its JDBC calls. The difference is that prepared statements allow the database to reuse information about the SQL that is being executed. That saves work for the database on subsequent executions of the prepared statement.

Reuse is the operative word here: the first use of a prepared statement takes more time for the database to execute, since it must set up and save information. If the statement is used only once, then that work will be wasted; it's better to use a regular statement in that case.

In a batch-oriented program that makes only a few database calls, the `Statement` interface will let the application finish faster. But even batch-oriented programs may make hundreds or thousands of JDBC calls to the same few SQL statements; later examples in this chapter will use a batch program to load a database with 10,000 stock records. Batch programs that have many JDBC calls—and application servers that will service many requests over their lifetime—are better off using a `PreparedStatement` interface (and database frameworks like JPA will do that automatically).

Prepared statements provide their performance benefit when they are pooled—that is, when the actual `PreparedStatement` object is reused. For proper pooling, two things must be considered: the JDBC connection pool, and the JDBC driver configuration. (Statement pooling is often called statement caching by database vendors.) These configuration options apply to any program that uses JDBC, whether directly or via JPA.

Setting up the statement pool

Prepared statement pools operate on a per-connection basis. If one thread in a program pulls a JDBC connection out of the pool and uses a prepared statement on that connection, the information associated with the statement will be valid only for that connection. A second thread that uses a second connection will end up establishing a second pooled instance of the prepared statement. In the end, each connection object will have its own pool of all the prepared statements used in the application (assuming that they are all used over the lifetime of the application).

This is one reason why a standalone JDBC application should use a connection pool (JPA transparently creates a connection pool for Java SE programs, or uses a connection pool from the application server when used in a Java EE environment). It also means that the size of the connection pool matters (to both JDBC and JPA programs). That is particularly true early in the program's execution: when a connection that has not yet used a particular prepared statement is used, that first request will be a little slower.

The size of the connection pool also matters because it is caching those prepared statements, which take up heap space (and often a lot of heap space). Object reuse is certainly a good thing in this case, but you must be aware of how much space those reusable objects take up and make sure it isn't negatively affecting the GC time.

Managing statement pools

The second thing to consider about the prepared statement pool is what piece of code will actually create and manage the pool. Prepared statement pooling was introduced in JDBC 3.0, which provides a single method (the `setMaxStatements()` method of the `ConnectionPoolDataSource` class) to enable or disable statement pooling. Statement pooling is disabled if the value passed to the `setMaxStatements()` method is 0. That interface specifically does not define where the statement pooling should occur— whether in the JDBC driver or some other layer, such as the application server. And that single interface is insufficient for some JDBC drivers, which require additional configuration.

So, when writing a Java SE application that uses JDBC calls directly, there are two choices: either the JDBC driver must be configured to create and manage the statement pool, or the pool must be created and managed within the application code. Java EE applications have two (slightly different) possibilities: the JDBC driver can create and manage the pool, or the application server can create and manage the pool.

The tricky thing is that there are no standards in this area. Some JDBC drivers do not provide a mechanism to pool statements at all; they expect to be used only within an application server that is doing the statement pooling and want to provide a simpler driver. Some application servers do not provide and manage a pool; they expect the JDBC driver to handle that task and don't want to complicate their code. Both arguments have merit (though a JDBC driver that does not provide a statement pool puts a burden on you if you are the developer of a standalone application). In the end, you'll have to sift through this landscape and make sure that the statement pool is created somewhere.

Since there are no standards, you may encounter a situation where both the JDBC driver and the application server are capable of managing the prepared statement pool. In that case, it is important that only one of them be configured to do so. From a performance perspective, the better choice will again depend on the exact combination of driver and server. As a general rule, you can expect the JDBC driver to perform better statement pooling. Since the driver is (usually) specific to a particular database, it can be expected to make better optimizations for that database than the more generic application server code.

To enable statement pooling (or caching) for a particular JDBC driver, consult that driver's documentation. In many cases, you need only set up the driver so that the maxStatements property is set to the desired value (i.e., the size of the statement pool). Other drivers may require additional settings (e.g., the Oracle JDBC drivers require that specific properties be set to tell it whether to use implicit or explicit statement caching).

Quick Summary

1. Java applications will typically execute the same SQL statement repeatedly. In those cases, reusing prepared statements will offer a significant performance boost.

2. Prepared statements must be pooled on a per-connection basis. Most JDBC drivers and Java EE frameworks can do this automatically.

3. Prepared statements can consume a significant amount of heap. The size of the statement pool must be carefully tuned to prevent GC issues from pooling too many very large objects.

JDBC Connection Pools

Connections to a database are time-consuming to create, so JDBC connections are another prototypical object that you should reuse in Java.

In a Java EE environment, all JDBC connections come from the application server's pool. In a Java SE environment with JPA, most JPA providers will use a connection pool transparently, and you can configure the connection pool within the *persistence.xml* file. In a standalone Java SE environment, the connections must be managed by the application. To deal with that last case, you can use one of several connection pool libraries that are available from many sources. Often, though, it is easier simply to create a connection and store it in a thread-local variable for each thread in a standalone application.

As usual, it is important to strike the right balance here between the memory occupied by the pooled objects, and the amount of extra GC the pooling will trigger. This is particularly true because of the prepared statement caches. The actual connection objects may not be very big, but statement caches (which exist on a per-connection basis) can grow to be quite big.

In this case, striking the correct balance applies to the database as well. Each connection to the database requires resources on the database (in addition to the memory held in the application). As connections are added to the database, the database needs more resources: it will allocate additional memory for each prepared statement used by the

JDBC driver. Database performance can be adversely affected if the application server has too many open connections.

The general rule of thumb for connection pools is to have one connection for every thread in the application. In an application server, start by applying the same sizing to the thread pool and the connection pool. In a standalone application, size the connection pool based on the number of threads the application creates. In the typical case, this will offer the best performance: no thread in the program will have to wait for a database connection to be available, and typically there are enough resources on the database to handle the load imposed by the application.

If the database becomes a bottleneck, however, this rule can become counterproductive. Having too many connections to an undersized database is another illustration of the principle that injecting load into a busy system will decrease its performance. Using a connection pool to throttle the amount of work that is sent to an undersized database is the way to improve performance in that situation. Application threads may have to wait for a free connection, but the total throughput of the system will be maximized if the database is not overburdened.

Quick Summary

1. Connections are expensive objects to initialize; they are routinely pooled in Java—either in the JDBC driver itself, or within Java EE and JPA frameworks.

2. As with other object pools, it is important to tune the connection pool so it doesn't adversely affect the garbage collector. In this case, it is also necessary to tune the connection pool so it doesn't adversely affect the performance of the database itself.

Transactions

Applications have correctness requirements that ultimately dictate how transactions are handled. A transaction that requires repeatable-read semantics will be slower than a transaction that requires only read-committed semantics, but knowing that is of little practical benefit for an application that cannot tolerate nonrepeatable reads. So while this section discusses how to use the least intrusive isolation semantics for an application, don't let the desire for speed overcome the correctness of the application.

Database transactions have two performance penalties. First, it takes time for the database to set up and then commit the transaction. This involves making sure that changes to the database are fully stored on disk, that the database transaction logs are consistent, and so on. Second, during a database transaction, it is quite common for the transaction to obtain a lock for a particular set of data (not always a row, but I'll use that as the example here). If two transactions are contending for a lock on the same database row, then the scalability of the application will suffer. From a Java perspective, this is exactly analogous to the discussion in Chapter 9 about contended and uncontended locks.

For optimal performance, consider both of these issues: how to program the transactions so that the transaction itself is efficient, and how to hold locks on the database during a transaction so that the application as a whole can scale.

JDBC transaction control

Transactions are present within both JDBC and JPA applications, but JPA manages transactions differently (those details are discussed later in this chapter). For JDBC, transactions begin and end based on how the `Connection` object is used.

In basic JDBC usage, connections have an autocommit mode (set via the `setAutoCommit()` method). If autocommit is turned on (and for most JDBC drivers that is the default), then each statement in a JDBC program is its own transaction. In that case, a program need take no action to commit a transaction (in fact, if the `commit()` method is called, performance will often suffer).

If autocommit is turned off, then a transaction implicitly begins when the first call is made on the connection object (e.g., by calling the `executeQuery()` method). The transaction continues until the `commit()` method (or the `rollback()` method) is called. A new transaction will begin when the connection is used for the next database call.

Transactions are expensive to commit, so one goal is to perform as much work in a transaction as is possible. Unfortunately, that principle is completely at odds with another goal: because transactions can hold locks, they should be as short as possible. There is definitely a balance here, and striking the balance will depend on the application and its locking requirements. The next section, on transaction isolation and locking, covers that in more detail; first let's look into the options for optimizing the transaction handling itself.

Consider some sample code that inserts data into a database for use by the stock application. For each day of valid data, one row must be inserted into the STOCKPRICE table, and five rows into the STOCKOPTIONPRICE table. A basic loop to accomplish that looks like this:

```
Connection c = DriverManager.getConnection(URL, user, pw);
PreparedStatement ps = c.prepareStatement(insertStockSQL);
PreparedStatement ps2 = c.prepareStatement(insertOptionSQL)) {
Date curDate = new Date(startDate.getTime());
while (!curDate.after(endDate)) {
    StockPrice sp = createRandomStock(symbol, curDate);
    if (sp != null) {
        ps.clearParameters();
        ps.setBigDecimal(1, sp.getClosingPrice());
        // Similar set calls for the remaining fields
        ps.executeUpdate();
```

```
            for (int j = 0; j < 5; j++) {
                ps2.clearParameters();
                ps2.setBigDecimal(1, ...);
                // Similar set calls for the remaining fields
                ps2.executeUpdate();
            }
        } // else curDate is a weekend and it is skipped
        curDate.setTime(curDate.getTime() + msPerDay);
    }
```

If the start and end dates represent the year 2013, this loop will insert 261 rows into the STOCKPRICE table (via the first call to the executeUpdate() method) and 1,305 rows into the STOCKOPTIONPRICE table (in the inner for loop). In the default autocommit mode, that means 1,566 separate transactions, which will be quite expensive.

Better performance will be achieved if autocommit mode is disabled and an explicit commit is performed at the end of the loop:

```
Connection c = DriverManager.getConnection(URL, user, pw);
c.setAutoCommit(false);
...
while (!curDate.after(endDate)) {
    ...
}
c.commit();
```

From a logical point of view, that probably makes sense as well: the database will end up with either an entire year's worth of data, or no data.

If this loop is repeated for multiple stocks, there is a choice of committing all the data at once or committing a year's worth of data at a time:

```
Connection c = DriverManager.getConnection(URL, user, pw);
c.setAutoCommit(false);
for (int i = 0; i < numStocks; i++) {
    curDate = startDate;
    while (!curdate.after(endDate)) {
        ...
    }
    //c.commit();    // To commit a year at a time
}
c.commit();    // To commit all the data at once
```

Committing all the data at once offers the fastest performance, which is why the other option is commented out. In this example, though, there is a reasonable case where the application semantics might dictate that each year of data be committed individually. Sometimes, other requirements intrude on attempts to get the best performance.

Each time the executeUpdate() method is executed in the above code, a remote call is made to the database and some work must be performed. In addition, some locking will occur when the updates are made (to ensure, at least, that another transaction cannot insert a record for the same symbol and date). The transaction handling can be further optimized in this case by batching the inserts. When inserts are batched, the JDBC driver holds them until the batch is completed; then all statements are transmitted in one remote JDBC call.

Here is how batching is achieved:

```
for (int i = 0; i < numStocks; i++) {
    while (!curdate.after(endDate)) {
        ...
        ps.addBatch();  // replaces executeUpdate() call
        for (int j = 0; j < 5; j++) {
            ...
            ps2.addBatch();  // replaces executeUpdate() call
        }
    }
}
ps.executeBatch();
ps2.executeBatch();
c.commit();
```

The code could equally well choose to execute each batch on a per-stock basis (after the while loop). Some JDBC drivers have a limitation on the number of statements they can batch (and the batch does consume memory in the application), so even if the data is committed at the end of the entire operation, the batches may need to be executed more frequently.

These optimizations can yield very large performance increases. Table 11-1 shows the time required to insert one year of data for 128 stocks (a total of 200,448 insertions).

Table 11-1. Seconds required to insert data for 128 stocks

Programming mode	Time required	DB calls	DB commits
Autocommit enabled, no batching	2220.53 seconds	200,448	200,448
1 commit for each stock	174.44 seconds	200,448	128
1 commit for all data	169.34 seconds	200,448	1
1 batch per commit for each stock	19.32 seconds	128	128
1 batch per stock; 1 commit	17.33 seconds	128	1
1 batch/commit for all data	11.55 seconds	1	1

Note one interesting fact about this table that is not immediately obvious: the difference between lines 1 and 2 is that autocommit has been turned off and the code is explicitly calling the commit() method at the end of each while loop. The difference between lines 1 and 4 is that statements are being batched—but autocommit is still enabled. A batch is considered one transaction, which is why there is a one-to-one correspondence between database calls and commits. In this example, then, a larger benefit accrued from batching than from explicitly managing the transaction boundaries.

Transaction isolation and locking

The second factor affecting transaction performance concerns the scalability of the database as data within transactions is locked. Locking protects data integrity; in database terms, it allows one transaction to be isolated from other transactions. JDBC and JPA support the four major transaction isolation modes of databases, though they differ in the way they accomplish that.

Isolation modes are briefly covered here, though since programming to a correct isolation mode isn't really a Java-specific issue, you are urged to consult a database programming book for more information.

The basic transaction isolation modes (in order from most to least expensive) are:

TRANSACTION_SERIALIZABLE
> This is the most expensive transaction mode; it requires that all data accessed within the transaction be locked for the duration of the transaction. This applies both to data accessed via a primary key, and to data accessed via a WHERE clause—and when there is a WHERE clause, the table is locked such that no new records satisfying the clause can be added for the duration of the transaction. A serialized transaction will always see the same data each time it issues a query.

TRANSACTION_REPEATABLE_READ
> This requires that all accessed data is locked for the duration of the transaction. However, other transactions can insert new rows into the table at any time. This mode can lead to *phantom reads*, where a transaction that reissues a query with a WHERE clause may get back different data the second time the query is executed.

TRANSACTION_READ_COMMITTED
> This mode locks only rows that are written during a transaction. This leads to *nonrepeatable reads*: data that is read at one point in the transaction may be different from data that is read at another point in the transaction.

TRANSACTION_READ_UNCOMMITTED
> This is the least expensive transaction mode. No locks are involved, so one transaction may read the written (but uncommitted) data in another transaction. This is known as a *dirty read*; the problem here arises because the first transaction may roll back (meaning the write never actually happens), and hence the second transaction is operating on incorrect data.

Databases operate in a default mode of transaction isolation: MySQL starts with a default of TRANSACTION_REPEATABLE_READ; Oracle and DB2 start with a default of TRANSACTION_READ_COMMITTED; and so on. There are lots of database-specific permutations here. DB2 calls their default transaction mode CS (for cursor stability) and has different names for the other three JDBC modes. Oracle doesn't support either TRANSACTION_READ_UNCOMMITTED or TRANSACTION_REPEATABLE_READ.

When a JDBC statement is executed, it uses the database's default isolation mode. Alternately, the `setTransaction()` method on the JDBC connection can be called to have the database supply the necessary transaction isolation level (and if the database doesn't support the given level, the JDBC driver will either throw an exception or silently upgrade the isolation level to the next strictest level it supports).

TRANSACTION_NONE and Autocommit

The JDBC specification defines a fifth transaction mode, which is TRANSACTION_NONE. In theory, this transaction mode cannot be specified via the `setTransactionIsolation()` mode, since if a transaction already exists, its isolation level cannot be set to none. Some JDBC drivers (notably for DB2) do allow that call to be made (and in fact even default to that mode). Other JDBC drivers will allow an isolation level of none to be specified in the properties used to initialize the driver.

In a strict sense, a statement executing from a connection with TRANSACTION_NONE semantics cannot commit data to the database: it must be a read-only query. If data is written, there must be some locking; otherwise, if one user is writing a long string to a table using TRANSACTION_NONE semantics, a second user could see a partial string written in the table. It's possible there are databases that operate in that mode, though that would be uncommon; at the very least, data written to a single table is expected to be written atomically. Hence an operation that writes will in reality have (at least) TRANSACTION_READ_UNCOMMITTED semantics.

A TRANSACTION_NONE query cannot be committed, but JDBC drivers that use TRANSACTION_NONE may allow queries to be written if autocommit is enabled. This means that the database is treating each query as a separate transaction. Even so, since the database is (likely) not allowing other transactions to see partial writes, TRANSACTION_READ_UNCOMMITTED semantics are really being used.

For simple JDBC programs, this is sufficient. More commonly—and particularly when used with JPA—programs may want to mix isolation levels on data within a transaction. In an application that queries my employee information so as to ultimately give me a large raise, access to my employee record must be protected: that data needs to be treated as TRANSACTION_REPEATABLE_READ. But that transaction is also likely to access data in other tables, such as the table that holds my office ID. There is no real reason to lock that data during the transaction, so access to that row could certainly operate as TRANSACTION_READ_COMMITTED (or possibly even lower).

JPA allows you to specifying locking levels on a per-entity basis (and of course an entity is [at least usually] simply a row in the database). Because getting these locking levels correct can be quite difficult, it is easier to use JPA rather than performing the locking in JDBC statements. Still, it is possible to use different locking levels in JDBC applications, employing the same pessimistic and optimistic locking semantics that JPA uses (and if you're not familiar with those semantics, this example should serve as a good introduction to them).

At a JDBC level, the basic approach is to set the isolation level of the connection to TRANSACTION_READ_UNCOMMITTED, and then to lock explicitly only that data that needs to be locked during the transaction:

```
Connection c = DriverManager.getConnection();  // Or...get it from a local pool
c.setAutoCommit(false);
c.setTransactionIsolation(TRANSACTION_READ_UNCOMMITTED);
PreparedStatement ps1 = c.prepareStatement(
    "SELECT * FROM employee WHERE e_id = ? FOR UPDATE");
... process info from ps1 ...
PreparedStatement ps2 = c.prepareStatement(
    "SELECT * FROM office WHERE office_id = ?");
... process info from ps2 ...
c.commit();
```

The ps1 statement establishes an explicit lock on the employee data table: no other transaction will be able to access that row for the duration of this transaction. The SQL syntax to accomplish that is nonstandard. You must consult your database vendor's documentation to see how to achieve the desired level of locking, but the common syntax is to include the FOR UPDATE clause. This kind of locking is called *pessimistic locking*. It actively prevents other transactions from accessing the data in question.

Locking performance can often be improved by using optimistic locking—the same way that the java.util.concurrent.atomic package approaches uncontended atomic operations. If the data access is uncontended, this will be a significant performance boost. If the data is even slightly contended, however, the programming becomes more difficult.

In a database, optimistic concurrency is implemented with a version column. When data is selected from a row, the selection must include the desired data plus a version column. To select information about me, I could issue the following SQL:

```
SELECT first_name, last_name, version FROM employee WHERE e_id = 5058;
```

This query will return my names (Scott and Oaks) plus whatever the current version number is (say, 1012). When it comes time to complete the transaction, the transaction updates the version column:

```
UPDATE employee SET version = 1013 WHERE e_id = 5058 AND version = 1012;
```

If the row in question requires repeatable-read or serialization semantics, this update must be performed even if the data was only read during the transaction—those isolation levels require locking read-only data used in a transaction. For read-committed semantics, the version column only needs to be updated when other data in the row is also updated.

Under this scheme, if two transactions use my employee record at the same time, each will read a version number of 1012. The first transaction to complete will successfully update the version number to 1013 and continue. The second transaction will not be able to update the employee record—there is no longer any record where the version number is 1012, so the SQL update statement will fail. That transaction will get an exception and be rolled back.

This highlights a major difference between optimistic locking in the database and Java's atomic primitives: in database programming, when the transaction gets that exception, it is not (and cannot be) transparently retried. If you are programming directly to JDBC, the commit() method will get an SQLException; in JPA, your application will get an OptimisticLockException when the transaction is committed.

Depending on your perspective, this is either a good or a bad thing. When the performance of the atomic utilities (which did transparently retry the operation) was discussed, I observed that performance in highly contended cases could suffer when there were a lot of retries chewing up a lot of CPU resources. In a database, that situation is far worse, since the code executed in a transaction is far more complicated than simply incrementing the value held in a memory location. Retrying a failed optimistic transaction in the database has a far greater potential to lead to a never-ending spiral of retries. Plus, it is often infeasible to determine automatically what operation(s) to retry.

So not retrying transparently is a good thing (and often the only possible solution), but on the other hand, that does mean the application is now responsible for handling the exception. The application can choose to retry the transaction (maybe only once or twice), it can choose to prompt the user for different data, or it can simply inform the user that the operation has failed. There is no one-size-fits-all answer here.

Optimistic locking works best, then, when there is very little chance of a collision between two sources. Think of a joint checking account: there is a slight chance that my husband and I may be in different parts of the city withdrawing money from our checking account at exactly the same time. That would trigger an optimistic lock exception for one of us. Even if that does happen, asking one of us to try again is not too onerous, and now the chance of an optimistic lock exception is virtually nil (or so I would hope; let's not address how frequently we make ATM withdrawals). Contrast that scenario to something involving the sample stock application. In the real world, that data is updated so frequently that locking it optimistically would be quite counterproductive. In truth, stock applications would frequently use no locking when possible just because of the volume of changes, although actual trade updates would require some locking.

Quick Summary

1. Transactions affect the speed of applications in two ways: transactions are expensive to commit, and the locking associated with transactions can prevent database scaling.

2. Those two effects are antagonistic: waiting too long to commit a transaction increases the amount of time that locks associated with the transaction are held. Especially for transactions using stricter semantics, the balance should be toward committing more frequently rather than holding the locks longer.

3. For fine-grained control of transactions in JDBC, use a default TRANSACTION_READ_UNCOMMITTED level and explicitly lock data as needed.

Result Set Processing

Typical database applications will operate on a range of data. The stock application, for example, deals with a history of prices for an individual stock. That history is loaded via a single SELECT statement:

```
SELECT * FROM stockprice WHERE symbol = 'TPKS' AND
        pricedate >= '2013-01-01' AND pricedate <= '2013-12-31';
```

That statement returns 261 rows of data. If the option prices for the stock are also required, a similar query would be executed that would retrieve five times that amount of data. The SQL to retrieve all data in the sample database (128 stocks covering 1 year) will retrieve 200,448 rows of data:

```
SELECT * FROM stockprice s, stockoptionprice o WHERE
        o.symbol = s.symbol AND s.pricedate >= '2013-01-01'
        AND s.pricedate <= '2013-12-31';
```

To use this data, code must scroll through the result set:

```
PreparedStatement ps = c.prepareStatement(...);
ResultSet rs = ps.executeQuery();
while (rs.next()) {
    ... read the current row ...
}
```

The question here is where that data for the 200,448 rows lives. If the entire set of data is returned during the executeQuery() call, then the application will have a very large chunk of live data in its heap, possibly causing GC and other issues. Instead, if only one row of data is returned from the call to the next() method, there will be a lot of back-and-forth traffic between the application and the database as the result set is processed.

As usual, there is no correct answer here; in some cases it will be more efficient to keep the bulk of the data in the database and retrieve it as needed, while in other cases it will be more efficient to load all the data at once when the query is executed. To control this, use the `setFetchSize()` method on the `PreparedStatement` object to let the JDBC driver know how many rows at a time it should transfer.

The default value for this varies by JDBC driver; for example, in Oracle's JDBC drivers, the default value is 10. When the `executeQuery()` method is called in the loop shown above, the database will return 10 rows of data, which will be buffered internally by the JDBC driver. Each of the first 10 calls to the `next()` method will process one of those buffered rows. The 11th call will return to the database to retrieve another 10 rows, and so on.

Other Ways to Set the Fetch Size

I've recommended using the `setFetchSize()` method here on the (prepared) statement object, but that method also exists on the `ResultSet` interface. In either case, the size is just a hint. The JDBC driver is free to ignore that value, or round it to some other value, or anything else it wants to do. There are no assurances either way, but setting the value before the query is executed is more likely to result in the hint being honored.

Some JDBC drivers also allow you to set a default fetch size when the connection is created by passing a property to the `getConnection()` method of the `DriverManager`. Consult your vendor's documentation if that path seems easier to manage.

Though the value varies, JDBC drivers will typically set the default fetch size to a fairly small number. That approach is reasonable in most circumstances; in particular, it is very unlikely to lead to any memory issues within the application. If the performance of the `next()` method (or the performance of the first getter method on the result set) is particularly slow every now and then, consider increasing the fetch size.

Quick Summary

1. Applications that process large amounts of data from a query should consider changing the fetch size of the data.
2. There is a trade-off between loading too much data in the application (putting pressure on the garbage collector) and making frequent database calls to retrieve a set of data.

JPA

The performance of JPA is directly affected by the performance of the underlying JDBC driver, and most of the performance considerations regarding the JDBC driver apply to JPA. JPA has additional performance considerations.

JPA achieves many of its performance enhancements by altering the bytecodes of the entity classes. In a Java EE environment, this happens transparently. In a Java SE environment, it is very important to make sure that the bytecode processing is set up correctly. Otherwise, JPA application performance will be unpredictable: fields that are expected to be loaded lazily might be loaded eagerly, data saved to the database might be redundant, data that should be in the JPA cache may need to be refetched from the database, and so on.

There is no JPA-defined way for the bytecodes to be processed. Typically, this is done as part of compilation—after the entity classes are compiled (and before they are loaded into JAR files or run by the JVM), they are passed through an implementation-specific postprocessor that "enhances" the bytecodes, producing an altered class file with the desired optimizations.

Some JPA implementations also provide a way to dynamically enhance the bytecodes as the classes are loaded into the JVM. This requires running an agent within the JVM that is notified when classes are loaded; the agent interposes on the classloading and alters the bytes before they are used to define the class. The agent is specified on the command line of the application; for example, for EclipseLink you include the `-javaagent:path_to/eclipselink.jar` argument.

Transaction Handling

JPA can be used within both Java SE and Java EE applications. The platform in use affects the way JPA transactions are handled.

In Java EE, JPA transactions are part of the application server's Java Transaction API (JTA) implementation. This offers two choices of how the transaction boundaries are handled: the application server can take care of the boundaries (using container-managed transactions, or CMT), or the transaction boundaries can be explicitly programmed in the application (using user-managed transactions, or UMT).

There is no significant difference in performance between CMT and UMT if they are used equivalently. However, it is not always possible to use them equivalently. In particular, user-managed transactions can have a larger or smaller scope than container-managed transactions, which can have a significant impact on performance.

Consider the following pseudocode:

```
@Stateless
public class Calculator {
    @PersistenceContext(unitName="Calc")
    EntityManager em;

    @TransactionAttribute(REQUIRED)
    public void calculate() {
        Parameters p = em.find(...);
        ...perform expensive calculation...
        em.persist(...answer...);
    }
}
```

The transaction scope here (using CMT) is the entire method. If the method requires repeatable read semantics for the data that is being persisted, then data in the table will be locked during the expensive calculation.

With user-managed transactions, there is more flexibility:

```
@Stateless
public class Calculator {
    @PersistenceContext(unitName="Calc")
    EntityManager em;

    public void calculate() {
        UserTransaction ut = ... lookup UT in application server...;
        ut.begin();
        Parameters p = em.find(...);
        ut.commit();
        ...perform expensive calculation...
        ut.begin();
        em.persist(...answer...);
        ut.commit();
    }
}
```

Splitting the transaction—which can only be done easily with user-managed transactions—limits the effect of the transaction on the scaling of the application. Strictly speaking, this could have been done with container-managed transactions by splitting the work into three different methods, each with a different transaction attribute. In general, the UMT approach is far more convenient.

Similarly, a servlet using user-managed transactions can establish a transaction boundary that spans multiple calls to an EJB. Using container-managed transactions to accomplish the same thing means adding into the EJB interface a new metamethod that calls those other methods within the same transaction.

In a Java SE application, the entity manager is responsible for providing the transaction object, but the application is responsible for demarcating the transaction boundaries on that object. The JPA example to populate the database of stock prices includes the following code:

```
public void run() {
    for (int i = startStock; i < numStocks; i++) {
        EntityManager em = emf.createEntityManager();
        EntityTransaction txn = em.getTransaction();
        txn.begin();
        while (!curDate.after(endDate)) {
            StockPrice sp = createRandomStock(curDate);
            if (sp != null) {
                em.persist(sp);
                for (int j = 0; j < 5; j++) {
                    StockOptionPriceImpl sop =
                        createRandomOption(sp.getSymbol, sp.getDate());
                    em.persist(sop);
                }
            }
            curDate.setTime(curDate.getTime() + msPerDay);
        }
        txn.commit();
        em.close();
    }
}
```

Similar to what was observed using transactions in JDBC, there are efficiency trade-offs here between the frequency of committing the transaction versus the natural transaction boundaries. Some timings for this example are included in the next section.

XA Transactions

JPA entities can frequently be involved in an XA transaction; that is, a transaction that uses more than one database resource, or a database resource and another transactional resource (such as a JMS resource).

Committing a transaction across different transactional resources is a very expensive operation—the algorithm to perform that implements the eXtended Architecture (XA) standard for committing data. It is a very clever and very complex operation that requires multiple back-and-forth exchanges among the resources involved in the transaction.

Most Java EE application servers will allow an optimization in this situation whereby the last resource can bypass the normal XA protocol. This optimization is known as the Last Agent Optimization (LAO), the Logging Last Resource (LLR) optimization, the Last Resource Commit Optimization (LRCO), the Last Resource Gambit, and probably other names.

Technically speaking, these optimizations are not exactly the same. In particular, the LLR and LRCO optimizations provide full ACID compliance as long as the last agent is a JDBC resource capable of storing the XA logs. Some implementations of LAO do that, and some do not. If the JPA database can be used as the transaction log in an application server that supports some form of LAO, then transactions will be noticeably faster because the database updates don't need to participate in the XA protocol. They will also be ACID compliant.

If the LAO implementation does not store the transactions logs like that, it will still give a large performance benefit—just be aware that if there is a crash in the middle of a transaction involving such a resource, the crash cannot be automatically recovered. Human intervention will be required to look at pending and recently committed data and manually roll back some items to achieve data consistency.

Quick Summary

1. Explicitly managing transaction boundaries with user-managed transactions can often improve the performance of an application.

2. The default Java EE programming model—a servlet or web service accessing JPA entities via EJBs—supports that model easily.

3. As an alternative, consider splitting JPA logic into separate methods depending on the transactional needs of the application.

Optimizing JPA Writes

In JDBC, we looked at two critical performance techniques: reusing prepared statements and performing updates in batches.

It is possible to accomplish both of those optimizations with JPA, but the way it is done depends on the JPA implementation in use; there are no calls within the JPA API to do that. For Java SE, these optimizations typically require setting a particular property in the application's *persistence.xml* file.

Writing Fewer Fields

One common way to optimize writes to a database is to write only those fields that have changed. The code the HR system uses to double my salary may need to retrieve 20 fields from my employee record, but only one (very important) field needs to be written back to the database.

JPA implementations should be expected to perform this optimization transparently. This is one of the reasons JPA bytecodes must be enhanced, since that is the process by which the JPA provider keeps track of when values in the code are changed. When the JPA code is properly enhanced, the SQL to write my doubled salary back to the database will update only that single column.

For example, using the JPA EclipseLink reference implementation, statement reuse is enabled by adding the following property to the *persistence.xml* file:

```
<property name="eclipselink.jdbc.cache-statements" value="true" />
```

Note that this enables statement reuse within the EclipseLink implementation. If the JDBC driver is capable of providing a statement pool, it is usually preferable to enable the statement caching in the driver and to leave this property out of the JPA configuration.

Statement batching in the reference JPA implementation is achieved by adding these properties:

```
<property name="eclipselink.jdbc.batch-writing" value="JDBC" />
<property name="eclipselink.jdbc.batch-writing.size" value="10000" />
```

JDBC drivers cannot automatically implement statement batching, so this is a useful property to set in all cases. The batch size can be controlled in two ways: first, the `size` property can be set, as is done in this example. Second, the application can periodically call the `flush()` method of the entity manager, which will cause all batched statements to be executed immediately.

Table 11-2 shows the effect of the statement reuse and batching to create and write stock entities into the database.

Table 11-2. Seconds required to insert data for 128 stocks via JPA

Programming mode	Time required
No batching, no statement pool	240 seconds
No batching, statement pool	200 seconds
Batching, no statement pool	23.37 seconds
Batching, statement pooling	21.08 seconds

Quick Summary

1. JPA applications, like JDBC applications, can benefit from limiting the number of write calls to the database (with the potential trade-off of holding transaction locks).

2. Statement caching can be achieved either at the JPA layer or the JDBC layer. Caching at the JDBC layer should be explored first.

3. Batching JPA updates can be done declaratively (in the *persistence.xml* file), or programmatically (by calling the `flush()` method).

Optimizing JPA Reads

Optimizing when and how JPA reads data from the database is much more complicated than it might seem. That's because JPA will cache data in the hope that it might be used to satisfy a future request. That's usually a good thing for performance, but it means that the JPA-generated SQL that is used to read that data may seem, on the face of it, sub-optimal. The data retrieval is optimized to serve the needs of the JPA cache, rather than being optimized for whatever particular request is in progress.

The details of the cache are covered in the next section. For now, let's look at the basic ways to apply database read optimizations to JPA. JPA reads data from the database in three cases: when the `find()` method of the `EntityManager` is called, when a JPA query is executed, and when code navigates to a new entity using the relationship of an existing entity. In the stock class, that latter case means calling the `getOptions()` method on a `Stock` entity.

Calling the `find()` method is the most straightforward case here: only a single row is involved, and (at least) that single row is read from the database. The only thing that can be controlled here is how much data is retrieved. JPA can retrieve only some of the fields in the row, it can retrieve the entire row, or it can prefetch other entities are related to the row being retrieved. Those optimizations apply to queries as well.

There are two possible paths: read less data (because the data won't be needed), or read more data at a time (because that data will definitely be needed in the future).

Reading less data

To read less data, specify that the field in question is loaded lazily. When an entity is retrieved, the fields with a lazy annotation will be excluded from the SQL used to load the data. If the getter of that field is ever executed, it will mean another trip to the database to retrieve that piece of data.

It is rare to use that annotation for simple columns of basic types, but consider using it if the entity contains large BLOB- or CLOB-based objects.

```
@Lob
@Column(name = "IMAGEDATA")
@Basic(fetch = FetchType.LAZY)
private byte[] imageData;
```

In this case, the entity is mapped to a table storing binary image data. The binary data is large, and the example assumes it shouldn't be loaded unless it is actually needed. Not loading the unneeded data in this case serves two purposes: it makes for faster SQL when the entity is retrieved, and it saves a lot of memory, leading to less GC pressure.

Fetch Groups

If an entity has fields that are loaded lazily, they are normally loaded one at a time as they are accessed.

What if there are, say, three fields in an entity that are subject to lazy loading, and if one field is needed, all of them will be needed? Then it is preferable to load all the lazy fields at once.

That is not possible with standard JPA, but most JPA implementations will allow you to specify a *fetch group* to accomplish this. Using fetch groups, it is possible to specify that certain lazily loaded fields should be loaded as a group whenever one of them is accessed. Typically, multiple independent groups of fields can be defined; each group will be loaded as needed.

Because it is not a JPA standard, code using fetch groups will be tied to one particular JPA implementation. But if it is useful, consult your JPA implementation documentation for details.

Note also that the lazy annotation is, in the end, only a hint to the JPA implementation. The JPA implementation is free to request that the database eagerly provide that data anyway.

On the other hand, perhaps some other data should be preloaded—for example, when one entity is fetched, data for other (related) entities should also be returned. That is known as *eager fetching*, and it has a similar annotation:

```
@OneToMany(mappedBy="stock", fetch=FetchType.EAGER)
private Collection<StockOptionPriceImpl> optionsPrices;
```

By default, related entities are already fetched eagerly if the relationship type is @OneToOne or @ManyToOne (and so it is possible to apply the opposite optimization to them: mark them as FetchType.LAZY if they are almost never used).

This also is just a hint to the JPA implementation, but it essentially says that any time a stock price is retrieved, make sure also to retrieve all related option prices. Beware here: a common expectation about eager relationship fetching is that it will employ a JOIN in the generated SQL. In typical JPA providers, that is not the case: they will issue a single SQL query to fetch the primary object, and then one or more SQL commands to fetch any additional, related objects. From a simple find() method, there is no control over this: if a JOIN statement is required, you will have to use a query and program the JOIN into the query.

Using JOIN in queries

JPQL doesn't allow you to specify fields of an object to be retrieved. Take the following JPQL query:

```
Query q = em.createQuery("SELECT s FROM StockPriceImpl s");
```

That query will always yield this SQL statement:

```
SELECT <enumerated list of non-LAZY fields> FROM StockPriceTable
```

If you want to retrieve fewer fields in the generated SQL, you have no option but to mark them as lazy. Similarly, for fields that are marked as lazy, there is no real option for fetching them in a query.

If there are relationships between entities, the entities can be explicitly joined in a query in JPQL, which will retrieve the initial entities and their related entities in one shot. For example, in the stock entities, this query can be issued:

```
Query q = em.createQuery("SELECT s FROM StockOptionImpl s " +
                          "JOIN FETCH s.optionsPrices");
```

That results in an SQL statement similar to:

```
SELECT t1.<fields>, t0.<fields> FROM StockOptionPrice t0, StockPrice t1
WHERE ((t0.SYMBOL = t1.SYMBOL) AND (t0.PRICEDATE = t1.PRICEDATE))
```

Other Mechanisms for a JOIN FETCH

Many JPA providers allow a join fetch to be specified by setting query hints on a query. For example, in EclipseLink, this code will produce a JOIN query:

```
Query q = em.createQuery("SELECT s FROM StockOptionImpl s");
q.setQueryHint("eclipselink.join-fetch", "s.optionsPrices");
```

Some JPA providers also have a special @JoinFetch annotation that can be used on the relationship.

The exact SQL will differ among JPA providers (this example is from EclipseLink), but this is the general process.

Join fetching is valid for entity relationships regardless of whether they are annotated as eager or lazy. If the join is issued on a lazy relationship, the lazily annotated entities that satisfy the query are still retrieved from the database, and if those entities are later used, no additional trip to the database is required.

When all the data returned by a query using a join fetch will be used, then the join fetch often provides a big improvement in performance. However, a join fetch also interacts with the JPA cache in unexpected ways. An example of that is shown in the section on caching; be sure you understand those ramifications before writing custom queries using join fetch.

Batching and queries

JPA queries are handled like a JDBC query yielding a result set: the JPA implementation has the option of getting all the results at once, getting the results one at a time as the application iterates over the query results, or getting a few results at a time (analogous to how the fetch size worked for JDBC).

There is no standard way to control this, but JPA vendors have proprietary mechanisms to set the fetch size. In EclipseLink, a hint on the query specifies the fetch size:

```
q.setHint("eclipselink.JDBC_FETCH_SIZE", "100000");
```

Hibernate offers a custom @BatchSize annotation instead.

If a very large set of data is being processed, the code may need to page through the list returned by the query. This has a natural relationship to how the data might be displayed to the user on a web page: a subset of data is displayed (say 100 rows), along with "next" and "previous" page links to navigate (page) through the data.

This is accomplished by setting a range on the query:

```
Query q = em.createNamedQuery("selectAll");
query.setFirstResult(101);
query.setMaxResults(100);
List<? implements StockPrice>  = q.getResultList();
```

This returns a list suitable for display on the second page of the web application: items 101–200. Retrieving only the range of data needed will be more efficient than retrieving 200 rows and discarding the first 100 of them.

Note that this example uses a named query (the createNamedQuery() method) rather than an ad hoc query (the createQuery() method). In many JPA implementations, named queries are faster: the JPA implementation will almost always use a prepared statement with bind parameters, utilizing the statement cache pool. There is nothing that prevents JPA implementations from using similar logic for unnamed, ad hoc queries, though implementing that is more difficult, and the JPA implementation may simply default to creating a new statement (i.e., a Statement object) each time.

1. JPA can perform several optimizations to limit (or increase) the amount of data read in a single operation.

2. Large fields (e.g., BLOBs) that are not frequently used should be loaded lazily in a JPA entity.

3. When a relationship exists between JPA entities, the data for the related items can be loaded eagerly or lazily. The choice depends on the needs of the application.

4. When eagerly loading relationships, named queries can be used to issue a single SQL statement using a JOIN statement. Be aware that this affects the JPA cache; it is not always the best idea (as the next section discusses).

5. Reading data via named queries will often be faster than a regular query, since it is easier for the JPA implementation to use a PreparedStatement for named queries.

JPA Caching

One of the canonical performance-related use cases for Java is to supply a middle tier that caches data from backend database resources. The Java tier performs a number of architecturally useful functions (such as preventing clients from directly accessing the database). From a performance perspective, caching frequently used data in the Java tier can greatly speed up response times for the clients.

JPA is designed with that architecture in mind. There are two kinds of caches in JPA. Each entity manager instance is its own cache: it will locally cache data that it has retrieved during a transaction. It will also locally cache data that is written during a transaction; the data is sent to the database only when the transaction commits. A program may have many different entity manager instances, each executing a different transaction, and each with its own local cache. (In particular, the entity managers injected into Java EE applications are distinct instances.)

When an entity manager commits a transaction, all data in the local cache can be merged into a global cache. The global cache is shared among all entity managers in the application. The global cache is also known as the Level 2 (L2) cache or the second-level cache; the cache in the entity manager is known as the Level 1, L1, or first-level cache.

There is little to tune within an entity manager transaction cache (the L1 cache), and the L1 cache is enabled in all JPA implementations. The L2 cache is different: most JPA implementations provide one, but not all of them enable it by default (e.g., Hibernate does not, but EclipseLink does). Once enabled, the way in which the L2 cache is tuned and used can substantially affect performance.

The JPA cache operates only on entities accessed by their primary keys; that is, items retrieved from a call to the find() method, or items retrieved from accessing (or eagerly loading) a related entity. When the entity manager attempts to find an object via either its primary key or a relationship mapping, it can look in the L2 cache and return the object(s) if they are found there, thus saving a trip to the database.

Items retrieved via a query are not held in the L2 cache. Some JPA implementations do have a vendor-specific mechanism to cache the results of a query, but those results are only reused if the exact same query is re-executed. Even if the JPA implementation supports query caching, the entities themselves are not stored in the L2 cache and cannot be returned in a subsequent call to the find() method.

There are many ways that the connections between the L2 cache, queries, and the loading of objects affects performance. To examine them, code based on the following loop will be used:

```
EntityManager em = emf.createEntityManager();
Query q = em.createNamedQuery(queryName);
List<StockPrice> l = q.getResultList(); ❶
for (StockPrice sp : l) {
    ... process sp ...
    if (processOptions) {
        Collection<? extends StockOptionPrice> options = sp.getOptions(); ❷
        for (StockOptionPrice sop : options) {
            ... process sop ...
        }
    }
}
em.close();
```

❶   SQL Call Site 1
❷   SQL Call Site 2

Because of the L2 cache, this loop will perform one way the first time it is executed, and another (generally faster) way on subsequent executions. The specific difference of that performance depends on various details of the queries and the entity relationships. The next few subsections will explain the results in detail.

The differences in this example are based in some cases on different JPA configurations, but also because some tests are executed without traversing the relationship between the Stock and StockOptions classes. In those tests without traversal of the relationship, the processOptions value in the loop is false; only the StockPrice objects are actually used.

Default caching (lazy loading)

In the sample code, the stock prices are loaded via a named query. In the default case, this simple query is executed to load the stock data:

```
@NamedQuery(name="findAll",
    query="SELECT s FROM StockPriceImpl s ORDER BY s.id.symbol")
```

The `StockPrice` class has a `@OneToMany` relationship with the `StockOptionPrice` class using the `optionsPrices` instance variable:

```
@OneToMany(mappedBy="stock")
private Collection<StockOptionPrice> optionsPrices;
```

`@OneToMany` relationships are loaded lazily by default. Table 11-3 shows the time to execute this loop.

Table 11-3. Seconds required to read data for 128 stocks (default configuration)

Test case	First execution	Subsequent executions
Lazy relationship	61.9 seconds (33,409 SQL calls)	3.2 seconds (1 SQL call)
Lazy relationship, no traversal	5.6 seconds (1 SQL call)	2.8 seconds (1 SQL call)

The first time the sample loop is executed in this scenario (for 128 stocks with one year of data), the JPA code executes one SQL statement in the call to the `executeQuery()` method. That statement is executed at SQL Call Site 1 in the code listing.

As the code loops through the stock and visits each collection of option prices, JPA will issue SQL statements to retrieve all the options associated with the particular entity (that is, it retrieves the entire collection for one stock/date combination at once). This occurs at SQL Call Site 2, and it results in 33,408 individual SELECT statements during execution (261 days * 128 stocks).

That example takes almost 62 seconds for the first execution of the loop. The next time that code is executed, it takes only 3.2 seconds. That's because the second time the loop is executed, the only SQL that is executed is the named query. The entities retrieved via the relationship are still in the L2 cache, so no database calls are needed in that case. (Recall that the L2 cache only works for entities loaded from a relationship or a find operation. So the stock option entities can be found in the L2 cache, but the stock prices —since they were loaded from a query—do not appear in the L2 cache and must be reloaded.)

The second line in Table 11-3 represents the code that does not visit each of the options in the relationship (i.e., the `processOptions` variable is `false`). In that case, the code is substantially faster: it takes 5.6 seconds for the first iteration of the loop, and 2.8 seconds for subsequent iterations. (The difference in performance between those two cases is due to the warm-up period of the compiler. Although it wasn't as noticeable, that warm-up occurred in the first example as well.)

Caching and eager loading

In the next two experiments, the relationship between the stock prices and option prices is redefined so that the option prices are loaded eagerly.

When all the data is used (i.e., the first lines in Tables 11-3 and 11-4, the performance of the eager and lazy loading cases is essentially the same. But when the relationship data isn't actually used (the second lines in each table), the lazy relationship case saves some time—particularly on the first execution of the loop. Subsequent executions of the loop don't save time since the eager-loading code isn't reloading the data in those subsequent iterations; it is loading data from the L2 cache.

Table 11-4. Seconds required to read data for 128 stocks (eager loading)

Test case	First execution	Subsequent executions
Eager relationship	60.2 seconds (33,409 SQL calls)	3.1 seconds (1 SQL call)
Eager relationship, no traversal	60.2 seconds (33,409 SQL calls)	2.8 seconds (1 SQL call)

Eager Loading of Relationships

Regardless of whether the relationship is fetched lazily or eagerly, the loop here will execute 33,408 SELECT statements to retrieve the stock options (as the last section mentioned, a JOIN will not be used by default).

The difference between eagerly and lazily loading the relationship in this situation applies to *when* those SQL statements are executed. If the relationship is annotated to load eagerly, when the query is executed the result set is processed immediately (within the call to the getResultList( ) method). The JPA framework looks at every entity returned in that call and executes an SQL statement to retrieve their related entities. All these SQL statements occur at SQL Call Site 1—in the eager relationship case, no SQL statements are executed at SQL Call Site 2.

If the relationship is annotated to load lazily, then only the stock prices are loaded at SQL Call Site 1 (using the named query). The option prices for individual stocks are loaded when the relationship traversal occurs at SQL Call Site 2. That loop is executed 33,408 times, resulting in the 33,408 SQL calls.

Regardless of when the SQL is issued, though, the number of SQL statements remains the same—assuming that all the data is actually used in the lazy-loading example.

Join fetch and caching

As discussed in the previous section, the query could be written to explicitly use a JOIN statement:

```
@NamedQuery(name="findAll",
    query="SELECT s FROM StockPriceEagerLazyImpl s " +
    "JOIN FETCH s.optionsPrices ORDER BY s.id.symbol")
```

Using that named query (with full traversal) yields the data in Table 11-5.

Table 11-5. Seconds required to read data for 128 stocks (JOIN query)

Test case	First execution	Subsequent executions
Default configuration	61.9 seconds (33,409 SQL calls)	3.2 seconds (1 SQL call)
Join fetch	17.9 seconds (1 SQL call)	11.4 seconds (1 SQL call)
Join fetch with query cache	17.9 seconds (1 SQL call)	1.1 seconds (0 SQL call)

The first time the loop is executed with a JOIN query, there is a big performance win: it takes only 17.9 seconds. That is the result of issuing only one SQL request, rather than 33,409 of them.

Unfortunately, the next time the code is executed, it still needs that one SQL statement, since query results are not in the L2 cache. Subsequent executions of the example take 11.4 seconds—because the SQL statement that is executed has the JOIN statement and is retrieving over 200,000 rows of data.

If the JPA provider implements query caching, this is clearly a good time to use it. If no SQL statements are required during the second execution of the code, only 1.1 seconds are required on the subsequent executions. Be aware that query caching works only if the parameters used in the query are exactly the same each time the query is executed.

Avoiding queries

If entities are never retrieved via a query, then after an initial warm-up period, all entities can be accessed through the L2 cache. The L2 cache can be warmed up by loading all entities, so slightly modifying the previous example gives this code:

```
EntityManager em = emf.createEntityManager();
ArrayList<String> allSymbols = ... all valid symbols ...;
ArrayList<Date> allDates = ... all valid dates...;
for (String symbol : allSymbols) {
    for (Date date = allDates) {
        StockPrice sp =
            em.find(StockPriceImpl.class, new StockPricePK(symbol, date);
        ... process sp ...
        if (processOptions) {
            Collection<? extends StockOptionPrice> options = sp.getOptions();
            ... process options ...
        }
    }
}
```

The results of executing this code are given in Table 11-6.

Table 11-6. Seconds required to read data for 128 stocks (L2 cache used)

Test case	First execution	Subsequent executions
Default configuration	61.9 seconds (33,409 SQL calls)	3.2 seconds (1 SQL call)
No query	100.5 seconds (66,816 SQL calls)	1.19 seconds (0 SQL calls)

The first execution of this loop requires 66,816 SQL statements: 33,408 for the call to the find() method, and an additional 33,408 for the call to the getOptions() method. Subsequent executions of that code are the fastest possible, since all the entities are in the L2 cache, and no SQL statements need to be issued.

Warming Up a Test

Java performance tests—and particularly benchmarks—usually have a warm-up period. As discussed in Chapter 4, that allows the compiler to compile the code optimally.

Here's another example where a warm-up period is beneficial. During the warm-up period of a JPA application, the most-frequently used entities will be loaded into the L2 cache. The measurement period of the test will see very different performance as those entities are first loaded. This is particularly true if, as in the last example, no queries are used to load entities.

Recall that in the sample database, there are five option prices for every date and symbol pair, or a total of 167,040 option prices for 128 stocks over one year of data. When the five stock options for a particular symbol and date are accessed via a relationship, they can all be retrieved at once. That's why only 33,408 SQL statements are required to load all the option price data. Even though multiple rows are returned from those SQL statements, JPA is still able to cache the entities—it is not the same thing as executing a query. If the L2 cache is warmed up by iterating through entities, don't iterate through related entities individually—do that by simply visiting the relationship.

As code is optimized, you must take into account the effects of the cache (and particularly the L2 cache). Even if you think you could write better SQL than what JPA generates (and hence should use complex named queries), make sure that code is worthwhile once the cache comes into play. Even if it seems that using a simple named query will be faster to load data, consider what would happen in the long run if those entities were loaded into the L2 cache via a call to the find() method.

Sizing the JPA cache

Like all cases where objects are reused, the JPA cache has a potential performance downside: if the cache consumes too much memory, it will cause GC pressure. This may require that the cache be tuned to adjust its size, or that you control the mode in which entities remain cached. Unfortunately, these are not standard options, so you must perform these tunings based on which JPA provider you are using.

JPA implementations typically provide an option to set the size of the cache, either globally or on a per-entity basis. The latter case is obviously more flexible, though it also requires more work to determine the optimal size for each entity. An alternative approach is for the JPA implementation to use soft and/or weak references for the L2 cache. EclipseLink, for example, provides five different cache types (plus additional deprecated types) based on different combinations of soft and weak references. That approach, while potentially easier than finding optimal sizes for each entity, still requires some planning: in particular, recall from Chapter 7 that weak references do not really survive any GC operation and are hence a questionable choice for a cache.

If a cache based on soft or weak references is used, the performance of the application will also depend on what else happens in the heap. The examples of this section all used a large heap so that caching the 200,448 entity objects in the application would not cause issues with the garbage collector. Tuning a heap when there are large JPA L2 caches is quite important for good performance.

Quick Summary

1. The JPA L2 cache will automatically cache entities for an application.

2. The L2 cache does not cache entities retrieved via queries. This means that in the long run it can be beneficial to avoid queries altogether.

3. Unless query caching is supported by the JPA implementation in use, using a JOIN query turns out to frequently have a negative performance effect, since it bypasses the L2 cache.

JPA Read-Only Entities

The JPA specification does not directly address the notion of a read-only entity, but many JPA providers do. A read-only entity will usually offer much better performance than a (default) read-write entity, because the JPA implementation knows that it does not need to keep track of the state of the entity, nor enroll the entity in transactions, nor lock the entity, and so on. In Java EE containers, read-only entities are often supported regardless of the JPA implementation used. The application server in that case ensures that the entities are accessed using a special, nontransactional JDBC connection. This usually offers a significant performance benefit.

In a Java EE container, transaction support for read-only entities is one area that the JPA specification does address: a business method that is annotated with

`@TransactionAttributeType.SUPPORTS` can be run outside a transaction (assuming no transaction is in progress when that method is called).

In that case, the entities accessed in that method must be, essentially, read-only, since they are not part of a transaction. However, if the method is called from another method that is part of a transaction, the entities still become part of the transaction.

Summary

Properly tuning JDBC and JPA access to a database is one of the most significant ways to affect the performance of a middle-tier application. Keep in mind these best practices:

- Batch reads and writes as much as possible by configuring the JDBC or JPA configuration appropriately.

- Optimize the SQL the application issues. For JDBC applications, this is a question of basic, standard SQL commands. For JPA applications, be sure to consider the involvement of the L2 cache.

- Minimize locking where possible. Use optimistic locking when data is unlikely to be contended, and pessimistic locking when data is contended.

- Make sure to use a prepared statement pool.

- Make sure to use an appropriately sized connection pool.

- Set an appropriate transaction scope: it should be as large as possible without negatively affecting the scalability of the application because of the locks held during the transaction.

## CHAPTER 12

Java SE API Tips

This chapter covers areas of the Java SE API that have implementation quirks that affect their performance. There are many such implementation details throughout the JDK; these are the areas where I consistently uncover performance issues (even in my own code).

Buffered I/O

When I joined the Java Performance Group in 2000, my boss had just published the first ever book on Java performance, and one of the hottest topics in those days was buffered I/O. Fourteen years later, I was prepared to assume the topic was old hat and leave it out of this book. Then, in the week I started this book's outline, I filed bugs against two unrelated projects where unbuffered I/O was greatly hampering performance. A few months later, as I was working on an example for this book, I scratched my head as I wondered why my "optimization" was so slow. Then I realized: stupid, you forgot to buffer the I/O correctly.

So let's talk about buffered I/O performance. The `InputStream.read()` and `OutputStream.write()` methods operate on a single character. Depending on the re-source they are accessing, these methods can be very slow. A `FileInputStream` that uses the `read()` method will be excruciatingly slow: each method invocation requires a trip into the kernel to fetch 1 byte of data. On most operating systems the kernel will have buffered the I/O and so (luckily) this scenario doesn't trigger a disk read for each invocation of the `read()` method. But that buffer is held in the kernel, not the application, and reading a single byte at a time means making an expensive system call for each method invocation.

The same is true of writing data: using the `write()` method to send a single byte to a `FileOutputStream` requires a system call to store the byte in a kernel buffer. Eventually (when the file is closed or flushed), the kernel will write out that buffer to the disk.

For file-based I/O using binary data, always use a `BufferedInputStream` or `BufferedOutputStream` to wrap the underlying file stream. For file-based I/O using character (string) data, always wrap the underlying stream with a `BufferedReader` or `BufferedWriter`.

Although this performance issue is most easily understood when discussing file I/O, it is a general issue that applies to almost every sort of I/O. The streams returned from a socket (via the `getInputStream()` or `getOutputStream()` methods) operate in the same manner, and performing I/O a byte at a time over a socket is quite slow. Here, too, always make sure that the streams are appropriately wrapped with a buffering filter stream.

There are more subtle issues when using the `ByteArrayInputStream` and `ByteArrayOutputStream` classes. These classes are essentially just big in-memory buffers to begin with. In many cases, wrapping them with a buffering filter stream means that data is copied twice: once to the buffer in the filter stream, and once to the buffer in the `ByteArrayInputStream` (or vice versa for output streams). Absent the involvement of any other streams, buffered I/O should be avoided in that case.

When other filtering streams are involved, the question of whether or not to buffer becomes more complicated. A common use case is to use these streams to serialize or deserialize data. For example, Chapter 10 discusses various performance trade-offs involving explicitly managing the data serialization of classes. A simple version of the `writeObject()` method in that chapter looks like this:

```
private void writeObject(ObjectOutputStream out) throws IOException {
    if (prices == null) {
        makePrices();
    }
    out.defaultWriteObject();
}

protected void makePrices() throws IOException {
    ByteArrayOutputStream baos = new ByteArrayOutputStream();
    ObjectOutputStream oos = new ObjectOutputStream(baos);
    oos.writeObject(prices);
    oos.close();
}
```

In this case, wrapping the `baos` stream in a `BufferedOutputStream` would suffer a performance penalty from copying the data one extra time.

In that example, it turned out to be much more efficient to compress the data in the `prices` array, which resulted in this code:

```
private void writeObject(ObjectOutputStream out) throws IOException {
    if (prices == null) {
        makeZippedPrices();
    }
    out.defaultWriteObject();
```

```
    }

    protected void makeZippedPrices() throws IOException {
        ByteArrayOutputStream baos = new ByteArrayOutputStream();
        GZIPOutputStream zip = new GZIPOutputStream(baos);
        BufferedOutputStream bos = new BufferedOutputStream(zip);
        ObjectOutputStream oos = new ObjectOutputStream(bos);
        oos.writeObject(prices);
        oos.close();
        zip.close();
    }
```

Now it is necessary to buffer the output stream, because the GZIPOutputStream operates more efficiently on a block of data than it does on single bytes of data. In either case, the ObjectOutputStream will send single bytes of data to the next stream. If that next stream is the ultimate destination—the ByteArrayOutputStream—then no buffering is necessary. If there is another filtering stream in the middle (such as the GZIPOutputStream in this example), then buffering is often necessary.

There is no general rule about when to use a buffered stream interposed between two other streams. Ultimately it will depend on the type of streams involved, but the likely cases will all operate better if they are fed a block of bytes (from the buffered stream) rather than a series of single bytes (from the ObjectOutputStream).

The same situation applies to input streams. In the specific case here, a GZIPInputStream will operate more efficiently on a block of bytes; in the general case, streams that are interposed between the ObjectInputStream and the original byte source will also be better off with a block of bytes.

Note that this case applies in particular to stream encoders and decoders. When you convert between bytes and characters, operating on as large a piece of data as possible will provide the best performance. If single bytes or characters are fed to encoders and decoders, they will suffer from bad performance.

For the record, not buffering the gzip streams is exactly the mistake I made when writing that compression example. It was a costly mistake, as the data in Table 12-1 shows.

Table 12-1. Time to serialize/deserialize 10,000 objects with compression

Operation	Serialization time	Deserialization time
Unbuffered compression/decompression	60.3 seconds	79.3 seconds
Buffered compression/decompression	26.8 seconds	12.7 seconds

The failure to properly buffer the I/O resulted in as much as a 6x performance penalty.

Quick Summary

1. Issues around buffered I/O are common due to the default implementation of the simple input and output stream classes.

2. I/O must be properly buffered for files and sockets, and also for internal operations like compression and string encoding.

Classloading

The performance of classloading is the bane of anyone attempting to optimize either program startup or deployment of new code in a dynamic system (e.g., deploying a new application into a Java EE application server, or loading an applet in a browser).

There are many reasons for that. The primary one is that the class data (i.e., the Java bytecodes) is typically not quickly accessible. That data must be loaded from disk or from the network, it must be found in one of several JAR files on the classpath, and it must be found in one of several classloaders. There are some ways to help this along: for example, Java WebStart caches classes it reads from the network into a hidden directory, so that next time it starts the same application, it can read the classes more quickly from the local disk than from the network. Packaging an application into fewer JAR files will also speed up its classloading performance.

In a complex environment, one obvious way to speed things up is to parallelize classloading. Take a typical application server: on startup, it may need to initialize multiple applications, each of which uses its own classloader. Given the multiple CPUs available to most application servers, parallelization should be an obvious win here.

Two things hamper this kind of scaling. First, the class data is likely stored on the same disk, so two classloaders running concurrently will issue disk reads to the same device. Operating systems are pretty good at dealing with that situation; they can split up the reads and grab bytes as the disk rotates. Still, there is every chance that the disk will become a bottleneck in that situation.

Until Java 7, a bigger issue existed in the design of the ClassLoader class itself. Java classloaders exist in a hierarchy as shown in Figure 12-1, which is an idealized version of the classloaders in a Java EE container. Normally, classloading follows a delegation model. When the classloader running the first servlet application needs a class, the request flows to the first web app classloader, but that classloader delegates the request to the its parent: the system classloader. That's the classloader associated with the classpath; it will have the Java EE–based classes (like the Java Server Faces, or JSF, interfaces) and the container's implementation of those classes. That classloader will also delegate to its parent classloader, in this case the bootstrap classloader (which contains the core JDK classes).

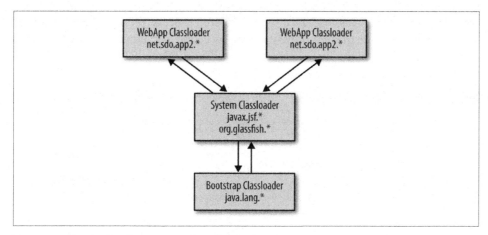

Figure 12-1. Idealized structure of multiple classloaders

The net result is that when there is a request to load a class, the bootstrap classloader is the first code that attempts to find the class; that is followed by the system (classpath) classloader, and then the application-specific classloader(s). From a functional point of view, that's what makes sense: the bytecodes for the java.lang.String class must come from the bootstrap classloader and not some other implementation that was accidentally (or maliciously) included in some other classloader in the hierarchy.

Prior to Java 7, the problem here was that the method to load the class was synchronized: only one classloader could delegate to the system classloader at a time. This drastically reduced any parallelization from using multiple classloaders, since each had to wait its turn for access into the system and bootstrap classloaders. Java 7 addresses that situation by using a set of locks based on the class name. Now, two classloaders that are looking for the same class will still contend for a lock, but classloaders that are looking for different classes can execute within the class hierarchy in parallel.

This benefit also applies if Java-supplied classloaders such as the URLClassLoader are used. In Java 6, a URL classloader that was the parent of additional classloaders would be a synchronization bottleneck for parallel operations; in Java 7, the classloader is able to be used in parallel. Java 7–supplied classloaders are termed *parallel-capable*.

Classloaders are not parallel-capable by default. If you want to extend the benefits of parallel use into your own classloaders, you must take steps to make them parallel-capable. There are two steps.

First, ensure that the classloader hierarchy does not contain any cycles. A cyclical class-loader hierarchy is fairly uncommon. It also results in code that is quite difficult to maintain, since at some point in the cycle, some classloader must directly satisfy the request rather than passing the request to its parent classloader (otherwise, the delegation would have an infinite loop). So while it is technically possible to enable parallelism for a cyclical series of classloaders, it is a convoluted process (on top of already convoluted code). Since one precept of performant Java code is to employ common idioms and write simple code that the compiler can easily optimize, that case will not be recommended here.

Second, register the classloader as parallel-capable in a static initializer within the class:

```
public class MyCustomClassLoader extends SecureClassLoader {

    static {
        registerAsParallelCapable();
    }


    ....

}
```

This call must be made within each specific classloader implementation. The SecureClassLoader is itself parallel-capable, but subclasses do not pick up that setting. If, within your own code, you have a second class that extends the MyCustomClassLoader class, that class must also register itself as parallel-capable.

For most classloaders, these are the only two steps that are required. The recommended way to write a classloader is to override the findClass() method. Custom classloaders that instead override the loadClass() method must also ensure that the defineClass() method is called only once for each class name within each classloader instance.

As with all performance issues involving scalability around a lock, the net performance benefit of this optimization depends on how long the code in the lock is held. As a simple example, consider this code:

```
URL url = new File(args[0]).toURL();
URLClassLoader ucl = new URLClassLoader(url);
for (String className : classNames) {
    ucl.loadClass(className);
}
```

The custom classloader here will look in a single JAR file (passed on the command line as the first element of args). Then it loops through an array of class names (defined elsewhere) and loads each of the classes from that JAR file.

The parent classloader here is the system classpath classloader. When two or more threads execute this loop concurrently, they will have to wait for each other as they delegate the lookup of the class into the classpath classloader. Table 12-2 shows the performance of this loop when the system classpath is empty.

Table 12-2. Time to load classes concurrently (no classpath)

Number of threads	Time in JDK 7	Time in JDK 6
1	30.353 seconds	27.696 seconds
2	34.811 seconds	31.409 seconds
4	48.106 seconds	72.208 seconds
8	117.34 seconds	184.45 seconds

The time here is for 100 executions of the loop with a classname list of 1,500 classes. There are a few interesting conclusions to draw here. First, the more complex code in JDK 7 (to enable the parallel loading) has actually introduced a small penalty in the simplest case—an example of the principle that simpler code is faster. Even with two threads, the new model is slightly slower in this case, because the code spends virtually no time in the parent classloader: the time spent while the lock is held in the parent classloader is greatly outweighed by the time spent elsewhere in the program.

When there are four threads, things change. To begin, the four threads here are competing for CPU cycles against other processes on the four-CPU machine (in particular, there is a browser displaying a flash-enabled page, which is taking some 40% of a single CPU). So even in the JDK 7 case, the scaling isn't linear. But at least the scaling is much better: in the JDK 6 case, there is now severe contention around the parent classloader lock.

There are two reasons for that contention. First, competition for the CPU has effectively increased the amount of time the classloader lock is held, and second, there are now twice as many threads competing for the lock.

Increasing the size of the system classpath also greatly increases the length of time the parent classloading lock is held. Table 12-3 repeats this experiment when the classpath has 266 entries (the number of JAR files in the GlassFish distribution). (GlassFish doesn't simply put all those files into a single classloader; it has been chosen here simply as an expedient example.)

Table 12-3. Time to load classes concurrently (long classpath)

Number of threads	Time in JDK 7	Time in JDK 6
1	98.146 seconds	92.129 seconds
2	111.16 seconds	316.01 seconds
4	150.98 seconds	708.24 seconds
8	287.97 seconds	1461.5 seconds

Now, the contention even with only two threads is quite severe: without a parallel-enabled classloader, it takes three times longer to load the classes. And as load is injected into the already-stressed system, scaling becomes even worse. In the end, performance is as much as seven times slower.

There is an interesting trade-off here: whether to deploy the more complex code and slightly hurt performance in the single-threaded case, or whether to optimize for other cases—particularly when, as in the last example, the performance difference is quite large. These are the sort of performance trade-offs that occur all the time, and in this case the JDK team opted for the second choice as a default. As a platform, it is a good idea to provide both choices (even though only one can be a default). Hence, the JDK 6 behavior can be enabled by using the -XX:+AlwaysLockClassLoader flag (which is false by default). Long startup cycles without concurrent threads loading classes from different classloaders may benefit slightly from including that flag.

Quick Summary

1. In complex applications (particularly application servers) with multiple classloaders, making those classloaders parallel-capable can solve issues where they are bottlenecked on the system or bootclass classloader.

2. Applications that do a lot of classloading through a single classloader in a single thread may benefit from disabling the parallel-capable feature of Java 7.

Random Numbers

Java 7 comes with three standard random number generator classes: java.util.Random, java.util.concurrent.ThreadLocalRandom, and java.security.SecureRandom. There are important performance differences among these three classes.

The difference between the Random and ThreadLocalRandom classes is that the main operation (the nextGaussian() method) of the Random class is synchronized. That method is used by any method that retrieves a random value, so that lock can become contended no matter how the random number generator is used: if two threads use the same random number generator at the same time, one will have to wait for the other to complete its operation. This is why the thread-local version is used: when each thread has its own random number generator, the synchronization of the Random class is no longer an issue. (As discussed in Chapter 7, the thread-local version also provides significant performance benefits because it is reusing an expensive-to-create object.)

The difference between those classes and the SecureRandom class lies in the algorithm used. The Random class (and the ThreadLocalRandom class, via inheritance) implements a typical pseudorandom algorithm. While those algorithms are quite sophisticated, they are in the end deterministic. If the initial seed is known, it is easy to determine the exact series of numbers the engine will generate. That means hackers are able to look at series of numbers from a particular generator and (eventually) figure out what the next number will be. Although good pseudorandom number generators can emit series of numbers that look really random (and that even fit probabilistic expectations of randomness), they are not truly random.

The SecureRandom class, on the other hand, uses a system interface to obtain random data. The way that data is generated is operating-system-specific, but in general this source provides data based on truly random events (such as when the mouse is moved). This is known as entropy-based randomness and is much more secure for operations that rely on random numbers. SSL encryption is the best-known example of such an operation: the random numbers it uses for encryption are impossible to determine with an entropy-based source. (There are other ways to break encryption methods for data, even when a SecureRandom random number generator is used in the algorithm.)

Unfortunately, computers generate a limited amount of entropy, so it can take a very long time to get a lot of random numbers from a secure random number generator. Calls to the nextRandom() method of the SecureRandom class will take an indeterminate amount of time, based on how much unused entropy the system has. If no entropy is available, the call will appear to hang, possibly as long as seconds at a time, until the required entropy is available. That makes performance timing quite difficult: the performance itself becomes random.

This is often a problem for applications that create many SSL connections or otherwise need a lot of secure random numbers; it can take such applications a long time to perform their operations. When executing performance tests on such an application, be aware that the timings will have a very large amount of variance. There really isn't any way to deal with that variance other than to run a huge number of sample tests as discussed in Chapter 2. The other alternative is to contact your operating system vendor and see if they have additional (or better) entropy-based sources available.

In a pinch, a third alternative to this problem is to run performance tests using the Random class, even though the SecureRandom class will be used in production. If the performance tests are module-level tests, that can make sense: those tests will need more random numbers (e.g., more SSL sockets) than the production system will need during the same period of time. But eventually, the expected load must be tested with the SecureRandom class to determine if the load on the production system can obtain a sufficient number of random numbers.

Quick Summary

1. Java's default Random class is expensive to initialize, but once initialized, it can be reused.

2. In multithreaded code, the ThreadLocalRandom class is preferred.

3. The SecureRandom class will show arbitrary, completely random performance. Performance tests on code using that class must be carefully planned.

Java Native Interface

If you are interested in writing the fastest possible code, avoid JNI.

Well-written Java code will run at least as fast on current versions of the JVM as corresponding C or C++ code (it is not 1996 anymore). Language purists will continue to debate the relative performance merits of Java and other languages, and there are doubtless examples you can find where an application written in another language is faster than the same application written in Java (though often those examples contain poorly written Java code). However, that debate misses the point of this section: when an application is already written in Java, calling native code for performance reasons is almost always a bad idea.

Still, there are times when JNI is quite useful. The Java platform provides many common features of operating systems, but if access to a special, operating-system-specific function is required, then so is JNI. And why build your own library to perform some operation, when a commercial (native) version of the code is readily available? In these and other cases, the question becomes how to write the most efficient JNI code.

The answer is to avoid making calls from Java to C as much as possible. Crossing the JNI boundary (the term for making the cross-language call) is quite expensive. Because calling an existing C library requires writing some glue code in the first place, take the time to create new, coarse-grained interfaces via that glue code: perform many, multiple calls into the C library in one shot.

Interestingly, the reverse is not necessarily true: C code that calls back into Java does not suffer a large performance penalty (depending on the parameters involved). For example, consider the following code:

```
public void main() {
    calculateError();
}

public void calculateError() {
    for (int i = 0; i < numberOfTrials; i++) {
        error += 50 - calc(numberOfIterations);
    }
}

public double calc(int n) {
    double sum = 0;
    for (int i = 0; i < n; i++) {
        int r = random(100);       // Return random value between 1 and 100
        sum += r;
    }
    return sum / n;
}
```

This (completely nonsensical) code has two main loops: the inner loop makes multiple calls to code that generates a random number, and the outer loop repeatedly calls that inner loop to see how close to the expected value it is. A JNI implementation could implement any subset of the calculateError(), calc(), and random() methods in C. Table 12-4 shows the performance from various permutations, given 10,000 trials.

Table 12-4. Time to calculate the error of the random method

calculateError	Calc	Random	JNI transitions	Total time
Java	Java	Java	0	12.4 seconds
Java	Java	C	10,000,000	32.1 seconds
Java	C	C	10,000	24.4 seconds
C	Java	Java	10,000	12.4 seconds
C	C	C	0	12.4 seconds

Implementing only the innermost method in a JNI call provides the most crossings of the JNI boundary (numberOfTrials * numberOfLoops, or 10 million). Reducing the number of crossings to numberOfTrials (10,000) reduces that overhead substantially, and reducing it further to 0 provides the best performance—at least in terms of JNI, though the pure Java implementation is just as fast as an implementation that uses all native code.

JNI code performs worse if the parameters involved are not simple primitives. Two aspects are involved in this overhead. First, for simple references, an address translation is needed. This is one reason why, in the example above, the call from Java to C experienced more overhead than the call from C to Java: calls from Java to C implicitly pass the object in question (the this object) to the C function. The call from C to Java doesn't pass any objects.

Second, operations on array-based data are subject to special handling in native code. This includes String objects, since the string data is essentially a character array. To access the individual elements of these arrays, a special call must be made to pin the object in memory (and for String objects, to convert from Java's UTF-16 encoding into UTF-8). When the array is no longer needed, it must be explicitly released in the JNI code. While the array is pinned, the garbage collector cannot run—so one of the most expensive mistakes in JNI code is to pin a string or array in code that is long-running. That prevents the garbage collector from running, effectively blocking all the application threads until the JNI code completes. It is extremely important to make the critical section where the array is pinned as short as possible.

Sometimes, this latter goal conflicts with the goal of reducing the calls that cross the JNI boundary. In that case, the latter goal is the more important one: even if it means making multiple crossings of the JNI boundary, make the sections that pin arrays and strings as short as possible.

Exceptions

Java exception processing has the reputation of being expensive. It is somewhat more expensive than processing regular control flows, though in most cases, the extra cost isn't worth the effort to attempt to bypass it. On the other hand, because it isn't free, exception processing shouldn't be used as a general mechanism either. The guideline here is to use exceptions according to the general principles of good program design: mainly, code should only throw an exception to indicate something unexpected has happened. Following good code design means that your Java code will not be slowed down by exception processing.

Two things can affect the general performance of exception processing. First, there is the code block itself: is it expensive to set up a try-catch block? While that might have been the case a very long time ago, it has not been the case for years. Still, because the Internet has a long memory, you will sometimes see recommendations to avoid exceptions simply because of the try-catch block. Those recommendations are out of date; modern JVMs can generate code that handles exceptions quite efficiently.

The second aspect is that (most) exceptions involve obtaining a stack trace at the point of the exception. This operation can be expensive, particularly if the stack trace is deep.

Let's look at an example. Here are three implementations of a particular method to consider:

```java
public ArrayList<String> testSystemException() {
    ArrayList<String> al = new ArrayList<>();
    for (int i = 0; i < numTestLoops; i++) {
        Object o = null;
        if ((i % exceptionFactor) != 0) {
            o = new Object();
        }
        try {
            al.add(o.toString());
        } catch (NullPointerException npe) {
            // Continue to get next string
        }
```

```
        }
        return al;
    }

    public ArrayList<String> testCodeException() {
        ArrayList<String> al = new ArrayList<>();
        for (int i = 0; i < numTestLoops; i++) {
            try {
                if ((i % exceptionFactor) == 0) {
                    throw new NullPointerException("Force Exception");
                }
                Object o = new Object();
                al.add(o.toString());
            } catch (NullPointerException npe) {
                // Continue to get next string
            }
        }
        return al;
    }

    public ArrayList<String> testDefensiveProgramming() {
        ArrayList<String> al = new ArrayList<>();
        for (int i = 0; i < numTestLoops; i++) {
            Object o = null;
            if ((i % exceptionFactor) != 0) {
                o = new Object();
            }
            if (o != null) {
                al.add(o.toString());
            }
        }
        return al;
    }
```

Each method here returns an array of arbitrary strings from newly created objects. The size of that array will vary, based on the desired number of exceptions to be thrown.

Table 12-5 shows the time to complete each method for 100,000 iterations given the worst case—an exceptionFactor of 1 (each iteration generates an exception, and the result is an empty list). The example code here is either shallow (meaning that the method in question is called when there are only 3 classes on the stack), or deep (meaning that the method in question is called when there are 100 classes on the stack).

Table 12-5. Time to process exceptions at 100%

Method	Shallow time	Deep time
Code exception	381 ms	10,673 ms
System exception	15 ms	15 ms
Defensive programming	2 ms	2 ms

There are three interesting differences here. First, in the case where the code explicitly constructs an exception in each iteration, there is a significant difference of time between the shallow case and the deep case. Constructing that stack trace takes time, which is dependent on the stack depth.

The second interesting difference is between the case where the code explicitly creates the exception, and where the JVM creates the exception when the null pointer is dereferenced (the first two lines in the table). What's happening is that at some point, the compiler has optimized the system-generated exception case; the JVM begins to reuse the same exception object rather than creating a new one each time it is needed. That object is reused each time the code in question is executed, no matter what the calling stack is, and the exception does not actually contain a call stack (i.e., the printStackTrace() method returns no output). This optimization doesn't occur until the full stack exception has been thrown for quite a long time, so if your test case doesn't include a sufficient warm-up cycle, you will not see its effects.

Finally, the case where defensive programming is used to test for a null value before accessing the object provides the best performance. In this example, that isn't surprising —it reduces the entire loop into a no-op. So take that number with a grain of salt.

Despite the differences between these implementations, notice that the overall time involved in most cases is quite small—on the order of milliseconds. Averaged out over 100,000 calls, the individual execution time differences will barely register (and recall that this is the worst-case example).

If the exceptions are used properly, then the number of exceptions in these loops will be quite small. Table 12-6 shows the time required to execute the loop 100,000 times generating 1,000 exceptions, 1% of the time.

Table 12-6. Time to process exceptions at 1%

Method	Shallow time	Deep time
Code exception	56 ms	157 ms
System exception	51 ms	52 ms
Defensive programming	50 ms	50 ms

Now the processing time of the toString() method dominates the calculation. There is still a penalty to pay for creating the exceptions with deep stacks, but the benefit from testing for the null value in advance has all but vanished.

So performance penalties for using exceptions injudiciously is smaller than might be expected. Still, there are cases where you will run into code that is simply creating too many exceptions. Since the performance penalty comes from filling in the stack traces, the -XX:-StackTraceInThrowable flag (which is true by default) can be set to disable the generation of the stack traces.

This is rarely a good idea: the stack traces are present to enable some analysis of what unexpectedly went wrong. That capability is lost when this flag is enabled. And there is code that actually examines the stack traces and determines how to recover from the exception based on what it finds there. (The reference implementation of CORBA works like that.) That's problematic in itself, but the upshot is that disabling the stack trace can mysteriously break code.

There are some APIs in the JDK itself where exception handling can lead to performance issues. Many collection classes will throw an exception when nonexistent items are retrieved from them. The Stack class, for example, throws an EmptyStackException if the stack is empty when the pop() method is called. It is usually better to utilize defensive programming in that case by checking the stack length first. (On the other hand, unlike many collection classes, the Stack class supports null objects, so it's not as if the pop() method could return null to indicate an empty stack.)

The most notorious example within the JDK of questionable use of exceptions is in classloading: the loadClass() method of the ClassLoader class throws a ClassNotFoundException when asked to load a class that it cannot find. That's not actually an exceptional condition. An individual classloader is not expected to know how to load every class in an application, which is why there are hierarchies of class-loaders.

In an environment with dozens of classloaders, this means a lot of exceptions are created as the classloader hierarchy is searched for the one classloader that knows how to load the given class. The classloading example earlier in this chapter, for example, runs 3% faster when stack trace generation is disabled.

Still, that kind of difference is the exception more than the rule. That classloading example is a microbenchmark with a very long classpath, and even under those circumstances, the difference per call is on the order of a millisecond.

Quick Summary

1. Exceptions are not necessarily expensive to process, though they should be used only when appropriate.

2. The deeper the stack, the more expensive to process exceptions.

3. The JVM will optimize away the stack penalty for frequently created system exceptions.

4. Disabling stack traces in exceptions can sometimes help performance, though crucial information is often lost in the process.

String Performance

Strings are central enough to Java that their performance has already been discussed in several other chapters. To highlight those cases:

String interning

It is common to create many string objects that contain the same sequence of characters. These objects unnecessarily take space in the heap; since strings are immutable, it is often better to reuse the existing strings. See Chapter 7 for more details.

String encoding

While Java strings are UTF-16 encoded, most of the rest of the world uses a different encoding, so encoding of strings into different charsets is a common operation. The encode() and decode() methods of the Charset class are quite slow if they process only one or a few characters at a time; make sure that they are set up to process full buffers of data, as discussed earlier in this chapter.

Network encoding

Java EE application servers often have special handling for encoding static strings (from JSP files and so on); see Chapter 10 for more details.

String concatenation is another area where there are potential performance pitfalls. Consider a simple string concatenation like this:

```
String answer = integerPart + "." + mantissa;
```

That code is actually quite performant; the syntactic sugar of the javac compiler turns that statement into this code:

```
String answer = new StringBuilder(integerPart).append(".").
                             append(mantissa).toString();
```

Problems arise, though, if the string is constructed piecemeal:

```
String answer = integerPart;
answer += ".";
answer += mantissa;
```

That code translates into:

```
String answer = new StringBuilder(integerPart).toString();
answer = new StringBuilder(answer).append(".").toString();
answer = new StringBuilder(answer).append(mantissa).toString();
```

All those temporary StringBuilder and intermediate String objects are inefficient. Never construct strings using concatenation unless it can be done on a single (logical) line, and never use string concatenation inside a loop unless the concatenated string is not used on the next loop iteration. Otherwise, always explicitly use a StringBuilder object for better performance. In Chapter 1, I argued that there are times to "prematurely" optimize when that phrase is used in a context meaning simply "write good code." This is a prime example.

Quick Summary

1. One-line concatenation of strings yields good performance.

2. For multiple concatenation operations, make sure to use a `StringBuilder`.

Logging

Logging is one of those things that performance engineers either love or hate—or (usually) both. Whenever I'm asked why a program is running badly, the first thing I ask for are any available logs, with the hope that logs produced by the application will have clues as to what the application was doing. Whenever I'm asked to review the performance of working code, I immediately recommend that all logging statements be turned off.

There are multiple logs in question here. GC produces its own logging statements (see Chapter 6). That logging can be directed into a distinct file, the size of which can be managed by the JVM. Even in production code, GC logging (with the -XX:+PrintGCDetails flag) has such low overhead and such an expected large benefit if something goes wrong that it should always be turned on.

Java EE application servers generate an access log that is updated on every request. This log generally has a noticeable impact: turning off that logging will definitely improve the performance of whatever test is run against the application server. From a diagnosability standpoint when something goes wrong, those logs are (in my experience) not terribly helpful. However, in terms of business requirements, that log is often crucial, in which case it must be left enabled.

Although it is not a Java EE standard, many application servers support the Apache mod_log_config standard, which allows you to specify exactly what information is logged for each request (and servers that don't follow the mod_log_config syntax will typically support some other log customization). The key here is to log as little information as possible and still meet the business requirements. The performance of the log is subject to the amount of data written.

In HTTP access logs in particular (and in general, in any kind of log), it is a good idea to log all information numerically: IP addresses rather than hostnames, timestamps (e.g., seconds since the epoch) rather than string data (e.g., "Monday, June 3, 2013 17:23:00 -0600"), and so on. Minimize any data conversion that will take time and memory to compute so that the effect on the system is also minimized. Logs can always be postprocessed to provide converted data.

There are three basic principles to keep in mind for application logs. First is to keep a balance between the data to be logged and level at which it is logged. There are seven standard logging levels in the JDK, and loggers by default are configured to output three of those levels (INFO and greater). This often leads to confusion within projects: INFO-level messages sound like they should be fairly common and should provide a description of the flow of an application ("now I'm processing task A," "now I'm doing task B," and so on). Particularly for applications that are heavily threaded and scalable (including Java EE application servers), that much logging will have a detrimental effect on performance (not to mention running the risk of being too chatty to be useful). Don't be afraid to use the lower-level logging statements.

Similarly, when code is checked into a group repository, consider the needs of the user of the project rather than your needs as a developer. We'd all like to have a lot of good feedback about how our code works once it is integrated into a larger system and run through a battery of tests, but if a message isn't going to make sense to an end user or system administrator, it's not helpful to enable it by default. It is merely going to slow down the system (and confuse the end user).

The second principle is to use fine-grained loggers. Having a logger per class can be tedious to configure, but having greater control over the logging output often makes this worthwhile. Sharing a logger for a set of classes in a small module is a good compromise. The point to keep in mind is that production problems—and particularly production problems that occur under load or are otherwise performance related—are tricky to reproduce if the environment changes significantly. Turning on too much logging often changes the environment such that the original issue no longer manifests itself.

Hence, you must be able to turn on logging only for a small set of code (and, at least initially, a small set of logging statements at the FINE level, followed by more at the FINER and FINEST levels) so that the performance of the code is not affected.

Between these two principles, it should be possible to enable small subsets of messages in a production environment without affecting the performance of the system. That is usually a requirement anyway: the production system administrators probably aren't going to enable logging if it slows the system down, and if the system does slow down, then the likelihood of reproducing the issue is reduced.

The third principle to keep in mind when introducing logging to code is to remember that it is quite easy to write logging code that has unintended side effects, even if the logging is not enabled. This is another case where "prematurely" optimizing code is a good thing: as the example from Chapter 1 shows, remember to use the isLoggable() method anytime the information to be logged contains a method call, a string concatenation, or any other sort of allocation (for example, allocation of an Object array for a MessageFormat argument).

Quick Summary

1. Code should contain lots of logging to enable users to figure out what it does, but none of that should be enabled by default.

2. Don't forget to test for the logging level before calling the logger if the arguments to the logger require method calls or object allocation.

Java Collections API

Java's collections API is quite extensive; there are at least 58 different collection classes supplied by Java 7. Using an appropriate collection class—as well as using collection classes appropriately—is an important performance consideration in writing an application.

The first rule in using a collection class is to use one suitable for the algorithmic needs of an application. This advice is not specific to Java; it is essentially Data Structures 101. A LinkedList is not suitable for searching; if access to a random piece of data is required, store the collection in a HashMap. If the data needs to remain sorted, use a TreeMap rather than attempting to sort the data in the application. Use an ArrayList if the data will be accessed by index, but not if data frequently needs to be inserted into the middle of the array. And so on...the algorithmic choice of which collection class is crucial, but the choice in Java isn't different than the choice in any other programming language.

There are, however, some idiosyncrasies to consider when using Java collections.

Synchronized Versus Unsynchronized

By default, virtually all Java collections are unsynchronized (the major exceptions being the Hashtable, Vector, and their related classes).

Synchronized Collection Classes

If you've ever wondered why the Vector and Hashtable (and related) classes are synchronized, here's a bit of history.

In the very early days of Java, these were the only collection classes in the JDK. Back then (before Java 1.2), there was no formal definition of the Collections Framework; these were just useful classes that the original Java platform provided.

When Java was first released, threading was poorly understood by most developers, and Java attempted to make it easier for developers to avoid some of the pitfalls of coding in a threaded environment. Hence, these classes were thread-safe.

Unfortunately, synchronization—even uncontended synchronization—was a huge performance problem in early versions of Java, so when the first major revision to the platform came out, the Collections Framework took the opposite approach: all new collection classes would be unsynchronized by default. Even though synchronization performance has drastically improved since then, it still is not free, and having the option of unsynchronized collections helps everyone to write faster programs (with the occasional bug caused by concurrently modifying an unsynchronized collection).

Chapter 9 posited a microbenchmark to compare CAS-based protection to traditional synchronization. That proved to be impractical in the threaded case, but what if the data in question will only ever be accessed by a single thread—what would be the effect of not using any synchronization at all? Table 12-7 shows that comparison. Because there is no attempt to model the contention, the microbenchmark in this case is valid in this one circumstance: when there can be no contention, and the question at hand is what the penalty is for "oversynchronizing" access to the resource.

Table 12-7. Performance of synchronized and unsynchronized access

Mode	Total time	Per-operation time
CAS operation	6.6 seconds	13 nanoseconds
Synchronized method	11.8 seconds	23 nanoseconds
Unsynchronized method	3.9 seconds	7.8 nanoseconds

The second column makes it clear that there is a small penalty when using any data protection technique as opposed to simple unsynchronized access. However, keep in mind this is a microbenchmark executing 500 million operations—so the difference in time per operation is on the order of 15 nanoseconds. If the operation in question is executed frequently enough in the target application, the performance penalty will be somewhat noticeable. In most cases, the difference will be outweighed by far larger inefficiencies in other areas of the application. Remember also that the absolute number here is completely determined by the target machine the test was run on (my home machine with a four-core AMD Athlon); to get a more realistic measurement, the test would need to be run on hardware that is the same as the target environment.

So, given a choice between a synchronized `Vector` and an unsynchronized `ArrayList`, which should be used? Access to the `ArrayList` will be slightly faster, and depending on how often the list is accessed, there can be a measurable performance difference here. (As noted in Chapter 9, excessive calls to the synchronized method can be quite painful for performance on certain hardware platforms as well.)

On the other hand, this assumes that the code will never be accessed by more than one thread. That may be true today, but what about tomorrow? If that might change, then it is better to use the synchronized collection now and mitigate any performance impact that results. This is a design choice, and whether future-proofing code to be thread-safe is worth the time and effort will depend on the circumstances of the application being developed.

If the choice is between using an unsynchronized collection and a collection using CAS principles (e.g., a HashMap compared to a ConcurrentHashMap), then the performance difference is even less important. CAS-based classes show virtually no overhead when used in an uncontended environment (but keep reading for a discussion of memory differences in the particular case of hashmaps).

Collection Sizing

Collection classes are designed to hold an arbitrary number of data elements and to expand as necessary, as new items are added to the collection. There are two performance considerations here.

Although the data types provided by collection classes in Java are quite rich, at a basic level those classes must hold their data using only Java primitive data types: numbers (integers, doubles, and so on), object references, and arrays of those types. Hence, an ArrayList contains an actual array:

```
private transient Object[] elementData;
```

As items are added and removed from the ArrayList, they are stored at the desired location within the elementData array (possibly causing other items in the array to shift). Similarly, a HashMap contains an array of an internal data type called HashMap$Entry, which maps each key-value pair to a location in the array specified by the hashcode of the key.

Not all collections use an array to hold their elements; a LinkedList for example, holds each data element in an internally defined Node class. But collection classes that do use an array to hold their elements are subject to special sizing considerations. You can tell if a particular class falls into this category by looking at its constructors: if it has a constructor that allows the initial size of the collection to be specified, then it is internally using some array to store the items.

For those collection classes, it is important to accurately specify the initial size. Take the simple example of an ArrayList: the elementData array will (by default) start out with an initial size of 10. When the 11th item is inserted into an ArrayList, the list must expand the elementData array. This means allocating a new array, copying the original contents into that array, and then adding in the new item. The data structure and algorithm used by, say, the HashMap class is much more complicated, but the principle is the same: at some point, those internal structures must be resized.

The ArrayList class chooses to resize the array by adding roughly half of the existing size, so the size of the elementData array will first be 10, then 15, then 22, then 33, and so on. Whatever algorithm is used to resize the array (see sidebar), this results in some wasted memory (which in turn will affect the time the application spends performing GC). Additionally, each time the array must be resized, an expensive array copy operation must occur to transfer the contents from the old array to the new array.

To minimize those performance penalties, make sure to construct the collection with as accurate an estimate of its ultimate size as possible.

Data Expansion in Noncollection Classes

Many noncollection classes also store lots of data in an internal array. For example, the ByteArrayOutputStream class must store all data written to the stream into an internal buffer; the StringBuilder and StringBuffer classes must similarly store all their characters in an internal char array.

Most of these classes use the same algorithm to resize the internal array: it is doubled each time it needs to be resized. This means that, on average, the internal array will be 25% larger than the data it currently contains.

The performance considerations here are similar: the amount of memory used is larger than in the ArrayList example, and the number of times data must be copied is less, but the principle is the same. Whenever you are given the option to size a object when it is constructed and it is feasible to estimate how much data the object will eventually hold, use the constructor that takes a size parameter.

Collections and Memory Efficiency

We've just seen one example where the memory efficiency of collections can be suboptimal: there is often some wasted memory in the backing store used to hold the elements in the collection.

This can be particularly problematic for sparsely used collections: those with one or two elements in them. These sparsely used collections can waste a large amount of memory if they are used extensively. One way to deal with that is to size the collection when it is created. Another way is to consider whether a collection is really needed in that case at all.

When most developers are asked how to quickly sort any array, they will offer up quicksort as the answer. Good performance engineers will want to know the size of the array: if the array is small enough, then the fastest way to sort it will be to use insertion sort. (Algorithms based on quicksort will usually use insertion sort for small arrays anyway; in the case of Java, the implementation of the Arrays.sort() method assumes that any array with less than 47 elements will be sorted faster with insertion sort than with quicksort.) Size matters.

Collection Memory Sizes in JDK 7u40

Because underused collections are quite problematic in many applications, JDK 7u40 introduced a new optimization into the `ArrayList` and `HashMap` implementations: by default (e.g., when no size parameter is used in the constructor), these classes no longer allocate any backing store for the data. The backing store is only allocated when the first item is added to the collection.

This is an example of the lazy-initialization technique discussed in Chapter 7, and in testing of several common applications, it resulted in an improvement in performance due to reduced need for GC. These applications had a lot of such collections that were never used; lazily allocating the backing store for those collections was a performance win. Because the size of the backing store already had to be checked on every access, there was no performance penalty for checking to see if the backing store had already been allocated (though the time required to create the initial backing store did move from when the object was created to when data was first inserted into the object).

Similarly, a `HashMap` is the fastest way to look up items based on some key value, but if there is only one key, then the `HashMap` is overkill compared to using a simple object reference. Even if there are a few keys, maintaining a few object references will consume much less memory than a full `HashMap` object, with the resulting (positive) effect on GC.

Along those lines, one important difference to know regarding the memory use of collection classes is the difference in size between a `HashMap` object and a `ConcurrentHashMap` object. Prior to Java 7, the size of an empty or sparsely populated `ConcurrentHashMap` object was quite large: over 1 KB (even when a small size was passed to the constructor). In Java 7, that size is only 208 bytes (compared to 128 bytes for an empty `HashMap` constructed without a specified size, and 72 bytes for a `HashMap` constructed with a size of 1).

This size difference can still be important in applications where there is a proliferation of small maps, but the optimizations made in Java 7 make that difference much less significant. There are existing performance recommendations (including some by me) that urge avoiding the `ConcurrentHashMap` class in applications where memory is important and the number of maps is large. Those recommendations center around the trade-off of possible faster access to the map (if it is contended) against the increased pressure on the garbage collector that the larger maps cause. That trade-off still applies, but the balance is now much more in favor of using the `ConcurrentHashMap`.

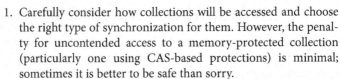

Quick Summary

1. Carefully consider how collections will be accessed and choose the right type of synchronization for them. However, the penalty for uncontended access to a memory-protected collection (particularly one using CAS-based protections) is minimal; sometimes it is better to be safe than sorry.

2. Sizing of collections can have a large impact on performance: either slowing down the garbage collector if the collection is too large, or causing lots of copying and resizing if it is too small.

AggressiveOpts

The `AggressiveOpts` flag (by default, `false`) affects the behavior of several basic Java SE operations. The purpose of this flag is to introduce optimizations on a trial basis; over time, the optimizations enabled by this flag can be expected to become the default setting for the JVM. Many of those optimizations that were experimented with in Java 6 became the default in Java 7u4. You should retest this flag with every release of the JDK to see if it is still positively affecting your application.

Alternate Implementations

The major effect of enabling the `AggressiveOpts` flag is that it substitutes different implementations for several basic JDK classes: notably, the `BigDecimal`, `BigInteger`, and `MutableBigDecimal` classes from the `java.math` package; the `DecimalFormat`, `DigitalList`, and `NumberFormat` classes from the `java.text` package; and the `HashMap`, `LinkedHashMap`, and `TreeMap` classes from the `java.util` package.

These classes are functionally the same as the classes in the standard JDK that they replace, but they have more efficient implementations. In Java 8, these alternate implementations have been removed; either they have been incorporated into the base JDK classes, or the base JDK classes have been improved in other ways.

The reason that these classes are enabled (in Java 7) only when the `AggressiveOpts` flag is set is because their behavior can trigger subtle bugs in application code. For example, the aggressive implementation of the `HashMap` class yields an iterator that returns the keys in a different order than the standard implementation. Applications should never depend on the order of items returned from this iterator in the first place, but it turns out that many applications made that mistake. For compatibility reasons, then, the more efficient implementation did not override the original implementation, and it is necessary to set the `AggressiveOpts` flag to get the better implementation.

Since Java 8 removes these classes, the bug compatibility they preserve may break when upgrading—which is an indication to write better code in the first place.

Miscellaneous Flags

Enabling the `AggressiveOpts` flag affects some other minor tunings of the JVM.

Setting the `AggressiveOpts` flag enables the `AutoFill` flag, which by default is `false` in JDK 7 though 7u4, when the default is set to `true`. That flag enables some better loop optimizations by the compiler. Similarly, this flag also enables the `DoEscapeAnalysis` flag (that is also set by default in JDK 7u4 and later versions).

The `AutoBoxCacheMax` flag (default 128) is set to 20,000—that enables more values to be autoboxed, which can slightly improve performance for certain applications (at the expense of using slightly more memory). The value of the `BiasedLockingStartupDelay` is reduced from its default of 2,000 to 500, meaning that biased locking will start sooner after the application begins execution.

Finally, this flag enables the `OptimizeStringConcat` flag, which allows the JVM to optimize the use of `StringBuilder` objects—in particular, the `StringBuilder` objects that are created (by the `javac` compiler) when writing code like this:

```
String s = obj1 + ":" + obj2 + ":" + obj3;
```

The `javac` compiler translates that code into a series of `append()` calls on a string builder. When the `OptimizeStringConcat` flag is enabled, the JVM just-in-time compiler can optimize away the creation of the `StringBuilder` object itself. The `OptimizeStringConcat` flag is `false` by default in JDK 7 until 7u4, when the default becomes `true`.

Quick Summary

1. The `AggressiveOpts` flag enables certain optimizations in base classes. For the most part, these classes are faster than their replacements, but they may have unexpected side effects.

2. These classes have been removed in Java 8.

Lambdas and Anonymous Classes

For many developers, the most exciting feature of Java 8 is the addition of lambdas. There is no denying that lambdas have a hugely positive impact on the productivity of Java developers, though of course that benefit is difficult to quantify. But we can examine the performance of code using lambda constructs.

The most basic question about the performance of lambdas is how they compare to their replacement, anonymous classes. There turns out to be little difference.

The usual example of how to use a lambda class begins with code that creates anonymous inner classes (the usual example often uses a Stream rather than the iterator shown here; information about the Stream class comes later in this section):

```java
private volatile int sum;

public interface IntegerInterface {
    int getInt();
}

public void calc() {
    IntegerInterface a1 = new IntegerInterface() {
        public int getInt() {
            return 1;
        }
    };
    IntegerInterface a2 = new IntegerInterface() {
        public int getInt() {
            return 2;
        }
    };
    IntegerInterface a3 = new IntegerInterface() {
        public int getInt() {
            return 3;
        }
    };
    sum = a1.get() + a2.get() + a3.get();
}
```

That is compared to the following code using lambdas:

```java
public void calc() {
    IntegerInterface a3 -> { return 3 };
    IntegerInterface a2 -> { return 2 };
    IntegerInterface a1 -> { return 1 };
    sum = a3.get() + a2.get() + a1.get();
}
```

The body of the lambda or anonymous class is crucial here: if that body performs any significant operations, then the time spent in the operation is going to overwhelm any small difference in the implementations of the lambda or the anonymous class. However, even in this minimal case, the time to perform this operation is essentially the same, as Table 12-8 shows.

Table 12-8. Time to execute the calc() method using lambdas and anonymous classes

Implementation	Time in microseconds
Anonymous classes	87.2
Lambda	87.9

Numbers always look impressively official, but we can't conclude anything from this other than that the performance of the two implementations is basically equivalent. That's true because of the random variations in tests, but also because these calls are measured using `System.nanoTime()`. Timing simply isn't accurate enough to believe at that level; what we do know is that for all intents and purposes, this performance is the same.

One interesting thing about the typical usage in this example is that the code that uses the anonymous class creates a new object every time the method is called. If the method is called a lot (as of course it must be in a benchmark to measure its performance), many instances of that anonymous class are quickly created and discarded. As we saw in Chapter 5, that kind of usage has very little impact on performance. There is a very small cost to allocate (and, more important, initialize) the objects, and because they are discarded quickly they do not really slow down the garbage collector.

Nonetheless, cases can be constructed where that allocation matters and where it is better to reuse those objects:

```java
private IntegerInterface a1 = new IntegerInterface() {
    public int getInt() {
        return 1;
    }
};
... Similarly for the other interfaces....
public void calc() {
        return a1.get() + a2.get() + a3.get();
    }
}
```

The typical usage of the lambda does not create a new object on each iteration of the loop—making this an area where some corner cases can favor the performance of the lambda usage. Nonetheless, it is difficult to construct even microbenchmarks where these differences matter.

Lambda and Anonymous Classloading

One corner case where this difference comes into play is in startup and classloading. It is tempting to look at the code for a lambda and conclude that it is syntactic sugar around creating an anonymous class (particularly since, in the long run, their performance is equal). But that is not how it works—the code for a lambda creates a static method that is called through a special helper class in JDK 8. The anonymous class is an actual Java class—it has a separate class file and will be loaded from the classloader.

As we saw previously in this chapter, classloading performance can be important, particularly if there is a long classpath. If this example is run such that every execution of the calc() method is performed in a new classloader, the anonymous class implementation is at a disadvantage. Table 12-9 shows the difference in that case.

Table 12-9. Time to execute the calc() method in a new classloader

Implementation	Time in microseconds
Anonymous classes	267
Lambdas	181

One point about these numbers: they have been measured after a suitable warm-up period to allow for compilation. But one other thing happens during the warm-up period: the class files are read from disk for the first time. The OS will keep those files in memory (in the OS filesystem buffers). So the very first execution of the code will take much longer, as the calls to the OS to read the files will actually load them from disk. Subsequent calls will be faster—they will still call the OS to read the files, but since the files are in the OS memory, their data is returned quickly. So the result for the anonymous class implementation is better than it might otherwise be, since it doesn't include any actual disk reading of the class files.

Quick Summary

1. The choice between using a lambda or an anonymous class should be dictated by ease of programming, since there is no difference between their performance.

2. Lambdas are not implemented as classes, so one exception to that rule is in environments where classloading behavior is important; lambdas will be slightly faster in that case.

Stream and Filter Performance

One other key feature of Java 8, and one that is frequently used in conjunction with lambdas, is the new Stream facility. One very important performance feature of streams is that they can automatically parallelize code. Information about parallel streams can be found in Chapter 9; this section discusses some general performance features of streams and filters.

Lazy Traversal

The first performance benefit from streams is that they are implemented as lazy data structures. Consider the example where we have a list of stock symbols, and the goal is to find the first symbol in the list that does not contain the letter A. The code to do that through a stream looks like this:

```
public String findSymbol(ArrayList<String> al) {
    Optional<String> t = al.stream().
            filter(symbol -> symbol.charAt(0) != 'A').
            filter(symbol -> symbol.charAt(1) != 'A').
            filter(symbol -> symbol.charAt(2) != 'A').
            filter(symbol -> symbol.charAt(3) != 'A').
                findFirst();
    return t.get();
}
```

There's obviously a better way to implement this using a single filter, but we'll save that discussion for later. For now, consider what it means for the stream to be implemented lazily in this example. Each `filter()` method returns a new stream, so there are in effect four logical streams here.

The `filter()` method, it turns out, doesn't really do anything except set up a series of pointers. The effect of that is when the `findFirst()` method is invoked on the stream, no data processing has been performed—no comparisons of data to the character A have yet been made.

Instead, the `findFirst()` asks the previous stream (returned from filter 4) for an element. That stream has no elements yet, so it calls back to the stream produced by filter 3, and so on. Filter 1 will grab the first element from the array list (from the stream, technically) and test to see if its first character is A. If so, it completes the callback and returns that element downstream; otherwise, it continues to iterate through the array until it finds a matching element (or exhausts the array). Filter 2 behaves similarly—when the callback to filter 1 returns, it tests to see if the second character is not A. If so, it completes its callback and passes the symbol downstream; if not, it makes another callback to filter 1 to get the next symbol.

All those callbacks may sound inefficient, but consider the alternative. An algorithm to process the streams eagerly would look something like this:

```
private <T> ArrayList<T> calcArray(ArrayLisr<T> src, Predicate<T> p) {
    ArrayList<T> dst = new ArrayList<>();
    for (T s : src) {
        if (p.test(s))
            dst.add(s);
    }
    return dst;
}
```

```
private static long calcEager(ArrayList<String> a1) {
    long then = System.currentTimeMillis();
    ArrayList<String> a2 = calcArray(a1, (String s) -> s.charAt(0) != 'A');
    ArrayList<String> a3 = calcArray(a2, (String s) -> s.charAt(1) != 'A');
    ArrayList<String> a4 = calcArray(a3, (String s) -> s.charAt(2) != 'A');
    ArrayList<String> a5 = calcArray(a4, (String s) -> s.charAt(3) != 'A');
    answer = a5.get(0);
    long now = System.currentTimeMillis();
    return now - then;
}
```

There are two reasons this alternative is less efficient than the lazy implementation that Java actually adopted. First, it requires the creation of a lot of temporary instances of the `ArrayList` class. Second, in the lazy implementation, processing can stop as soon as the `findFirst()` method gets an element. That means only a subset of the items must actually pass through the filters. The eager implementation, on the other hand, must process the entire list several times until the last list is created.

Hence, it should come as no surprise that the lazy implementation is far more performant than the alternative in this example. In this case, the test is processing a list of 456,976 four-letter symbols, which are sorted in alphabetical order. The eager implementation processes only 18,278 of those before it encounters the symbol BBBB, at which point it can stop. It takes the iterator two orders of magnitude longer to find that answer, as shown in Table 12-10.

Table 12-10. Time to process lazy versus eager filters

Implementation	Seconds
Filter/findFirst	0.359
Iterator/findFirst	48.706

One reason, then, why filters can be so much faster than iterators is simply that they can take advantage of algorithmic opportunities for optimizations: the lazy filter implementation can end processing whenever it has done what it needs to do, processing less data.

What if the entire set of data must be processed—what is the basic performance of filters versus iterators in that case? For this example, we'll change the test slightly. The previous example made a good teaching point about how multiple filters worked, but hopefully it was obvious that the code would perform better with a single filter:

```
private static long countFilter(ArrayList<String> al) {
    long then = System.currentTimeMillis();
    Stream<String> stream = al.stream();
    stream.filter(
            symbol -> symbol.charAt(0) != 'A' &&
            symbol.charAt(1) != 'A' &&
            symbol.charAt(2) != 'A' &&
            symbol.charAt(3) != 'A').
```

```
            forEach(symbol -> { count++; });
    long now = System.currentTimeMillis();
    return now - then;
}
```

The example here also changes the final code to count the symbols, so that the entire list will be processed. On the flip side, the eager implementation can now use an iterator directly:

```
private static long countIterator(ArrayList<String> al) {
    long then = System.currentTimeMillis();
    for (String symbol : al) {
      if (symbol.charAt(0) != 'A' &&
          symbol.charAt(1) != 'A' &&
          symbol.charAt(2) != 'A' &&
          symbol.charAt(3) != 'A')
          count++;
    }
    return System.currentTimeMillis() - then;
}
```

Even in this case, the lazy filter implementation is faster than the iterator (see Table 12-11).

Table 12-11. Time to process single filter versus an iterator

Implementation	Time required
Multiple filters	18.0 seconds
Single filter	6.5 seconds
Iterator/count	6.8 seconds

For the sake of comparison, Table 12-11 includes (as its first line) the case where the entire list is processed using four separate filters as opposed to the optimal case: one filter, which is slightly faster even than an iterator.

Quick Summary

1. Filters offer a very significant performance advantage by allowing processing to end in the middle of iterating through the data.

2. Even when the entire data set is processed, a single filter will slightly outperform an iterator.

3. Multiple filters have some overhead; make sure to write good filters.

Summary

This look into some key areas of the Java SE JDK concludes our examination of Java performance. One interesting theme of most of the topics of this chapter is that they show the evolution of the performance of the JDK itself. As Java developed and matured as a platform, its developers discovered that repeatedly generated exceptions didn't need to spend time providing thread stacks; that using a thread-local variable to avoid synchronization of the random number generator was a good thing; that the default size of a `ConcurrentHashMap` was too large; that classloaders were not able to run in parallel due to a synchronization lock; and so on.

This continual process of successive improvement is what Java performance tuning is all about. From tuning the compiler and garbage collector, to using memory effectively, to understanding key performance differences in the SE and EE APIs, and more, the tools and processes in this book will allow you to provide similar ongoing improvements in your own code.

Summary of Tuning Flags

Table A-1. Flags to tune the just-in-time compiler

Flag	What it does	When to use it	See also
-server	Chooses the server compiler.	For long-running applications that need fast performance.	"Hot Spot Compilation" on page 75
-client	Chooses the client compiler.	For applications where startup is the most important factor.	"Hot Spot Compilation" on page 75
-XX:+TieredCompilation	Uses tiered compilation (both client and server).	For applications where you want the best possible performance and have enough available native memory for the extra compiled code.	"Hot Spot Compilation" on page 75
-XX:ReservedCodeCacheSize=<*MB*>	Reserves space for code compiled by the JIT compiler	When you see a warning that you are out of code cache, and generally when using tiered compilation.	"Tuning the Code Cache" on page 85
-XX:InitialCodeCacheSize=<*MB*>	Allocates the initial space for code compiled by the JIT compiler.	If you need to preallocate the memory for the code cache, which is very uncommon.	"Tuning the Code Cache" on page 85
-XX:CompileThreshold=<*N*>	Sets the number of times a method or loop is executed before compiling it.	When using the server compiler, this can cause more methods to be compiled, and methods to be compiled sooner. The first case is sometimes an advantage if you aren't using tiered compilation.	"Compilation Thresholds" on page 87

Flag	What it does	When to use it	See also
`-XX:+PrintCompilation`	Provides a log of operations by the JIT compiler.	When you suspect an important method isn't being compiled, or are generally curious as to what the compiler is doing.	"Inspecting the Compilation Process" on page 90
`-XX:+CICompilerCount=<N>`	Sets the number of threads used by the JIT compiler.	When using tiered compilation and too many compiler threads are being started (particularly on large machines running multiple JVMs).	"Compilation Threads" on page 94

Table A-2. Flags to choose the GC algorithm

Flag	What it does	When to use it	See also
`-XX:+UseSerialGC`	Uses a simple, single-threaded GC algorithm.	For small (100 MB) heaps.	"The serial garbage collector" on page 109
`-XX:+UseParallelOldGC`	Uses multiple threads to collect the old generation while application threads are stopped.	When your application can tolerate occasional long pauses and you want to maximize throughput while minimizing CPU usage.	"The throughput collector" on page 110
`-XX:+UseParallelGC`	Uses multiple threads to collect the young generation while application threads are stopped.	Use in conjunction with UseParallelGC.	"The throughput collector" on page 110
`-XX:+UseConcMarkSweepGC`	Uses background thread(s) to remove garbage from the old generation with minimal pauses.	When you have available CPU for the background thread, you do not want long GC pauses, and you have a relatively small heap.	"The CMS collector" on page 110
`-XX:+UseParNewGC`	Uses multiple threads to collect the young generation while application threads are stopped.	Use in conjunction with Use ConcMarkSweepGC.	"The CMS collector" on page 110
`-XX:+UseG1GC`	Uses multiple threads to collect the young generation while application threads are stopped, and background thread(s) to remove garbage from the old generation with minimal pauses.	When you have available CPU for the background thread, you do not want long GC pauses, and you do not have a small heap.	"The G1 collector" on page 111

Table A-3. Flags common to all GC algorithms

Flag	What it does	When to use it	See also
-Xms	Sets the initial size of the heap.	When the default initial size is too small for your application.	"Sizing the Heap" on page 119
-Xmx	Sets the maximum size of the heap.	When the default maximum size is too small (or possibly too large) for your application.	"Sizing the Heap" on page 119
-XX:NewRatio	Sets the ratio of the young generation to the old generation.	Increase this to reduce the proportion of the heap given to the young generation; lower it to increase the proportion of the heap given to the young generation. This is only an initial setting; the proportion will change unless adaptive sizing is turned off (except for CMS, when the young-generation size is constant). As the young-generation size is reduced, you will see more frequent young GCs and less frequent full GCs (and vice versa).	"Sizing the Generations" on page 122
-XX:NewSize	Sets the initial size of the young generation.	When you have finely tuned your application requirements.	"Sizing the Generations" on page 122
-XX:MaxNewSize	Sets the maximum size of the young generation.	When you have finely tuned your application requirements.	"Sizing the Generations" on page 122
-Xmn	Sets the initial and maximum size of the young generation.	When you have finely tuned your application requirements.	"Sizing the Generations" on page 122
-XX:PermSize=N (JDK 7 only)	Sets the initial size of the permgen.	For applications that use a lot of classes, increase this from the default.	"Sizing Permgen and Metaspace" on page 124
-XX:MaxPermSize=N (JDK 7 only)	Sets the maximum size of the permgen.	For applications that use a lot of classes, increase this from the default.	"Sizing Permgen and Metaspace" on page 124
-XX:MetaspaceSize=N (JDK 8 only)	Sets the initial size of the metaspace.	For applications that use a lot of classes, increase this from the default.	"Sizing Permgen and Metaspace" on page 124
-XX:MaxMetaspaceSize=N (JDK 8 only)	Sets the maximum size of the metaspace.	Lower this number to limit the amount of native space used by class metadata.	"Sizing Permgen and Metaspace" on page 124

Flag	What it does	When to use it	See also
-XX:ParallelGCThreads=N	Sets the number of threads used by the garbage collectors.	Lower this value on systems running many JVMs. Consider increasing it for JVMs with very large heaps on very large systems.	"Controlling Parallelism" on page 126
-verbose:gc	Enables basic GC logging.	GC logging should always be enabled, but other, more detailed logs are generally better.	"GC Tools" on page 128
-Xloggc:<path>	Directs the GC log to a special file rather than standard output.	Always, the better to preserve the information in the log.	"GC Tools" on page 128
-XX:+PrintGC	Enables basic GC logging.	GC logging should always be enabled, but other, more detailed logs are generally better.	"GC Tools" on page 128
-XX:+PrintGCDetails	Enables detailed GC logging.	Always, even in production (the logging overhead is minimal).	"GC Tools" on page 128
-XX:+PrintGCTimeStamps	Prints a relative timestamp for each entry in the GC log.	Always, unless datestamps are enabled.	"GC Tools" on page 128
-XX:+PrintGCDateStamps	Prints a time-of-day stamp for each entry in the GC log.	Has slightly more overhead than timestamps, but may be easier to process.	"GC Tools" on page 128
-XX:+PrintReferenceGC	Prints information about soft and weak reference processing during GC.	If the program uses a lot of those references, add this flag to determine their effect on the GC overhead.	"Weak, Soft, and Other References" on page 208
-XX:+UseGCLogFileRotation	Enables rotations of the GC log to conserve file space.	In production systems that run for weeks at a time when the GC logs can be expected to consume a lot of space.	"GC Tools" on page 128
-XX:NumberOfGCLogFiles=N	When logfile rotation is enabled, indicates the number of logfiles to retain.	In production systems that run for weeks at a time when the GC logs can be expected to consume a lot of space.	"GC Tools" on page 128
-XX:GCLogFileSize=N	When logfile rotation is enabled, indicates the size of each logfile before rotating it.	In production systems that run for weeks at a time when the GC logs can be expected to consume a lot of space.	"GC Tools" on page 128
-XX:+UseAdaptiveSizePolicy	When set, the JVM will resize various heap sizes to attempt to meet GC goals.	Turn this off if the heap sizes have been finely tuned.	"Adaptive Sizing" on page 127

Flag	What it does	When to use it	See also
-XX:+PrintAdaptiveSizePolicy	Adds information about how generations are resized to the GC log.	Use this flag to gain an understanding of how the JVM is operating. When using G1, check this output to see if full GCs are triggered by humongous object allocation.	"Adaptive Sizing" on page 127
-XX:+PrintTenuringDistribution	Adds tenuring information to the GC logs.	Use the tenuring information to determine if and how the tenuring options should be adjusted.	"Tenuring and Survivor Spaces" on page 159
-XX:InitialSurvivorRatio=N	Sets the amount of the young generation set aside for survivor spaces.	Increase this if short-lived objects are being promoted into the old generation too frequently.	"Tenuring and Survivor Spaces" on page 159
-XX:MinSurvivorRatio=N	Sets the adaptive amount of the young generation set aside for survivor spaces.	Decreasing this values reduces the maximum size of the survivor spaces (and vice versa).	"Tenuring and Survivor Spaces" on page 159
-XX:TargetSurvivorRatio=N	The amount of free space the JVM attempts to keep in the survivor spaces.	Increasing this value reduces the size of the survivor spaces (and vice versa).	"Tenuring and Survivor Spaces" on page 159
-XX:InitialTenuringThreshold=N	The initial number of GC cycles the JVM attempts to keep an object in the survivor spaces.	Increase this number to keep objects in the survivor spaces longer, though be aware that the JVM will tune it.	"Tenuring and Survivor Spaces" on page 159
-XX:MaxTenuringThreshold=N	The maximum number of GC cycles the JVM attempts to keep an object in the survivor spaces.	Increase this number to keep objects in the survivor spaces longer; the JVM will tune the actual threshold between this value and the initial threshold.	"Tenuring and Survivor Spaces" on page 159

Table A-4. Flags for the throughput collector

Flag	What it does	When to use it	See also
-XX:MaxGCPauseMillis=*N*	Hints to the throughput collector how long pauses should be; the heap is dynamically sized to attempt to meet that goal.	As a first step in tuning the throughput collector if the default sizing it calculates doesn't meet application goals.	"Adaptive and Static Heap Size Tuning" on page 136
-XX:GCTimeRatio=*N*	Hints to the throughput collector how much time you are willing to spend in GC; the heap is dynamically sized to attempt to meet that goal.	As a first step in tuning the throughput collector if the default sizing it calculates doesn't meet application goals.	"Adaptive and Static Heap Size Tuning" on page 136
-XX:-AggressiveHeap	Enables a set of tuning flags that are "optimized" for machines with a large amount of memory running a single JVM with a large heap.	It is better not to use this flag, and instead use specific flags as necessary.	"AggressiveHeap" on page 171

Table A-5. Flags for the CMS collector

Flag	What it does	When to use it	See also
-XX:CMSInitiatingOccupancyFraction=*N*	Determines when CMS should begin background scanning of the old generation.	When CMS experiences concurrent mode failures, reduces this value.	"Understanding the CMS Collector" on page 140
-XX:+UseCMSInitiatingOccupancyOnly	Causes CMS to use only CMSInitiatingOccupancyFraction to determine when to start CMS background scanning.	Whenever CMSInitiatingOccupancyFraction is specified.	"Understanding the CMS Collector" on page 140
-XX:ConcGCThreads=*N*	Sets the number of threads to use for CMS background scanning.	When lots of CPU is available and CMS is experiencing concurrent mode failures.	"Understanding the CMS Collector" on page 140
-XX:+CMSPermGenSweepingEnabled	Directs CMS to sweep the permgen.	When using CMS with an application server that performs lots of class unloading.	"Understanding the CMS Collector" on page 140

Flag	What it does	When to use it	See also
-XX:CMSInitiatingPermOccupancyFraction=*N*	Determines when CMS should scan permgen.	When CMSPerm GenSweepingEn abled is set and full GCs occur because CMS didn't clean up permgen fast enough.	"Understanding the CMS Collector" on page 140
-XX:+CMSClassUnloadingEnabled	Directs CMS to unload classes after the permgen is scanned.	Whenever CMSPerm GenSweepingEn abled is set.	"Understanding the CMS Collector" on page 140
-XX:+CMSIncrementalMode	Runs CMS in incremental mode.	If CPU is limited and you still must run CMS.	"Incremental CMS" on page 149
-XX:CMSIncrementalModeSafetyFactor=*N*	Affects how often incremental CMS background threads run.	When using incremental CMS and experiencing concurrent mode failures, increase this value.	"Incremental CMS" on page 149
-XX:CMSIncrementalDutyCycleMin=*N*	Affects how often incremental CMS background threads run.	When using incremental CMS and experiencing concurrent mode failures, increase this value, though setting CMSIncremen talModeSafety Factor is preferred.	"Incremental CMS" on page 149
-XX:CMSIncrementalDutyCycleMax=*N*	Affects how often incremental CMS background threads run.	When using incremental CMS and experiencing concurrent mode failures, increase this value, though setting CMSIncremen talModeSafety Factor is preferred.	"Incremental CMS" on page 149
-XX:+CMSIncrementalDutyCycle	Affects how often incremental CMS background threads run.	When using CMSIn crementalDuty CycleMin, set this flag.	"Incremental CMS" on page 149

Table A-6. Flags for the G1 collector

Flag	What it does	When to use it	See also
-XX:MaxGCPauseMillis=N	Hints to the G1 collector how long pauses should be; the G1 algorithm is adjusted to attempt to meet that goal.	As a first step in tuning the G1 collector; increase this value to attempt to prevent full GCs.	"Understanding the G1 Collector" on page 150
-XX:ConcGCThreads=N	Sets the number of threads to use for G1 background scanning.	When lots of CPU is available and G1 is experiencing concurrent mode failures.	"Understanding the G1 Collector" on page 150
-XX:InitiatingHeapOccupancyPercent=N	Sets the point at which G1 background scanning begins.	Lower this value if G1 is experiencing concurrent mode failures.	"Understanding the G1 Collector" on page 150
-XX:G1MixedGCCountTarget=N	Sets the number of mixed GCs over which G1 attempts to free the garbage old generation regions.	Lower this value if G1 is experiencing concurrent mode failures; increase it if mixed GC cycles take too long.	"Understanding the G1 Collector" on page 150
-XX:G1HeapRegionSize=N	Sets the size of a G1 region.	Increase this value for very large heaps, or when the application allocates very, very large objects.	"G1 region sizes" on page 168

Table A-7. Flags for memory management

Flag	What it does	When to use it	See also
-XX:+HeapDumpOnOutOfMemoryError	Generates a heap dump when the JVM throws an out of memory error.	Enable this flag if the application throws out of memory errors due to the heap space or permgen, so the heap can be analyzed for memory leaks.	"Out of Memory Errors" on page 184
-XX:HeapDumpPath=<path>	Specifies the filename where automatic heap dumps should be written.	To specify a path other than *java_pid<pid>.hprof* for heap dumps generated on out of memory errors or GC events (when those options have been enabled).	"Out of Memory Errors" on page 184
-XX:SoftRefLRUPolicyMSPerMB=N	Controls how long soft references survive after being used.	Decrease this value to clean up soft references more quickly, particularly in low-memory conditions.	"Weak, Soft, and Other References" on page 208

Flag	What it does	When to use it	See also
-XX:MaxDirectMemorySize=N	Controls how much native memory can be allocated via the allocateDir ect() method of the ByteBuffer class.	Consider setting this if you want to limit the amount of direct memory a program can allocate. Note that it is no longer necessary to set this flag to allocate more than 64 MB of direct memory.	"Footprint" on page 223
-XX:+UseLargePages	Directs the JVM to allocate pages from the operating system's large page system, if applicable.	If supported by the OS, this option will generally improve performance.	"Large Pages" on page 230
-XX:+LargePageSizeInBytes=N	Directs the JVM to allocate large pages of the given size (Solaris only).	On large Solaris systems, increase this value (to, say, 256 MB) for best performance.	"Large Pages" on page 230
-XX:+StringTableSize=N	Sets the size of the hashtable the JVM uses to hold interned strings.	Increase this value if the application performs a significant amount of string interning.	"String Interning" on page 198
-XX:+UseCompressedOops	Emulates 35-bit pointers for object references.	This is the default for heaps that are less than 32 GB in size; there is never an advantage to disabling it.	"Compressed oops" on page 234
-XX:+PrintTLAB	Prints summary information about TLABs in the GC log.	When using a JVM without support for JFR, use this to ensure that TLAB allocation is working efficiently.	"Thread-local allocation buffers" on page 164
-XX:TLABSize=N	Sets the size of the TLABs.	When the application is performing a lot of allocation outside of TLABs, use this value to increase the TLAB size.	"Thread-local allocation buffers" on page 164
-XX:-ResizeTLAB	Disables resizing of TLABs.	Whenever TLABSize is specified, make sure to disable this flag.	"Thread-local allocation buffers" on page 164

Table A-8. Flags for thread handling

Flag	What it does	When to use it	See also
-Xss<N>	Sets the size of the native stack for threads.	Particularly on 32-bit JVMs, decrease this size to make more memory available for other parts of the JVM.	"Tuning Thread Stack Sizes" on page 267
-XX:-BiasedLocking	Disables the biased locking algorithm of the JVM.	Often helps performance of the thread pool based applications.	"Biased Locking" on page 268

Table A-9. Miscellaneous JVM flags

Flag	What it does	When to use it	See also
`-XX:+AlwaysLockClassLoader`	Revert the Java 7 parallel classloading scheme to the Java 6 nonparallel scheme.	On large systems loading classes in only a single thread, startup performance may slightly benefit by using this flag.	"Classloading" on page 358
`-XX:-StackTraceInThrowable`	Prevents the stack trace from being gathered whenever an exception is thrown.	On systems with very deep stacks where exceptions are frequently thrown (and where fixing the code to throw fewer exceptions is not a possibility).	"Exceptions" on page 366
`-XX:-RestrictContended`	Allows non-JDK code to use the @Contended annotation.	Set this if application code uses the @Contended annotation to pad variables to prevent false sharing.	"The @Contended Annotation" on page 266
`-XX:-EnableContended`	Disables JDK code from using the @Contended annotation.	This should likely be left enabled. Disabling may save a small amount of space in certain JDK classes.	"The @Contended Annotation" on page 266
`-XX:+AggressiveOpts`	Enables certain optimizations for the JVM. These optimizations are likely to become defaults in future releases.	You can test with this flag to determine if it helps, but be aware that it may not work the same when JVM versions change.	"AggressiveOpts" on page 378

Table A-10. Flags for Java Flight Recorder

Flag	What it does	When to use it	See also
`-XX:+FlightRecorder`	Enables Java Flight Recorder.	Enabling Flight Recorder is always recommended, as it has very little overhead unless an actual recording is happening (in which case, the overhead will vary depending on the features used, but still be relatively small).	"Java Flight Recorder" on page 60
`-XX:+FlightRecorderOptions`	Sets options for a default recording via the command line.	Control how a default recording can be made for the JVM.	"Java Flight Recorder" on page 60
`-XX:+UnlockCommercialFeatures`	Allows the JVM to use commercial (non-open-source) features.	If you have the appropriate license, setting this flag is required to enable Java Flight Recorder.	"Java Flight Recorder" on page 60

Index

Symbols

-client, 387
-server, 387
-verbose:gc, 390
-Xloggc:<path>, 390
-Xmn, 389
-Xms, 389
-Xmx, 389
-Xss<N>, 395
-XX:+AggressiveOpts, 396
-XX:+AlwaysLockClassLoader, 396
-XX:+AlwaysTenure, 161
-XX:+CICompilerCount=<N>, 388
-XX:+CMSClassUnloadingEnabled, 393
-XX:+CMSIncrementalDutyCycle, 393
-XX:+CMSIncrementalMode, 393
-XX:+CMSPermGenSweepingEnabled, 392
-XX:+FlightRecorder, 396
-XX:+FlightRecorderOptions, 396
-XX:+HeapDumpAfterFullGC, 186
-XX:+HeapDumpBeforeFullGC, 186
-XX:+HeapDumpOnOutOfMemoryError, 186, 394
-XX:+LargePageSizeInBytes=N, 395
-XX:+NeverTenure, 161
-XX:+PrintAdaptiveSizePolicy, 391
-XX:+PrintCompilation, 90, 388
-XX:+PrintGC, 390
-XX:+PrintGCDateStamps, 390
-XX:+PrintGCDetails, 390
-XX:+PrintGCTimeStamps, 390
-XX:+PrintInlining, 96
-XX:+PrintReferenceGC, 390
-XX:+PrintTenuringDistribution, 391
-XX:+PrintTLAB, 395
-XX:+ScavengeBeforeFullGC, 172
-XX:+StringTableSize=N, 395
-XX:+TieredCompilation, 387
-XX:+UnlockCommercialFeatures, 396
-XX:+UseAdaptiveSizePolicy, 390
-XX:+UseCMSInitiatingOccupancyOnly, 392
-XX:+UseCompressedOops, 395
-XX:+UseConcMarkSweepGC, 388
-XX:+UseG1GC, 388
-XX:+UseGCLogFileRotation, 390
-XX:+UseGCOverheadLimit, 188
-XX:+UseLargePages, 395
-XX:+UseParallelGC, 388
-XX:+UseParallelOldGC, 388
-XX:+UseParNewGC, 388
-XX:+UseSerialGC, 388
-XX:+UseSpinning, 269
-XX:-AggressiveHeap, 392
-XX:-BiasedLocking, 395
-XX:-EnableContended, 396
-XX:-Inline, 96
-XX:-ResizeTLAB, 395
-XX:-RestrictContended, 396

We'd like to hear your suggestions for improving our indexes. Send email to index@oreilly.com.

C

C1/C2 compilers, 77
  (see also JIT (just-in-time) compiler)
caching (database results)
  avoiding queries, 350
  cache sizing, 352
  cache types, 346
  default (lazy loading), 348
  eager loading and, 349
  joined with fetching, 349
cardinality, 206
classes
  atomic classes, 254, 261
  class information, 51
  classloader memory leaks, 185, 215
  classloader performance tips, 358
  concurrent classloading, 92
  lambda/anonymous classloading, 382
client compilers, 77
  (see also JIT (just-in-time) compiler)
client-class machines, 5
code cache tuning, 85, 226
committed memory, 224
common code examples, for performance testing, 20
Compare and Swap (CAS) instruction, 254
compilation policies, 172
compilation threads, 94
compilation thresholds, 87
compiled languages, 73
compiler, determining default, 84
  (see also JIT (just-in-time) compiler)
compressed oops, 234
concatenation, 370
concurrent (CMS) garbage collector
  adaptive sizing, 145
  adjusting background threads, 147
  algorithm overview, 110
  basics of, 108, 140
  incremental CMS (iCMS), 149
  running background threads more often, 146
  troubleshooting, 175
  tuning flags for, 392
  tuning for permgen, 148
  vs. G1, 118
concurrent classloading, 92, 358–362
concurrent reset phase (CMS), 143
concurrent utilities, 254

D

concurrent-mode failures, 145, 155, 175
confidence levels, 31
connection pools, 325, 326
container-managed transactions (CMT), 337
contended atomic classes, 261
CPU run queue, 41
CPU usage, 38–41, 114
CSS resources, 278
cycles per instruction (CPI), 265

data
  compressing serialized, 311
  effect of size on performance, 290
  expansion of in noncollection classes, 376
  reading less, 342
  sample payloads, 290
  sizing data transfers, 316
databases
  best practices, 321, 353
  effect on performance, 8, 17, 321
  Java Persistence API (JPA)
    bytecode processing and, 337
    caching, 346–352
    fetch groups, 343
    JDBC performance and, 337
    optimizing JPA reads, 342
    optimizing JPA writes, 340
    read-only entities, 352
    transaction handling, 337
    XA transactions, 339
  JDBC (Java Database Connectivity)
    connection pools, 326
    driver evaluation, 322
    driver types, 323
    JPA framework for, 322
    prepared statements/statement pooling, 324
    result set processing, 335
    setting the fetch size, 336
    transactions, 327–334
deep object size, 180
default compiler, determining, 84
default flag values, 4, 48
deinitialization, 195
deoptimization
  not entrant code, 98
  zombie code, 101
disk usage, 43

low-pause garbage collectors, 108, 175

M

macrobenchmarks, 16
main memory vs. registry values, 76
marshalling/parsing
  choosing a parser, 293
  overview of, 291
  parser factories, 296
  reusing parsers, 296
memory
  adaptive vs. static tuning, 136
  allocated vs. reserved, 224
  analyzer tools for, 180
  efficiency in Java Collections API, 377
  HTTP session state memory, 280
  memory leaks, 185, 215
  native memory
    best practices, 223
    footprint measurement, 224
    footprint minimization, 225
    JVM tunings, 230
    Native Memory Tracking (NMT), 227
    native NIO buffers, 226
    vs. heap memory, 223
  out of memory errors, 184, 187, 267
  pooled objects and, 326
  reserved vs. allocated, 87
  total footprint of, 224
  tuning flags for, 394
mesobenchmarks, 18
metaspace
  default size of, 125
  in CMS garbage collection, 144
  memory errors, 184
  sizing during GC tuning, 124
microbenchmarks, 11–16
Microsoft Management Center, 233
middleware, 323

N

native memory
  best practices, 223
  footprint measurement, 224
  footprint minimization, 225
  JVM tunings
    compressed oops, 234
    large page sizes, 233

large pages, 230
  Linux huge pages, 231
  transparent huge pages, 232
  Windows large pages, 233
Native Memory Tracking (NMT), 227
native NIO buffers, 226
out of memory errors, 184, 267
over-reserving, 224
tuning flags for, 394
vs. heap memory, 223
vs. total footprint, 224
native NIO buffers, 204, 223, 226
native profilers, 57
NetBeans, 79
netstat, 45
network encoding, 370
network lookups, 205
network usage, 45
networking APIs
  protocols available, 316
  sizing data transfers, 316
nicstat, 45
NIO buffers, 205, 223, 226
not entrant code, 98

O

object lifecycle management
  finalizers/final references, 216
  indefinite references, 208
  normal lifecycle, 202
  object reuse
    common techniques, 202
    garbage collection efficiency and, 203
    object pools, 205
    thread-local variables, 206
    when and how to use, 204
  soft references, 212
  weak references, 214
objects
  alignment of, 190
  allocation of, 204
  canonical, 196
  deep size, 180
  dominators, 181
  immutable, 196
  initialization of, 204
  Java object models, 305
  locking in synchronization, 255
  object pools, 205

volatile, 260

W

warm-up periods
    elapsed time (batch) measurements and, 24
    microbenchmarks and, 14
    queries and, 351
web container performance
    combining CSS/JavaScript resources, 278
    compressing output, 278
    forgoing dynamic JSP compilation, 278
    pre-encoding strings, 279
    producing less output, 277
    producing less whitespace, 277
well-formed documents, 299
whitespace
    in XML/JSON, 290
    producing less, 277
Windows large pages, 233
Woodstox parser, 298

X

XML and JSON processing
    data payload samples, 290
    data size, 290
    document models, 303
    filtering XML and JAX-WS, 306
    functional differences between, 289
    Java object models, 305
    parser factories, 296
    parser reuse, 296
    parser selection, 293
    parsing/marshalling overview, 291
    XML validation, 299

Z

ZIP encoders/decoders, 205, 217
zombie code, 101

About the Author

Scott Oaks is an architect at Oracle Corporation, where he works on the performance of Oracle's middleware software. Prior to joining Oracle, he worked for years at Sun Microsystems, specializing in many disparate technologies from the SunOS kernel to network programming and RPCs to Windows systems and the OPEN LOOK Virtual Window Manager. In 1996, Scott became a Java evangelist for Sun and in 2001 joined their Java Performance Group—which has been his primary focus ever since. Scott also authored O'Reilly's *Java Security*, *Java Threads*, *JXTA in a Nutshell*, and *Jini in a Nutshell* titles.

Colophon

The animals on the cover of *Java Performance: The Definitive Guide* are saiga antelopes (*Saiga tatarica*), commonly known as saigas. Their most distinctive feature is an oversized flexible nose, which hangs partially over their mouths. The saigas' noses help filter out dust in the summer, and heat up air in the winter before it goes to their lungs.

Saiga coats also adapt to both seasons: in the cold, it is thick and white, but turns a cinnamon color and thins out significantly in the summer. The animals are around 2-3 feet tall at the shoulder, and weigh between 80-140 pounds. Saigas have long thin legs, and are able to run up to 80 miles an hour to avoid predators. Their habitat is in semidesert steppes, where they spend their days grazing on various grasses and shrubs (including some that are poisonous to other animals).

Saigas normally live in herds of 30-40 individuals, but gather in the thousands for migration in the winter. Rut begins in late November, after the herds move south. During this time males don't eat much and violently fight with each other, causing many to die from exhaustion. The survivors collect and impregnate a harem of females, who will each give birth to one or two young in late April.

The saiga population is almost exclusively within Kazakhstan, with a small isolated subspecies in Mongolia. Though they used to range all across the steppes of Central Asia, saigas have been severely overhunted in the last few decades and are designated as "critically endangered." The collapse of the USSR led to uncontrolled hunting and a dramatic 97% decrease in the saiga herds. Recovery has also been much more difficult because male saigas are the only sex with horns, a commodity much in demand in traditional Chinese medicine. As a result, hunters have nearly wiped out male saigas and crippled the species' ability to breed.

The cover image is from a loose plate, origin unknown. The cover fonts are URW Typewriter and Guardian Sans. The text font is Adobe Minion Pro; the heading font is Adobe Myriad Condensed; and the code font is Dalton Maag's Ubuntu Mono.

Have it your way.

Get even more for your money.

Join the O'Reilly Community, and register the O'Reilly books you own. It's free, and you'll get:

- $4.99 ebook upgrade offer
- 40% upgrade offer on O'Reilly print books
- Membership discounts on books and events
- Free lifetime updates to ebooks and videos
- Multiple ebook formats, DRM FREE
- Participation in the O'Reilly community
- Newsletters
- Account management
- 100% Satisfaction Guarantee

Signing up is easy:

1. Go to: oreilly.com/go/register
2. Create an O'Reilly login.
3. Provide your address.
4. Register your books.

Note: English-language books only

To order books online:
oreilly.com/store

For questions about products or an order:
orders@oreilly.com

To sign up to get topic-specific email announcements and/or news about upcoming books, conferences, special offers, and new technologies:
elists@oreilly.com

For technical questions about book content:
booktech@oreilly.com

To submit new book proposals to our editors:
proposals@oreilly.com

O'Reilly books are available in multiple DRM-free ebook formats. For more information:
oreilly.com/ebooks

O'REILLY®

CPSIA information can be obtained at www.ICGtesting.com
Printed in the USA
BVOW09s1146160316

440571BV00004B/31/P

9 781449 358457